The Outsider

DAN ROTTENBERG

THE OUTSIDER

ALBERT M. GREENFIELD

and the Fall

of the Protestant Establishment

TEMPLE UNIVERSITY PRESS   PHILADELPHIA

TEMPLE UNIVERSITY PRESS
Philadelphia, Pennsylvania 19122
www.temple.edu/tempress

Library of Congress Cataloging-in-Publication Data

Rottenberg, Dan, author.
    The outsider : Albert M. Greenfield and the fall of the Protestant establishment /
Dan Rottenberg.
       pages cm
    Includes bibliographical references and index.
    ISBN 978-1-4399-0841-9 (hardback : alk. paper) —
ISBN 978-1-4399-0843-3 (e-book)   1. Greenfield, Albert M., 1887–1967.   2. Jews—
Pennsylvania—Philadelphia—Biography.   3. Jewish capitalists and financiers—
Pennsylvania—Philadelphia—Biography.   4. Capitalists and financiers—United
States—Biography.   5. Philadelphia (Pa.)—Biography.   I. Title.
    F158.9.J5R88 2014
    974.8′04092—dc23
    [B]
                                                                          2014008381

♾ The paper used in this publication meets the requirements of the American
National Standard for Information Sciences—Permanence of Paper for Printed Library
Materials, ANSI Z39.48-1992

Printed in the United States of America

9 8 7 6 5 4 3 2 1

In memory of my father,

HERMAN ROTTENBERG,

who left the business world to spread joy in every land

But seek the welfare of the city where I have sent you into exile, and pray to the Lord on its behalf, for in its welfare you will find your welfare.

—JEREMIAH 29:7

He does not have a chance—he has not had a chance to absorb the American ideals. There are any number of foreign boys to whom that situation applies.

—PHILADELPHIA LAWYER HENRY S. DRINKER,
SPEECH TO AMERICAN BAR ASSOCIATION, 1929

Contents

Illustrations follow page 144

Preface

The Jews, the WASPs,
and the New American Dream

The celebrated "American Dream" of the twentieth century evolved from two conflicting visions. The first was the dream of the Puritans, of Benjamin Franklin's Poor Richard, of Thomas Jefferson's yeoman farmer: the dream of prosperity accumulated through patience and hard work. The second was the dream of the Spanish conquistadors, of the forty-niners during the California Gold Rush, of entrepreneurs like Andrew Carnegie and John D. Rockefeller: the dream of instant wealth acquired through sheer brilliance, audacity, timing, and luck.

The rise of the modern corporation in the twentieth century represented an ingenious attempt to combine the best of both impulses, harnessing huge pools of capital and labor to the energy and brainpower of gifted entrepreneurs. Yet this financial transformation occurred at the very moment that waves of European immigrants were asserting their own vision of the American Dream.

In effect, their pursuit of wealth and status pitted ambitious and innovative Catholic and Jewish newcomers against a dominant class of native-born Protestants who considered themselves the custodians of American values. This conflict was played out to some degree in every major American city, but nowhere were the fault lines drawn as sharply as in Philadelphia.

That most insular and provincial American metropolis witnessed the most dramatic confrontation between the new arrivals and the native business establishment: the ascent of Albert M. Greenfield, a feisty and combative Russian Jewish immigrant who rose from office boy to ruler of an immense business empire, encompassing real estate, department stores, banks, finance companies, hotels, newspapers, and transportation companies.

Greenfield was the prototypical ambitious immigrant outsider challenging an entrenched business elite—Jewish as well as gentile. To Philadelphia's cautious and proper old-family business leaders, he seemed a bull in their china shop. At a critical moment, Philadelphia's leading bankers joined forces to shut him down, only to see him bounce back, more resilient than ever, even replacing them as the favored confidant of mayors, senators, governors, and U.S. presidents.

Conventional wisdom in Greenfield's day (and indeed ever since) held that immigrants required at least a generation or two to absorb American values. But it was Greenfield's perverse yet fiercely held belief that immigrants—especially Jewish immigrants, because of their long history as a persecuted minority—appreciated American values better than the natives and consequently made better citizens.

The sociologist E. Digby Baltzell, a keen student of this debate, observed that America's WASPs—his acronym for "White Anglo-Saxon Protestants"—became obsessed with asserting the purity of their bloodlines when they should have been asserting the authority of their valuable democratic traditions; consequently, the Protestant Establishment suffocated from its refusal to open its doors to fresh air. By the end of Greenfield's life, America's Protestant Establishment was retreating on a broad front, from Wall Street to City Hall to academia. Philadelphia's last white Protestant mayor left office in 1962. Albert Greenfield's story, to a large extent, illustrates Baltzell's thesis in microcosm.

Like many of his Jewish contemporaries, Greenfield embraced America as the Diaspora's New Zion—the ultimate destination where Jews could finally unleash their potential for the benefit of humankind. Thus when Jews were denied opportunities in mainstream U.S. companies, they started their own. American Jews created entire new industries (movies, theater, public relations, advertising, real estate, scrap metal) and revolutionized many more (clothing, publishing, retailing, banking, investments, liquor). In these fields and others, they relentlessly broke down class lines among consumers through such products as the blue jeans of Levi Strauss, the shopping malls of Melvin Simon and Alfred Taubman, the suburban housing developments of William Levitt, and, of course, motion pictures. In the process, Jews played a major role in restructuring America's formerly clubby corporate world and opening it up to broader participation, at least among white Americans from European backgrounds.

From the time of Abraham until the twentieth century, Jewish culture was essentially defensive: Even in the Diaspora's "New Zions" of the past— Spain, Holland, Poland, Lithuania—that culture assumed that Jews would relate to the rest of the world as underdogs and, consequently, would voluntarily keep to themselves even when they were not being segregated in Jewish ghettoes. Albert Greenfield gleefully rejected such assumptions. In a world that believed society functions best when people stick to their own kind, Greenfield crossed social, religious, and ethnic boundaries with impunity. In the process he demonstrated the rich rewards—emotional as well as financial—that await anyone willing to venture beyond his or her immediate familiar circle.

The story of Albert Greenfield's long evolution from driven young real estate broker to avuncular champion of intercultural relations bears retelling but not necessarily as a guide to business or personal success: Greenfield benefited from a rare combination of genes, background, education, ambition, talent, personal magnetism, good health, opportunities, connections, and luck. His lifetime of audacious risk taking, while remarkable, was not necessarily exemplary. His vast but precariously constructed corporate empire collapsed shortly after he died. Ultimately, Greenfield's story merits our attention as a dazzling prism through which to examine four major themes of his century: the transformation of American cities, the evolution of America's immigrant experience, the rise of the American Jewish business class, and the decline of America's Protestant Establishment.

For better or worse, this uniquely brilliant and energetic man spent his life testing society's limitations on individual potential. In the process Albert Greenfield redefined the nature of American citizenship by demonstrating the extent to which a single individual, even of humble foreign birth, can make a difference in his community and his nation.

Author's Disclosure

lbert M. Greenfield was a controversial figure who maintained tight control over his personal narrative. Those who revered or despised him cherish their own narratives of the man. As Greenfield's biographer, I have sought to provide an independent assessment of his life, which has necessarily required sifting the available accounts and narratives dispassionately. If you find observations in this book that strike you as mistaken or misguided, please bear in mind that they are mine alone and are not necessarily shared by the book's funders, its publisher, or anyone else.

My research was supported by four funders (see the Acknowledgments), two of which—the Albert M. Greenfield Foundation and Jack Farber—are interested parties in Albert Greenfield's story. In both cases I accepted their support only on the condition that they would exercise no control over the book's contents; nor would they even have the opportunity to see the manuscript before its publication.

Coincidentally, at the time I was approached by Temple University Press to write this book in 2010, I had recently finished editing the memoirs of Jack Farber, who took over Greenfield's largest business after Greenfield's death. This experience gave me a solid grounding in the aftermath of Greenfield's death but also, obviously, may have compromised my ability to write objectively about Farber.

Some of the material in this book is derived from two dozen interviews I conducted in 1975 and 1976 while researching a magazine article about Greenfield. Those interviews were conducted on a "not for attribution" basis—that is, I could use the information as long as I concealed the source.

An academic book like this one requires the author to cite his sources where possible, and in the best of all worlds I would seek out these sources and ask them to release me from my "not for attribution" pledge. Indeed I have done so with the two who survive at this writing. But the others, having died years ago, have left me with an ethical quandary that journalism schools seem not to have addressed—to wit, is there such a thing as a statute of limitations for rules like "not for attribution"?

The respected ethicists whom I consulted about this issue (see the Acknowledgments) were hardly unanimous in their verdicts. That being the case, I have chosen to attribute these interviews but only sparingly and not in cases in which I feel the person interviewed would have objected.

Finally, I should disclose that one figure mentioned in this book, whom I interviewed in 1975—Greenfield's longtime lieutenant, the late Alfred Blasband—was a relative of mine, albeit a very distant one: specifically, my second cousin, twice removed.

The Outsider

Philadelphia's leading bankers assembled at the Merion home of William Purves Gest on the night of December 21, 1930, to decide the fate of Albert M. Greenfield's Bankers Trust Company. *(Lower Merion Historical Society)*

Prologue

Merion Station, December 1930

B y 8:00 P.M. the winds had shifted slightly from southwest to northwest; the sky over the Main Line, clear and crisp all afternoon, had
turned cloudy. The thermometer was quickly falling toward the freez-
ing level. Snowflakes were beginning to settle on the lawns and hedges of
Merion. Winter would arrive the next morning.[1]

Inside the stone mansion on Hazelhurst Avenue, the air was warm with
the smell of burning logs and lighted cigars. William Purves Gest had built
this manor house in 1897, when he was thirty-six and rising through the
ranks at the Fidelity Trust Company along a seemingly preordained path
toward the presidency then held by his father. At the time, Gest had been sufficiently confident of his future to purchase three and a half acres just west
of Philadelphia's city line and had commissioned the architectural team of
William and Frank Price to design an elegant home. Now Gest was nearly
seventy, a banker of bushy whiskers, aristocratic bearing, and impressive
accomplishments, noted equally as chairman of the Fidelity-Philadelphia
Trust, the city's largest trust company; founder of the Philadelphia Foundation, America's second oldest community foundation; and author of *The
Philosophy of American History*.[2]

Gest was the first member of his family in more than two centuries
to live beyond the city limits of Philadelphia.[3] William Penn's Holy Experiment—the world's first planned community—had been based on a fundamen-
tal belief that while the countryside may provide food for humanity, cities
are the building blocks of civilization. No bucolic farm, village, small town,
or country estate, Penn perceived, offered a great city's opportunities for the

sort of cooperation and collaboration that produced commerce, art, science, and, indeed, all human progress.

But in Philadelphia that certainty had been crumbling since the mid-nineteenth century, when the Pennsylvania Railroad began laying the tracks for its Main Line to Pittsburgh and points west.[4] As early as the 1850s the upper-class Philadelphia diarist Sidney Fisher had marveled, "One may now have a villa ten, twenty or thirty miles from town and yet go in half an hour and return after the work of the day is over to dinner. In consequence . . . cottages and country estates, some of them very beautiful and costly, are multiplying."[5] To boost passenger traffic along its Main Line, in the 1870s and 1880s the Pennsylvania Railroad created a whole series of suburban towns, most of them bearing Welsh names in memory of the original "Welsh Tract" granted there by William Penn to a group of Quakers from Wales. Here the railroad erected high-toned housing developments, opened elegant hotels, and induced or browbeat its executives to settle.[6] The Pennsylvania Railroad was an awesome human phenomenon, a combination of industrial might and organizational ingenuity never before seen; by 1880 it was the world's largest corporation twice over, with thirty thousand employees and $400 million in capital.[7] Wherever it ventured, ambitious and successful men followed.

As a consequence, by the time Gest moved out to Merion with his wife, his two daughters, and their five servants in 1897, the Main Line was quickly becoming the Philadelphia gentleman's preferred refuge from the city's corrupt politics, onerous taxes, and increasingly teeming and squalid streets—a place where, after a busy day in the city, a man of affairs could retreat to the peaceful embrace of his family, his home, and his gardens.[8] The last of the city's elegant townhouses had gone up just about the time Gest left, and from then on the concept of fashionable city life was doomed. By the 1920s the automobile had completed the process begun by the railroad, almost entirely removing upper- and upper-middle-class Philadelphians from the city to the suburbs.[9] Property values on the Main Line had risen to such an extent that now Gest's Merion home was valued at $135,000, even in the midst of a crippling economic depression.[10] So many of the city's leaders now lived out on the Main Line that sometimes they found it easier to conduct the city's business out there, among themselves, rather than downtown.

In Merion alone, Gest's neighbors included such formidable figures as Dr. Albert Barnes, who had amassed perhaps the world's greatest collection of impressionist art just a few blocks from Gest's home, and Henry Drinker—head of one of Philadelphia's most prestigious law firms and descendant of one of the city's oldest and most illustrious families (an ancestor, Edward

Drinker, was said to have been born in a cave along the Delaware River before Philadelphia was even built).[11] Drinker's house, also just a few blocks
from Gest's, was home to the "Drinker Sing," a chorus of a hundred or more
amateurs who assembled periodically, by invitation only, in a special room
housing two grand pianos and a Hammond organ that Henry and Sophia
Drinker had designed specifically for that purpose.[12] Just across Hazelhurst
Avenue from Gest's home stood the Merion Tribute House, a community
center like almost none other in America: a huge Gothic stone mansion,
modeled after an English country manor, with wood-beamed ceilings, slate
floors, stained glass windows, a walk-in fireplace, and ornamental ironwork
designed by the famous studio of Samuel Yellin. Gest and his neighbors had
erected this building—said to be "the most beautiful structure of its kind in
this locality"—in 1924 as a tribute to Merion's soldiers in World War I and
also as a tribute to the English civilization of their ancestors.[13]

On just such an evening as this, Gest and his neighbors might have been
singing Christmas carols at the Merion Tribute House or at the Drinkers'
home over on Merion Road. But there would be no carols on this Sunday,
December 21, 1930. Like the undertow from a great wave at the beach, the
aftershocks of the most devastating stock market crash in history were now
rolling in, bringing the sort of financial panic that few people, rich or poor,
had ever experienced. Money was tight, businesses were overextended, companies were cutting back, unemployment lines were growing, homes were
being repossessed, banks were beginning to totter.

In this moment of crisis, Gest had gathered in his home Philadelphia's
leading bankers, a formidable combination of financial talent and impeccable bloodlines within a single room. Here, for example, was the dapper
but aging Edward Townsend "E. T." Stotesbury, senior partner of Drexel &
Co., which by virtue of its tie to the Morgans in New York was Philadelphia's
most influential (albeit private) banking concern—the same Ned Stotesbury who as a drummer boy during the Civil War had tagged along beside
Philadelphia's departing Union troops and whose banking career stretched
back to the time when his mentor, Anthony Drexel, had transformed the
obscure J. Pierpont Morgan into the greatest banker of his age. Here too
was the large, ruddy, white-haired Joseph Wayne Jr.—former baseball player
and cricketer, now president of the Philadelphia National Bank, the city's
largest. Here was soft-spoken, beaver-like C. Stevenson Newhall, executive
vice president of the city's second largest bank, the Pennsylvania Company,
as well as rector's warden of Philadelphia's historic Episcopal Church of St.
James the Less, which his ancestors had founded in 1846.[14] And here was the
noted host himself, William Purves Gest, head of Philadelphia's largest trust

company, whose own ancestors had arrived in Philadelphia in 1683, just two years after William Penn.[15] Yet for all their apparent power and prestige, the bankers assembled in Gest's home now confronted a decision that would be painful no matter which way they turned.

The problem was the Bankers Trust Company, Philadelphia's tenth largest bank, with $50 million in deposits. A run on the bank had started in September, and by now more than $17 million had been withdrawn, more than exhausting the bank's supply of available cash. If Bankers Trust were forced to close its doors, the bankers in Gest's home knew, the resulting loss of public confidence could lead to withdrawal stampedes at every bank in the city. Indeed, to avoid such a closing, two of these bankers had already loaned more than $7 million to Bankers Trust. But the end of the run on Bankers Trust was nowhere in sight: Tens of millions of dollars more might be needed—and who could be certain that, even with that infusion, Bankers Trust might not fold anyway?

The prime stockholder of Bankers Trust, Albert M. Greenfield, had assured these gentlemen that his bank was indeed sound. He had agreed to their demands that he personally put up funds and collateral to guarantee any future loans to Bankers Trust. That commitment had satisfied the members of the banking coalition only twenty-four hours earlier. But now they were plagued by second thoughts.

In subdued tones that masked the tension of the moment, the bankers discussed the value of Greenfield's collateral—his real estate properties, his diverse financial companies, his supposed wealth. Finally, a single voice pierced the stale air in the drawing room.

The speaker reminded his colleagues of the basic principle laid down by Pierpont Morgan eighteen years earlier—a principle that Morgan himself had learned from *his* patron, the Philadelphia banker Anthony Drexel: The primary basis of credit is neither money nor property, but character. As Morgan had put it, "A man I do not trust could not get money from me on all the bonds in Christendom." In that moment a great calm suddenly descended on the group. After three days of confusion and conferences, someone had finally cut through to the heart of the matter, had pinpointed the nagging doubt in the bankers' minds: When all was said and done, they simply did not trust Albert Greenfield.

It was nothing any of them could put his finger on. All of them had done business with Greenfield, and many of them had accepted the favors that he so eagerly bestowed on them through his seemingly endless web of financial and political connections. Greenfield appeared to possess money and property, and he was so persuasive that it was difficult to argue with his contention that his bank was sound.

The fact remained that he made them uncomfortable. He was an immigrant and a Jew, yes, but the problem transcended his background: Greenfield did not operate according to Philadelphia tradition. He did not look back longingly to the golden age of Benjamin Franklin or the "Athens of America" of Nicholas Biddle or the steel age of William McKinley; he refused to genuflect before the Pennsylvania Railroad or the Main Line. On the contrary, Greenfield sought to *change* Philadelphia, to transform their oasis of civility into a cosmopolitan boomtown like New York or Chicago.

He had come too far too fast from too little, but now the laws of economics had inevitably caught up with him. The closing of Bankers Trust would be painful for every man in this room, but then, their ancestors had suffered with William Penn aboard the *Welcome* and with George Washington at Valley Forge and with Ulysses S. Grant at Cold Harbor; they could stand to suffer too, for the cause of sound business practices.

So they would let the Bankers Trust Company go; it would never open its doors again. Albert Greenfield, at age forty-three, would be ruined, they knew, but they assured themselves that he had only himself to blame. Opportunists came and went, but Philadelphia's great enterprises had been nurtured slowly, carefully, over centuries.

Thirty-six years later, long after the men in that room had gone to their heavenly rewards—long after Gest's mansion had been dismantled and subdivided into four tract homes, and long after Greenfield had acquired and shuttered Drexel & Co.'s headquarters building and subdivided Stotesbury's palatial Georgian estate into a suburban village—the once portly but now emaciated figure of Albert Monroe Greenfield gazed out the second-floor bedroom window of his Chestnut Hill estate, atop a high and winding hill in Philadelphia's northwest corner. Beyond the balcony he looked down on a city whose businesses and politics were dominated by Jews and Catholics, a city in which Anglo-Saxon Protestants had become almost superfluous. Hundreds of thousands of Philadelphians—including the descendants of the bankers who had met at Gest's house that December night—lived in or worked in or conducted business in buildings he owned, managed, leased, or sold. He had controlled a chain of department stores with 112 units in nineteen states stretching from New York to New Orleans, a mortgage banking company, Philadelphia's largest cab company, and the Loft Candy Corporation, as well as six major downtown hotels. Governors and mayors had paid court to him; so had presidents from Herbert Hoover to Lyndon Johnson. And he *had* changed not only Philadelphia's face but also its soul, just as those bankers in Merion had feared. His influence extended into so many aspects of the city's life that it could well be said that he had acquired more local power than anyone in the history of Philadelphia—or, perhaps, any city in a democracy. To some Philadelphians Greenfield was reviled and feared as a calculating octopus, monopolizing and choking everything within the grasp of his many tentacles; but Greenfield saw himself as a happy warrior, exuberantly harnessing the creative forces of a free society to shatter the entrenched structures of a repressive past.

The bankers on Gest's committee, the Pennsylvania Railroad, the publisher Moses Annenberg, the Philadelphia Republican political machine, the department store magnate Rudolph Goerke, Tsar Alexander II, Adolf Hitler—all had, in the course of seventy-nine years, in one way or another, sought to destroy this combative little man with that homely dome-like head and those hooded eyes. Greenfield had outlasted them all, often graciously extending the hand of friendship to his defeated rivals. In a society that believed there are no second acts in American lives, he had reinvented himself half a dozen times. He had raced through life at full speed while others had sauntered. And when he closed his eyes for the last time on January 5, 1967, it could be said that the man had not merely survived; he had prospered. He had not merely endured but triumphed.

But to what end? What was the point of those seemingly endless reinventions, those victories and defeats, those rivalries and alliances, those peripatetic wheelings and dealings? That was the question.

[PART I]

BEGINNINGS

[1]

The Wealth in Your Head

For centuries before Albert M. Greenfield was born, many gentiles and
even some Jews themselves believed that the descendants of Abraham, Isaac, and Jacob possessed some sort of cultural if not genetic
gift for finance and commerce. "The glory of our town would be augmented
a thousandfold if I were to bring Jews to it," declared Rüdiger Huozmann,
the Bishop of Speyer, in 1084. That was his rationale for granting Jews "the
free right of exchanging gold and silver, and of buying everything they use."[1]
Such notions were understandable in the Middle Ages, when Jews dominated trade between Europe and Asia and the "Court Jew," who handled the
finances of European kings and nobles, was thought to be indispensable to
any functioning European government.[2]

Yet when Albert Greenfield was born in Russia in 1887 this prototype
of the innovative Jewish capitalist was barely eight centuries old—a relatively recent development in a Jewish civilization that stretched back more
than three thousand years. With a few exceptions (like King Solomon, the
first great Jewish exporter), the Hebrews of ancient Israel were largely farmers, craftsmen, and warriors who for the most part lacked commercial acumen. The Torah, for all its complex regulations concerning the conduct of
everyday life, said little about the conduct of business, most likely because
commerce played such a minor role among the Jews of antiquity. The entrepreneurs of that age were not the Hebrews, who lived in inland isolation, but
the Phoenicians and the Canaanites, whose proximity to trade routes and
the seacoast naturally disposed them to commercial occupations. "We do
not dwell in a land by the sea," remarked the first century Roman historian

Flavius Josephus, himself a Jew, "and do not therefore indulge in commerce either by sea or otherwise."[3]

Only after the loss of their homeland in the first century C.E. were Jews forced to seize whatever economic prospects they could find as outsiders living in other people's homelands. When Christians were barred from trade in Muslim countries, and vice versa, Jews found opportunities as commercial intermediaries between the two. When Jews were barred from owning land or merchandise, they gravitated into money lending, pawn broking, and managing wealth for landowners and even kings. When early Christians were banned from lending money at interest to their fellow Christians, they turned to Jews—who faced no such religious sanction—to fill the void.

In effect, the Jews' status as outsiders granted them a flexibility to experiment and innovate that was denied to the dominant Christians and Muslims. In the process, Jews were liberated from the narrow roles—noble, burgher, peasant—prescribed for Christians. In this way, paradoxically, the Jews came to be perceived simultaneously as totally marginal and also uncannily powerful.

As outsiders, Jews suffered constant persecution in Europe and the Near East, not only because they rejected Christianity and Islam but also because killing or ransoming Jews was a convenient way to expunge debts. For centuries Jews and non-Jews performed a delicate dance with each other: On one hand, Jews nervously refrained from blatantly asserting their power in the non-Jewish world, even as they worked assiduously to preserve it. On the other hand, gentiles sought to limit Jewish access to power even as they granted Jews access to specific *kinds* of power.[4]

Frederick II of Prussia summarized his quandary in the eighteenth century:

We have too many Jews in the towns. They are needed on the Polish border because in these areas Hebrews alone perform trade. As soon as you get away from the frontier, the Jews become a disadvantage, they form cliques, they deal in contraband and get up to all manner of rascally tricks which are detrimental to Christian burghers and merchants. I have never persecuted anyone from this or any other sect; I think, however, it would be prudent to pay attention so that their numbers do not increase.[5]

Inevitably, survival as a Jew in the medieval and early modern world required an ability to live by one's wits and devise ways to profit amid adversity. The Sassoon family, for example, prospered in Baghdad for centuries until the early 1830s, when the pasha, strapped for cash, began seizing rich Jews for ransom in order to pay his debts. At that moment, for all his family's wealth and prestige, David Sassoon was forced to escape from Baghdad by boat in the dead of night, muffled under a turban and cloak, with a money belt around his waist and pearls sewn inside his clothes. Eventually, he made his way to Bombay, where he set up a trading house and dispersed his eight sons to open branches in India, China, Japan, and London, effectively globalizing the Far Eastern trade.[6]

By the nineteenth century, Jews epitomized entrepreneurship to such an extent that Karl Marx, who came from a Jewish family, perceived capitalism as an ancestral Jewish curse from which his people could be rescued only by revolution.[7] But Sassoon's experience, like that of many other Jewish businessmen, reinforced the received wisdom that Eurasian Jewish culture had passed down for centuries—the same perception it would ultimately bequeath to Albert M. Greenfield: that the only permanent wealth in this world is what you carry in your head.

At its root, the Greenfield family story is a tale of human connections skillfully deployed over centuries. Albert Greenfield's ancestors probably fled Western or Central Europe during the Black Death of the fourteenth century, when Jews were widely accused of instigating the plague by poisoning the wells of Europe. These refugees found relative freedom and comfort for several centuries in Poland, which as Europe's last Christianized land was also the most tolerant toward non-Christians. Since neither the landowning upper classes nor the peasant lower classes in Poland cared to engage in commerce, trade of all sorts became the default Jewish career there. Polish Jews were held in sufficiently high regard that in 1587 the wealthy Jewish merchant Saul Wahl of Brest-Litovsk, who held a state-granted monopoly of the salt mines in Polish Lithuania, was chosen to sit as interim king of Poland for a week or two before the parliament elected Sigismund III to the throne. And when Poland annexed western Russia in the sixteenth century, Polish Jews were routinely dispatched to administer the newly conquered lands.[8]

The Russian kingdom recovered these lands in the late eighteenth century and, together with Prussia and Austria, carved the old Kingdom of Poland out of existence. Yet the descendants of the occupying Polish Jewish bureaucrats remained in Russia—and so, to be sure, did the descendants of those Slavs and Ukrainians who resented the Jews for their role in the Polish occupation as well as their rejection of Christianity. Under laws promulgated in 1795 and 1835, some two and a half million Russian Jews were confined to the "Pale of Settlement," an arid piece of western Russia stretching from the

Black Sea north almost to the Baltic. Most Jews herded into the Pale suffered lives of abject poverty. Yet if only by virtue of the survival skills they had honed over many generations, by the mid-nineteenth century a relatively small circle of Polish Jewish contractors largely monopolized Russia's trade in lumber, produce, and liquor.

Above all, Jews dominated Russia's grain trade, a business that involved multitudes of buyers, commission agents, bankers, and brokers, all of them operating through a network of branch offices spread across Russia's "breadbasket," the Ukraine. Each autumn, Jewish agents fanned out through this grain belt to purchase harvested crops, which were then sold to Jewish dealers who had set themselves up in market towns and (later) at railroad stations, and these dealers in turn forwarded the grain to ports on the Black Sea or to German frontier towns like Danzig or Konigsberg.[9]

At a far distant end of this chain of connections in the 1860s stood a remote outpost called Lozovata, a wheat-farming village of some 350 souls located in the Russian governorate of Podolia, roughly 225 kilometers southwest of Kiev and fully 430 kilometers northwest of Odessa. Here a Jewish peddler named Jacob Serody lived with his wife, Hannah, and their large brood of children in a log cabin with a straw roof—the straw insulation having been fashioned from bunches of excess wheat and rye plucked from nearby fields. Since Lozovata lacked a general store, at some point in the early 1870s, Jacob Serody opened his own general store in his cabin.[10]

To stock the store, once or twice each month Jacob Serody spent two or three hours driving his horse and wagon each way to Nemirov, a good-sized town of roughly ten thousand souls about thirty viersts to the north.[11] Jews comprised some three-fifths of Nemirov's population, and virtually all the Jews there made their living as merchants or shopkeepers, a logical trade at a time when Jews were forbidden to live in industrial districts where factory jobs were available.[12] And since Jacob Serody's clan was one of only two Jewish families in Lozovata, it was equally logical that Jacob traveled to Nemirov not merely for merchandise but also to find a husband for his daughter, Esther Vita.

A trader in Nemirov named Moshe Grunfeld, with whom Serody conducted much of his business there, had a son named Jacob who struck Serody as a promising prospect: Among his other virtues, Jacob Grunfeld spoke Ukrainian and Yiddish and some German as well—prerequisites for doing business with both gentile peasants and Jewish dealers.[13] So when Serody returned from one of his trips to Nemirov, about 1876, Jacob Grunfeld came with him. Jacob Grunfeld and Esther Vita Serody, ages twenty-two and eighteen, respectively, were married shortly after.[14]

Once installed with his new bride in Jacob Serody's cabin in Lozovata, Jacob Grunfeld made his living buying excess grain and livestock from peasants nearby and shipping the goods to Kiev or Odessa. Esther, a forceful young wife with what was said to be a prodigious memory, came to be perceived as something of a *savant* among the local peasants, who often sought her advice in resolving disputes.[15]

In the young couple's efforts to raise a family, Esther lost several babies as well as a son who died young. But in 1880 Esther gave birth to a healthy daughter; a son followed less than two years later; another daughter followed about four years after him; and on or about August 4, 1887, their fourth surviving child was born.[16]

This baby boy was named Moshe Abba ben Yakov in Hebrew, but he seems to have been known more familiarly as Abishe Moishe or Avrum Moishe.[17] Even at birth this child already distinguished himself from his siblings—not to mention 98 percent of the world's population—by virtue of his bright auburn hair. As the result of a rare gene on chromosome 16 that affects the melanocortin-1 receptor gene, the future Albert Greenfield would benefit not only from the Jewish commercial heritage that produced Sassoons and Rothschilds but also from the gene structure that for centuries had produced overachieving and often hyperactive redheads, from Erik the Red, William the Conqueror, Titian, Vivaldi, and Columbus to Henry VIII, Elizabeth I, and Oliver Cromwell to Thomas Jefferson, Mark Twain, Emily Dickinson, Sarah Bernhardt, Vincent Van Gogh, and Jesse James.

Jacob and Esther Grunfeld had barely begun creating a family when, in 1881, Tsar Alexander II was assassinated in Saint Petersburg by revolutionists, some of them Jews. In retaliation, the tsar's son and successor, Alexander III, announced his intention to eliminate Russia's Jewish population altogether, either through emigration, conversion, or a series of murderous anti-Jewish pogroms that began the following year. Under the so-called May Laws of 1882, Jews were forbidden to own rural property or hold mortgages; more than one and a half million Russian Jews who had previously managed to live outside the Pale were now forced into it, and some half-million Jews already living in rural areas of the Pale were forced to leave their homes and live in towns or townlets known as *shtetls.*

Yet even as pogroms swept the villages of the northern Ukraine for five years, peace prevailed in the south, where the Grunfelds lived. The Russian peasants there, Albert Greenfield's older brother later recalled, were "fine fellows, generous to Jews."[18]

Jacob Grunfeld's more immediate concern as a grain merchant was not the pogroms but the May Laws that prevented Jews from living in towns or cities (where better jobs could be found) or from owning or renting farm-land. Moreover, the May Laws were constantly being revised to further re-strict Jews' access to education, to professions like law and medicine, and to their right to sell alcohol. Hundreds of thousands of Jews, having caught the scent in the wind, were decamping for the United States—the first of the great waves that over the next forty years brought some 3.2 million Russian and Polish Jews to America.[19] But Jacob Grunfeld, to judge from his subse-quent life, was a cautious man who hesitated to give up his relative prosperity in Russia in order to start life anew in a land where he enjoyed no connec-tions and did not speak the language.

As his descendants later told it, Jacob circumvented the restrictions against Jewish landowning by finding a trustworthy peasant to pose as a straw owner when government officials made their inspections.[20] But as the May Laws grew more onerous, Jacob was less inclined to rely on the peasant's loyalty. And as Jacob prospered, a rival grain merchant went into competi-tion with him.[21] So in June 1891, with five small children at home and his wife expecting a sixth, Jacob said good-bye to his family and his in-laws and left Lozovata for New York.[22] There Jacob found work ironing shirts in a gar-ment factory and apparently changed his surname to Greenfield.[23]

Esther followed him to New York late in 1891, bringing young Avrum with her as well as two infants—including a four-month-old daughter whom Jacob had yet to meet—but leaving her three eldest children behind in Lozovata.[24] Their journey in December 1891 began with a horse and wagon excursion of four or five hours to Vinnitsa, some thirty viersts to the west, where Jacob Serody sometimes conducted business with merchants. There Esther's group boarded a train to Austria and then another train to Ham-burg, Germany, where on December 18, 1891, they boarded the steamer Co-blenz, bound for Glasgow, Scotland. Here they transferred to the Devonia, which arrived in New York on January 6, 1892. In this circuitous manner, Avrum Moishe Grunfeld, at somewhere between the age of four and six, was removed from a tiny village in the Ukraine to the greatest city in the world.[25]

The three eldest children, led by fifteen-year-old Molly, finally arrived in New York in the spring of 1896, apparently after having been stranded in the English port of Liverpool for months or even a year.[26] A charming family legend contends that Avrum Moishe ultimately styled himself "Al-bert Monroe" after a Liverpool gentleman by that name who befriended the stranded siblings and possibly advanced them the funds they needed for their journey to America.[27] Conversely, another family legend holds that an Albert Monroe was captain of the ship that brought the Greenfield siblings to America.[28] Both stories may be spurious, but some support for either one lies in the curious fact that the eldest sibling in that threesome, fifteen-year-old Molly, named her first son Albert as well, just five years after her arrival in America.[29]

When those three eldest Grunfeld children finally arrived in New York on May 19, 1896, they were welcomed not only by their parents and younger siblings but also by a newborn sister named Rebecca.[30] They also learned that their family name had been changed to Greenfield. And somewhere around this time, their brother Avrum Moishe anglicized his first and middle names as well, to the name he would subsequently splash on houses and buildings throughout Philadelphia in the decades to come: Albert Monroe Greenfield.

Unlike his father (who after four years among Russian Jewish immigrants on New York's Lower East Side still spoke almost no English) and his older brother, Albert was young enough to attend school and learn to speak English with hardly a trace of accent. But he was also old enough to appreciate the difference between his native land and his adopted country. "To me," he put it many years later, "America is the fulfillment of a promise and hope which brought my own parents to these shores from a country dedicated to the aggrandizement of the few at the expense of the many."[31]

The Greenfields' arrival in New York coincided with the Panic of 1893, one of the longest and most severe economic depressions in American history. In the nation's rural heartland, the newly organized Populist Party bemoaned "a nation brought to the verge of moral, political, and material ruin."[32] Yet most of the immigrants then arriving by the hundreds of thousands saw only an empowering and energizing land of opportunity.

Immigrants, whether fleeing from persecution or merely seeking better jobs and homes, tend to be optimists, and consequently, they become agents of change wherever they settle. By the same token, a nation that welcomes immigrants becomes an incubator for change. What happens, then, when millions of immigrants, descended from ancestors who spent centuries surviving by their wits, suddenly arrive in a land conceived as a haven for immigrants—a place where, at least in theory, they may rise or fall not as members of a group but on their individual merits?

Many years would pass before Albert Greenfield would pause to reflect on that question. For the moment, at the age of eight going on nine, he was a very minor actor in a larger drama that had barely begun to unfold. Two separate historical threads—one triggered by the Romans' destruction of the Second Temple in Jerusalem in 70 C.E., the other by a group of lawyers and gentlemen farmers who gathered in Philadelphia in 1776 to stake their lives and fortunes on an unproven concept called democracy—were about to meet. America was about to change the way that Jews conducted business. And Jews—not least of them Albert M. Greenfield—were about to change the way that Americans conducted business.

[2]

The New World

In the fall of 1896, less than six months after the Greenfield family was reunited in New York, Jacob Greenfield received a letter from one of his former factory coworkers. The friend had moved to Philadelphia, where he had found a better job ironing shirts and where, he wrote, Jacob could do the same.[1]

The friend's letter arrived on a Friday. As an observant Orthodox Jew, Jacob could not travel on Saturday. But that Sunday Jacob took a train to Philadelphia to investigate the opportunity. After staying there with his friend for two weeks, he wrote to Esther, telling her to sell whatever possessions she could and ship the rest to Philadelphia.[2] Their son Avrum—now Albert Monroe Greenfield—was nine years old.[3]

Many years later, Albert Greenfield bristled whenever his career was described as a "rags to riches" story. The notion that he or his family had ever struggled was anathema to his perception of himself as a man to whom success had come "early and without any great difficulty."[4] He and his family, he suggested, were always masters of their fate, never victims. Yet the alacrity with which Jacob seized on this letter from Philadelphia suggests a man who was, if not desperate, at least lacking any assurance that another such offer would soon come his way on the crowded sidewalks of New York's Lower East Side.

When the Greenfields arrived in Philadelphia, the city was in the process of reinventing itself for perhaps the fifth time in its long history. Having been created in the seventeenth century as a utopian community, Philadelphia was not only the world's first planned city but also the world's only city founded and profoundly influenced by Quakers. In the eighteenth century it had evolved first into a maritime commercial center and then into the birthplace of American democracy as well as the nation's capital. In the early nineteenth century, Philadelphia gained prominence in still other guises: as the cultural "Athens of America" and as the nation's financial center.

But since the Civil War, Philadelphia's illustrious heritage had been largely discarded in favor of the more alluring possibilities of a modern industrial city. In this brave new urban world, railroads connected cities; streetcars connected neighborhoods within cities; and telegraphs and telephones connected people at great distances without their moving at all. A community's waking hours, once restricted by the rising and setting of the sun, were now extended as Thomas Edison's powerful electric lights illuminated homes, factories, businesses, and streets.

Thus the potential of a modern city seemed unlimited; and thanks to Philadelphia's unique proximity to the industrial holy trinity of coal, iron, and railroads, William Penn's "greene country towne" had once again reinvented itself—this time as "the workshop of the world," a manufacturing behemoth whose diverse capabilities had scarcely been matched anywhere before or since.

More than seven thousand Philadelphia mills and factories produced everything from Baldwin locomotives, battleships, telephones, and carpets to banjos, brooms, buttons, Stetson hats, and dental equipment.[5] The mightiest of all corporations, the Pennsylvania Railroad, was headquartered here. By 1900 Philadelphia's population had exploded to 1.3 million, almost double its size thirty years earlier, and it showed no sign of slowing down.

In this dynamic economy most Philadelphians worked not for large corporations but in small shops. The city's nearly five hundred cigar manufacturers each employed only a few workers, many of them recently arrived Russian Jews. Philadelphia's textile industry, the world's largest and most diversified, accounted for one-third of Philadelphia's jobs, but the city's eighty thousand textile workers were spread among more than thirteen hundred different companies. Two-fifths of that garment labor force consisted of Jews. As a member of that workforce, Jacob Greenfield enjoyed a built-in social network with which to ease his assimilation into his new homeland.[6]

Yet compared with immigrants in other cities, foreign-born Philadelphians exerted little presence or political power. The old Philadelphia families that constituted the city's social establishment had surrendered America's political leadership to Washington, D.C., in 1800, its financial leadership to New York in 1836 (when Andrew Jackson closed the Second Bank of the United States), and its intellectual leadership to Boston somewhere in between, and they had responded to these rejections in turn by rejecting the world outside their narrow group. The result was an ossified social elite that cherished bloodlines and local roots above merit or even wealth, a city that prompted Mark Twain's famous quip: "In Boston they ask, 'What does he know?' In New York, 'How much does he make?' In Philadelphia, 'Who were his parents?'"

Because of this emphasis on background and tradition, ambitious new-comers even before the Civil War tended to gravitate to New York rather than to Philadelphia; and after the Civil War, Philadelphia became the one Northern metropolis where native-born Americans remained not only in the majority but also in firm control of the city's political and economic life.

In a place where freshly arrived immigrants like the Greenfields were routinely relegated to low-paying jobs with long hours and abominable work-ing conditions, the one certain friend immigrants could count on was their neighborhood Republican ward committeeman. He would find them jobs, locate dwellings for them, help them obtain citizenship papers, and provide handouts: a bucket of coal, a basket of food, and free beer on holidays at the local taproom, which was usually owned by the committeeman himself or one of his relatives. In exchange for this material help, grateful immigrants were usually happy to vote as they were directed.[7]

But whereas New York, Boston, and Chicago developed Irish-run Demo-cratic political machines that catered to immigrants' needs while com-mandeering their votes, Philadelphia's Protestant Republican political ma-chine—run by men with names like Quay, Vare, and Penrose—frustrated the aspirations of immigrant Jews and Catholics alike (not to mention black Americans). Not coincidentally, this exclusionary political system operated one of America's most corrupt city governments, using public construction contracts to generate support and reinforce its control.[8] Public schools—in most cities the most likely vehicle for immigrant advancement—were run in Philadelphia by neighborhood boards populated by racetrack runners, sa-loon operators, and other political insiders, who routinely demanded kick-backs from the teachers they hired and fired.[9] This was the "corrupt and con-tented" city that the journalist Lincoln Steffens, in his 1903 study of big-city politics, labeled "the worst-governed city in the country."[10]

Of course, it still remained possible for outsiders to succeed in Phila-delphia. A long line of *auslanders*—from the Boston transplant Benjamin Franklin to the Frenchman Stephen Girard to the Austrian Catholic Fran-cis Martin Drexel to the Pew family from western Pennsylvania—had not merely survived but had flourished in Philadelphia despite the local estab-lishment's rejection. But doing so required ingenuity, determination, and a

thick skin. It also required the vision to perceive that the past and present
need not dictate the future—the sort of vision most likely to be found in the
fresh eyes of a newcomer from a foreign land.

L ike more than fifty thousand other Russian Jews, many of them from the
Ukraine, the Greenfield family settled in South Philadelphia.[11] Within
that vast neighborhood the family moved almost every year, and sometimes
more than once a year—a common pattern among newly arrived immigrants, who often changed flats because of conflicts with a landlord or to
take advantage of the free month's rent offered by a rival landlord as an in-
ducement to move.[12]

Albert, even at age nine, became the logical repository for the family's
hopes and dreams, and not just because he was the family's only school-age
male. He was, in the words of his older brother William, "a very smart boy, a
genius."[13] By most accounts Albert was not only smart but, with his auburn
hair and blue eyes, quite handsome as well. "If there had been a men's exhibition, he'd have won a prize," William later recalled.[14]

Albert demonstrated the benefits of his instinctive charm at an early age
when, according to family lore, a cousin anxious to show off his new horse
and buggy took the family for a drive and was stopped for a traffic violation
by a large and intimidating Irish policeman. In the midst of his harangue,
the cop sneezed, and Albert piped up, "God bless you!" The cop, momen-
tarily disarmed, put away his summons book and waved them on.[15]

Education for such a precocious child was a challenge. Waves of immigrants into South Philadelphia had created such crowded conditions in public schools that students often shared desks and books and sometimes sat on
milk crates instead of chairs. In some cases where schools were filled beyond
capacity, the overflow received instruction in homes nearby. Throughout the
city the school day was split into two sessions, with the result that grammar
school pupils attended for only three and a half hours a day instead of five.[16]

Almost immediately on the Greenfield family's arrival in Philadelphia,
Albert was enrolled at the Horace Binney School on Spruce Street near Sixth,
just a few blocks from Independence Hall. In this antiquated and unsanitary two-story structure, erected as a Presbyterian church school in 1814
and more recently named for a lawyer and congressman who had dominated
Philadelphia's bar through most of the nineteenth century, boys and girls
were taught separately. In Albert's class a single teacher took charge of more
than fifty boys.[17] Nevertheless, the Binney School provided Albert's first exposure to the larger and more sophisticated city beyond South Philadelphia's
Russian Jewish ghetto.[18] The fact that the school was not in his immediate

neighborhood—it was actually at least a mile from his home—may suggest the lengths to which his parents were willing to go to provide him a decent education.

Here Albert studied civics and rhetoric from McGuffey Readers. As an immigrant who likely enrolled at Binney a month or more into the school year, Albert was subjected to the hazing and bullying of his classmates. At a reunion years later he recalled "some of my more studious colleagues" who "used to shout me down when my answer to one of Miss Emma's questions was wrong."[19] On one occasion, when Albert was sent home for fighting, his older sister Rose presented herself to the principal on the pretense that their mother was ill, and promised that Albert would behave in the future—an incident that suggests both the difficulties Albert experienced at school and the tribal loyalty with which he and his siblings shielded each other from the outside world and even from their parents.[20] ("We'd have cut our arms off for each other," Albert's brother William recalled many years later.)[21]

Whatever hardships he may have suffered at the Binney School, at least in retrospect Albert embraced his rigorous free education there as the first of many blessings he experienced in his adopted homeland. "Doesn't it seem a Heaven-sent privilege to you," he asked his classmates more than a quarter-century later, "that the State should see to it that we, who were young urchins, should be given a lady of the sterling character of Miss Emma to be taught by her the obligations that we owed to each other and to ourselves?"[22]

At the same time, Albert gained his first taste of business at the street level. When he was ten, if his later account is to be believed, he sold scorecards outside ballparks and then (against his father's advice) branched out into peddling newspapers.[23] After school he worked at a drugstore.

Albert graduated from the Binney School's eighth grade in June 1899,[24] when he was not quite twelve, and enrolled in high school the following fall. At a time when most children's schooling ended in eighth grade and Philadelphia's Board of Education operated only four high schools, this was a remarkably ambitious act in itself.[25] But Greenfield exaggerated it in later life, claiming to have attended the elite Central High School, the city's only purely academic high school for boys. There is no evidence that he attended Central; more likely he was enrolled at Central Manual Training School, which was located not far from Central High in North Philadelphia.[26]

In any case, Albert attended high school for no more than two years and probably less.[27] Years later he said that he left school because he had to pay off debts that he had run up playing pool,[28] and perhaps he did play some pool: As a teenager, Albert was said to have run with a rough crowd of neighborhood boys, Catholics as well as Jews.[29] In addition to pool, they liked to sneak into musical comedies or burlesque shows, where they would sit in the front row and make funny faces and gestures to distract the performers.[30]

Yet Albert's private, and probably more genuine, passion as a boy was reading, especially history and biography. Without apparent direction from any teacher, he consumed books and articles about inspirational leaders like Napoleon ("as great a man as a man without a conscience could be," Albert later described him)[31] and organizational geniuses like J. P. Morgan and John Wanamaker. His favorite role model was Benjamin Franklin, who, as Albert later characterized him, "arrived in Philadelphia both homeless and penniless—a mere printer's apprentice, but with an ambition that knew no bounds." Albert was especially impressed by a quotation from the French writer Alexandre Dumas: "When I found out that I was black, I resolved to live as if I were white, and so force men to look below my skin." In the process of his reading, the thought first occurred to Albert: "Most of the world's great achievements were accomplished by men who were born poor," as he put it later.[32]

When Americans spoke of the "land of opportunity," they usually thought only in narrow economic terms: Here a poor man could become a rich man. But Albert's exposure to Philadelphia, as well as the Binney School and his books, planted the seeds of a much more audacious notion: If Alexandre Dumas could reinvent himself as a white man, and if Avrum Moishe Grunfeld could reinvent himself as Albert Monroe Greenfield, could an immigrant Russian Jew reinvent himself as an established German Jew, or even as an Old Philadelphia gentleman? If the "Athens of America" could reinvent itself as "the workshop of the world," could Albert Greenfield reinvent himself as J. P. Morgan or John Wanamaker or Benjamin Franklin, or even a combination of all three?

Ultimately, Albert's decision to drop out of high school at age fourteen was most likely prompted not by any poolroom debts but by his impatience with the academic process and his eagerness to begin making his own way in the world. "I was always in a hurry, I guess," Greenfield acknowledged years later.[33]

Once having quit school, Albert ran away from home to sell encyclopedias door-to-door in Harrisburg, a hundred miles to the west. He sold his first set on the first day and settled back to enjoy the fruits of his labors: a $25 commission, the equivalent of two weeks' wages for most working people in 1901. But he used up his expense money while waiting for the commission to arrive and finally was forced to look about for other means of support. When Albert answered an ad for a trolley car motorman, he was accepted immediately despite his youth, only to discover on the first day—when angry pedestrians along his route began pelting his vehicle with stones—that

he had been hired as a strikebreaker. Although the encyclopedia commission money still had not arrived, Albert hastily returned the trolley car to its
barn, pawned his watch to repay the Harrisburg landlady who had trusted
him for his rent, and wired home for the fare back to Philadelphia, where he
discovered that the encyclopedia company had ceased operations.

For a time Albert tried his hand as a book wrapper at John Wanamaker's,
the first of the world's great department stores.[34] He also worked briefly as
a reporter for a daily newspaper, the *Public Ledger*, earning $8 a week. After
he scored a scoop on a large fire that he reported firsthand, he asked for a
$2 raise; when his request was declined, he resigned.[35]

Whether any of these adventures really occurred is impossible to confirm; we have only Greenfield's word, as he later reconstructed his childhood
years in narratives that he no doubt embellished for the benefit of impressionable journalists as well as his adoring grandchildren. At the very least,
this picaresque account reflects the image Greenfield cherished for himself
throughout his life: that of a young man who was independent, entrepreneurial, plucky, and indefatigably upbeat from the very beginning.

In any case, before he turned fifteen Albert found his career path.

At some point in 1901 or 1902 he was hired as a clerk in the downtown
office of J. Quincy Hunsicker, a prominent real estate and mechanics
lien lawyer then in his late fifties—by one description, "a tall, fine looking
man of good figure" who, "while dignified, has a genial and attractive manner."[36] Here Albert learned conveyancing—a term that covers the transfer of
legal title from one person to another—as well as the granting of mortgages
or liens. At a time when typewriters were new and scarce, Albert was put to
work writing deeds and mortgages in longhand, a task he took to assiduously,
especially since he was paid by the job: $1.00 for every deed and $1.50 for
each bond and mortgage. "There's a mark here yet on my finger from writing
those deeds and mortgages by hand," he claimed a half-century later.[37]

Neither Hunsicker nor his son and associate, J. Quincy Jr., was Jewish;
they were descended from a Dutch farmer who had arrived near Philadelphia in the seventeenth century.[38] The Hunsickers' young associate, the huge
John J. McDevitt Jr., who had just joined their practice out of law school, was
not Jewish either.[39] But several of their clients were. Having been denied the
right to own land in Europe, many Russian Jews cherished an almost mystical reverence for real property, at precisely the time when America's real
estate market desperately needed their services.

In the past, landowners had typically held onto their properties for generations—believing, with the great nineteenth-century Philadelphia banker

Anthony J. Drexel, that "there is no more certain or reliable property to be held than real estate."[40] When landowners needed to sell, they usually did so directly, without a middleman. But from the 1880s onward, the huge influx of immigrants (as well as African Americans from the South) to cities like Philadelphia increased housing demands exponentially. In this seller's market, no license or professional credentials—or even much capital—was required to represent buyers or sellers, so a man with no real estate experience could call himself a broker and make a killing by selling a single house or lot. Consequently, the field was inundated with fly-by-night brokers who bought and sold properties at arbitrarily low or high prices.

In the process, these rogue brokers destabilized land values and undermined consumer confidence in real estate altogether. Amid such anarchy, even Anthony Drexel's successors were rethinking their faith in the certainty of real estate and shifting their assets into more liquid and seemingly more rational investments like stocks and bonds.

What American real estate operators needed at the turn of the twentieth century was someone who could do for them what Anthony Drexel and his partner J. P. Morgan had done for Wall Street a generation earlier, during the age of the robber barons: impose order on a chaotic market so as to make it safe and respectable for investors and sellers. That would require devising standard contracts, commission scales, valuation formulas, and professional codes of ethics.[41] Because Jewish immigrants were for the most part hungrier and more inventive than other men in the field, and also because the field was wide open to them, Jewish brokers came to dominate Philadelphia's real estate market by the turn of the twentieth century. The ingenious deals and projects concocted by Jewish Philadelphia brokers like Felix Isman, Alfred Fleisher, and the brothers Jules and Stanley Mastbaum attracted attention even from the *New York Times*.[42]

It was not unusual for Jewish real estate brokers in Philadelphia to rely almost exclusively on gentile lawyers for their legal needs. Unlike real estate, the practice of law was effectively closed to Jews. In Philadelphia at the turn of the century only a handful of Jews made their living practicing law; given the widespread anti-Semitism of judges, court clerks, and jurors, it was simply imprudent for clients—even Jewish clients—to hire Jewish lawyers.[43] Years later the noted Philadelphia lawyer Henry S. Drinker, an authority on legal ethics, candidly (and not unsympathetically) discussed the prevailing concern about Jewish lawyers, especially Russian Jews. One thing he noticed as chairman of the Philadelphia Bar Association's grievance committee, Drinker said, was that of the men who came before us who had been guilty of professional abuses, an extraordinarily large proportion were Russian Jew boys, young fellows who had been at the Bar a few years, and I could not understand why that was. I have known many splendid Jewish lawyers and judges and have had such great admiration for them, and I could not see why such a large proportion were this way. I asked some of my good friends among the Jewish lawyers why this was, and they told me that the Russian Jews, and the other foreign Jews too, who come over to this country, are all afire with an ambition that somebody in their family shall make good, and that if they have four or five boys and two or three girls, when they get big enough, they pick out the one that is the smartest, and they all make a sacrifice to let that boy get an education, and they put him through school and try to get him to be a professional man, and lots of them become lawyers and doctors. Well, the boy comes on, works in a sweat shop or somewhere in the daytime and he studies law at odd times mostly— some of them send them through college, but most cannot; and he comes to the Bar with no environment at all except that out of which he came, and, with the tremendous pressure back of him to succeed, he has to make good, the whole family have been sacrificing themselves so he can. He does not have a chance—he has not had a chance to absorb the American ideals. There are any number of foreign boys to whom that situation applies.[44]

Two of John McDevitt's clients—Benjamin Finberg, a Russian Jew, and David E. Simon, a German Jew—were among the biggest Jewish real estate brokers in Philadelphia, and both men took a liking to Albert and the industrious way this bright young clerk wrote out deeds and mortgages in longhand.

Having sniffed what his brother later called "the smell of real estate," Albert yearned to immerse himself further. He also was impatient with the life of an office clerk. After a year or so, when McDevitt left Hunsicker's office to open his own real estate law practice in 1903, Albert followed him to McDevitt's new office in the Land Title Building, a new complex of two office towers located at Broad and Chestnut Streets, then the very center of Philadelphia's business district.[45] Here, notwithstanding the barriers to Jews in the law, he conceived the notion of becoming a lawyer himself.

In the fall of 1903, while still working for McDevitt, Albert enrolled as one of thirteen night students at the University of Pennsylvania Law School.[46]

In so doing he may have been encouraged by the example of two friends from South Philadelphia, David Bortin (who was Jewish himself) and John Monaghan.[47] Albert financed his tuition by continuing to write deeds and mortgages, not only for McDevitt but also for one of his law school instructors.[48] Many of his nights were spent studying in Penn's law library, where the building's inadequate heat required him to wear his hat in the winter. Albert later blamed the building's frigid temperatures for accelerating his balding process, which began about this time, when he was only sixteen. Whatever the reason, by the time he turned twenty-one Albert was quite bald.[49]

In any case, after barely a year of law school, Albert became disillusioned with the law. "I thought law was a science," he remarked years later. "I was seventeen when I found out it wasn't."[50] More likely, as in high school, Albert had once again grown impatient with formal education and perceived a brighter future as a broker like Finberg or Simon rather than a lawyer like Hunsicker or McDevitt. He began casting about for ways to go into business for himself.[51]

Through McDevitt's clients, the real estate brokers Finberg and Simon, Albert had met Louis Cahan, a printer then in his late twenties, who in 1903 moved into a shop on Fourth Street below Walnut that Finberg had formerly occupied.[52] Cahan was a rare Russian Jew with a real estate *yichus*, of sorts: His father had built homes for the Russian nobility before fleeing the country in the mid-1880s.[53] Cahan lived with his family above his print shop, but he had an empty room—probably more like a cubicle—on the first floor behind his shop.[54] Albert approached a paperhanger named Earl Kunze and suggested that they set up a real estate office there. He harbored a vague notion that both Cahan the printer (as his landlord) and Kunze the paperhanger (as his partner) would be motivated to steer their customers to Albert when they had homes to buy or sell, and Albert, in turn, would steer *his* clients to them for printing real estate documents and papering walls, respectively.[55]

Notwithstanding his independent ways, his natty attire, and his red moustache, Albert was still only seventeen years old and living with his parents and siblings at this point.[56] For the $500 needed to set up the business, Albert approached his father. Jacob Greenfield had become a partner in a wholesale food plant about the time Albert left high school; by 1902 he had saved enough to open a grocery store and move his family in above the store. Over the next five years, Jacob owned as many as nine different groceries, some of them concurrently, often moving the family and relying on Esther and the oldest children to run the stores when he was not there.[57] Not all of these stores succeeded, but this little chain brought Jacob an income of

$3,000 to $4,000 a year—a comfortable living at a time when an annual income of as little as $500 was considered middle class.[58]

Still, Jacob was reluctant to lend Albert the necessary $500. What capital he had was tied up in his business; he had a wife and six children to support, and he was determined to give his other children the same high school education that (he felt) Albert had squandered. He told Albert to finish law school before going into business.[59]

Probably more to the point, Albert's independence seems to have rankled Jacob. As a schoolboy Albert had peddled newspapers against his father's advice. Although Jacob practiced Orthodox Judaism largely in the breach—sneaking Albert out of synagogue on the High Holidays to a restaurant and saloon next door—Albert had drifted away from Orthodoxy altogether; he does not appear to have become a bar mitzvah.[60] His intention to drop out of law school probably widened the gulf between father and son.

Undeterred by his father's rejection, Albert now turned to his mother. By most accounts, Esther was the family's business head as well as its backbone, and as such not the sort to hand out money frivolously. But unlike her husband, Esther perceived Albert not as a rebellious youth but as a kindred soul, as well as the family's best hope for the future. Her role, as she saw it, was not to stifle Albert's ambitions but to encourage them.[61] So Esther borrowed the necessary $500 from her brother, Michael Serody, then a young lawyer. Albert may have borrowed an additional $500 from his older brother William as well.[62]

With this cash, Albert bought himself a rolltop desk, a flattop desk for the outside office, a typewriter, a typewriter desk, and a few rugs and chairs. He also hired, at $12 a week, a young woman roughly his own age to serve as his stenographer.[63]

Probably in late 1904 Albert and his paperhanger partner Kunze opened their office in the rear of Louis Cahan's print shop.[64] Early in 1905 Albert dropped out of Penn's law school.[65] But the business went nowhere. Albert's partnership with Kunze appears to have dissolved almost immediately when Kunze opted to return to his paperhanging trade.[66]

Albert—no more daunted by this setback than he had been by his father's refusal to lend him $500 or by the failure of the encyclopedia company or by the taunts of his Binney School classmates—enlisted his landlord Cahan to replace Kunze. Cahan, in turn, brought an insurance broker named Israel Grossman into the partnership. Albert took no money from either man; making them his partners, he figured, would motivate them to steer their customers to him when they had real estate to buy or sell.[67]

Perhaps because Albert was not yet old enough to sign legal documents, the firm at first was styled Grossman, Cahan & Co. Albert was listed only as its secretary. But anyone who ventured into Cahan's printing shop got a very different impression. "The only well-dressed man in that grimy shop, you wore an extra-high starch collar," one of Cahan's customers recalled years later in a letter to Greenfield.[68] Between his fastidious attire and the red hair conveniently receding from his forehead, Albert conveyed an image of maturity and success even as he was just getting started.

On the day the firm opened for business in May 1905, horses and cows still outnumbered automobiles in Philadelphia. Farmers sometimes herded sheep downtown along Broad Street, Philadelphia's primary north–south boulevard. A burial ground occupied the heart of the business district at Fifteenth and Chestnut, and a stockyard operated on Market Street, the city's main east–west thoroughfare.[69] Albert Greenfield was seventeen years old and entering a business to which he brought no experience whatsoever—only his supreme confidence that the future would be different and that he would help to bring it about. Within a year he would make twice as much money as his father would ever make; within four years he would own, among other properties, the house where his parents lived;[70] within seven years he would be earning $60,000 annually; within twelve years he would be worth about $15 million; and within twenty-five years his company would be the largest real estate concern in the United States.

To everyone who crossed Albert Greenfield's path, what unfolded from that moment in 1905 was an astonishing story. To Greenfield it was simply a matter of seizing the opportunities that seemed, to his mind, to abound wherever a young man of limitless energy might turn in this brave new land.

[PART II]

POWER

[3]

Broker

Greenfield launched his business career at a time when businessmen of all stripes, native and immigrant alike (and even people not engaged in business at all), instinctively operated within the comfort zone of their relatives, friends, coreligionists, or *landsmen*—familiar faces they could trust. This was a logical approach at a time when most businesses were sole proprietorships or partnerships rather than corporations.

A partnership was much like a marriage: Any partner could be held liable for the partnership's debts. A single rogue partner could destroy not only the business but his individual partners as well. This unlimited liability explained why most partnerships were restricted either to blood relatives or close friends. Yet by its very inbred nature, this limitation usually prevented partnerships from taking risks and seizing broader opportunities.

From the outset Greenfield bridled at such restraints, in part because his sheer love of the game far outweighed his fear of financial failure. Like other immigrant entrepreneurs, he was happy to exploit his Russian Jewish contacts, or to cater to gentile stereotypes about Jews in order to build relationships. But he refused to be pigeonholed by his Jewishness and yearned to break out of that stereotype. As he saw it, this was the new world, not the old one.

"We didn't experience any anti-Semitism," his brother William later recalled of Albert's earliest real estate days. "The *goyim* liked to hear the Russian stories. We tried to set an example for them by being 'better' Jews than the Bainbridge–South Street second-hand storekeepers. They always said we were different Jews from any they knew."[1]

Albert began with the perception that capital mattered less than con-tacts. These he obtained at first from his landlord and partner, Cahan, who introduced Albert to his many printing customers. John McDevitt's law cli-ents, the real estate brokers Finberg and Simon, also gave young Albert some of their business to help him get started, sharing their commissions with him when he helped them sell properties.[2]

But it soon became clear that Albert did not need much help. Word spread quickly that young Greenfield was somehow able to move property that other brokers could not. He owed this success partly to his persuasive personality and his instinctive sense of timing in dealing with other people and partly because he knew—or gave the impression of knowing—so much that was important in Philadelphia. But his main asset was simply the fact that Albert, unlike most other Philadelphia brokers, did his homework.

Many brokers knew little or nothing about the properties they were given to buy or sell, but when Albert Greenfield was asked to sell a home or store, he immediately launched a thorough investigation not only of the property itself but also of the neighborhood where the property was located. He reasoned that people buy real estate based on their expectation of what the property will be worth five years later, and the best way to determine that is to examine the condition of the stores and businesses nearby: If they are prospering, property values are likely to rise. So he would scour the neigh-borhood where his client's property was located, interviewing merchants and coming up with so many examples of business prosperity that no potential buyer could argue with him. If a neighborhood's businesses were struggling, Greenfield studied these, too, to discover why. He did not, of course, discuss these failures with prospective buyers, but if a potential customer happened to mention them, Greenfield would be ready with an answer.

"What about Jacobson's Shoe Store?" the customer might ask. "It isn't do-ing well. Nobody ever goes in there."

"That's true," Greenfield would acknowledge. "But have you seen the shoes Jacobson is stocking? It isn't the neighborhood's fault that he's doing badly." He had an answer for everything, and thus it was hard to turn him down.

To Greenfield, success was a simple matter of common sense: Do it now. Get the facts first and then follow up with a call. Meet people, make them like you, and leave them with a smile. Smile over the telephone too. Take joy with you wherever you go.[3] "I knew that if I could make people satisfied with me, they would do business with me," Greenfield told a group of young professionals in 1922 while recalling those early days.

And to make people satisfied I had to do more than merely please them—I had to give them ideas or practical suggestions from which they would benefit in a material way. People are hungry for ideas—for worthwhile suggestions from those who think—most of us, you know, do not really think.

Therefore, I learned early that the way to sell real estate is not to sell real estate, but to convince my prospect that he needs the piece of ground, the building or the dwelling I have to offer. . . . Through this transaction I have done two things instead of one: I have sold my merchandise and also myself as a trustworthy counselor. Many of us simply sell our product and not the quality of confidence that inspires the customer to come back for a second order.[4]

Greenfield possessed one other unique asset: an apparently photographic mind, capable of flipping through deed and mortgage books and retaining all the figures he found. In effect, he became a walking encyclopedia of Philadelphia's real estate market—and, as such, the only broker with a genuine sense of property values, his own clients' and everyone else's. In the vast poker game that Philadelphia's real estate market had become, Greenfield effectively enjoyed the advantage of knowing which cards the other players held.

Of course, success did not come as smoothly as Greenfield claimed: During one bad spell he had to borrow money for postage stamps. But even his sixteen-year-old stenographer, who saw the flawed mortal behind his upbeat façade, confessed herself "frightened" by his formidable mind.[5]

Fostering the illusion of success quickly expanded Greenfield's clientele beyond the narrow circle of South Philadelphia Jews for whom he sold his first homes and stores. In his first year in business, Greenfield made $12,000 in commissions—this at a time when the average American worker made less than $400 a year and even the average dentist made only $2,500.[6]

By that time his partner Israel Grossman, the insurance man, had withdrawn because he could not tolerate Greenfield's one-man-band style of operation. Albert shrugged and reconstituted the partnership in 1906 as Cahan, Greenfield & Co.

He was still only nineteen years old at this point and thus legally dependent on the partnership of adults. But in 1906 Albert applied for and obtained U.S. citizenship—nine years before his father did so. In the process he added two and a half years to his real age. This kind of age inflation was common practice among teenage male immigrants in South Philadelphia, who were encouraged by Republican ward leaders to become citizens so they could vote in exchange for favors like extra lumps of heating coal in the winter. (Albert's older brother William had done the same thing four years earlier, claiming in 1902 to have been born in 1880 rather than 1882.) The impatient Albert was surely eager to ingratiate himself with the city's ruling political party too, but certifying his age as twenty-one in 1906 also enabled him to sign legal papers and applications for bank loans.[7]

At first his clients were mostly buyers and sellers of homes. But almost from the outset Albert perceived far more lucrative opportunities in serving the needs of business—especially fledgling businesses whose potential might be recognized only by a visionary like Greenfield himself.

One such business that seemed obvious, at least to Greenfield, was motion pictures. The process of sequencing photographs in rapid succession to create the impression of movement had been developed in the 1880s.[8] The first "Life Motion Photographs" were primitive flickering images projected onto bedsheets hung in halls, churches, and vacant storerooms for no more than a few minutes. Yet as crude as these "movies" may have seemed, their sheer novelty brought a small ray of sunshine into the otherwise gloomy working days of immigrants toiling in urban sweatshops. Inevitably, the first movie pioneers—men like William Fox, Louis B. Mayer, Adolph Zukor, Samuel Goldwyn, and the Warner brothers—were immigrants themselves, men who had dealt with immigrant families as garment peddlers, junk collectors, and grocers. In this manner, a crude amusement dismissed by the business establishment as a passing fad quickly expanded from makeshift halls into nickelodeons and peepshows specifically dedicated to movies.[9]

Full-length feature films were still on the horizon when Greenfield went into the real estate business, but Greenfield recognized, as much as the movie pioneers themselves did, that the future of their industry would require large and even palatial movie theaters where, for a few hours, ordinary workers, clerks, and shop girls could escape into the world of fantasy. In short, he perceived that the movie industry's future was inextricably linked to real estate.

The year 1907 saw the opening of the Market Street Subway and Elevated—Philadelphia's first rapid transit railway—connecting Philadelphia's downtown with the city's western limits. Where rapid transit goes, Greenfield theorized, new development follows. Amid the cow paths and country lanes of undeveloped West Philadelphia, he envisioned thriving complexes of theaters, stores, and apartments. The Breberman brothers, manufacturers who had known Greenfield's father in Russia, introduced him to two banks in South Philadelphia, and with their support Greenfield began buying up lots in West Philadelphia.[10] In the process he graduated from a mere real estate broker to a real estate speculator.

In 1908, as agent for movie theater interests, Greenfield bought several lots along the two blocks of Fifty-Second Street between Walnut and Market. He also organized a syndicate that built several stores along that strip. Two years later, when Philadelphia's biggest real estate brokers—Felix Isman and Mastbaum Brothers & Fleisher—were ready to move into West Philadelphia, Greenfield was their logical choice to attempt to corral all the real estate on Fifty-Second Street between Spruce and Market Streets. Working quickly and secretively, he assembled virtually every available property on that four-block strip before any of the property owners realized what he was doing, thus holding the purchase prices down. Isman and the Mastbaum Brothers' firm paid $2.5 million for the entire package; Greenfield's two-and-a-half percent commission came to $62,500.[11] The following year he performed the same service for Mastbaum Brothers & Fleisher along Sixtieth Street. There the transaction amounted to $1.8 million.[12]

Greenfield's commissions on these deals were so astonishing that by this point Albert's partner, Cahan, had abandoned his printing business to focus exclusively on real estate.[13] But, of course, by now Albert no longer needed Cahan's services or even his office (Albert had moved a few doors down Fourth Street from Cahan in 1907).[14] Even at this early stage of his career, Albert was uncomfortable working with partners. What he needed now was not the connections Cahan had provided to get him started but the capital with which to buy properties and, ultimately, build and manage them.

In 1911, when Cahan inexplicably rejected Albert's request to be promoted from secretary to vice president of Cahan & Greenfield, Albert quit the partnership. Now he installed himself in the Real Estate Trust Building, a sixteen-story skyscraper on Broad Street downtown, a far cry from the cubicle he had occupied at Cahan's print shop just a few years earlier. Here he formed a new company, entirely his own, as its title suggested: Albert M. Greenfield & Co.[15] His older brother William joined him as secretary-treasurer—the first of dozens of relatives Albert would hire over the next four decades.[16]

The next four years found Albert venturing into the Logan neighborhood north of downtown, buying up what he saw as undervalued real estate and then developing it into a business district along North Broad Street. Eventually, he sold properties there for several million dollars.[17] When a seven-mile stretch of the new Roosevelt Boulevard was opened from North Broad Street into Philadelphia's vast but largely rural northeast section, Greenfield bought and resold properties there, astutely anticipating that land values would soon rise with the opening of the new boulevard, just as they had risen with the opening of the subway to West Philadelphia.[18]

Out of necessity, Greenfield's ventures into West Philadelphia, Logan, and Northeast Philadelphia shared a common pattern: In each place he acquired properties and mortgages that were either undervalued or in default, if only because he possessed little capital of his own to invest. His success at packaging theater properties for Isman and the Mastbaums had whetted his appetite to develop, own, and manage real estate rather than merely sell it for clients. He was also eager to try his hand at changing the face of Philadelphia's downtown as he had done along Fifty-Second and Sixtieth Streets. But how could he raise the necessary capital without giving up control to partners or lenders?

While mulling this question in 1913, Greenfield serendipitously encountered Solomon C. Kraus, a prominent real estate broker some twenty years his senior. Kraus's parents had arrived from Bohemia a generation before the Greenfields, and Kraus had begun as a coal dealer before gravitating into real estate. Now he was acknowledged as the leading real estate man in North Philadelphia, with a home in Philadelphia's relatively fashionable Strawberry Mansion section, off Fairmount Park near Thirty-Third Street (just two blocks from Louis Cahan's home).[19]

Sol Kraus was also known as the "father" of South Philadelphia's building and loan associations. These were cooperative organizations that functioned like banks—paying interest to immigrants who made monthly deposits, then offering them mortgages to buy homes—without a conventional bank's overhead expenses, like bricks, mortar, and salaried employees. This ingenious scheme gave Kraus access to idle capital as well as the ability to provide financing for the homes he sold, which in turn further enhanced his reputation as a successful broker. He was a man of many charities and extensive fraternal connections, including B'rith Sholom, the largest Jewish fraternal order in the United States (of which he ultimately became grand master). Kraus was also a sought-after personality who enjoyed sports as well as card games like pinochle.[20] In any given project Kraus insisted on being the boss; his associates even *called* him "Boss."[21]

The two men had actually met seven years earlier, when Greenfield called on Kraus about a piece of property.[22] In many respects their personalities were similar—aggressive, competitive, overbearing, tempestuous, but also charming—and, consequently, they had taken an instant dislike to each other. However, as businessmen Kraus and Greenfield both instinctively recognized that successful men rarely possess placid personalities and that each might benefit from working with the other.

When their paths crossed again in 1913, Albert noticed another potential benefit of working with Kraus. Kraus's daughter Edna Florence was nineteen and terribly pretty, with reddish hair, clear white skin, and huge blue eyes. She dressed stylishly and smelled of lavender. She took singing lessons and played the piano. She had attended Philadelphia's elite Girls' High School and then had spent a year at an even more prestigious institution: Bryn Mawr College, on Philadelphia's exclusive Main Line. She was said to be the first Jewish girl at Bryn Mawr since its founding in 1885.[23]

It is perhaps a reflection on Albert's preoccupation with his work to the exclusion of everything else that at this point he was still single and living with his parents and his younger siblings. Although Albert was seven years older than Edna Kraus (and claiming to be older than that), he was instantly smitten with this walking vision of the good and beautiful life to which every immigrant aspired. He was also no doubt attracted by the prospect of advancing his social and financial status through an advantageous marriage. In due course he began pursuing Sol Kraus's young and impressionable daughter with all the charm and energy that he had previously reserved for his real estate deals.

The resistance he encountered came not from Edna but from her family. For all of Albert's success, Sol Kraus's opinion of him had not changed since their first meeting: He regarded the young Greenfield as an upstart. Edna's maternal grandparents, the Mayers, were urbane and proud German Jews from Frankfurt am Main who had emigrated along with many other German Jews after the failed revolution of 1848. These Jewish Germans had experienced difficulties gaining acceptance from gentile America, but as Western Europeans their backgrounds were at least somewhat enlightened and comfortable. So they shrank from the prospect of being associated in gentile minds with the much larger wave of Russian Jewish immigrants to which Albert Greenfield belonged: In Philadelphia, for example, Russians accounted for 70 percent of the city's hundred thousand Jews by 1905.[24]

As nations, Poland and Russia had always been more backward than the states of Western Europe, and within Poland and Russia themselves the Jews occupied society's lower rungs. Thus, in contrast to their cultivated German brethren, the Jews from Poland and Russia seemed poor, dirty, ignorant, and pushy—"peasants," as one of Greenfield's Philadelphia contemporaries put it.[25] To avoid the stigma of the new arrivals, America's German Jewish community perpetrated the very sort of rigid caste system they would have condemned had it been practiced by gentiles: German Jewish businesses, clubs, synagogues, and even charities were closed to the Russian and Polish Jews, who had to start their own.

Greenfield felt no resentment toward German Jews; on the contrary, he aspired to become one himself. He wore high collars in the German style and, about this time, began attending services at Philadelphia's Reform (that is, German) Congregation Keneseth Israel.[26] To the Krauses and Mayers, these attempts to Germanize himself merely reinforced Albert's image as a parvenu interloper. But ultimately their objections proved irrelevant. As Greenfield's daughter-in-law later remarked, "If he could sell all that real estate without owning any, he could obviously sell a girl to marry him."[27]

Edna later confessed that she married Albert because he sent her "the nicest box of chocolates"—perhaps the first example of Greenfield's lifelong pattern of sending chocolates, fruit baskets, flowers, or birthday greetings to anyone likely to be useful to him.[28] Sol Kraus—perhaps as mindful as Albert of the business advantages—reluctantly consented to their marriage.

Six weeks after their wedding in June 1914, Albert further ingratiated himself with his new in-laws by joining the Reform Congregation Keneseth Israel.[29] Shortly after, he began teaching with the Hebrew Sunday School Society under the direction of his fellow congregant, the prominent German Jewish lawyer Horace Stern, who within a few years would become a Common Pleas Court judge and later the first Jewish justice on the Pennsylvania Supreme Court.[30]

The newlyweds set up housekeeping in the St. James Hotel, a stylish downtown building designed ten years earlier by the noted architect Horace Trumbauer.[31] Within a year they had moved to a house on Broad Street deep in South Philadelphia, where in June 1915 Edna delivered their first son.[32]

Albert, eager to seize every opportunity to Americanize himself, proposed to name the child Albert Jr. By suggesting such a thing he horrified not only Edna and her family but his own family as well: According to Ashkenazic Jewish tradition, children were to be named only for deceased ancestors, never for the living. To Greenfield these Old World rules no longer applied; this was a new world, where any man of pluck and ingenuity could fashion his own rules. But Albert was in no position to alienate the Krauses, who at this point represented his best ticket to the higher reaches of financial, political, and social status. So Albert shelved his idea and apparently conceded the naming rights to his in-laws: Gordon Kraus Greenfield was named not for a relative but for a local judge with whom the Krauses had been friendly.[33] Albert's dream of passing his name directly to a son would remain on the back burner for another day.[34]

Sometime after delivering Gordon, Edna began to demonstrate signs of obsessive/compulsive disorder and in particular a germ phobia that caused her to wear white gloves at all times and to shrink from physical contact with anyone. Although she delivered a second child—a daughter named Elizabeth—in 1917, she refused to hold or even touch the baby.[35] The fact that she bore three daughters between 1917 and 1923 indicates that she had at least some physical contact with her husband; but as a consequence of her germ phobia, those three daughters grew up without ever being held by their mother. The children's cuddling and general motherly attention would be left almost entirely to nannies and housekeepers.[36]

Further emboldened by his alliance with Kraus, between late 1913 and 1915 Greenfield created a syndicate that built four or five more movie theaters in South and West Philadelphia. These he sold in 1916 to the Stanley Company, an organization created by the brothers Jules and Stanley Mastbaum, for more than $2 million.[37] Even Greenfield's headquarters seemed constantly on the move: By 1915 he had left the Real Estate Trust Building for an office one block away, at Thirteenth and Chestnut, and a few years later he moved again, to much more visible offices on the upper floors of a four-story building at the northeast corner of Fifteenth and Chestnut Streets. Here a huge nameplate between the building's second and third stories proclaimed the presence of "Albert M. Greenfield & Co., Real Estate" to all who passed through one of Philadelphia's busiest intersections.[38]

A major setback—or at least what would have been a major setback to anyone else—in Greenfield's relentless upward trajectory occurred in 1917 when one of his clients died. Greenfield had endorsed notes for the client amounting to hundreds of thousands of dollars, and he was held liable for the full amount when the client died insolvent. "It took everything I had," he later claimed.

This reversal raised a question about Greenfield's motivations that would be debated throughout his career: Was he driven (as he and his friends insisted) by sheer optimism and a joy of serving others that caused him always to see his cup as half full? Or was he driven (as others suggested) by a sublimated lack of self-esteem that caused him to refuse to acknowledge problems and to insist that everything was fine even when it was not? Whatever the answer, both interpretations suggest that money or the lack of it never concerned Greenfield terribly. In the case of the insolvent client, he seems to have welcomed the challenge of bouncing back, almost as if it helped him sharpen his blade. He sold properties to pay off his debt and gamely set about rebuilding his operation from scratch, with such apparently quick success that by 1920 he had reestablished his fortune, capitalizing on the post–World War I depression through what was becoming his typical practice: purchasing property in foreclosure proceedings and reselling it for a profit.[39]

A more cautionary lesson began that same year, 1917, in Greenfield's efforts to join Philadelphia's political establishment. For immigrants— Irish and Italian as well as Jewish—politics represented a conduit not only to money and power but also to status and prestige, intangible commodities that seemed unobtainable through the private sector.[40] And in a city dominated by Republicans there was no question as to which party an ambitious real estate operator should join. Philadelphia's Republican machine had been dominated since the 1880s by three Vare brothers—George, Edwin, and Bill—who had used their political clout to build their family's small contracting business in South Philadelphia into a major street-cleaning operation. Between 1888 and 1921 the Vares collected $28 million from 341 public contracts for street cleaning, sewer construction, bridge building, and street resurfacing.[41]

In theory these contracts were determined by the city's two councils, but these were large and unwieldy legislatures, with 146 members between them, where all matters had to be considered by committees before being discussed in Council chambers. Thus, any committee could obstruct a bill by holding it back, and of the twenty-seven Council committees, the Vare organization controlled the most important ones—as Philadelphia's reform mayor, Rudolph Blankenburg, discovered when the Vares thwarted virtually all his initiatives during his single term from 1912 to 1916.

"The whole body is organized so that a very few strong-willed and corrupt men at points of vantage arrange everything," noted Blankenburg's director of public works, Morris L. Coke. "A bare half dozen absolutely dictate to twenty times their number."[42]

Any Philadelphian who aspired to power, or at least the appearance of power (which often amounted to the same thing), would need to be visibly identified with the Vare camp, or so Greenfield believed at this point in his career. To conduct business with the city or develop land required friends in City Hall and the courts, or at least the illusion of such friendships. Greenfield was only too happy to play the game.

George Vare had died in 1908, but Edwin Vare had succeeded his brother as a state senator, and William, the youngest Vare brother, held Philadelphia's First District seat in the U.S. Congress beginning in 1915. Greenfield cultivated their support not only by raising funds and making generous donations to the machine's candidates but also by handling their real estate matters. The Vares reciprocated by granting him access to city business. In 1917, for example, Greenfield first began handling real estate transactions for the Philadelphia Rapid Transit Company (PRT), the privately owned concern that managed the city's public streetcars and elevated trains. Later that year the Vares slated Greenfield for a seat in the Common Council, the lower of Philadelphia's two legislatures.

This recognition should have been a feather in Greenfield's cap. But it came at a rare moment of bitter factional warfare within Philadelphia's Republican machine that would soon result in the demise of the two city councils altogether. In 1917 a group of ostensible reformers led by the patrician U.S. senator Boies Penrose broke with the Vares and threw their strength behind a reform "Town Meeting" ticket.[43] Amid the contentiousness, Greenfield—who stuck with the Vares—seemed largely irrelevant. He campaigned for his Council seat with his customary gusto and ingenuity, calling on the women in his district who were usually overlooked at election time because they could not vote; his ploy was to charm them into influencing their husbands to vote for him.[44]

Greenfield's campaign efforts were surely wasted. The Vares barely maintained their majority in the councils overall, but in South Philadelphia their efficient organization easily elected its entire slate, including the three Common Council seats in Greenfield's Thirty-Ninth Ward. Once installed, Greenfield found himself one of ninety-seven members, most of whom were mere errand boys for the Vares or their Town Meeting adversaries. At the end of his first year in office, a charter revision movement, aimed at eliminating the two-council structure, was launched at a dinner attended by more than nine hundred patrons. Greenfield, who fancied himself a community visionary, was not with them; instead, his loyalty to the Vares had boxed him into a hoary vestige of Philadelphia's past.

In mid-1918 Greenfield spent $50,000 to purchase a spacious stone and stucco home with grounds at Johnson and Greene Streets in Germantown. Then he and Edna set about rebuilding it—installing ornate moldings, semicircular balconies, and a Greek rotunda guarding the front doorway; adding a pool, playhouse, tennis court, and a large garage with chauffeur's quarters; and converting a barn on the property into a stable for the family's horses.[45]

This neighborhood in Philadelphia's northwest section was home to many influential civic figures but precious few of the Jews who had composed his Council constituency. Greenfield's purchase of property outside his councilmanic district—miles away, in fact—suggests that he had grown disaffected with the life of a councilman and had already decided not to seek reelection but to invest his political energies elsewhere.[46]

While the Greenfields awaited the completion of their Germantown home renovations, they remained in their house on South Broad Street. Early in the morning of Monday, November 25, 1918, as Albert and Edna slept in their second-story rear bedroom, Albert—always a light sleeper—awoke to a room filled with smoke. He sprang out of bed, awakened Edna, and ran into the hall, only to find the hall in flames and his access to the rear stairway cut off. A few crossed electric wires at the base of the front stairway had apparently set off the blaze, which then made its way up the stairs.

Wrapping Edna in a blanket, Greenfield carried her through the smoke and flames of the hallway, down the front stairway, and then out the front door. Although he had been burned about the face and hands, he went back into the house in search of their two children. Smoke filled their bedrooms, but Greenfield wrapped them carefully in blankets and groped his way through the smoke-filled hallways to the outdoor front stoop, first with Elizabeth (then twenty months old) and then with Gordon (age three and a half).

Two domestic servants—a maid and the cook—awakened by the shouting, made a futile effort to escape from their rooms on the third floor. Believing their escape route was cut off, both women ran to a rear window and leaped to the shed roof in the rear, where they scaled down the side of the shed to the backyard.

Firefighters responded quickly and doused the blaze, limiting the damage to what Greenfield estimated as some $2,500 worth of valuable paintings and draperies. Greenfield was treated by a physician but insisted his injuries were not serious; the maid was taken to Methodist Hospital nearby.[47]

That, at least, is the account of the fire as it was provided to firefighters and the Philadelphia newspapers, presumably by Greenfield himself. At a family gathering more than four decades later he provided a slightly less heroic version: While he ran downstairs to phone the fire department, Edna awoke the rest of the house; a nanny carried baby Elizabeth out in a blanket, and Greenfield broke down the door to Gordon's room and carried him to safety as well. Edna presumably escaped under her own steam.[48]

But if the original account—in which Greenfield wrapped up his wife and carried her to safety before returning for the two children—is correct, it must give one pause. What mother would want to be carried from a fire without first making sure that her children were safe? What father would accommodate such a request?

In moments of panic, of course, people respond unpredictably and irrationally. It is possible that Albert rescued Edna first on the presumption that the children would be saved by one or more of the servants. But it is

BROKER 43

also possible that Edna's germ phobia was foremost in her mind as well as Albert's. In that case, Edna's reaction to the fire provided an early hint of the sort of psychological issues that would subsequently develop into a major burden on their marriage.

By the end of Greenfield's two-year term in Common Council, the state legislature had enacted a new charter for Philadelphia that in 1919 replaced the two councils and their 146 delegates with a single City Council of just twenty-one seats.[49] In effect, Greenfield's seat was eliminated, along with those of most of his Council colleagues, which was just as well with him. "There was little I could contribute to a city where the political machine dictated to the Council," he told an interviewer years later, eliding his own involvement in that machine.[50] More likely he perceived that, in politics as in business, he operated best as a leader rather than a team member.

He remained an active fund-raiser and supporter of the Vare brothers for years thereafter. When Edwin Vare died in 1922, Greenfield handled the real estate matters for his estate.[51] By 1923 Greenfield was sending periodic fruit baskets to Edwin's younger brother and successor, Congressman William Vare, in Washington, and William Vare was reciprocating by sending postcards from vacations in France addressed to "Friend Al."[52] But after 1919 Greenfield related to the Vares not as a subservient officeholder but as an equal who operated from his own independent power base. He never sought public office again. Instead, he found other outlets to satisfy his hunger to be at the center of things.

When the United States entered the Great War in 1917, Greenfield offered his services to the Four-Minute Men, an organization of notable Americans who gave patriotic speeches and led patriotic songs in support of Liberty Loan bond drives at movie houses across the country. It was an opportunity to enhance his public profile while demonstrating the patriotism of Jews in general. He also supervised the Philadelphia campaign for the Foreign Relief Committee, a role that threw him in contact for the first time with the campaign's national chairman, the entrepreneur-turned-humanitarian philanthropist Herbert Hoover.[53]

In his quest for acceptance among Philadelphia's German and Sephardic Jews, Greenfield now became active in Jewish fund-raising campaigns as well. As early as 1906 his name had appeared on a list of subscribers to the campaign to build Philadelphia's Mount Sinai Hospital, a Russian Jewish institution that finally opened in 1921.[54] After World War I he became active in raising funds for relief of Russian Jewish war refugees, donating an astonishing $92,000 to a campaign that raised $1.5 million in Philadelphia and $20 million nationwide.[55]

In the process, Greenfield discovered that his skills as a real estate promoter could be put to equal use in raising funds for worthy causes as well as bridging the gulf between Russian and German Jews. He became a master of the famous, or infamous, Jewish charity tactic of inviting wealthy men to a luncheon or dinner and then, when the meal was over, forcing them to stand up and pledge a contribution in such a way that each was embarrassed into giving more than he intended.

"Five thousand?" Greenfield would shout incredulously from the dais at a shame-faced contributor. "What do you mean, only five thousand? On the X-Y-Z deal last year you made ten thousand alone. On that deal with me in West Philly you made twenty thousand." The implications of such a harangue were twofold: First, the man could afford to give much more than he proposed, and second, if he wanted to continue doing business with Albert Greenfield, he had better increase his pledge to this worthwhile cause. And so, to silence Greenfield's stinging recitation of the man's private business affairs—and Greenfield knew more about people's private business affairs than anyone else—the man would reluctantly agree to increase his contribution.

After World War I, Philadelphia's Federation of Jewish Charities— created in 1901 to raise funds for the city's German Jewish organizations— voted for the first time to combine with the city's Russian charitable organizations in a single fund-raising drive. This new unity was partly a reaction to the rise of anti-Semitism across the United States, but it was also motivated by the growing wealth of the Russian Jews, especially Greenfield.[56]

His help in aggressively soliciting and collecting pledges was welcomed by the more reticent Germans and Sephardim; Dr. Cyrus Adler, the prominent Judaica scholar and a leader of a national Jewish war relief drive in 1921, readily acknowledged that Greenfield possessed one of the "best business heads available."[57]

Greenfield's leadership of Federation fund-raising campaigns in 1922 and 1923 were so successful—the two campaigns raised more than $5 million—that one of his Federation colleagues teased him, "Even the Protestant Episcopal Church wishes you'd consent to being chairman of their present campaign."[58]

At about this time Greenfield became one of the first two non-German members of the Jewish upper-class Mercantile Club. In the process he took his place not only among his Kraus and Mayer relatives but also among the Wolfs, Gimbels, Fleishers, and Philadelphia's other leading German Jewish families.[59]

Within five years of his marriage to Edna Kraus, Greenfield's wealth and influence easily overshadowed that of his father-in-law, Sol Kraus, to such an extent that in 1920 Kraus merged his own real estate company into Albert's and became first vice president of Albert M. Greenfield & Co.[60] In this seeming victory over his erstwhile rival, Greenfield was gracious and accommodating; as in most relationships throughout his life, he preferred to focus his energies on turning enemies into friends rather than nurse grudges. He cheerfully continued to address his father-in-law by Kraus's preferred sobriquet—"Boss"—but a 1921 "Dear Boss" letter from Greenfield to Kraus left little doubt as to who was really in charge. Responding to Kraus's request that one of their building and loan associations should lend an additional $5,000 to a Mr. Anderson, Greenfield wrote back:

> Have concluded not to ask the Association to do this. I know that you are a friend of Mr. Anderson's and would like to help him, but that is not the relationship he bears to me, and I am unwilling to advance any additional sums to Mr. Anderson, because he has been continuously in arrears, and has been a source of trouble to the officers of the building associations. . . . At best it is . . . an undesirable loan for a building association. . . . I would thank you if you would not press me to go any further with this proposition, as I really do not wish to do it, and whilst I would not hesitate to refuse Mr. Anderson a further loan, because my relationship with him is purely business, and on that basis he has no claims, I do hesitate not to follow any suggestion you make, but it does seem to me that in this case, it will be best if we get Mr. Anderson to gradually pay up his arrearages with the hope that finally the loan will be repaid to us at a not too distant date.[61]

By the early twenties, Philadelphians' seemingly insatiable appetites for homes of their own had given rise to literally thousands of building and loan associations: At that time Philadelphia had more single-family homes than New York and Boston combined, and more than 50 percent of these were owner-occupied.[62] By this time, Kraus and Greenfield had gained control of twenty-seven building and loan associations with total assets of $35 million, thus enhancing Greenfield's value as a broker by giving himself control over the financing of his real estate. A Greenfield & Co. brochure in 1922 listed the firm as conveyancer for twenty-two building and loan associations, many of them named for Kraus and Greenfield relatives—"S. C. Kraus," "Gilbert," "Gordon," "Lillian," and "Almar," for example.[63] No longer could a potential customer turn down a Greenfield house by saying he had no money: Greenfield would *lend* him the money, through one of his loan associations.

But, of course, by this time Greenfield had outgrown his dependence on Kraus, just as, a decade earlier, he had outgrown his dependence on his partner Louis Cahan. Another ally had entered his life who offered Greenfield a possible entrée to the national stage.

The movie mogul William Fox was a Hungarian Jew, born Vilmos Fuchs in 1879.[64] His parents brought him to the United States when he was nine months old, and he grew up on New York's Lower East Side. Fox entered the arcade and nickelodeon business by opening a small movie theater in Brooklyn in 1904. After a rocky first few months, that venture succeeded, and he subsequently opened other small theaters in New York, gradually developing larger, more upscale ventures. In 1907 he began distributing films, and by 1914 he was making movies himself from a rented studio in Fort Lee, New Jersey, across the Hudson River from Manhattan.

Like most pioneering filmmakers, Fox perceived movies as a potentially lucrative business; but unlike his fellow movie moguls, Fox was an idealistic socialist who cherished the hope that movies could inspire the masses to create a better world. Given the chaotic nature of the movie business, Fox valued real estate as a stabilizing factor. In any case, both his film company and his theater operation proved successful. By 1916, Fox was established in Hollywood, but he continued to make movies in the New York area and to maintain his headquarters there.[65]

About this time Fox encountered trouble booking his films into the Mastbaum brothers' two theaters on Market Street in downtown Philadelphia. Fox felt the Mastbaums were discriminating against him because of their connection with the dominant studio of the day, Famous Players-Lasky (later to become Paramount). The Mastbaums—Greenfield's friends—insisted that Fox's films were not good enough to play in their theaters. In October 1920 Fox threatened to build his own theater if he could not find adequate outlets in Philadelphia, and the following June—apparently with Greenfield's representation—Fox took a fifty-year lease on a lot at Sixteenth and Market Streets adjoining the Mastbaums' 1,600-seat Stanton Theatre.[66]

The feud was settled in August 1921—presumably by Greenfield—when the Mastbaums signed a two-year pact promising to show Fox's features (especially his extravaganza, *Over the Hill*, about a woman abandoned by her children) at the Stanton; in return, Fox agreed to shelve his plans to build a rival theater for at least two years.[67] Fox's sixteen-story office building and

2,423-seat theater (called the Fox) opened in November 1923, after the pact expired.[68]

In the process of these maneuverings, and somehow without alienating the Mastbaums, Greenfield acquired a valuable client and friend. Greenfield was surely no socialist, but in Fox he found a kindred soul who shared Greenfield's conceit that a single inspired individual possessed the power to remake the world.

B y the dawn of the 1920s, Greenfield was owner of the largest real estate business in Pennsylvania and one of the largest in the entire United States, doing about $125 million worth of transactions a year.[69] Yet for all his success to this point, Greenfield remained a peripheral figure to Philadelphia's business establishment. He yearned to test himself not just against his fellow immigrant real estate brokers but also against the city's movers and shakers in their own downtown bailiwick.

His first opportunity arose in 1920 when, during the nationwide recession that followed World War I, Philadelphia's Metropolitan Opera House went on the auction block. That huge, block-long structure on North Broad Street—the largest and perhaps most sumptuous theater of its kind in the world, seating more than four thousand people—had been built in 1908 by the theatrical impresario Oscar Hammerstein I. But it had been a white elephant from the start. A year after its opening, with no hope of paying off a $400,000 mortgage, the great building had faced closure. It was saved by the grand old man of Philadelphia banking, E. T. Stotesbury himself, the senior partner of Drexel & Co., and, as such, a partner of J.P. Morgan & Co. in New York, whose financial resources dwarfed those of other Philadelphia banks. Stotesbury had been employed at Drexel & Co. since 1866—had been there, in fact, when Anthony Drexel offered a partnership to the young J. P. Morgan Sr. in 1871.

Like Greenfield, Stotesbury was a shrewd, energetic, peppery, and peripatetic little man (it was said that he never read a book because he never sat down for more than a few minutes).[70] Unlike Greenfield, Stotesbury towered over Philadelphia's business scene, both by virtue of his longevity and his bank's vast wealth and prestige. Not incidentally, Stotesbury was an opera lover and a personal patron to such noted singers as Mary Garden and Titta Ruffo. In short order Stotesbury formed a syndicate that raised $1.25 million and turned the troubled building over to the Metropolitan Opera Company of New York, which used the building for its touring performances.[71]

When the Met put the building up for sale in April 1920, it was said to be worth at least $1.5 million. Greenfield was enlisted to bid for it on behalf of the Nixon-Nordlinger theatrical company, which then owned three Philadelphia theaters and was jockeying for dominance in the Philadelphia market with the Shuberts, who owned four. The Nixon-Nordlinger people wanted the Met but instructed Greenfield to bid no higher than $900,000 for it. If Greenfield longed to be tested in the big leagues, here was his opportunity.

Yet because of the rumored steep price, most of the New York theater operators who were said to be interested in the Met—including the Shuberts—failed to show up for the auction. When the sale started, Greenfield found himself competing with just one other bidder: Stotesbury himself, who still held a $400,000 mortgage against the property that he was anxious to satisfy.

Stotesbury opened the auction with a bid of $650,000—the property's assessed value. Greenfield countered with a bid of $655,000, just $5,000 higher. At that point, to Greenfield's astonishment, Stotesbury declined to bid further. In just five minutes, Greenfield had secured a storied opera house for his clients at less than half its presumed value—"one of the greatest real estate bargains here in the last twenty years," the theater trade newspaper *Variety* called it. After the sale, Greenfield himself expressed surprise at the ease with which the Met had fallen into his hands.[72]

In retrospect, Stotesbury seems to have had no interest in acquiring the Met at all—only in recovering his mortgage. Greenfield seems not to have wondered why no one else bid for the Met, or why a shrewd operator like Stotesbury had refused to engage in a bidding contest for it. In this case, as in most others, Greenfield simply assumed that he perceived value that others overlooked, and that he possessed boldness that others lacked. The possibility that Stotesbury may have seen something that *he* had overlooked did not occur to Greenfield.

"I have never been afraid to take a chance," Greenfield told an interviewer shortly after. "At one time or another, business men of my acquaintance, having heard of a move I had made, held up their hands in surprise and called me on the telephone to forecast catastrophe. At times, events called for courage and daring, particularly when I staked such a tremendous thing as my future on my own foresight as to the future trend of realty in various quarters."[73]

Almost immediately, Greenfield announced that, on behalf of the Nixon-Nordlinger group, he would make a bid for an equally troubled but far more celebrated Philadelphia institution: the Academy of Music, which the Nixons proposed to convert into a movie theater. The Philadelphia Orchestra, the Academy's owner and principal tenant, resisted that gambit, but Greenfield remained unfazed: A year later he resold the Met for $1 million in cash, generating a profit of better than 50 percent for his clients, the Nixons.[74]

The Met transaction convinced Greenfield, if any convincing were needed, that he was ready for big-time competition. In what may have been his first encounter with Stotesbury, he had not merely survived but had prevailed. Since Greenfield aspired to become what Stotesbury already was—a man of such wide-ranging influence that no important deal could be transacted in Philadelphia without him—it was inevitable that their paths would cross again.

[4]

Developer

G reenfield turned his sights downtown at the very moment that America's cities seemed poised for a growth spurt. Across the country, the urban downtown remained the focal point for virtually all important business, government, social, and cultural activities. And Philadelphia posed a typical combination of postwar challenges and opportunities.

Center City, as Philadelphia's downtown was known, had become a "nomad city," occupied each morning by some half-million office workers and shoppers from outlying neighborhoods and the suburbs. A quarter of a million people—many of whom had once lived within a mile or two of City Hall—passed through the intersection of Broad and Chestnut Streets every day, only to vanish again at 5:00 P.M.[1] As a consequence, Center City seemed inundated with abandoned houses. Yet at the same time, commercial space downtown failed to match the soaring demand, which had driven office and store rental rates to exorbitant levels.[2] "This city," Greenfield wrote in the *Public Ledger* in 1921, "has less space and greater demand for this section than any other city in the Union."[3] The comment was typical of his hyperbolic salesmanship, but in this case it was unerringly accurate.

Other major cities, like New York and Chicago, responded to this quandary by constructing new (and often very tall) office buildings. But Philadelphia's downtown growth was constrained by two seemingly insurmountable obstacles, one physical and one psychological: the Pennsylvania Railroad's "Chinese Wall"—a rail viaduct that since 1891 had sliced westward from City Hall along Market Street, effectively preventing Center City from expanding north of it—and a "gentleman's agreement" not to erect any building higher than William Penn's hat atop City Hall, a 548-foot-high tower completed in 1901. Philadelphia was equally hampered by what one observer called an "anti-leadership vaccine" handed down from the city's timid Quaker founders.[4]

The solution seemed clear to Greenfield: First, accept the limitations of the "Chinese Wall" and start collecting properties within the rectangle south of the Wall and west of Broad Street—the city's likely new business hub. Second, replace old buildings there with new ones while encouraging other speculators to invest in Center City real estate as well. Third, count on the consequent rise in property values to drive up the values of the properties you already own.

This strategy required Greenfield to evolve from a mere real estate broker into what was then known as an "operator" and later became known as a "developer"—that is, someone who takes the prime responsibility for improving a piece of real estate, either by constructing a new building or renovating an old one. The developer is, in effect, an orchestra leader whose complex ensemble includes investors, an architect, a contractor, a short-term financier (to underwrite the construction period), and a long-term financier (to cover the life of the building), as well as marketing experts, property managers, and lawyers. Since a building can take years to finish and no one can predict the future rental market with certainty, development is no job for the faint of heart. Consequently, most developers are characterized by their self-confidence, outgoing personalities and massive egos—traits necessary to persuade people that they can control the multitude of factors that actually lie beyond any individual's control. Greenfield's company was already well stocked with property managers and lawyers, so he enjoyed a good head start in the minds of investors. And few real estate men anywhere exuded Greenfield's confidence.

To pursue his vision for Center City, Greenfield organized a series of investment syndicates, each created to construct or renovate a specific building. Typically, Greenfield invested little or none of his own money but took a percentage of the building's equity in exchange for his leadership services—a pattern that subsequently became standard among twentieth-century real estate developers.

Greenfield announced his arrival downtown with a relatively inexpensive purchase of a prestigious name in retailing: In April 1921 he acquired 60 percent of the stock of Bonwit Teller, the fashionable women's specialty shop, then located east of Broad Street.[5] But Greenfield's designs were focused on the more prestigious blocks west of Broad Street.

Later that year he acquired the Colonnade Hotel, catty-corner from his own office at Fifteenth and Chestnut Streets—a cherished institution that had hosted grand military and naval reunions since the Civil War. Greenfield replaced this decaying symbol of the past with "The Greenfield Building," a modern twenty-story structure housing 250 offices and seemingly blessed with every modern technological innovation: draftless ventilation, modulated heating, special lighting fixtures, and seven passenger elevators, all topped by a tower visible from every entrance to the city. The total effect was calculated to bolster faith in Center City in general and in Greenfield's image as a forward-thinking visionary in particular.[6] Even before the building was completed, Greenfield recouped his investment by selling it to the Franklin Trust Company, which promptly changed the building's name to its own.[7]

Greenfield quickly followed this venture in January 1922 with a publicity blitz extolling the virtues of investing in Center City real estate. In advertisements placed in four Philadelphia newspapers, he claimed that downtown land values would rise by 6 to 10 percent annually.[8] To demonstrate his faith, Greenfield began acquiring hotels, office buildings, and other undervalued downtown properties, thus conveying the message that he was putting his money where his mouth was (even though he invested very little of his own money and often sold the buildings almost as soon as he bought them). In the process he typically demanded that his company be appointed as the building's manager and rental agent.[9]

In the spring of 1923 a Greenfield syndicate acquired an unfinished but elegant seventeen-story office building at Walnut and Juniper that the noted architect Horace Trumbauer was designing for Greenfield's former partner, Louis Cahan. Cahan had obtained the state charter for a bank that he hoped to open on the ground floor, bearing the grandiloquent name of Bankers Trust Company. Cahan had even gone so far as to fight and win a suit contesting his use of the name, filed by the Bankers Trust Company of New York, the prominent major bank created in 1903 by J. P. Morgan Sr. and other New York bankers to provide trust services to customers of state and national banks throughout the country. But once having won his case, Cahan apparently suffered second thoughts about entering banking, a field in which he lacked experience.

Greenfield suffered no such qualms. Before the roof was placed on this putative Bankers Trust Building, Greenfield's syndicate acquired it. The price paid for this unfinished building—as well as the bank charter plus all the capital stock of the potential bank—was $3.5 million, then one of the largest real estate transactions in Philadelphia history. But Greenfield's syndicate put up just $500,000 in cash.[10] Greenfield quickly resold the building—retaining the bank charter and the building's management contract—by guaranteeing the new buyer the presence of a long-term major tenant: himself and his growing family of operations. The following year Greenfield moved his offices into this new Bankers Trust Building and set himself up in a walnut-paneled office on the second floor that would become his headquarters for the next forty years.[11]

Here he surrounded himself with a cadre of assistants and clerks characterized above all by their unquestioning willingness to carry out Greenfield's wishes. "It wasn't pleasant working around Al," one such assistant from those days later recalled. "He couldn't work with other strong personalities. He had to dominate the show. He'd listen to you, but you could never change his mind."[12]

Greenfield was quick to reciprocate his employees' loyalty, however. One day in the 1920s a distraught homeowner burst into Greenfield's office with a gun, declaring, "Mr. Greenfield, you've foreclosed on my house; now I'm going to foreclose on your life." The would-be assassin was tackled by a previously obscure clerk named Chester Cincotta; Greenfield promptly promoted the young man to vice president for real estate, one of several executive positions Cincotta held in Greenfield's employ over the next half-century.[13]

Greenfield's grandest project, announced in 1923, was the Benjamin Franklin Hotel, one of the nation's largest, with 1,210 rooms, each with a private bath. As was the case with the Greenfield Building, "the Ben" seemed calculated to erase anyone's notion that Philadelphia was a second-rate city. Its lobby on Chestnut Street and Ninth, designed along with the rest of the building by Horace Trumbauer, was two stories high, 60 feet wide, and 140 feet long. It offered 13 "high-speed elevators," 1,500 "telephone stations," and 20,000 electric light outlets. The Ben, gushed one newspaper account, combined "better than any other building in the city the idea of great size and spaciousness with architectural beauty."[14]

With its $13 million price tag, the Ben was the most expensive building ever constructed in Philadelphia, aside from City Hall and the John Wanamaker department store. Greenfield raised the funds from what he called "a group of leading citizens and business men of this city," most of whom, with a few notable exceptions (the publisher Cyrus H. K. Curtis, the Federal Reserve Bank governor George Norris, the Strawbridge & Clothier department store) were Jews.

Like the Greenfield Building, the Ben replaced a proud but outmoded vestige of the old Philadelphia: the Continental Hotel, which had opened in

1860 and had hosted Presidents Lincoln, Harrison, and McKinley; the Prince of Wales; Emperor Dom Pedro of Brazil; and the stage personalities Lillian Russell and Joseph Jefferson.[15] The opening of the Ben in January 1925 effectively announced the ascendance of a new, forward-looking Philadelphia business community, with Greenfield as its impresario.

Greenfield was beginning to change the face of Philadelphia, just as he had hoped. There was no longer any question as to who was the city's predominant real estate force: His deals for the Colonnade Hotel, the seventeen-story Pennsylvania Building (also at Fifteenth and Chestnut), and the Ben Franklin Hotel were said to be three of Philadelphia's four largest transactions in several decades.[16]

"It seems to me that you have not put up a big office building or a new hotel for several weeks," the auctioneer Samuel Freeman, scion of a family business established in Philadelphia in 1805, quipped in a note to Greenfield, "and it is about time you started on another."[17]

"If God spares you to live many more years," wrote an old friend, "you will buy the Universe and lease it to God."[18] At a party in 1923, a fellow broker—presumably more talented as a salesman than as a lyricist—serenaded Greenfield to the tune of "The Sheik of Araby":

> *Al's the Sheik of Chestnut Street;*
> *He looks so mild and meek*
> *But when upon the trail*
> *Of a property for sale*
> *The other men despair,*
> *Their chances then are rare;*
> *You must admit he's there*
> *The Sheik of Chestnut Street.*[19]

At a testimonial dinner in 1926—held at the Ben, of course—three hundred officers and directors of building and loan associations showered praise on Greenfield while honoring his father-in-law Sol Kraus as "the father of building and loan associations in South Philadelphia."[20]

Much of this praise was orchestrated by Greenfield himself. He worked hard, and constantly, to promote an image of himself as a man of substance. To advance his sense of dignity, he took to wearing a pince-nez, however painful it might have felt when clamped on his nose. To distinguish himself from other businessmen, he wore vests of light green, a play on his name.[21] His ubiquitous green-and-white "Albert M. Greenfield & Co." signs were posted conspicuously on buildings, homes, and lawns wherever Philadelphians turned, so that it was impossible to travel downtown from an outlying neighborhood without passing twenty or thirty of them.

He began affecting many of the trappings of a traditional Philadelphia gentleman. His house in Germantown was photographed in *Country Home* magazine.[22] In the manner of the great nineteenth-century Philadelphia banker Anthony J. Drexel—as well as Drexel's successor, E. T. Stotesbury—he took up horseback riding, and as early as 1924 he was described in a newspaper profile as "an accomplished equestrian," one who "may frequently be seen astride a fine saddle horse along the bridle paths of Fairmount Park or the roads of the neighboring countryside."[23] He acquired Oak Crest Farm in suburban Montgomeryville as a weekend retreat for his family, which by the mid-1920s numbered four children.[24] In 1926 he also purchased the seashore home of U.S. Senator Walter Edge in Ventnor, New Jersey.[25] Notwithstanding his lack of interest in the Old World, Greenfield and Edna began taking grand tours of Europe. Typically, Greenfield would accompany Edna across the Atlantic for a few days, then leave her there for weeks with their traveling companions while he scurried back to Philadelphia to attend to business.

Greenfield sought and received so many civic awards that some prominent Philadelphians complained of a kind of Greenfield fatigue. "Greenfield was in good company," the *Philadelphia Jewish Times* publisher Philip Klein later recalled.

In those days, there was a small clique around this town. . . . And every year they would arrange to have the others receive all the awards that were given around in town. . . . Each one of them would get two awards a year at two dinners. You just got tired going to those dinners because you knew the same faces all the time.[26]

One failure in Greenfield's bid for social acceptance was his children's rejection for admission to Germantown Friends School in 1921, apparently because they were Jewish. Greenfield subsequently sent his children to the Oak Lane Country Day School, a new nonsectarian private school largely supported by prominent Jewish families like his own, and he pledged $10,000 to the school's campaign fund in 1925.[27]

Increasingly, Greenfield became the first person Philadelphians turned to for any major project—business, civic, or political. He raised funds for Freeland Kendrick's successful mayoral campaign in 1923, in return for which the Republican boss William Vare consulted with Greenfield about

pending legislation affecting his businesses. His financial support to Pennsylvania's Republican State Committee gave him input concerning legislative strategies and the slating of candidates. When Vare himself ran for the
U.S. Senate in 1926, Greenfield became his principal fund-raiser, contributing $125,000 personally and raising another $50,000 from his associates.[28]

Greenfield kicked off Philadelphia's U.S. Sesquicentennial Exposition
of 1926 by donating $100,000, then canvassed the city in a lightning fund-
raising drive, pressuring his business contacts to chip in or risk losing his
favor in the future. In just ten days he raised $3 million, exceeding the drive's
initial projections and far exceeding the funds allocated by the state and by
Philadelphia's City Council.[29] At the same time, he personally reorganized
the Chamber of Commerce's Convention and Exhibition Committee.[30]

The Exposition's ancillary benefits to Greenfield were, of course, potentially enormous: It would bring guests to his hotels and stimulate real estate
values in South Philadelphia, where he controlled many properties; it would
also earn the gratitude of his political ally William Vare, by funneling some
four hundred contracts for street, sewer, and water service as well as mos-
quito extermination to Vare's contracting company.[31]

Meanwhile, sensing that the time was ripe to shift the city's upper-class
shopping district westward, in 1927 Greenfield moved Bonwit Teller from its
six-story building on the east side of Broad Street to a renovated eight-story
building, nearly three times the size of the old Bonwit's, on the west side,
at Seventeenth and Chestnut Streets. In doing so he took a calculated risk
that upper-class customers accustomed to Wanamaker's and Strawbridge &
Clothier on the east side would change their shopping patterns. But Greenfield hedged his risk: As landlord, renovator, and manager of the new Bonwit's building, Greenfield's real estate company would profit even if Bonwit's
struggled.[32]

Much of Greenfield's purported success derived from his talent for painting his failures as successes. The Sesquicentennial Exposition of 1926
suffered construction delays, long stretches of rain, and poor attendance that
resulted in losses of $1 million a month over its six-month duration.[33] The
Ben Franklin Hotel, for all its glowing publicity, lost more than $1 million
during its first three years of operation, despite a good volume of business
during the Sesquicentennial celebration. Although Greenfield predicted that
the Ben would rejuvenate its East Chestnut Street textile factory district into
a vibrant commercial area, hotel guests found its location too far from the
best shops closer to Broad Street. Greenfield's lack of hotel management experience compounded the Ben's problems: To generate more revenue, the

hotel raised its room and food rates, driving still more guests away. At one point, struggling to pay its bills, the Ben had to postdate checks.[34]

Yet in Greenfield's strategic vision, the Ben's disastrous financial performance was a minor problem. Instead of withdrawing from the hotel business, he expanded his investments in floundering Center City hotels, the better to camouflage the Ben's losses. As head of an increasingly integrated operation, he was not interested in the hotel business per se but in the land that the hotels occupied and the management fees they generated for Albert M. Greenfield & Co. He may have persuaded himself that his business acumen could salvage an ailing hotel; but if it could not, he could still sell the property and earn a commission in the process. As long as his company made a profit on a commission or on servicing fees, it did not matter whether the actual investment was solid or even if his syndicate partners lost money. The Ben, to Greenfield's way of thinking, was a "loss leader" that generated other intangible benefits: prestige for himself and his city, as well as prominent guests who might develop into partners or customers or allies somewhere down the road.

As Greenfield's real estate projects grew in size and number, so did his appetite for capital. Financial services like banking, mortgage lending, and insurance were generally unwelcome to Jews, but Greenfield refused to acknowledge any such obstacle. The market for mortgages was huge: Mortgaged residences in the United States had increased by 43 percent between 1890 and 1920, and the number was still growing. Between 1923 and 1929, seventy thousand new homes were built in Philadelphia.[35] Control of a bank or mortgage company, Greenfield realized, would give him an advantage over his competitors: He could guarantee prospective clients a mortgage on one of his properties, retain or increase his interest in those properties, and make a profit in the process.[36]

In 1924, with his father-in-law, Sol Kraus, Greenfield created Bankers Bond & Mortgage Company, with offices above Greenfield's in the Walnut Street building. By that time, Philadelphians were so keen to get title to homes that 3,400 building and loan companies operated in the city, with total assets of $625 million and 1,250,000 shareholders.[37] In effect, Bankers Bond extended Kraus's concept of building and loan associations to the burgeoning market in first mortgages and first mortgage bonds.[38]

Next, Greenfield turned his attention to life and property insurance. At a time when life insurance companies constituted the nation's third largest source of home mortgage loans, they also presented another obvious tool for expanding his control over real estate—or, as he saw it, his ability to serve his clients' needs. In 1926 Greenfield bought control of the Commonwealth Casualty Company, Philadelphia's oldest casualty insurance company; within two years the insurance department of Albert M. Greenfield & Co. was generating premium income of more than $1 million annually.[39]

In creating Bankers Bond and acquiring Commonwealth Casualty, as in his downtown syndicates, Greenfield encountered little trouble raising capital, and not just because of his persuasiveness: By the mid-1920s real estate projects everywhere seemed to be making money, and Greenfield's projects had cultivated a reputation for making more money than most. At the end of 1924 Bankers Bond reported a profit of more than $30,000 in less than a year and paid an 8 percent dividend to its common stockholders.[40]

Of course, Greenfield owed much of his success to questionable business practices whose sole redeeming virtue was Greenfield's cheerful refusal to conceal or disguise them. Chief among these was his practice of buying and selling real estate for himself in addition to acting as a broker for others. At the time, most rival brokers lacked the capital to buy property for themselves and, consequently, earned their living solely from commissions on sales. But Greenfield was in a position to act as both broker and buyer if he saw a good deal for himself. If a property owner asked Greenfield to sell a building that Greenfield himself was interested in buying, the owner could never be sure that Greenfield would seek the best possible price for the building. But in Greenfield's own mind, his ability to act simultaneously as broker and buyer was an added service he could offer to his client, and indeed his clients rarely objected. Only later was this practice seen as unethical; the rival firm of Jackson-Cross, for example, for years boasted in its advertisements, "We do not own, nor have we owned, any part of any real estate we buy, sell or lease."[41]

Some brokers, to be sure, bought property for themselves secretly, through the use of "straw men"—that is, people who posed as buyers of property but were actually stand-ins for brokers. Greenfield was the only Philadelphia broker to buy for himself openly. And since he *did* engage in it openly, he disarmed much of the criticism. After all, any client who was dissatisfied with Greenfield's style could take his business elsewhere.

But could he really? In the 1920s Albert Greenfield's influence began to extend into virtually every aspect of Philadelphia business life. Through his building and loan associations and his mortgage banking company he enjoyed instant access to financing, whereas other brokers had to work out financing arrangements just like any other bank customer. Greenfield's seemingly peripatetic trading of Center City properties meant that anyone with Center City real estate aspirations would do well to cultivate his friendship. His political contributions to the Vare brothers gave him powerful influence in Philadelphia's City Council. And so the word got around: Even if you had doubts about Al Greenfield, it was a good idea to cultivate him as an ally, for you never could tell when you might need him.

Since the turn of the century, the real estate business had struggled to establish itself as a respectable profession with standards and codes of ethics. Greenfield openly flouted such constraints; to him, real estate was intrinsically connected to everything else in life, and any real estate man who accepted limitations on his activities undermined his effectiveness for his clients. Smart real estate men, just like smart retailers and bankers, sought to offer their customers the broadest possible variety of services. "Do you know which is the most ethical real estate concern in the country?" Greenfield liked to ask friends. Then, with what the newspapers described as "a twinkle in his eye," he would reply, "Albert M. Greenfield & Co. It has to be. It's the most closely watched."[42]

Only a man who refused to abide by society's conventions would have cultivated what became—on the surface, at least—Greenfield's most remarkable alliance. His rise in real estate circles after World War I coincided with the rise of Dennis Dougherty, whom the pope appointed archbishop of Philadelphia in 1918, when the city's Catholic archdiocese was poised for its greatest period of real estate expansion. By 1921, when Dougherty became the first bishop of Philadelphia to be made a cardinal, Greenfield was already showering Dougherty with small favors and donations, and the cardinal was routinely responding with written assurances that "you will be remembered at Mass and in our prayers by the Sisters and myself."[43]

On the surface, Greenfield and Dougherty seemed an unlikely pair: a glib and extroverted Russian Jew of no strong religious faith on the one hand and, on the other, a stern, square-jawed, introverted Irish Catholic of military bearing, implacable beliefs, and a strong mystical streak who was virtually devoid of people skills.[44] Dougherty was a cardinal who without hesitation banned his flock from attending motion pictures, condemning "the much-married, much-divorced actors and actresses and the Russian producers of lascivious filth, and theater owners who purvey crime and sex films." Such an edict struck at the souls and wallets of some of Greenfield's best clients, virtually all of whom happened to be Jewish.[45]

Yet one of Greenfield's strengths was his refusal to dwell on or even acknowledge animosity or insults. And for all their differences, both men were sufficiently shrewd to perceive that they shared much in common despite their outward differences. Greenfield and Dougherty were both overachieving empire builders, usually held in awe by those they dealt with; both were autocratic, tough-minded, hard-working, and totally committed to their respective enterprises, and both represented sizable immigrant ethnic groups that had largely been excluded by Philadelphia's dominant Protestant business establishment—the chummy circle of bankers, lawyers, and Pennsylvania Railroad executives who tolerated Philadelphia's political status quo because, after all, they lived in the suburbs. Philadelphia's Jews and Catholics, by contrast, had to walk the city's dirty streets and drink the city's rancid water. Separately, these two previously antagonistic religious groups had developed their own power bases. Together they might alter the city's power structure.

The two men developed a friendship that blossomed through the 1920s to such an extent that Greenfield became the exclusive real estate agent for the Archdiocese of Philadelphia. With Greenfield's active assistance, over the next thirty-three years "God's bricklayer," as Dougherty styled himself, would oversee the establishment of 105 parishes, 75 churches, 146 schools, 7 nursing homes, and 7 orphanages.[46] Eventually, Greenfield became the cardinal's personal financial adviser as well.

Precisely because of his august role as Christ's personal emissary to Philadelphia Catholics, Dougherty could never relax among his coreligionists; he could let his hair down only among his few close friendships from outside the church. Greenfield, for his part, saw in Dougherty a unique opportunity to expand his business and gratify his ego while improving relations between Catholic and Jews.

Thus, often on Sundays the cardinal would call Greenfield and the two men would drive around the city, looking over prospective sites for schools, churches, hospitals, and cemeteries. Sometimes these jaunts wound up at Greenfield's Oak Crest Farm, where they talked business and sang songs.[47] During the week, Dougherty sometimes took lunch at Greenfield's office on Walnut Street, where Greenfield had installed a dining room with a Japanese cook and waiter.[48] And the cardinal was a frequent dinner guest at Greenfield's Germantown home, where his Catholic servants invariably knelt and kissed the cardinal's ring, to the wonder of Greenfield's children.[49]

Greenfield cemented this relationship by contributing heavily to Catholic charities and to Catholic institutions like Villanova University, St. Joseph's College, and St. Mary's Home for Children in Ambler. In 1927 he donated an organ to St. Charles Borromeo Seminary in Overbrook in honor of his childhood friend John Monaghan, a Philadelphia Common Pleas Court judge then running for district attorney. As a result of these benefactions, in 1930 Cardinal Dougherty arranged for the pope to confer on Greenfield the title of Commander of the Order of Pius IX. He was the first American Jew to receive the honor.[50]

Greenfield's children were amused by this papal knighthood as well as by the costume he wore to receive it—"Hello, Pope Albert!" they would greet him—and Greenfield's detractors scoffed at his tribute as more of a business deal than a religious honor. And indeed it was. But the fact remained that, through his business operations, Greenfield had opened up the first lines of communications between two Philadelphia groups that had long been enemies.

Undoubtedly, Greenfield was sincere in his fondness for Catholicism. He often spoke of his high regard for Catholics and especially for their school system. "If I weren't a Jew, I'd be a Catholic," he remarked at least once.[51] Catholic visitors to his office were invariably impressed by a large photo of St. Peter's Basilica in Rome that hung just outside Greenfield's inner sanctum. And if Jewish visitors expressed dismay at finding the picture there, Greenfield would take them by the arm with a sly wink and point to one obscure corner of the photo where, imperceptible at first glance, a man could be seen relieving himself against a wall.[52]

Greenfield's alliance with Cardinal Dougherty continued the pattern by which Greenfield constantly expanded his relationships beyond conventional boundaries. Yet each alliance, no matter how formidable, eventually reached a saturation point for Greenfield, if only because few people operated at his level. Sol Kraus was an important financial figure among Philadelphia's German Jews but enjoyed few connections beyond them. William Fox, by the mid-1920s, was an immensely wealthy and celebrated film executive, but withal a socialist son of immigrants. Bill Vare's success as an entrepreneur depended entirely on the coercive and often debilitating power of government. Cardinal Dougherty, when all was said and done, was no entrepreneur at all—just a capable administrator who had climbed through the ranks of an existing bureaucracy. Each of these men had something useful to offer Greenfield, but none was the sort he might aspire to emulate.

Such an ultimate role model entered Greenfield's life during World War I in the person of Thomas E. Mitten, the traction magnate who had rescued the tangled streetcar systems of Buffalo, Milwaukee, and Chicago before E. T. Stotesbury of Drexel & Co. recruited him in 1911 to perform a similar miracle in Philadelphia. Mitten was a genuine WASP, descended from a knight who had fought alongside William the Conqueror at the Battle of Hastings; he was born in mid-Victorian England in 1864 and raised in Indiana. Mitten came of age at a time when urban transportation systems were evolving from horse-drawn trolleys to electrified streetcars and subways, and when cities were increasingly desperate to solve the congestion caused by the growing numbers of automobiles on city streets.[53]

In Philadelphia a coalition of politicians and private streetcar operators attempted to get a handle on the problem in 1902 by creating the Philadelphia Rapid Transit Company (PRT), a private concern contracted to electrify the streetcar lines and to build and run the Market Street subway and elevated as well as a parallel underground trolley line to West Philadelphia. But the cumulative cost of these projects nearly bankrupted the PRT: By 1910 the company was losing $1.5 million a year. After the PRT's overworked and underpaid employees staged two long and violent strikes in 1909 and 1910, Drexel & Co. agreed to refinance the PRT in exchange for a controlling stake and the right to install new management. Mitten, who had brought labor peace to three other cities, was the "white knight" chosen for the job by Drexel's senior partner, E. T. Stotesbury.

Having already made several fortunes, Mitten by this point believed he had transcended mere empire building. When business acquaintances asked, "Why do you stick it out?" Mitten's assistant later recalled:

Usually he replied that his reason for sticking was that he loved the task because of its very difficulty. This, he said, was his game, his food, his drink. He needed business opposition as the poor man needed his beer and skittles, or the rich man his poker and champagne.[54]

Here was a surrogate father figure after Albert Greenfield's own heart, perhaps the first man Greenfield could both admire and respect, as Greenfield himself all but acknowledged in a fawning letter he wrote to Mitten in 1926:

There are certain propositions which await only the right mind to unfold them and the right man to state them, when they strike the hearer as so self-evident it seems impossible that they were not always clearly understood. . . . America cannot but benefit immeasurably from the results of your work.[55]

Only one thing interested Mitten in the long run, the traction king insisted on his arrival in Philadelphia. "It isn't money and it isn't freedom from worry," he explained while declining an offer to run John Wanamaker's famous department store. "It is to see if something can be done to prove that men and management can get along in industry without eternally fighting."[56]

Before he took the Philadelphia job, Mitten demanded and obtained assurance that he would have a free hand. To boost ridership on PRT lines, he purchased more than a thousand new streetcars of his own modern design. To buy labor peace, he implemented his own ingenious "Co-operative Plan," under which 22 percent of fares would be earmarked for wages, pensions, and benefits. In effect, he made the PRT's employees his partners so that they resisted union organizing drives.

But just as Greenfield concealed his hotel failures by buying more hotels, Mitten's approach to the rising cost of subway and elevated construction was to increase the PRT's ridership—and, consequently, its revenues—through acquisitions. It was a classic pyramid scheme that worked only as long as the company continued to grow.

Greenfield, by virtue of his Republican connections with the Vare brothers, began handling the PRT's real estate transactions in 1917, just when the PRT was beginning its most expansive phase.[57] The Frankford Elevated, connecting City Hall with Philadelphia's vast and mostly empty northeast, opened in 1922, and a Broad Street subway to the city's northern reaches was in the works as well. As the city expanded from its traditional core in the 1920s, Mitten sought to create a fully integrated transit system by acquiring bus lines and trackless trolley systems in the city and suburbs, as well as interurban bus lines linking Philadelphia to New York and Atlantic City. In 1926 Mitten purchased the Yellow Cab Company of Philadelphia as yet a further source of growth for the PRT.

Greenfield's friendship with Mitten appears to have been deep and genuine. Greenfield occasionally visited Mitten at his camp in Maine, and Mitten was often seen strolling the Atlantic City boardwalk as Greenfield's guest in Ventnor. Greenfield's children rode horses on Mitten's estate in the Pocono Mountains in northeastern Pennsylvania; Mitten named three of his horses for Greenfield's children (Greenfield subsequently bought all three).[58] And Greenfield showered Mitten with volumes by such diverse writers as Shakespeare, the nineteenth-century socialist philosopher Ferdinand Lassalle, and Georg Brandes (including such books as *On Reading, Creative Spirits of the 19th Century, The Jesus Myth,* and *Hellas*)—the sort of gifts that few of his other business acquaintances would have appreciated and that reinforced the mutual notion that Greenfield and Mitten were no mere hustlers but gentlemen of taste and intellect.[59]

By 1926 the PRT's ridership had more than doubled since Mitten's arrival, to 975 million from 443 million in 1910. No one, least of all Mitten, seems to have pondered what might happen to the PRT when its last competitors were acquired and its enormous growth inevitably slowed or ceased. When newspaper editorials accused Mitten of creating a transportation monopoly, he self-righteously replied:

> If the word is interpreted for any reason to mean a soulless corpora-
> tion trying to drive poor men out of business to get inordinate profits
> for itself, then this is not a monopoly. If, however, it is interpreted as
> meaning that all the transportation facilities for the public carrying
> of passengers shall be handled most economically so as to produce
> the best service for the lowest price and leave as much as possible in
> the box to help support city-built subway investment, then I am talk-
> ing about a "monopoly."[60]

Just as Greenfield refused to confine himself to real estate, Mitten refused to restrict himself to transportation. When his cautious patrons at Drexel & Co. bridled at his ambitious expansion plans, Mitten dropped them and incorporated his own firm, Mitten Management Inc., to operate the PRT on a contract basis while pursuing other ventures as well, including a labor bank that he called the Producers & Consumers Bank.

To raise capital for these ventures, Mitten enlisted the support of the Central Labor Union, selling shares in small lots to the union's members, his own employees, and even to PRT passengers. He persuaded some 1,500 of these novice capitalists to deposit funds in "their" bank.[61] He also dipped into the assets of the employee stock fund he had created. Greenfield assisted his friend by buying 178 shares in the Producers & Consumers Bank—not in his own name, but in the name of his secretary.[62]

When the PRT's extraordinary growth inevitably slowed and then stopped, it became increasingly difficult for Mitten to juggle the competing demands of employees, riders, and the city. He needed new sources of growth. Here Greenfield saw his chance to perform a service for his friend for which he was uniquely qualified.

When the Quaker City Cab Company went bankrupt in 1926, the trustee in bankruptcy asked Greenfield to find a buyer. The assets of the bankrupt Quaker City Cab Company were inventoried at $387,500, and in 1927 Greenfield, as agent for the bankruptcy trustee, sold the company for that amount to one Frank Sawyer of Boston. The public did not know it at the time, but Sawyer was acting as a straw man for Mitten, who actually financed the purchase.

Then in January 1928 Greenfield negotiated the sale of Quaker City Cab from Sawyer to the PRT for $1,360,000. In effect, the PRT, managed by Mitten, bought the cab company from a straw man for Mitten in a deal that netted Mitten a profit of nearly $1 million. At the same time, the PRT awarded Mitten Management a contract to operate the newly acquired cab company.

The ultimate victims of these manipulations were the PRT stockholders and Philadelphia's taxpayers, for the PRT was supposed to share its profits with the city, and Greenfield's finaglings on behalf of Mitten had assured that the PRT made no profits whatsoever. More than a year would pass before that deal attracted public attention, or before it became known that Greenfield had acted as agent for *both* the buyer (the PRT) and the seller (Sawyer); that both had paid him a 5 percent commission, amounting to a total of $190,000; and that Greenfield's total fees from the PRT since 1917 had exceeded $700,000.[63]

Meanwhile, Mitten's Producers & Consumers Bank encountered financial problems just three years after its creation. The bank had loaned $154,000 to a smooth-talking swindler named Alexander Roseman, who had gained control of seventeen building and loan associations and then used their funds to pyramid the value of homes by taking out second and third mortgages on them. When Roseman's scheme collapsed, Mitten's bank held $154,000 in virtually worthless notes and faced imminent collapse.[64]

As a result of Greenfield's political connections with the Pennsylvania Republican administration in Harrisburg, as well as his growing reputation as a financial genius, in 1925 he was appointed the troubled bank's permanent receiver.[65] Here was another opportunity for Greenfield to apply his ingenuity in his friend Mitten's behalf while simultaneously dipping his toes into a new field: commercial banking.

Greenfield had not forgotten the bank charter he had acquired from Louis Cahan when he bought the unfinished Bankers Trust Building two years earlier. The Bankers Trust Company had never been launched, but anyone armed with the charter and sufficient capital could legally do so. In the process, such a go-getter could join the rarefied ranks of men qualified to call themselves legitimate bankers.[66]

Of course, the receiver of the Producers & Consumers Bank was technically required to be a disinterested party, which Greenfield was not, because of his personal and financial relationships with Mitten. But prior to his appointment he denied any connection to the Producers & Consumers Bank, conveniently overlooking the 178 shares he had purchased in his secretary's name.[67]

Under the agreement Greenfield reached on February 1, 1926, Mitten agreed to reorganize the Producers & Consumers Bank under a new name—the Mitten Men & Management Bank—and to supply the necessary funds, which subsequently amounted to about $1 million.[68] Greenfield himself became a director of the new bank.[69]

Of course, the new Mitten Bank, like its predecessor, was no conventional bank but an instrument of Mitten's romantic vision of empowering workingmen with the tools of capitalism. At first, Mitten tried to make up the bank's shortfall by offering stock to PRT employees, as he had done before. By the following year he had extended the offer to the general public. In an open letter to "The people of Philadelphia," Mitten sketched his dream of letting "every member of this community . . . share in the proceeds of the community's industry in proportion to what he puts in."[70]

When Greenfield was appointed receiver of the Producers & Consumers Bank in 1925, the seventeen building and loan associations swindled by Alexander Roseman were seized by the state as insolvent.[71] Once again, Greenfield was appointed receiver and asked to reorganize them.[72] Since Greenfield himself already controlled (with his father-in-law, Sol Kraus) twenty-seven building and loan associations, there were inherent conflicts in Greenfield's being asked to reorganize his competitors, just as there were conflicts in his being asked to reorganize a bank—Mitten's—in which he personally held a financial interest, and just as there were conflicts in a real estate broker's acting as a banker in the first place. But these concerns were overshadowed by the urgent needs of the moment: Greenfield, everyone knew, would cut through the complexities to get the job done. Someone else with no conflicting involvements might not.

Businessmen of Greenfield's era were typically too busy to spend much time with their families, and Greenfield was busier than most. "I work all the hours I don't sleep, and I don't sleep much," he was fond of saying.[73] When Greenfield *was* home, his children often found him, as one relative put it, "caring, interested, and dictatorial." Another said that the children "had to do things for him that pleased him, like get good grades, and be well dressed all the time, and be very proper."[74]

But whatever difficulties Greenfield's children suffered because of Greenfield's parenting—or lack of it—paled beside their exposure to Edna's neuroses. Having Edna for a mother, her children generally agreed, was even more difficult than having Albert for a father.[75] Because of Edna's germ phobia, the mothering of her children was largely delegated to the household servants, many of whom were themselves unpleasant and difficult people. Edna believed that the French and the Germans made the classiest nannies; one newspaper advertisement she placed for a nanny stipulated that knowledge of English was not necessary. One nanny punished childish misbehavior by holding the offender's head over the toilet and sometimes pushing it in.[76]

Edna was rarely around to object; at some point she began to travel by herself—first to various spas and sanatoriums in New York and New England and then to Europe to engage in therapy with followers of Freud and other therapists. In New York she apparently developed a relationship with a progressive private school teacher named Berta Rantz, who communicated with Edna at a level of sensitivity beyond Albert's ken. "I was once a patient person," Berta Rantz wrote in a heartfelt eight-page response to one of Edna's letters in 1924. "I do not know you well enough to know how to amuse you. That is why I want to see you again—to know you better. Something in our last day's talk brought us a little closer together; perhaps we are sympathetic in our valuations of life."[77]

Greenfield lacked the patience or interest to delve into this seemingly intimate relationship of his wife's. A month later he dictated a response to Miss Rantz's long handwritten letter:

Edna has asked me to send you a word and say that she received your recent note to her. Edna has not been at all well, and has been ordered by the doctor to take a rest in bed for a few weeks. She will probably be confined to her room for the next month, but will be glad to write you when she is about again.[78]

Albert approached the obligations of fatherhood much as he handled his relations with his parents, in-laws, siblings, and indeed all other relatives: as a cheerful and generous provider of financial assistance, often before it was requested. Yet this man who believed so strongly in building relationships in his business life often struggled helplessly with the same task in his personal life.

By the mid-1920s Albert's father, Jacob Greenfield, had aged into a sweet, white-haired man in his seventies, long removed from the grocery business but still operating a small furniture store in the Strawberry Mansion neighborhood where he and Esther lived. To Albert's frustration, his parents refused to shed their parsimonious Old World habits and behave like the high-class parents of a successful tycoon. Without being asked, Albert often sent Jacob and Esther funds to cover summers at the New Jersey seashore; had he not done so, it seems likely they would have been content to remain in their city house near the edge of the Fairmount reservoir. In January 1925 Albert sent them a check for $1,000 to pay for their trip to Florida, adding,

"Please make arrangements as speedily as possible to make the trip and stay as long as you wish. Should this amount not be enough for you to stay for the balance of the entire winter please let me know and I will send you any additional sum you need."[79]

For her part, Esther kept a tight rein on Jacob's finances. When Albert's children visited Jacob's furniture store, Jacob customarily gave them a nickel or a dime, usually with the admonition, "Don't tell your grandmother!" Jacob customarily displayed furniture on the sidewalk in front of his store; one day, when a thief snatched a piece and ran off with it, Jacob gave chase for a block without success. Albert was furious when he found out. "You have no business running after someone who's stealing furniture," he upbraided his father. "You'll get hurt!"[80]

The last of Albert and Edna's five children, their second son, arrived in June 1927. Twelve years had passed since Albert's abortive attempt to name his first son after himself, but his dream still burned as brightly as ever, and now no one was in a position to object. Albert no longer needed the good graces of the Krauses; indeed, Sol Kraus and both of Albert's parents would be gone in barely a year.[81] So the baby was named Albert M. Greenfield Jr.

As it turned out, though, one significant person remained in a position to object: Edna herself. Greenfield's insistence on overriding her wishes and breaking Ashkenazic Jewish naming traditions apparently became the final wedge that drove an already unraveling relationship irretrievably apart. The heir to Albert Greenfield's name later remarked that he had never been held by his mother even once—only by nannies, maids, and butlers. For some ten years, because of her germ phobia, Edna had been a mother in name only; now she became Greenfield's wife in name only.[82]

During lags in the real estate market, Greenfield kept busy by negotiating the sale of other businesses. In 1925 he brokered the sale of a Philadelphia daily newspaper, the *North American*, to its morning rival, the *Public Ledger*, netting himself a $25,000 commission for the transaction.[83] At the time, Philadelphia had five morning newspapers and three evening papers, but the market was in flux: The publisher Cyrus H. K. Curtis was in the process of buying and absorbing several of them into his morning and evening *Ledgers*.[84] The *North American* deal whetted Greenfield's interest in newspapers and the potential influence they offered to a man of rapidly expanding operations.[85]

In the process he reconnected with an old acquaintance, J. David Stern, whom he had first met in 1905 when Stern had stopped by Louis Cahan's print shop to supervise the lock-up of the *YMHA Review,* a Jewish publication that Stern edited. Stern was a nervous, nail-biting, robust and fairly short dynamo with large intelligent blue eyes behind his glasses.[86] He was Philadelphia-born and -bred, from an established German Jewish family, educated at upper-class institutions like the Penn Charter School and the University of Pennsylvania, and related by marriage to the family that owned Philadelphia's Lit Brothers department store downtown.[87] But his abiding passion was the ink-stained newspaper business.

After starting out as a reporter at the *Ledger,* Stern had bought the *New Brunswick Times* in New Jersey in 1911, then moved the following year to Illinois, where he bought two newspapers in Springfield. He returned to Philadelphia in 1919 to take over the moribund *Camden Courier* across the river and then its rival, the *Camden Post-Telegram.* By 1926, thanks to his enterprising journalism and aggressive promotion, Stern's combined *Camden Courier-Post* had increased its circulation from the *Courier's* seventy-eight hundred in 1919 to more than eighty-three thousand.[88]

Stern and Greenfield were barely a year apart in age and shared the same entrepreneurial zeal for their respective businesses. Stern admired Greenfield for the very reason that many prominent Philadelphia businessmen feared him. "He was the shrewdest wheeler-dealer in Philadelphia," Stern later recalled. "The older men he had outsmarted were jealous and vented their spleen. But Al, blessed with a rhinoceros hide, and not disturbed by such attacks, was riding high."[89]

Greenfield bought a small interest in Stern's *Camden Courier-Post,* and the two men soon developed a close friendship in which each instinctively compensated for the other's shortcomings: Greenfield provided the persuasiveness and financial support to goad Stern into taking bigger publishing risks; Stern provided the journalistic detachment to bring Greenfield down to earth when his enthusiasms threatened to carry him off. Greenfield was a Republican and Stern was a liberal Democrat, but Greenfield was never one to be constrained by definitions, political or otherwise.

In June 1926 Thomas Mitten received an unsolicited letter from an admiring Philadelphia resident urging him to create "a fearless, uncontrolled, independent newspaper" in Philadelphia. The writer urged Mitten to purchase the venerable but financially troubled *Philadelphia Record* for that purpose.[90] Mitten, who had no interest in newspapers, passed the letter on to Greenfield, and soon Greenfield was urging Stern to buy the *Record* and offering to go in as Stern's silent partner. With Greenfield's encouragement, Stern spoke about transforming the *Record* into "a strong, liberal, independent newspaper" such as did not then exist in Philadelphia—one that, Stern said, placed public confidence and respect over profits.[91]

On election night in November 1926 the two men discussed the plan over dinner, then walked over to Mayor W. Freeland Kendrick's office in City Hall to hear the election returns on the radio. There Stern was dismayed by the effusive greetings Greenfield received from the assembled Republican politicians, especially the party boss, William Vare, who that night was elected to the U.S. Senate, largely through Greenfield's fund-raising efforts.

After they left, according to Stern's later recollection, Stern told Greenfield, "If I came to Philadelphia, my first job would be to attack your friends, and you would be in the doghouse. Thanks for your offer, but it wouldn't work."[92] But the seeds of a future newspaper collaboration between Stern and Greenfield had been planted.

Throughout the 1920s Greenfield was widely perceived by friends and critics alike as a man blessed with an uncanny gift for positioning himself at the right place at the right time: He had gone into business just when movie theaters began to take off; he had moved into Center City just when demand for Center City office space accelerated; he had formed alliances with William Fox, Cardinal Dougherty, Thomas Mitten, and David Stern just as all four men were about to expand their respective domains.

Yet one could validly argue that Greenfield was the cause of all this activity as much as its beneficiary: that without his unique ability to make things happen—things that had not occurred to others—his allies and partners might never have felt emboldened to expand their operations, or at least not so aggressively. Now, with his receivership of Mitten's bank, Greenfield was poised to segue into commercial banking.

In some respects that seemed a logical development. Many if not most of history's great bankers—the Fuggers, say, or the Barings, the Hambros, the Rothschilds, the Lazards, or the Lehmans—had started out in some other field, evolving into banking only after discovering that they could make more money by extending credit to their customers than they could by selling dry goods or fabrics or cotton. Why could a real estate developer not make the same transition?

Yet each new triumph for Greenfield inevitably created enemies who bridled at his refusal to play by conventional rules. In early 1927 a state senator named George Woodward claimed that large real estate operators were "wrecking building and loan associations by organizing them into large syndicates for construction and purchase programs"; he did not mention

Greenfield by name, but everyone, including Greenfield, understood Woodward's intended target.[93] Among Greenfield's rival real estate brokers, foreclosed mortgagees, jealous politicians, and nervous investors in the money-losing projects that he blithely painted as great successes, a growing number waited patiently for the day when—inevitably, they believed—the perpetually ebullient Albert Greenfield would overplay his hand.

[5]

Banker

When Greenfield bought a controlling stake in the Bank and Trust Company of West Philadelphia late in 1926, it was a mere cipher among Philadelphia's 128 operating banks. Its deposits amounted to just $2.5 million at a time when the Philadelphia National Bank, the city's largest, had more than $200 million.[1] Yet few Philadelphians—least of all Greenfield himself—believed for a minute that Greenfield would be content with a small neighborhood bank. "I regard my activity in banking as a means of contributing to the growth and progress of my world and leaving an impress [sic] upon my time," he wrote to his friend Thomas Mitten, sounding every bit as grandiose as Mitten himself.[2]

Yet this newest business in Greenfield's growing bouquet differed in important respects from the other fields—real estate, hotel management, insurance, newspapers, politics, charitable fund-raising—that he had jumped into with such alacrity and apparent success. Banking was not merely a clubby profession, restricted at its highest levels to a tight circle of Old Philadelphia patricians who shared common backgrounds and values. It was also a mysterious business that few people understood, even at society's highest levels. President Andrew Jackson had shut down the Second Bank of the United States in 1836 because, he naïvely explained, "Ever since I read about the South Sea bubble I have been afraid of banks."[3]

To most Americans, banks and bankers were wealthy individuals or institutions that made money by lending it out at interest. In fact, the wealth of bankers was largely irrelevant to their function, which was to serve their customers and society by putting idle monetary assets to use in greasing the wheels of commerce. At different times in history that definition had meant different things. But at least since the turn of the twentieth century it had meant raising funds from depositors (or, in the case of investment banks, from investors) to be loaned or invested. The banker was essentially a fundraiser, a middleman extracting a fee for matching depositors with borrowers while performing a delicate dance to assure that each party's assets were protected. A real estate developer's greatest asset was his ability to generate enthusiasm, but a banker's greatest asset was his reputation for good character.

Precisely because few people understood banking, every bank had a vested interest in the health of the banking community as a whole. Just as a single rogue partner could destroy a partnership, so a single rogue bank, by undermining public confidence, could bring down the entire banking community.

Thus, conventional banking wisdom in Philadelphia called for increasing an institution's assets only slowly and cautiously. To avoid the unseemly appearance of cutthroat competition, Philadelphia bankers tended not to chase after each other's customers, and, consequently, banking tended to be a leisurely industry that valued prudence above ingenuity. The perceived key to banking success was the "3-6-3" rule—that is, pay depositors 3 percent interest, invest their money at 6 percent, and head for the country club by 3:00 P.M.

Such formulas, of course, were anathema to Greenfield. His plan was to grow his bank quickly, much the way Mitten had grown the PRT: by acquiring competitors. Quick growth would feed on itself, creating an image of success that would attract more business, thereby generating still greater growth—the same dazzling formula that had worked so well for Greenfield in real estate.

Almost immediately after the acquisition, Greenfield moved the bank's headquarters from West Philadelphia to the ground floor of his own building downtown, renamed it the Bankers Trust Company—the name on the charter that Louis Cahan had obtained—and began casting about for more acquisitions.[4]

These were not difficult to find because by 1927 many banks were suffering from a downturn in the real estate market. Thanks in large part to Greenfield's efforts, Center City, once underbuilt, had now become overbuilt to such an extent that Greenfield himself urged a moratorium on new downtown construction (even as he assembled and sold a site for the construction of the Market Street National Bank Building east of City Hall).[5] Thousands of homes—sold through mortgages of 80 percent or more to Philadelphians who could not really afford them—were now in default or foreclosure.[6]

Consequently, many banks that had made loans to downtown developers or homebuyers found themselves holding mortgages of dubious value.

Acquiring such banks was a risky tactic, of course. Even in the best of times, Greenfield's strategy of growth by acquisition seemed dangerous, if only because, at some point, Bankers Trust would run out of banks to buy (just as Greenfield's friend Mitten had run out of transportation companies to buy). But no business operates in a vacuum. The alternative to growth was to remain small and impotent at a time when bold speculation seemed to be paying off on Wall Street, not to mention everywhere else investors turned outside the real estate market. By the time Greenfield launched Bankers Trust in late 1926, even Philadelphia's bankers had caught the speculative fever and were growing more aggressive about taking over smaller banks. Greenfield would need to expand faster than his competitors, lest they wind up forcing him to sell out to them.

But of course this was a game that Greenfield relished. The big Philadelphia banks, by contrast, were making acquisitions reluctantly and defensively, to preserve their relative rank. An unspoken element of Greenfield's game plan was his political clout. From the start, he set about drumming up deposits for Bankers Trust from his Republican allies in state and local governments. He showered public officials and even rival bankers with petty favors—birthday greetings, fruit baskets, help with court cases or zoning approvals—gestures that were too small to cause anyone to self-righteously reject but significant enough to create a sense of obligation.

When Jack Dempsey fought Gene Tunney for the world heavyweight boxing title in Philadelphia in September 1926, Greenfield acquired a coveted set of tickets and invited key officials to join him as his guests. One invitee, Pennsylvania Secretary of Banking Peter G. Cameron, initially expressed qualms about the propriety of accepting and being seen in Greenfield's company. "Will you attend?" he asked Greenfield in a handwritten letter marked "Personal and Confidential." "Perhaps I should not. What do you think?" Greenfield replied reassuringly the next day: "I am confident it will be perfectly in accord with your official position to be present. I shall be delighted to have you with me, and from all indications, the fight should be a corker."[7] The cumulative net effect of these favors was to reinforce the impression that Greenfield had friends in high places and that one should tread cautiously before challenging him.

Although Greenfield's office was one flight above the Bankers Trust and he was its largest stockholder and depositor, he remained sufficiently cautious to keep an uncharacteristically low profile there. He took no executive title for himself at Bankers Trust; technically, he was merely one of the bank's seventeen board members.[8] To operate the bank as president, he made what appears to have been his first quality hire after more than twenty years of surrounding himself with yes-men. But his handpicked bank president came not from the banking community but from the ranks of financial journalism.

Samuel Barker had been born in 1872 into an old established Quaker family. His father, the soldier-financier-publicist Wharton Barker, had run for president of the United States on the Middle-of-the-Road Populist Party ticket in 1900 and had been a prime mover behind Thomas Mitten's idealistic Producers & Consumers Bank that had fallen into Greenfield's receivership in 1925.[9] Samuel's brother Rodman Barker had been chief financial officer to the merchant king John Wanamaker.[10] Samuel had been financial editor of the Philadelphia *North American* from 1907 to 1925, when the *North American* closed (in a sale negotiated by Greenfield) and Barker gave up writing about business to go into business for himself. Both Sam and Rodman Barker were "gentle men in every sense of the word," as one of Greenfield's associates later described them.[11] How Samuel Barker met Greenfield is unclear, although he probably covered Greenfield's deals for his newspaper.

In some respects, Barker was an inspired choice. Having written about business for eighteen years, he was eager to try it himself and unburdened by the cautiousness that seemed to infect most experienced Philadelphia bankers. On one hand, like Mitten (as well as his own Populist father), Barker believed in reaching out to depositors and sharing profits with employees. On the other hand, from Greenfield's perspective, he lacked the experience or credentials to question Greenfield's unorthodox banking style.

Over the next three and a half years, with Barker running the day-to-day operations and Greenfield directing acquisition strategy, Bankers Trust staged an astonishing series of mergers in Philadelphia, beginning with the National Bank of Commerce in 1927 and the Logan Bank and Trust Company in 1928.

To entice more depositors, Barker reinforced the bank's growth strategy by extending hours at most Bankers Trust branches to the outlandish hour of 10:30 P.M.[12] Barely two years after Greenfield acquired his little bank in West Philadelphia, Bankers Trust had seven locations throughout the city, with thirty-six thousand depositors and $24.6 million in deposits—nearly ten times its size at the time Greenfield acquired it.[13]

As another populist gesture, in May 1929 the bank distributed bonus checks equal to 1.5 percent of the annual salary of all employees below the officer level—significantly, on the same day that the bank mailed 1.5 percent quarterly dividend checks to its stockholders.

The bank's progress, Barker exulted in a letter to Bankers Trust employees, "whether in size, earnings position or prestige, has exceeded that of any financial institution in Philadelphia. And it has just started. I am counting on you as you can count on me. A wonderful future is ahead for this company in doing useful, helpful, constructive things as well as they can be done."[14]

As Greenfield had expected, the bank's phenomenal growth spurt attracted investors eager to relieve him of his own financial stake but happy to leave him in control. Stock in Bankers Trust, of course, was another of the carrots Greenfield could offer as gifts to public officials and anyone else likely to be of use to him, and stockholders, in turn, were only too happy to deposit funds in Bankers Trust as a way of assuring the success of the venture. As early as June 1927—just six months after the bank was purchased—Bankers Trust had about five hundred shareholders.[15] Five months later, Barker asked the bank's directors to come up with $20 million in deposits within four days, apparently successfully.[16] The following July, Greenfield's friend William Fox acquired $78,309 worth of Bankers Trust stock, and his Fox Film Corporation opened an account there.[17]

Yet this remarkable growth seemed only to stoke the appetites of Greenfield and his colleagues. Even before Bankers Trust had opened, Greenfield and Barker had a bigger idea.[18] As early as 1927, both Fox and Barker urged Greenfield to make Bankers Trust the launching pad for a still more ambitious financial venture: a securities company, allied with the bank, that could borrow funds from the bank and trade in stocks and bonds to an extent not permitted to banks themselves.[19] Although Bankers Trust's future "is assured," Barker wrote Greenfield, "we need to increase its business, which means creation of more, with the resulting profits which are absolutely necessary to its fullest success."

In another memo to Greenfield, Barker argued that Bankers Trust would have "a greater latitude of action through a securities corporation, with a limited liability which is impossible where the business is conducted directly by a banking institution." The proposed Bankers Securities Corporation, Barker suggested, could be organized by giving Bankers Trust stockholders the privilege of subscribing pro rata to 25 percent of Bankers Securities stock while Bankers Trust owned half the stock and the remaining 25 percent was sold to other investors.[20]

Thus was born, barely a year after Bankers Trust opened, the brightest jewel in Greenfield's crown: the Bankers Securities Corporation, organized in May 1928 with $12 million in capital that Greenfield raised from 1,628 investors, among them Mayor Harry A. Mackey and Joseph Wayne, president of the Philadelphia National Bank.[21] Half the original stock in Bankers

Securities—that is, $6 million worth—was subscribed to by Greenfield's Bankers Trust, which promptly offered roughly half that stock to its depositors and the other half to the bank's own stockholders on a share-for-share basis.[22]

Bankers Trust was not the first Philadelphia bank to create a securities company—the Franklin National Bank had organized the Franklin Securities Company in 1919[23]—but Philadelphians had never seen such a company of this scale and determination before. At its very first meeting, the Bankers Securities board voted extraordinary powers to Greenfield as its chairman: "He shall in general have power to do all things expedient and necessary to be done and performed in the general management of the corporation," the resolution noted.[24]

The offered shares were snapped up within a matter of months, solely on the new company's promise of a 5 percent return on investment. By tapping his existing constituency of Bankers Trust stockholders and depositors, Greenfield had created a new company entirely out of thin air without spending a dollar on underwriting or commissions.[25]

Bankers Securities entered the financial marketplace at the very time that the mighty Pennsylvania Railroad was seeking $62 million in a new public stock issue. Yet the railroad—"the largest system in the country, with splendid traffic position, long established business and financial history unsurpassed among American corporations," as Barker gleefully noted in an early report to his directors—had found it necessary to offer a 7 percent return on its earnings in order to raise that $62 million. By contrast, the stock offering for Bankers Securities—a company with no product, no customers, and no track record—had been oversubscribed while promising only 5 percent.[26]

The remaining half of Bankers Securities stock was sold to Greenfield, who distributed some of it to clients and friends. The corporation's first and largest individual shareholders, each with an initial stake of $600,000, were Greenfield and Fox.[27] Given the complex (and constantly shifting) weighting of Bankers Securities' common and preferred stock, it was never easy to pin down the extent of anyone's stake, but within a year or so Greenfield and Fox each wound up owning about a quarter of Bankers Securities.

At the same time, Bankers Securities wound up owning about half the stock of Bankers Trust, which had created Bankers Securities; it also kept large deposits there.[28] In addition, Greenfield and Fox each had deposits and loans with Bankers Trust. In late 1928 a syndicate managed by Greenfield and Fox also borrowed more than 10 percent of Bankers Trust's capital to acquire much of the Bankers Securities common and preferred stock owned by Bankers Trust.[29]

Anyone who tried to make sense out of these arrangements was doomed to perpetual confusion. In effect, Bankers Trust was the parent of Bankers Securities, and Bankers Securities became the parent of Bankers Trust. Few people questioned this setup as long as it seemed to work. Indeed, the very complexity of the arrangement enhanced Greenfield's mystique, reinforcing the perception that he was a financial magician capable of proving, as Barker put it in a memo to Greenfield, that "two and two make not four, but five or six or more where real energy and virile initiative and wisely applied belief are thrown, with all their compelling force, into any soundly based, constructive project."[30] Greenfield became chairman of Bankers Securities, with Barker as president of both Bankers Securities and Bankers Trust.

Like most of Greenfield's enterprises, Bankers Securities did not exist for the purpose of making or doing anything, as most people thought of those terms; its sole function was to make money from money. The success of the Bankers Securities offering was a commentary on the speculative exuberance of the late 1920s but also a tribute to Greenfield's reputation as a financial genius.

There remained the question of precisely how Bankers Securities would make money, aside from soliciting deposits from its stockholders and selling its own stock to Bankers Trust depositors. Barker's first communication with Bankers Securities shareholders, on May 19, was less than encouraging about this matter: Barker urged them to "help swell the earnings and so make dividends for yourself." He reminded them that "close interrelation exists between Bankers Securities Corporation and Bankers Trust Company. . . . Each of you 1,628 stockholders should be a depositor in Bankers Trust Company."[31]

To justify the huge expectations that Greenfield had raised, Bankers Securities needed to transact some major deal, and soon. As Greenfield had shrewdly, or perhaps instinctively, perceived, the widespread public knowledge that he had raised a pool of $12 million to invest increased the likelihood that such a deal might come his way.

Early in September 1928 Greenfield was approached by Jacob Lit with a proposition. Lit's older sister Rachel Lit Wedell had opened a dress shop on Market Street downtown in 1891, and two years later her brothers Samuel and Jacob had enlarged it into Lit Brothers, which subsequently expanded into a five-story, block-long, moderately priced department store that grossed some $38 million a year. Now Rachel was gone and the two Lit brothers were in poor health (Samuel died the following February).[32] Almost all their wealth was tied up in the store, and they were eager to cash out.[33]

Greenfield lacked any retailing experience, but in Lit Brothers he saw a prime parcel of real estate at Eighth and Market Streets that happened to be occupied by a profitable business. (Of real estate, Greenfield liked to say, "Unlike most commodities, the more it is used the more valuable it becomes.")[34] He also saw a company with the second-largest department store volume in Philadelphia and annual earnings of $2 million despite a stagnant management. "With active leadership," Greenfield wrote his friend Thomas Mitten, "Lit's could have volume of $50 million and profit of $3–4 million."[35] And he saw in the life of Colonel Samuel Lit—"a young Jewish boy who built a monument to himself and his fellowmen from very humble beginnings," as the *Jewish Times* eulogized him—a story very similar to his own.[36] It was a deal Greenfield was reluctant to refuse. If he could buy Lit's at the right price, he assumed he could make money from it one way or another.

So later that month Bankers Securities took nearly $10.3 million—or nearly all its initial capital—to buy a controlling 51 percent interest in Lit Brothers.[37] Almost immediately, Greenfield began exploring methods of marketing the Lit's stock to the public. If he could sell the 501,000 Lit's shares for two dollars per share above the price he had paid, Bankers Securities could turn a quick profit of $1 million.

These explorations had barely begun when Greenfield was approached by the Newark retailer Rudolph J. Goerke, who had leveraged his own dry goods empire into a controlling stake in City Stores Company, which owned four of the finest retailing names in the Southern states: Maison Blanche of New Orleans, Loveman, Joseph & Loeb of Birmingham, B. Lowenstein's of Memphis, and Kaufman-Straus of Louisville.[38] In October, scant weeks after Bankers Securities had bought the controlling share of Lit Brothers for $10.2 million, City Stores acquired it for $13 million.[39]

This quick $2.8 million profit—equivalent to more than 26 percent appreciation in less than a month—enabled Bankers Securities to pay its first dividend on common and preferred stock in October 1928. That action in turn drove the price of Bankers Securities stock up to $156 per share in late October, just seven months after it had been issued at $60.[40] It also enabled Bankers Securities to raise an additional $19 million in a second public stock offering in November 1928.[41] Although this second offering would dilute the stake of existing Bankers Securities common shareholders, no one challenged the euphoric joint statement issued by Greenfield and Barker: The offering, they argued, was impelled "by the firm conviction that the country is now entering upon an epoch of progress such as will transcend anything in the past, and in the belief that every sound business should therefore place itself in position to do much more than ever before."[42]

The secondary offering, together with the profit from the Lit's sale, more than doubled Bankers Securities' paid-in surplus. Although Bankers Securities had consummated only one transaction at this point, the *Wall Street Journal* referred to it as "one of the largest corporations of its kind in the country."[43]

On the surface the sale seemed a triumph of financial ingenuity. Not only did it give Bankers Securities an instant paper profit of $2.8 million; it also relieved Greenfield of the expense and bother of marketing the Lit's stock to the public.[44] Yet in fact City Stores had paid Bankers Securities hardly anything for Lit's. Instead, City Stores had given Bankers Securities a three-year note for $8 million and borrowed the rest from the investment banking firm of Halsey Stuart & Co. In effect, Bankers Securities had loaned money it did not have to enable City Stores to purchase Lit's from Bankers Securities.

Also, in effect, Bankers Securities had not unloaded Lit Brothers at all, but instead had entered into a hasty partnership with Goerke and City Stores without adequately investigating their creditworthiness. The deal had all the soundness of a chain letter, but it was typical of the speculative environment of the late 1920s in that nobody questioned it as long as it seemed to work.

To be sure, the $8 million loan was fully secured by the 501,000 shares of Lit's stock, valued at $13 million (whereas Halsey Stuart's loan to City Stores was unsecured).[45] And Bankers Securities would collect 6 percent interest on the loan. So to most observers the deal seemed brilliant.

The resultant sharp rise in Bankers Securities stock greatly increased the company's total assets and provided it with collateral—that is, its own inflated stock—with which to make further investments. In March 1929 the grateful board of Bankers Securities voted Greenfield, its previously unpaid chairman, an annual salary of $100,000—an amount that represented two-fifths of the company's entire payroll.[46]

The new infusion of capital at Bankers Securities enabled Greenfield and Fox to expand their respective holdings in real estate and the movie business. Greenfield, who already controlled the Bonwit Teller women's specialty store in Philadelphia, now loaned $1 million to Paul J. Bonwit and took as collateral 52 percent of the stock of the Bonwit's store in New York.[47] Fox, seizing on the death of the film pioneer Marcus Loew in September 1927, now borrowed $10 million from Bankers Securities—the lion's share of the new firm's capital—to help finance his purchase of the Loew family's controlling share in Loew's Inc., parent of Fox's rival, Metro-Goldwyn-Mayer studio.[48]

In the wake of Bankers Securities' success, Philadelphia's more established banks scrambled to create similar securities companies of their own. Over the next year, five major Philadelphia banks launched securities companies; the last bank to join the parade was the city's largest, the Philadelphia National Bank.[49] But these were defensive moves forced on them by Greenfield's inventive strategy; the sudden success of Bankers Securities, based on a single deal, exacerbated the alarm and apprehension with which Philadelphia's leading bankers viewed Greenfield and his activities.

Even as he launched Bankers Securities, Greenfield moved to shore up his political connections within both parties. When the struggling *Philadelphia Record* again became available barely a year after Greenfield had sold it to the Curtis interests, he was approached by his publisher friend, David Stern of the *Camden Courier-Post*.

"Why haven't you bought the *Record*?" Stern asked him, according to Stern's later recollection.

"I'm not interested without you," Greenfield replied.

Stern intimated that he was indeed thinking of buying the *Record*, "but I won't step in if you're in the picture"—a reference to Stern's reluctance as a liberal Democrat to embarrass Greenfield among his Republican friends.

Greenfield, to Stern's surprise, was adamant: "For the good of Philadelphia," Greenfield replied, "buy the *Record* with or without me. If I can be of help in financing or in any other way, I am at your service."[50]

To Stern, this encouragement exemplified Greenfield's exceptional broad-mindedness. "I found you unique among the business leaders of our city," he wrote Greenfield years later. "You did not have a closed mind like the rest of them. You wanted to hear the liberal side."[51]

In June 1928, with Greenfield as silent partner, Stern bought the *Record* from the Rodman Wanamaker estate and crossed the Delaware River from Camden to become a Philadelphia newspaper publisher for the first time. The sale price was $1,750,000, of which Greenfield personally invested $400,000 and Bankers Trust and Bankers Securities together put up $1.2 million in loans.[52] Following Greenfield's example at Bankers Trust, Stern's Courier-Post Company of Camden bought about half the stock of the newly created Record Company and sold the rest to the public, with an ease that astonished Stern. "In booming 1928 it was as easy to sell securities as pink lemonade at a circus," Stern later recalled. The stock issue of the new Record Company was quickly oversubscribed. "When I started to explain the financial plan," Stern recalled, "many friends cut me short with, 'Dave, I don't want details. Where do I sign and for how much?'"

The sale package included the Record Building, valued at $500,000, which Stern believed he could sell for working capital while remaining as its tenant. Greenfield, in his role as real estate sage, advised Stern to postpone the sale until the *Record* relocated to a new plant elsewhere. "Real estate values are soaring," he told Stern. "Next year I believe I can get seven hundred and fifty thousand for your equity instead of the half-million you're now asking. Meanwhile, my bank will advance you what you need for the new plant."[53] Those were the words of a loyal friend and—given the increasingly shaky condition of the real estate market—an incurable optimist.

The same month that Greenfield assisted Stern's entry into Philadelphia as the city's only Democratic newspaper publisher, he took his seat as a delegate to the Republican National Convention in Kansas City. National politics, especially Republican politics, was another area in which Jews had preferred to operate quietly and behind the scenes rather than openly and flamboyantly, at least until Greenfield came along.

In June 1928, as the convention approached, the incumbent Republican president, Calvin Coolidge, had not yet decided whether to seek reelection. Greenfield preferred Herbert Hoover, the secretary of Commerce, whom Greenfield had worked with in two successful food relief drives for European refugees following World War I. Hoover struck Greenfield as the prototype of a new kind of public-spirited politician.

"The trouble with present-day politics is that men use their political organization as a means for revenue only," Greenfield told a reporter. "Herbert Hoover is my type of public man, a new type of leader and the kind the country needs." When the reporter asked him whether Greenfield himself was such a "new type of leader," Greenfield encouraged the notion: "If the people of our city think that I am worthy of being their new-type leader, and a distinct departure from bosses and bossism," he replied, "why, then, I'm happy and flattered."[54]

Philadelphia's convention delegates—uncommitted to any candidate at a time when few states held primary elections—traveled together to Kansas City aboard a special train. The two-day journey left the delegates with nothing to do but plot convention strategy and try to influence the delegation's leader, Senator William Vare. Greenfield, by virtue of his role as Vare's leading fund-raiser during the 1926 senatorial campaign, gained access to Vare's stateroom and spent several hours closeted there while trying to persuade Vare to support Hoover for the nomination.

Vare at that point had reason to wonder whether Greenfield's support of his Senate candidacy had been a blessing or a curse. Greenfield's zealous efforts for Vare in 1926 had built a war chest capable of competing with rival party factions led by the wealthy Mellon family and the equally wealthy textile manufacturer Joseph Grundy, both from western Pennsylvania. As a result, Vare defeated two formidable rivals in the Republican primary: Pennsylvania's incumbent U.S. senator, George Wharton Pepper, and the incumbent governor, Gifford Pinchot.[55] But Greenfield's exertions focused so much attention on his fund-raising that it prompted a Senate investigation to determine whether Vare should be denied his seat for excessive campaign spending. That investigation was still under way when the Republican National Convention convened in Kansas City nearly two years later.[56]

Greenfield was not so naïve as to discuss the relative presidential merits of Hoover and Coolidge with a hard-nosed politician like Vare. Instead, he argued that control of the state's Republican organization was at stake. In the past, the Pennsylvania delegation had always voted as a unit. Andrew Mellon of Pittsburgh, secretary of the Treasury and one of America's wealthiest men, was trying to force Coolidge's candidacy on the entire Pennsylvania delegation, which Vare resented. But Greenfield had learned that Mellon would not arrive in Kansas City until Monday morning. In that case, Greenfield suggested to Vare, why not let Philadelphia's Republicans vote independently of the rest, and announce on Sunday night—the night before the convention opened—that the Philadelphia delegation supported Hoover?[57]

Greenfield also raised a more personal reason for Vare to undercut Mellon. If Mellon succeeded in returning Coolidge to the White House, Greenfield suggested, Vare would lose his Senate seat, because Coolidge was Mellon's man, and Mellon was Vare's enemy.[58]

As Vare later recalled, while still on board the train he tacitly agreed that the Philadelphia delegates would support Hoover; but in order to preserve their influence, they would not tip their hand until they arrived at Kansas City.

Immediately on arriving on Sunday, however, Vare learned from one of Hoover's managers that Hoover's support was slipping: He had lost three delegations during the day and seemed in danger of losing more without some new expression of support. Vare also received word from western Pennsylvania delegates that Mellon had scheduled a press conference at which he intended to deliver the coup de grâce to Hoover's hopes by announcing Pennsylvania's support of Coolidge. At this news, Vare—a far cannier politician than Mellon—organized a preemptive strike: Minutes before Mellon's press conference was to begin on Monday morning, Vare issued a press release announcing his support of Hoover.

"The Vare bomb," as Greenfield called it, "detonated in the midst of a gathering of some 200 journalists waiting the pleasure of the secretary of the Treasury to name his choice." When Mellon and Pennsylvania's other U.S. senator, David Reed, entered the room, they discovered that Vare had stolen

their thunder, forcing them to support Hoover rather than risk a split delegation. Other state delegations, eager to align themselves with the likely win-
ner, now stampeded to the Hoover camp, so that within a few hours Hoover's
nomination was all but assured.[59]

At the convention itself the next day, it was Greenfield who seconded
Hoover's nomination, and during the campaign that followed, Greenfield
served as vice-chairman of the Republican National Campaign Committee.[60]

Soon after the convention, Greenfield escorted Fox to Washington to
meet Hoover. Fox, pointing to Greenfield, told Hoover, "You can blame that
little bald-headed Hebrew Jew who made it possible for you to become the
President of the United States." Hoover, Fox later recounted, "naturally was
vitally interested to learn the details of how this came about."[61]

That Vare turned the tide in Hoover's favor at Kansas City seems beyond
dispute, but the extent of Greenfield's role remains unclear. Vare himself,
in his account of his conversations aboard the train to Kansas City, made
no mention of Greenfield; he tilted toward Hoover, he said in his memoirs,
after talking with Colonel James Elverson Jr., publisher of the *Philadelphia
Inquirer*.[62] Whatever the truth, Hoover believed Greenfield had helped advance his presidential career, and, consequently, Greenfield now had a friend
in the White House who to some degree felt beholden to him. And Fox's
pointed reference to Greenfield's Jewishness emphasized the fact that Jews,
who had previously influenced national politics only quietly and behind the
scenes, were becoming a more direct and assertive force.

Vare may have had another motive for writing Greenfield out of his
account: By the time Vare wrote his memoirs in 1933, Greenfield had
rendered himself persona non grata with his former friend and political ally.

Two months after the 1928 Kansas Convention, while vacationing at
his Atlantic City summer home, Vare suffered a stroke, possibly brought on
by the stress of those two years he had spent fighting for his Senate seat.[63]
During his long absences while he recuperated, Vare relied on Greenfield
and Mayor Harry Mackey to run Philadelphia's Republican organization. In
the inevitable vacuum that developed, a new Republican coalition emerged,
consisting (among others) of Greenfield, Mackey, Greenfield's friend and
partner Thomas Mitten, and Greenfield's childhood friend, District Attorney John Monaghan.

Publicly, these men promoted themselves as political reformers: "I have
no desire to have power politically in this city," Greenfield insisted in the
spring of 1929 in a speech at the Union League, Philadelphia's leading private club. "I believe that it is the civic duty of every business man to take an

interest in the development of his city, and this I shall always do."[64] Green-field may well have believed that his purposes were altruistic. Yet, inevitably, the reformers' actions advanced their own narrow purposes while threaten-ing Vare's control.

To eradicate corruption within the police department, District Attorney Monaghan launched grand jury investigations and Mayor Mackey replaced Director of Public Safety Harry C. Davis, a stalwart of the Vare machine, with Major Lemuel B. Schofield, a lawyer who often did legal work for Greenfield. The result was the dismissal, discharge, or transfer of roughly half of Philadelphia's police force by the beginning of 1929. In January 1929 the Mackey-Greenfield coalition successfully challenged the Vare machine by supporting Judge Charles L. Brown against a Vare loyalist for president judge of the municipal courts, a position that controlled more than five hun-dred patronage jobs.

In the ensuing brutally contested primary election in the spring of 1929, much of the vitriol was directed not at the candidates for the various row offices but at Greenfield, who was denounced as an "octopus." One politi-cal brochure pictured Greenfield swallowing the mayor above a caption that read, "Isn't he aware HAM isn't kosher?"[65] The United Businessmen's As-sociation denounced Schofield as a "right-hand man of Greenfield."[66] State senator Sam Salus accused Greenfield of sponsoring a train trip to Chicago in the fall of 1927 to see the Dempsey-Tunney heavyweight championship rematch and of paying for $1,700 worth of liquor on board; Greenfield and his allies, Salus said, were trying "to bury Mr. Vare while he is still alive." (Greenfield, in a nondenial denial, admitted that alcohol was consumed on the train but said he did not pay for it.)[67]

Yet ultimately the Vare machine prevailed convincingly in the Republi-can primaries, which were tantamount to victory in the general election that fall. In the aftermath of that bitter primary campaign, Greenfield found him-self disillusioned with politics and alienated from a machine that still domi-nated Philadelphia's municipal government.[68] Vare's bitterness was probably compounded when, in 1929, the U.S. Senate concluded its three-year investi-gation of his 1926 campaign financing by voting to deny Vare his seat.[69]

Without Vare's support, Greenfield's customarily risky operating style grew even riskier. In January his bizarre role in the PRT's acquisition of the Quaker City Cab Company in 1926 came to light, and a city councilman gave Greenfield a new sobriquet: "The old manipulator."[70] In September 1929, two months before the general election, the Vare organization struck back at its perceived tormentors when the city filed suit against Mitten and the PRT for alleged excessive fees and improper diversion of funds.[71] The suit threatened to expose Thomas Mitten's entire scheme of pyramiding the PRT's growth through acquisitions, many of them arranged by Greenfield. And in these proceedings Vare would no longer be Greenfield's ally but his adversary.

Still, Vare at that point was clearly a man whose star was fading while Greenfield's continued to rise. In October 1928 Greenfield took over two mortgage companies in Newark, New Jersey, and merged them into his Bankers Bond & Mortgage Co. (now grandiloquently renamed Bankers Bond & Mortgage Co. of America); the acquisition expanded the company's resources to $42.7 million and gave it a foothold in the New York market.[72] In February 1929 Greenfield's real estate company acquired the highly re-garded rival firm of Mastbaum Brothers & Fleisher, which had struggled following the deaths of its two leaders (both of them Greenfield's friends), Jules Mastbaum in December 1926 and Jules's partner, Alfred Fleisher, in December 1928. With this consolidation, Albert M. Greenfield & Co. was said to be one of the nation's largest real estate concerns, with management of more than $200 million worth of real estate and annual rent collections exceeding $14 million.[73]

Bankers Trust, meanwhile, accelerated its acquisition pace in 1929, pick-ing up the Federal Trust Company in March, the Empire Title and Trust Company in April, the Tioga Trust Company in May, and the Merchants and Drovers Bank in October.[74]

To Greenfield the secret of his success was not monopolization of any business but the unprecedented synergy among his various businesses—all headquartered in the Bankers Trust Building at Juniper and Walnut—which enabled him to serve his existing clients and attract new ones. "Why," mar-veled an anonymous banker quoted in an insurance newspaper, "a young married man can go in there, buy a house, get a mortgage, open a bank ac-count, buy securities, have his house insured, his furniture, his car and him-self insured all by simply walking from one department to another."[75]

Greenfield, for all the awe and fear he provoked, made himself remark-ably accessible to anyone who ventured to approach him. If a total stranger piqued his interest, he tended to drop everything else, although soon enough the visitor would find Greenfield preoccupied with other matters.

"It is difficult to interview Mr. Greenfield," wrote one reporter who tried. "He is courteous to you, answers your questions and acts the perfect host. But your thoughts and his, too, are 'lost' in the constant ringing of his tele-phone."[76] (If the phone rang in the midst of a meeting, Greenfield custom-arily excused himself and took the call in a standup phone booth he had installed in his office for privacy.)[77]

Greenfield's headquarters on the second floor of the Bankers Trust Building was dominated not by his personal office but by its great board-room, with an immense long table, which was mostly used not for board meetings but for property settlements.[78] Greenfield himself operated in a walnut-paneled office that was surprisingly small and dark, in part because the windows, looking out on narrow Juniper Street, admitted little light. This was Greenfield's preference (as, indeed, it had been the preference of the great J. Pierpont Morgan): He worked at a quaint rolltop desk, wrote with stubby pencils, and generally prided himself on maintaining the façade of a small-town real estate brokerage.[79]

Nevertheless, another reporter who visited Greenfield's office in January 1929 concluded that the office "has an air of elegance about it":

The furniture is mahogany, and on the walls are hung many beau-tiful pictures, some depicting important events in American his-tory. In one corner is a handsome clock, presented to Mr. Greenfield by building and loan associations with which he had co-operated. Near it is a picture of the Eiffel Tower, presented by a friend, who painted on it, "For Sale, Apply Albert M. Greenfield."[80]

The reporter added that "Riding horseback once or twice a week in the winter and swimming daily in the ocean at Ventnor in the summer are the principal exercises of this busy real estate man." Then the reporter turned to Greenfield for a description of his typical business day:

I arise every morning at 6:30 o'clock. The barber comes in at 7. I eat breakfast at 7:30 and play with the children from 8 until 8:15. That is the time allotted to them during the week, as I frequently do not get home for dinner.

I leave my home at 310 West Johnson Street, Germantown, at 8:30, arriving at the office shortly before 9 o'clock. Then the usual routine starts.

I work something like a physician, granting five and ten-minute interviews to between forty and fifty persons a day, in addition to answering an average of about 100 telephone calls. I do not go out for lunch, as we have our own dining room here, thereby saving time.

I leave the office at 6 in the evening or later, and often go home for dinner and return to the center of the city for a meeting. I retire shortly before 1 A.M. and need only six hours sleep.

This may sound like a busy routine, day after day, but I really don't feel the need of a change. I can stand the work. I like it and I save my energy for it, preferring that to playing bridge late in the night several times a week.[81]

Since Greenfield was almost completely bald, his reference to the daily visit from his barber may have amused some of his acquaintances. Yet the barber played a significant role in creating a presence that compensated for Greenfield's short stature and otherwise unappealing physical appearance. "He was always immaculately tailored," one acquaintance recalled—"rosy, glowing, always had an aura about him, as if he'd just had a rub, a shave and a steam. Nothing was out of place. He always wore a vest."[82]

The net effect was that Greenfield became the center of attention wherever he went. When he walked into lunch at the Bankers Trust dining room, the assembled guests would rise in unison—not just the men, but the women, and not just young women but women who were older than Greenfield himself. One woman who had observed this phenomenon later recalled that the people who rose so deferentially at Greenfield's entrance seemed to do so automatically, reflexively, just as one might on encountering Louis XIV.[83]

As 1929 wore on, Bankers Securities continued to captivate the investment world. In late September an independent stock analyst concluded that Bankers Securities "has already demonstrated its earning power beyond any doubt," having earned profits of $3.6 million in its first sixteen months while building up a pool of $26 million that was still available for further investments. Of course, most of those earnings had come from a single transaction—the 1928 purchase and subsequent sale of Lit Brothers to City Stores. And at this moment Bankers Securities' assets included debt obligations for two huge loans: $8 million loaned to City Stores for the purchase of Lit's and $10 million loaned to William Fox's film company to help him buy control of Loews Inc. Yet the analyst, like most observers and like Greenfield himself, chose to see the glass as half full. The Lit's transaction, the analyst wrote, "proves the ability of management to conduct operations of magnitude." And even excluding the Lit Brothers transaction, he added, Bankers Securities had shown better than a 10 percent annual rate of return on its capital. "The directorate of the company, headed by Albert M. Greenfield, of Philadelphia, contains names of outstanding strength," the report concluded. "The national contacts which they afford the company will doubtless contribute materially to bringing it lucrative business in the future, as they have in the past."[84]

"Your company," Greenfield and Barker assured Bankers Securities stockholders in a joint letter that same month, "is now in sounder condition than at any time, and its future more promising than ever."[85]

L ess than three weeks after he issued that rosy pronouncement, Greenfield opened his morning paper to the stunning news that his friend and patron, Thomas Mitten, had drowned while fishing on his private lake at Sunnylands, Mitten's four-thousand-acre estate near Milford in northeastern Pennsylvania. "All agree the drowning was accidental," the *Philadelphia Inquirer* reported.[86] That seemed a logical conclusion, at first. After all, Mitten was a sixty-five-year-old man with a heart condition. Only a few weeks earlier a federal agency had summoned him to Washington to explain how his "Philadelphia Plan" could be applied to labor problems in other municipal street railway systems. He still had much to live for.

The tributes that poured in included one from Greenfield:

I am greatly shocked at the news of Mr. Mitten's tragic death. He was the most unusual man with whom I ever came in contact. . . . He proved to the world at large that it was possible to harmonize capital and labor unceasingly toward a common goal . . . Thomas E. Mitten was a remarkable man, who accomplished much during his lifetime, and his death will come as great shock to men in every walk of life.[87]

Yet in the days that followed, many people began to wonder whether Mitten's drowning was indeed an accident. Why, they asked, would a sixty-five-year-old man with a heart condition take a boat out alone on a lake, beyond the sight of anyone else—in October, no less? And was it not convenient that the drowning had occurred scant weeks after the city filed its suit against Mitten and the PRT, accusing him of diverting funds and charging excessive fees?

Four weeks after Mitten's drowning, the stock market crashed. Mitten's death, accidental or not, had come at a more convenient moment than he could have imagined. Death would spare him any reckoning for the excesses of the twenties. Those who survived would not be so fortunate.

[PART III]

DOWNFALL

[6]

The Great Crash

For six years beginning in 1923, Wall Street had enjoyed a remarkable run that seemed to justify Greenfield's irrepressible optimism. Everywhere Americans turned, ordinary people—chauffeurs, teachers, housekeepers—seemed to be making millions in the stock market.

The key to this overnight affluence was a seemingly ingenious leveraging scheme that enabled stockbrokers and their clients alike to buy stock by putting up a "margin" of as little as 10 percent of the purchase price; the rest could be repaid in the future, presumably after the investor sold his or her stock at a profit.

To be sure, if the stock price fell, the broker would ask the customer for additional funds to maintain his or her margin of at least 10 percent of the sale value. If the stock continued to fall, the investor would have to keep meeting calls for additional margin or let the investment house sell the stock, wiping out almost all the investor's original outlay.

Trading stocks on margin was precisely the sort of leveraging strategy that Greenfield had employed in acquiring Center City office buildings and hotels, as well as in creating the Bankers Trust Company and Bankers Securities. It was a risky strategy for anyone who lacked Greenfield's exceptional nerve. Yet as of September 1929, Americans owed more than $8.5 billion in outstanding loans—more than the entire amount of currency circulating in the United States. At a time when individual investors owned some 80 percent of publicly traded stocks, any serious break in the market could trigger a stampede of investors unloading their stocks in order to meet margin calls.

Yet through most of the twenties, buying stock on margin seemed a sound and even prudent philosophy. When the stock market hit its peak on September 3, 1929, the Dow Jones Industrial Average had increased fivefold during the previous six years. "Stock prices have reached what looks like a permanently high plateau," the highly regarded economist Irving Fisher proclaimed on October 21.[1]

Just three days later, amid widespread apprehension about the pending Smoot-Hawley Tariff bill, the market suddenly lost 11 percent of its value at the opening bell in heavy trading. On that "Black Thursday," as it was later dubbed, a group of leading Wall Street bankers attempted to stem the tide by placing overpriced bids on the thirty blue-chip stocks that composed the Dow Jones Industrial Average. But this ploy failed to reassure investors: The following Monday, the twenty-eighth, the Dow Jones Average lost another 13 percent; on the twenty-ninth, still another 12 percent. So heavy was the volume of trading that "Black Tuesday" that the ticker did not finish recording all the transactions until 7:45 that evening, nearly five hours after the market had closed. In the space of two days, investors had lost more than $30 billion on Wall Street.

The greatest financial collapse in American history was under way. Yet many Americans, including Greenfield, at first failed to realize the extent of the debacle. At the time of the crash, Bankers Securities had at least $1.1 million invested in the stock market[2]—about 5 percent of its total assets—and much of that value was decimated by the crash. But Bankers Securities was primarily a lender, not a borrower, and so was Bankers Trust. What might happen to these businesses if borrowers were unable to repay their loans did not immediately concern Greenfield. The fact that real estate values were falling as precipitously as securities did not seem to trouble him either; it simply meant that more good properties would become available at bargain prices—properties that his companies could manage and insure profitably until values recovered.

For the first forty-two years of his life, Greenfield had seemed constitutionally incapable of acknowledging the downside of any situation; every problem was simply a challenge to be relished. He had been wiped out in 1917 and had bounced back, he liked to remind people whenever a crisis arose. In any case, as he told an interviewer years later, "I've always treated both success and failure as impostors. I like making money, but I can get along without it. I never worried about not having it because I knew I could make more."[3]

The flaw in this cheerful insouciance was not merely Greenfield's inability to comprehend the magnitude of the impending disaster; it also exposed his inability to empathize with other men who were traumatized by the crash—among them two of his closest friends and partners.

When J. David Stern bought the *Philadelphia Record* in 1928 with Greenfield's advice and support, Greenfield had advised him not to sell the Record Building at its $500,000 value, in the belief that it might fetch much more in another year or two. Stern had counted on that $500,000 equity to pay for new presses and working capital for his newspaper. Yet when the stock market crashed, the building's equity—and Stern's ability to borrow against it—evaporated almost overnight. Greenfield, perhaps feeling responsible for his friend's fix, came to the rescue. "Nothing to get excited about," he told Stern, according to Stern's later recollection. "Bankers Securities Corporation will give the *Record* a long-term loan." And so it did.[4]

William Fox's crisis was more complicated and involved much more money. At the time of the crash, Fox was anticipating a Justice Department investigation of possible antitrust violations in his purchase of Loew's Inc., which was finalized in early 1929.[5] Fox was also recovering from an auto accident on Long Island in July—his car was hit by an unlicensed driver—that killed his chauffeur and incapacitated Fox himself for three months.[6]

During the crash of October 28–29, Fox's Loew's shares, valued at $72 million, lost more than half their value. Worse, two-thirds of those shares were held by bankers as collateral against the loans Fox had incurred to acquire them. The $10 million that Fox had borrowed from Bankers Securities in the summer of 1928 was merely one of several loans Fox had taken out for that purpose: He also owed $15 million to American Telephone & Telegraph (AT&T) and $12 million to the investment bank Halsey Stuart, and both loans were due in early 1930.[7]

The remaining one-third of Fox's Loew's shares was in the hands of brokers, having been purchased on margin by Fox and his relatives. To hold onto these stocks—and therefore his empire—Fox would need to sell his other stocks and use the proceeds to meet the margin calls on his shares of Loew's Inc.[8]

The day after the crash, Fox's brokers told him that he owed them $10 million. They gave him twenty-four hours to raise the funds; if he could not, they said, they would sell nearly a quarter-million of those shares for the best offer, which would probably drive the price of the remaining Loew's shares down close to zero.

While Fox mulled his limited options at his apartment in the Ambassador Hotel in New York, the telephone rang. On the wire, providentially, was his friend and partner Albert Greenfield. Six months earlier Fox had enlisted Greenfield to sell a block of his stock in First National Pictures. Greenfield had received an offer of $2.1 million from Warner Brothers that Fox rejected, insisting the stock was worth at least $15 million. Now Greenfield told Fox he thought he could get $5 or $6 million for the First National shares; in view of the market panic the previous day, Greenfield said, Fox should be willing to take it.

At this point Greenfield had no idea that Fox was in trouble, and Fox— who may have been an even cannier negotiator than Greenfield—made no effort to enlighten him. "I would have been happy to sell them [the shares] for any price whatever, provided it was for cash," Fox later acknowledged.[9] But to Greenfield he dismissed the $6 million offer as ridiculously low. He invited Greenfield to come to New York for dinner, and Greenfield—who salivated at the scent of any deal—readily complied.

Before the dinner, as Fox later told the story, Fox invited his friend Jacob Rubinstein—secretary and treasurer of the Namquist Worsted Company, who had been injured in the auto accident with Fox the previous July—to join them. Fox rehearsed Rubenstein to "agree with Greenfield in whatever he says, and disagree with me." And so the dinner proceeded, by Fox's account:

> Halfway through the meal he [Greenfield] referred to the First National shares. I said, "You know we have always quoted the $15 mil-lion price. I realize there was a panic yesterday, and if these men still want these shares they can get them for $12,500,000." Greenfield went from $5 million up the scale to $10 million, and finally said to Rubinstein, "Don't you think if I could sell these shares at $10 mil-lion today that would be a fine piece of business for Fox?" Rubinstein said yes, he thought it would be. I told Rubinstein I wished he would keep out of this deal, that this was not his affair. So we got into a ter-rific row. I said to Greenfield, "I think you can sell these shares for $12.5 million." Greenfield came back that night at midnight with an offer of $10 million. He said he would consummate the deal the next morning.[10]

What are we to make of this incident, in which Fox, by his own tell-ing, deceived his friend and partner? In retrospect, Greenfield's supreme self-confidence blinded him to Fox's financial condition. The stock market crash had not bothered Greenfield yet, and he presumed it had not bothered Fox either. Fox, for his part, probably saw nothing deceitful in withholding information about his financial state from Greenfield. Like Greenfield, Fox had built an empire by making all the major decisions himself. He knew his business better than anyone else. Since he and Greenfield had never been through such a shattering crisis, he could not be sure how Greenfield would react to one. Had Fox revealed the true facts to Greenfield, Greenfield might (as Fox saw it) have panicked. In Fox's mind, it would be better for everyone concerned if things were done Fox's way. And, indeed, by deceiving Greenfield—who in this case was acting as Fox's agent—Fox pushed his friend to bargain for a higher price and bought himself a reprieve.

Yet Fox's supreme confidence in himself—again, like Greenfield's—blinded *him* to the grim truth that this reprieve was necessarily only very brief. As the market continued to slide, Fox would inevitably need Greenfield's help again. So Fox's question remained: How would Greenfield respond once he learned the true extent of Fox's desperation?

The answer came a month later, in November 1929. Fox's $15 million loan from AT&T would be due in February 1930, and the $12 million from Halsey Stuart on April 1.[11] Repaying the $10 million that Fox had borrowed from Bankers Securities was out of the question. Defaulting on that loan—which represented more than 40 percent of Bankers Securities' assets—would drive Bankers Securities' stock price down every bit as sharply as the Lit Brothers deal in 1928 had driven it up. Fox would have to break the bad news to Greenfield and enlist his help in selling other Fox assets in order to maintain his control of Fox Film Corporation and Fox Theatres.

But when Fox contacted Greenfield in November, he learned that Edna Greenfield was in the hospital, and Greenfield refused to leave Philadelphia while she was ill.[12] (Whatever his emotional deficiencies as a husband and father, Greenfield steadfastly honored his financial and physical obligations to his family.) After a few weeks, when Fox learned that Edna's temperature was normal, he urged Greenfield to come to New York. (Fox presumably could not travel because he had not totally recovered from his auto accident.)

Greenfield said he would make the trip, but five hours was all he could spare away from his wife. The train from Philadelphia to New York took two hours each way, door to door, so Fox would have just an hour of face-to-face conversation with Greenfield. Fox agreed. According to his plan, Greenfield would arrive by train at 7 in the evening and come to Fox's suite in the Ambassador Hotel on Park Avenue, where Fox would have dinner waiting for him. Then Greenfield could return to Penn Station in time to board the 8 o'clock train back to Philadelphia.[13]

As the meeting approached, Fox reflected that it might be better for Greenfield to hear the bad news *after* dinner rather than during the meal. He urged Greenfield to eat first, arrive an hour later, and take the 9 o'clock train home. But Greenfield was adamant: He must return home on the 8 o'clock train.

At the subsequent meal, Fox again invited his friend Rubinstein to join them. What happened was described by Fox three years later:

> I can recall that he [Greenfield] had a mouth full of food, eating very rapidly, and insisting that I tell him what was on my mind. When I informed him about my companies, that they were in serious difficulties, that there were rumors that a receiver might be appointed, it may be that he swallowed the food that was in his mouth; I am not sure, but I know he became violently ill. We sent for a bellboy to get all kinds of medicine. He didn't go back to Philadelphia for at least fourteen days thereafter, and that night when he engaged a room on the floor above me, he asked my friend Rubinstein to sleep with him, to see that nothing happened. I thought that was a fine plan, because I feel that Rubinstein himself was contemplating suicide, and they would be watching each other, and nothing would happen to either one.[14]

By the following morning, apparently, Greenfield felt better. He remembered that the Warner Brothers studio had large sums of cash on hand. He also remembered that Fox controlled West Coast Theatres, a chain of five hundred movie theaters in eleven states west of the Rocky Mountains. Surely, Greenfield reasoned, the Warners would be interested in buying such a chain. What, he asked, would Fox take for it? Fox, basing his estimate on West Coast's 1929 earnings, said he would take $55 million—if the purchaser would agree to continue renting Fox's films in the theaters at the same level it had done in 1929.

The prospect of rescuing his friend as well as Bankers Securities, while perhaps earning a commission on a $55 million deal, sent Greenfield whirling into action. Amid the financial exigencies of the moment, Edna's relatively minor malady was apparently forgotten. In any case, here was a matter uniquely suited to Greenfield's talents; for Edna, as he saw it, he could serve only as a passive observer.

That very day Greenfield visited the Warners in Manhattan and came back that evening to tell Fox that the Warner brothers were "vitally interested"; from their perspective, the news that Warner's had acquired this huge theater chain would boost Warner's stock and consequently increase its credibility in the bond markets. With that $55 million, Fox could pay off his debts—including the $10 million he owed to Bankers Securities—and retain control of his film empire, and still have some $15 million left over.

But now complications arose. The Warners offered to buy only half of West Coast Theatres. Then Greenfield learned that Fox was obligated to disclose the offer to his primary creditor, AT&T, which viewed Warner Brothers as a business rival. When Fox's contact at AT&T, John E. Otterson, got wind of Greenfield's proposed deal, he went to Fox with a counteroffer: Rather than let the West Coast chain fall into the Warners' hands, AT&T itself—in tandem with Fox's other creditor, Halsey Stuart—would buy the West Coast chain from Fox for the specified $55 million; then it would sell half the chain to the Paramount Studio and hold the remaining half, giving Fox an option to buy it back within three years.[15] "That sounded wonderful to me," Fox later recalled, and he authorized Otterson to negotiate with Paramount.

But now Greenfield got wind of the plan, and he was not so pleased. As he told Fox, according to Fox's later recollection:

In the transaction over the First National [Pictures] I was a broker and wanted a commission. But then I didn't know you were in trouble. Now you are in trouble and I am no longer a broker but a friend. I say to you now that if I make a sale I will not ask for a commission. But as a friend, I think you are walking into a trap. I think you made a mistake to authorize Otterson and Stuart to buy these shares. I have a feeling that this thing is not going to come out right, and I had better keep on dealing with Warner Brothers, because I think these men are stringing you. Will you please let me continue to hold on to the Warners for you? I have an engagement and want to continue these negotiations; in fact, Harry Warner is now in my room upstairs at this time and I want you to come upstairs and meet him.[16]

With his selective incisiveness, Greenfield clearly perceived the conflict between his role as Fox's broker and Fox's friend, but he failed to acknowledge his equally conflicting roles as Fox's creditor and partner, which must have weighed heavily on him, at least subconsciously. Greenfield and Fox each owned about 25 percent of the equity in Bankers Securities, which had loaned Fox $10 million; yet as Fox's friend, Greenfield made no effort to recover that loan and refused to bring any suit, theoretically to the detriment of other Bankers Securities shareholders.[17] (In Greenfield's eyes, however, as well as those of his shareholders, his interests and those of Bankers Securities were one and the same.)

Fox, who had been functioning on two hours' sleep per night since the crash and was surely wearing down, responded to Greenfield's scolding by accompanying Greenfield upstairs to meet Harry Warner, who now told Fox that he wanted to buy all of West Coast, but at a lower price.[18] Fox told Warner of the negotiations with Paramount, and Warner said he might share the ownership fifty-fifty with Paramount. But they failed to reach an agreement, and Fox returned to his apartment downstairs.

A few minutes later, Otterson of AT&T and Harry Stuart of Halsey Stuart appeared in Fox's suite, furious that Fox had double-crossed them. He had authorized *them* to make this sale, they said; yet while they were negotiating with Adolph Zukor of Paramount, Fox and Greenfield had been upstairs negotiating with Harry Warner. They no longer wanted any part of the deal, they said; further, as Fox's creditors, they had concluded that Fox's companies were insolvent, and they threatened to seek a proxy for Fox's voting shares that would enable them to take control of Fox's two companies themselves.[19]

Amid this negotiating dance it may have occurred to Fox that Otterson and Stuart were native-born Episcopalians and he and Greenfield were immigrant Jews, as were Harry Warner and Adolph Zukor.[20] (It may have occurred to Greenfield as well, although Greenfield, unlike Fox, preferred to pretend that such distinctions did not exist.) The suggestion by Otterson and Stuart that Fox and Greenfield had done "the most contemptible thing they ever heard of" (as Fox recalled it) may have been a subtle (or even unconscious) attempt to use their superior social status as a bargaining card.

In the ensuing months, all thirteen banks to which Fox and his companies owed money brought suits against him, demanding that his companies be placed in receivership, preferably with Otterson and Stuart as trustees. (AT&T apparently coveted Fox Film not for its movie business but for the patent to a German sound-on-film process owned by Fox.)[21] Greenfield himself urged Fox to accept this course.

Yet Fox stubbornly resisted giving up control. In December 1929, after entering a voting trust with Otterson and Stuart, Fox repudiated the trust and came up with a plan to fend off the bankers by marketing $35 million in bonds to sixteen thousand movie exhibitors across the country. The bonds would be issued not through an investment house but directly through a new company to be called Fox Securities Corporation and modeled very much after Greenfield's Bankers Securities.[22] But by early January 1930, shares of Fox Film—which had traded above $100 in October 1929—were down to $16.[23] Even an unlikely sudden infusion of $35 million would not have paid off all of Fox's debts, which he needed to do in order to liberate himself from Otterson and Stuart.[24]

Finally, early in April 1930, Fox sold his voting shares in both Fox Film and Fox Theatres to the buyer Greenfield recommended: Harley L. Clarke, a Chicago utilities magnate whose primary credentials for running a movie company were his friendship and business connections to Fox's primary creditors, Otterson and Stuart. Clarke's experience in the entertainment business came not as a creator but as an acquirer, through his General Theatres Equipment company.[25]

Greenfield, whom Fox described as "tireless" in trying to help him out of his difficulties, acted as agent for the sale. But, of course, Greenfield was no disinterested broker in this matter, as he reminded Fox days before the deal was consummated. As Fox later recalled:

> Greenfield frankly said that he could not be an impartial friend and adviser in this matter. The securities company, of which he was chairman, was my creditor for $10 million, and he had to think about that money. So throughout all this difficulty, Greenfield, who had constant access to my home, was urging that the thing to do was to sell these voting shares.[26]

Both Greenfield and Fox emerged whole from the deal, at least financially. Greenfield recovered the $10 million that Fox owed to Bankers Securities. Fox, for his part, received some $15 million after his debts were paid off; he was also appointed to an advisory board at his former companies, with an annual salary of $500,000 for five years.[27] But this was a meaningless figurehead role; without his creative genius at the top, Fox's film empire soon declined. By the end of 1931, Clarke's own company was close to financial ruin, and Clarke himself was gone from the Fox companies by early 1932.[28]

To Fox, who was still something of a socialist at heart, the loss of his companies signified the triumph of cold-blooded money interests (controlled by native-born Protestants) over struggling but warm-blooded and creative immigrants (mostly Jewish).[29] When the dust had settled, according to Fox's amanuensis, Upton Sinclair, Fox "warned Greenfield to watch his step, the banking ring would certainly punish him; and sure enough, they did it that very summer."[30]

The Fox negotiations, like many of Greenfield's deals, raised a question that was often asked by New Yorkers and Philadelphians alike: Was Greenfield operating in the wrong city? In many respects he seemed temperamentally more of a New Yorker than a Philadelphian. He was combative and aggressive, surely, but not unpleasantly so. As such he would have been totally accepted in New York, whereas many Philadelphians felt threatened by him.

Indeed, Felix Isman, the most ambitious of Philadelphia's Jewish real estate brokers when Greenfield first broke into the field, had subsequently moved to New York, where he blended in so easily that he was barely heard from again.[31] Greenfield himself was often approached by successful New York businessmen to move his operations there, and in the early 1920s he went so far as to open a New York office, which he generally visited on Tuesdays.[32] Had his marriage to Edna been on sounder footing, some of his friends speculated, he might well have moved there full-time. (Ironically, about this time Edna took an apartment in New York and increasingly spent time there—not to be with Albert but essentially to avoid confronting her deficiencies as a wife and mother.) In his later years Greenfield remarked privately that he would have been "infinitely more successful" had he moved to New York. But material success mattered less than community: He loved Philadelphia, and that was that.[33]

Back in Philadelphia after his Fox interlude, Greenfield reacted to the crash in his customary counterintuitive fashion: by seeking out and acquiring underpriced properties, including banks, at what he believed were bargain prices. He assumed that the stock market and property values alike would inevitably recover sooner or later. His real estate firm assembled a group of properties at Thirtieth and Market Streets for the Pennsylvania Railroad, which used the land to build a magnificent new railroad terminal and post office.[34] In the spring of 1930 his Bankers Trust Company made its seventh acquisition—of the Metropolitan Trust Company—thus expanding its domain to eleven offices with $35 million in deposits.[35] At that point, Greenfield later claimed, Bankers Trust had repaid all the moneys it had borrowed from other banks: "It was in splendid condition, well manned and officered, efficiently conducted, amply liquid, and rendering a real service to the city."[36]

But then in July 1930 a bank in North Philadelphia called the Bank of Philadelphia & Trust Company, which had $15 million in deposits and a big business in construction mortgages, showed signs of going under. Amid the building frenzy of the late 1920s, it had invested in land whose value was now negligible. With the real estate market in a deflationary cycle, its assets were largely frozen. Among its other obligations, the Bank of Philadelphia owed $3 million to the city's two largest commercial banks: the Philadelphia National Bank and the Pennsylvania Company.[37]

At this point, according to Greenfield's later account, he was approached by the heads of those two banks, who "urged upon me and my committee that Bankers Trust Company was the one best able to render a noble service to the banking structure of Philadelphia by coming to the aid of the distressed uptown bank."[38]

Greenfield had cultivated relationships with both men. Joseph Wayne of the Philadelphia National Bank owned stock in Bankers Securities,[39] and the previous year Greenfield had earned Wayne's gratitude by using his political clout to get Wayne excused from jury duty. ("Thank you for getting me out of jail this morning," Wayne had quipped in a note to Greenfield.)[40] After Greenfield opened an account at the Pennsylvania Company for Bankers Securities in 1928, he received an effusive "Dear Al" letter from Stevenson Newhall that concluded, "You are a real friend, and I know it!"[41]

Of course bankers, like diplomats, rarely expressed their true feelings openly—about Greenfield or anyone else. In truth, one knowledgeable observer recalled, "The bankers hated him. They saw him as a threat, as very devious. He was smarter than they'd ever be. He took chances, while they always held on to their dough and dribbled it out."[42] A prominent banker said much the same thing: "Greenfield was seen as too sharp. The heads of banks genuinely didn't like him, although some held him in awe."[43]

Newhall and Wayne apparently believed that Greenfield was better suited than they were to take charge of a bank whose collateral was almost entirely based in real estate.[44] Greenfield insisted eight years later:

I expressed doubt as to the wisdom of Bankers Trust Company assuming such a heavy burden. They replied by emphasizing what a danger it would be if Bank of Philadelphia and Trust Company would go under, and they said they would stand by Bankers Trust Company if aid were needed to carry the load. With this assurance, but still against my own judgment, we agreed to go along on the program. It was difficult for us then to refuse to respect the views of the two men we regarded as the outstanding banking leaders of Philadelphia.[45]

Wayne and Newhall, for their part, subsequently insisted that the idea of buying up the Bank of Philadelphia had been Greenfield's alone and that they were surprised when he decided to proceed.[46] The question of which version is accurate has never been resolved, and from the available evidence it is possible to credit both parties' recollections, to some extent. Wayne and Newhall were surely relieved to have Greenfield rescue the Bank of Philadelphia & Trust Co. And Greenfield was no doubt hungry to further expand Bankers Trust, especially if he could ingratiate himself with Wayne and Newhall in the process.

In any case, Greenfield did not agree to the merger until he received assurances from Wayne and Newhall that they would extend loans to Bankers
Trust "upon good and sufficient collateral."[47] The collateral consisted largely
of real estate mortgages held by Bankers Trust.

So on July 21, 1930, following a hectic weekend of negotiations, all
nine branches of the Bank of Philadelphia opened for business under the
name of Bankers Trust Company.[48] The acquisition expanded Greenfield's
bank to twenty-one branches and increased its deposits to more than
$50 million.[49]

Unfortunately, in buying up weak banks in order to avert the public disaster of a bank failure, Greenfield deluded not only the public but also himself. Real estate mortgages, which had seemed like such good collateral in
the twenties, had become almost worthless after the crash, as home buyers—
many of whom had borrowed 80 percent of the price of their homes—lost
their jobs and stopped making their mortgage payments.

Nevertheless, just ten days after the takeover, Bankers Trust blithely paid
a bonus to all its employees, accompanied by a statement from the bank's
president, Samuel Barker:

This company, for which 322 of us are now working, does some
things differently from usual practice, and I believe better. You know
that on all sides many are being laid off, more are working part time,
and a great number see their pay reduced. Your salaries are going
along with your work.[50]

And on August 11, Greenfield wrote to his lawyer, Harry Sundheim, who
was vacationing in Biarritz, France:

The acquisition of the Bank of Philadelphia and Trust Company
by the Bankers Trust Company is, I think, a step in the right direction. . . . More than ever, I am of the opinion, that our efforts with
Bankers Trust Company are fruitful of a real contribution to the
banking life of Philadelphia and some day Bankers Trust will stand
in the foreground of financial institutions of this city. I think its future is probably now assured and that its scope of usefulness will become increasingly larger as time goes on.[51]

The letter perhaps refutes Greenfield's later claim that he was reluctant to acquire the Bank of Philadelphia. More likely it reflects Greenfield's instinctive
tendency to put the best face on any situation.

Greenfield later acknowledged that, after the merger, "almost immediately friction began to develop. The former directors of the uptown bank failed to instill in their depositors the feeling of confidence in the new arrangement." Appraisals of the former bank's real estate properties revealed them to be worth far less than Greenfield had imagined.[52]

In fact, the problem involved more than a mere decline in property values. Under the terms of the merger, Leon A. Lewis, president of the Bank of Philadelphia & Trust Co., had been made a Bankers Trust vice president and director. Yet soon after the merger, Lewis became the target of whispered allegations that he had misappropriated funds from the Bank of Philadelphia in 1929—allegations that subsequently proved to be valid.[53] On August 20, just a month after the merger, Lewis resigned. In his resignation letter to Greenfield he spoke of "a persistent and relentless movement to destroy my usefulness," adding, "I have been done a terrible injury, but my greater regret is that you at Bankers Trust Company have been made to suffer too. Your problem has been made a great deal harder."[54]

Instead of relieving the problem, Lewis's departure appeared to confirm the rumors. Now the whispers suggested that Greenfield had overextended himself in assuming the Bank of Philadelphia's vast liabilities. For once, Greenfield was unable to transfer the public's confidence in him to a property he had acquired. Instead, the public's doubts about the stability of the Bank of Philadelphia were now transferred to its new owner, Bankers Trust.

The first run on the former Bank of Philadelphia's branches began in September as a handful of depositors closed their accounts. Greenfield professed himself unconcerned: Bankers Trust, he said later, was "amply able to take care of all normal requirements."[55]

As if to reinforce his confidence, on October 6 Bankers Trust was admitted to full membership in Philadelphia's Clearing House Association, a venerable cooperative organization formed by local banks after the Panic of 1857 to restore public confidence by providing stopgap funding to troubled members during financial panics and other rough patches. At the time Bankers Trust was admitted, membership was limited to some thirty-four of the city's soundest commercial banks; Joseph Wayne himself had just assumed the association's presidency.[56] Acceptance by such a group at such a time, Greenfield later insisted, was "evidence that even after the assumption of the obligations of the Bank of Philadelphia & Trust Company, Bankers Trust Company was regarded by the Philadelphia Clearing House as being in sound and liquid condition."[57]

The rude awakening was just around the corner. During October and November 1930, withdrawals at the former Bank of Philadelphia branches gained momentum. "It was evident," Greenfield later contended, that "a more or less concerted effort was at work to spread discontent among the depositors, and they were uneasy." True to their promise, Wayne and Newhall provided a steady infusion of loans to Bankers Trust throughout November, the lion's share apparently from Wayne's Philadelphia National Bank.[58] But by December the withdrawals had spread to the original main office of the Bank of Philadelphia at Broad and Erie Streets.[59]

Greenfield did what he could to instill confidence by his own personal example. He increased his personal deposits at Bankers Trust to $300,000 and those of Bankers Securities to more than $2 million. In all, by mid-December Greenfield and his companies had nearly $3.5 million deposited at Bankers Trust.[60] He also procured large deposits in Bankers Trust from William Fox and from David Stern's Philadelphia Record Company— indeed, "from every business and individual with whom I had any influence," he later recalled. And by mid-December the Philadelphia National and the Pennsylvania Company had provided between them $7.5 million worth of emergency support as well.[61]

Nevertheless, by mid-December Bankers Trust had paid out on demand more than $12 million of the roughly $50 million it had had in deposits as of September, and the run showed no signs of abating. On December 16, Samuel Barker, the bank's president, sought to relieve depositors' fears. Without referring specifically to the bank's liquidity crisis, he issued a report to stockholders announcing that Bankers Trust had reduced its own indebtedness by nearly $8 million since the takeover in July. By selling off assets of the former Bank of Philadelphia, he said, Bankers Trust had reduced its indebtedness to $10.1 million. The remaining assets of the Bank of Philadelphia, he added, had a total book value of $15.2 million.[62]

Before the crash, numbers of this sort would have been willingly accepted by credulous investors and depositors; now Barker's report merely triggered greater skepticism, and for good reason: The "book value"—the value at which an asset is carried on a balance sheet—bore little relation to the actual market value of Bankers Trust's assets in December 1930. Bankers Trust had already converted most of the Bank of Philadelphia's sound assets to cash in order to pay off depositors over the past three months. The remaining assets, as Barker acknowledged, consisted of securities, loans on collateral, mortgages, real estate, and commercial paper, all of which had fallen sharply in value since the crash of 1929. "While the greater part of these assets are good," Barker told reporters, "many, however, are of doubtful value. Time will be required to liquidate to advantage those assets."[63]

But time was the commodity Greenfield's bank lacked. By Friday, December 19, more than $17 million had been withdrawn from Bankers Trust—nearly $5 million that week alone. The bank's cash resources were exhausted to the point that it was no longer able to honor checks.[64] Clearly, the dike would not hold with the sort of patchwork that Wayne and Newhall were providing; as Greenfield later acknowledged, "The tide was getting beyond our control."[65]

On December 18, Bankers Trust sought relief from the Clearing House Association.[66] Greenfield also put in emergency calls to two influential friends who were directly affected: Peter G. Cameron, Pennsylvania's secretary of banking, in Harrisburg, and William Fox, Greenfield's partner in New York.

The eight members of the Clearing House Committee to which Greenfield's request was referred effectively constituted a shorthand definition of Philadelphia's Protestant banking establishment. Joe Wayne of Philadelphia National had assumed the Clearing House Association's presidency earlier that year.[67] The committee's chairman, William Purves Gest, sixtynine-year-old chairman of the Fidelity-Philadelphia Trust Company, had joined his bank in 1889 and assumed its presidency in 1915. The Pennsylvania Company was represented on the committee not by Stevenson Newhall but by another vice president, John H. Mason.

The committee also included one Jew: Howard A. Loeb, chairman of the Tradesmens National Bank, said to be the only Jew in Philadelphia employed in a significant role in a gentile institution.[68] At least one committee member could be described as a Greenfield ally: C. Addison Harris Jr., president of the Franklin Trust Company, was simultaneously a vice president and director of Greenfield's Bankers Securities.[69]

Yet for all practical purposes, the committee's official composition was largely irrelevant. For lack of a world-class bank, Philadelphia banking—at least since the death of Anthony J. Drexel in 1893—had been overshadowed by New York, either directly through accounts held there or through Drexel & Co., whose senior partner was J. P. Morgan Jr. of New York and whose other partners were Morgan partners as well.

As a private Philadelphia investment bank, Drexel & Co. did not belong to the Clearing House Association, but because of its vast resources, Drexel & Co. was usually the first place Philadelphia bankers turned for help in a crisis. Only the previous year, the Clearing House Association had asked Drexel & Co. to help the Corn Exchange National Bank assume the assets and liabilities of the failed Union Bank and Trust Company.[70] Before the Federal Reserve Act of 1913 prohibited bank cross-directorships, E. T. Stotesbury, Drexel's senior partner, had served on the boards of five of Philadelphia's largest banks, and two of his Drexel partners had served on five others. So pervasive was the Philadelphia influence of J.P. Morgan and other New York investment banks that Philadelphia bankers often felt obligated to maintain accounts with New York banks and subscribe to their bond offerings, even against their better judgment, in order to retain what one observer called the New York banks' "friendly regard."[71]

In this manner Stotesbury, a man of Quaker roots and conservative instincts, had dominated Philadelphia finance for more than a quarter-century.[72] No less an authority than the great J. Pierpont Morgan Sr. had remarked that Stotesbury knew more about the details of the banking business than any man in the United States.[73] He was, by one account, "lightning-like in his decisions, and as there was no appeal from the Stotesbury court the arguments were swift and the business was dispatched with an amazing quickness, considering the enormous amounts involved."[74] The same description, of course, could have been applied to Albert M. Greenfield as well.

Preoccupied as he was with the run on Bankers Trust, Greenfield probably failed to notice that a very similar drama was playing out at the same time just ninety miles to the north. The Bank of United States, founded in New York in 1913, had grown rapidly through mergers until it was that city's fourth largest deposit bank, with 450,000 depositors and sixty-two branches by 1930.[75] Like Greenfield's Bankers Trust, Bank of United States was created and owned by Jews and was heavily oriented toward real estate. Like Bankers Trust, Bank of United States bore a deceptively pretentious name (a play on the similarly titled Bank of *the* United States that Andrew Jackson had closed in 1836), a title deliberately designed to fool its immigrant customers into thinking it enjoyed government support. (The bank reinforced its misleading message by hanging a large oil portrait of the U.S. Capitol in its lobby.)

Beginning in mid-October 1930 a combination of legal problems and subpar real estate mortgages and loans triggered a run on the Bank of United States that depleted its deposits by more than $50 million.[76] On November 24, three leading New York banks announced an agreement to rescue the Bank of United States by including it in a four-way merger that would create a megabank, headed by the president of the Federal Reserve Bank of New York and supported by a $30 million loan from New York's Clearing

House Association.[77] But two weeks later, on December 8, the Wall Street bankers who dominated New York's Clearing House Association suddenly withdrew their support, and the merger plan fell apart. Two days later, the Bank of United States closed—the largest bank failure in the United States since the crash the previous year.[78]

Years later, financial historians concluded that Bank of United States was indeed mismanaged and deserved to fail. But at the time, its failure was widely attributed to the anti-Semitism of Wall Street bankers.[79] Joseph Broderick, the New York state superintendent of banks, noted that only two or three weeks before, these same bankers "had rescued two of the largest private bankers of the city, and had willingly put up the money needed."[80] The J.P. Morgan partner Russell Leffingwell described the Bank of United States dismissively as "an uptown bank with many branches and a large clientele among our Jewish population of small merchants and persons of small means and small education, from whom all its management was drawn."[81]

J. P. Morgan Jr. himself, the Morgan firm's titular head, was an outspoken anti-Semite who sincerely perceived Jews as a global fifth column that feigned loyalty to host governments while furtively advancing foreign plots. "The Jew is always a Jew first and an American second," Morgan wrote to Harvard's president in 1920.[82] "I cannot stand the German Jews," he wrote to the president of the Museum of Natural History in 1916, explaining his refusal to attend any board meeting where Felix Warburg was present, "and will not see them or have anything to do with them. . . . In my opinion they have made themselves impossible as associates for any white people for all time."[83] E. T. Stotesbury, as Morgan's senior representative in Philadelphia, was known to spend much of his time in New York and was presumed to be sensitive to his senior partner's concerns.[84]

But Bank of United States shared more than Jewishness and real estate mortgages in common with Greenfield's Bankers Trust: Both banks counted William Fox among their largest stockholders, depositors, and debtors. At Fox's request, two years earlier Greenfield had provided him a three-page analysis of a new Bank of United States stock plan;[85] and at the height of Fox's struggles to hold on to his film and theater empire earlier in 1930, Fox Film had owed Bank of United States $1.6 million, and Fox personally owed it $1 million. The loss of his film companies to Wall Street bankers, followed now by the demise of the Bank of United States at the hands of Wall Street bankers, intensified Fox's belief in the existence of a capitalist, and probably anti-Semitic, conspiracy to punish him and his allies.

Greenfield issued his desperate appeal to the Philadelphia Clearing House Association on behalf of Bankers Trust on December 18, just one week after the Bank of United States closed. That struck Fox as more than a coincidence.[86] That very day he boarded a train for Philadelphia in the hope of doing for Greenfield what Greenfield had tried to do for him barely a year earlier: rescue a friend in need and salvage his own sizable investment from the clutches of the Protestant Establishment.

The Protestant Establishment

The Old Philadelphia families who exemplified America's ruling class to immigrants like Fox and Greenfield had once been outsiders themselves. Before coming to America the English ancestors of the Stotesburys, Waynes, Newhalls, and Gests had lived for centuries on an increasingly crowded island whose population—some three million when Columbus discovered America in 1492—had nearly doubled by 1650, to roughly five million.[1]

Under the English system of primogeniture, all of a family's land passed to the oldest son upon the father's death, thus assuring that the estates of the wealthy would remain intact in the hands of "gentlemen" whose fortunes, in theory, endowed them with both the leisure time and the independence to devote themselves to the common good.[2]

For centuries the inequities of primogeniture had seemed like a reasonable trade-off for maintaining what was, after all, the world's most civilized society. But in preindustrial England the rich tended to bear more children who survived than the poor,[3] and for the excluded younger members of such landed families, the British inheritance system offered little promise.

England's North American colonies, by contrast, held millions of unoccupied acres, virtually free for the taking.[4] Above all, America offered the hope that people might elevate their social status. Consequently, younger children of the landed gentry who could afford the transatlantic passage often leaped at the opportunity.

In this manner the European population of America's thirteen original colonies, which numbered just a handful at the dawn of the seventeenth century, expanded to 2.75 million by 1790, more than four-fifths of them of British and Protestant stock.[5] Yet for the most part these immigrants were not refugees driven from their homelands by plague or famine or war or religious persecution; they were Britons, well grounded in all the familiar pursuits of life in the world's most advanced and secure society. That is, they were calculating, risk-taking capitalists, eager to seize opportunities that had not been available to them in the mother country.[6] In this respect they shared much in common with the Eastern European Jewish immigrants who followed them to America one or two centuries later.

But where the English immigrants perceived land ownership as critical to their destiny, the Jews—prohibited from owning or exploiting land in much of Europe—placed their highest priority on "portable wealth": the knowledge and skills that they carried in their heads. It was a minor irony of Albert Greenfield's career that by the twentieth century, Protestant bankers like E. T. Stotesbury were falling out of love with real estate at the very moment that Jewish immigrants like Greenfield, Felix Isman, and the Mastbaum brothers were embracing it so enthusiastically.

The new American nation that these English Protestants created in 1776 as the world's first modern democracy was necessarily a fragile experiment and, consequently, something that its founding families never took for granted. For want of evidence to the contrary, the founding families saw in America's English and Protestant character the foundation on which America would survive and flourish, and they saw themselves as the indispensable guardians of that character. "Providence has given to our people the choice of their rulers," wrote John Jay, America's first chief justice, "and it is the duty as well as the privilege and interest of our Christian nation to select and prefer Christians for their rulers."[7]

Robert Walker, secretary of the Treasury under President James K. Polk in the 1840s, professed to have found in the Bible a prophesy that "a time shall come when the human race shall become as one family, and that the predominance of our Anglo-Celt-Sax-Norman stock shall guide the nations to that result."[8]

George Baer, installed by the elder J. P. Morgan as president of the Philadelphia & Reading Railroad in 1901, attributed his authority to a covenant through which the world would be "protected and cared for by the Christian men to whom God in his infinite wisdom has given control of the property interests of this country."[9] These self-congratulatory beliefs received academic support in 1905 when the German sociologist Max Weber published *The Protestant Ethic and the Spirit of Capitalism*, which argued that modern capitalism was "born from the spirit of Christian asceticism"—specifically the Protestant form.[10]

The waves of Catholic and Jewish immigrants to America in the middle and late nineteenth century inevitably challenged these assumptions with an alternative theory: that capitalism derived not from Protestantism per se but from the experience of being a migrant. In this view, immigration—in its own right an expression of individualism, ambition, self-reliance, and even religious tolerance—may incline people more toward capitalistic tendencies than any particular religious creed.[11] Between their alternative belief structures as well as their sheer numbers, the new immigrants threatened to undermine the authority of white Anglo-Saxon Protestants—WASPs, as they later were labeled—and transform them into a minority in the country they had created.[12]

To Charles W. Eliot, president of Harvard from 1869 to 1909, the solution was to maintain control in order to transmit Anglo-Saxon values to the new (and presumably benighted) arrivals. "If society as a whole is to gain by mobility and openness of structure," Eliot observed, "those who rise must stay up in successive generations, that the higher level of society may be constantly enlarged, and that the proportion of pure, gentle, magnanimous and refined persons may be steadily increased."[13] The rector of St. Paul's School in New Hampshire similarly urged his students to preserve their enlightened traditions by raising large families and entering politics.[14]

The trouble with this solution was that politics, as a "status-conferring occupation," appealed more to immigrants than to native-born Anglo-Saxons, who already possessed status by virtue of their ancestry alone, especially in Philadelphia. "It is for this reason," observed one Philadelphia social critic, "that so few Protestants are to be found in the dirty trade of politics."[15]

But sheer numbers were not the only challenge that immigration posed to Protestant ascendance; the new immigrants also exposed a theoretical conflict between the egalitarian ideals expressed in the Declaration of Independence and the Calvinist notions ingrained in the Protestant Ethic itself.

In theory, the Protestant Ethic approved of hard work and the accumulation of capital but frowned on the spending of it. Consequently, America's Anglo-Saxon Protestants instinctively saw their role as conservators, not innovators. So in a country theoretically dedicated to enabling those on the bottom of society to climb to the top according to their merits, the ambition to preserve things as they are became a peculiarly Anglo-Saxon Protestant characteristic. "All we ask," wrote a WASP memoirist even in the twenty-first century, "is to maintain. So success, while vital, came to be understood as not blazing a trail but as waging a culture- or comfort-preserving rear-guard action."[16]

In such an environment, the Jews, who as underdogs for centuries had equated survival and success with innovation and ingenuity, were instinctively perceived even by relatively enlightened native Protestants as a threat to American values. "We are in the hands of the Jews," lamented Henry Adams, the descendant of two U.S. presidents. "They can do what they please with our values." In that case, Adams advised, the only safe investment was gold locked in a vault: "There you have no risk but the burglar. In any other form you have the burglar, the Jew, the Czar, the socialist, and, above all, the total irremediable, radical rottenness of our whole social, industrial, financial and political system."[17]

To the author and literary critic Henry James, the Jew was an alien whose presence on American soil aroused uneasiness if not acute distrust.[18] As late as 1933 the poet T. S. Eliot—like his cousin Charles Eliot of Harvard, a descendant of Boston Brahmins—declared, at a university lecture, "What is still more important [than cultural homogeneity] is unity of religious background, and reasons of race and religion combine to make any large number of free-thinking Jews undesirable."[19]

Consciously or unconsciously, America's Protestants tended to accept the view articulated by Oswald Spengler, in his magisterial 1918 work, *The Decline of the West*: that Jews were survivors and representatives of an earlier human type, aliens whose adaptive strategies or mimicries were based on blind survival methods or deceits.[20]

In Philadelphia, the preservation of Protestant values manifested itself above all in a preoccupation with bloodlines—the one barrier that seemed impregnable to outsiders. Social status in Philadelphia's upper class was conferred neither by wealth nor by knowledge but by descent from an Old Philadelphia family, usually confirmed by service in the First City Troop (which had served as George Washington's bodyguard) or by membership in the Philadelphia Club (Philadelphia's oldest and most patrician club, founded in 1834) or by participation in the Assembly, old Philadelphia's antique annual ball.[21]

"I always feel socially superior to a man who is not a gentleman by birth," explained Sidney George Fisher, the distinguished nineteenth-century Philadelphia diarist, "and I never yet saw one who had risen to a higher position whose mind and character, as well as his manners, did not show the taint of his origins."[22] Not by coincidence were Philadelphia heirs and heiresses chosen as convenient symbols for idle foppery and snobbery in Anita Loos's comic 1925 novel, *Gentlemen Prefer Blondes*, as well as countless books, plays, and films thereafter.

In retrospect, the exalted status that Philadelphians attached to ancestry seems almost as comical as the incestuous nature of their banking relationships. In 1926 E. T. Stotesbury recruited to a partnership at Drexel & Co. the lawyer Edward Hopkinson Jr., whose lack of banking experience paled beside the sort of impeccable family credentials that no training or experience could ever match: Hopkinson's great-great-great-grandfather had been a close friend of Benjamin Franklin, his great-great-grandfather had signed the Declaration of Independence, his great-grandfather wrote the patriotic song "Hail, Columbia," and his grandfather lived to be the oldest graduate of the University of Pennsylvania.[23] Two other Drexel partners, Thomas Gates and Horatio Gates Lloyd, traced their Philadelphia ancestry back before the Revolutionary War.[24] So did their cousin Stacy B. Lloyd, the tall, Quaker-like president of the Philadelphia Saving Fund Society, America's oldest mutual savings bank (founded in 1816), whose bloodline was buttressed by his wife's even more impressive lineage: Eleanor Morris Lloyd was descended from a *Mayflower* pioneer as well as from Philadelphia's second mayor, and her formidable father, Effingham Morris, dominated seven Philadelphia banks after spending forty years building the Girard Trust Company into Philadelphia's largest trust institution.[25]

If immigrants could breach the walls of politics or new business fields like real estate with alacrity, the Anglo-Saxons would preserve their values within a few restricted professions, most notably banking and the law, both of which came to assume many of the characteristics of a Protestant priesthood.

Harlan Fiske Stone, dean of Columbia University Law School from 1910 to 1923 and later a U.S. Supreme Court justice, once observed that he did not want Columbia to admit too many Jewish law students because then there would be too many Jewish lawyers. The Philadelphia lawyer Robert T. McCracken, who later served as president of the Pennsylvania Bar Association, once explained to a meeting of New York lawyers that the Pennsylvania bar had solved "the question of the social origins of men" by instituting a "character examination" that reduced the proportion of immigrant applicants (mostly Russian Jewish) from 76 percent to 60 percent.[26] When J. P. Morgan Sr. declared in 1912 that "a man I do not trust could not get money from me on all the bonds in Christendom," he did so in the confident belief that "Christendom" constituted the bounds of the known respectable world.[27]

It followed, then, that most Protestant-run banks and law firms took pains to resist or conceal any hint of Jewish or Catholic influence. In 1930 the Pennsylvania Company, Philadelphia's oldest and second largest commercial bank, acquired the Colonial Trust Company of Philadelphia, which itself had recently acquired the Peoples Bank and Trust, a Jewish-owned bank that specialized in sending foreign remittances back to the old country for its immigrant customers.[28] The People's Bank had been run by Maurice Wurzel, who was also a business associate of Albert Greenfield.[29] After the Colonial's merger into the Pennsylvania, Wurzel paid a visit to the acquiring bank's headquarters. As Wurzel's son later recalled:

> I remember my father telling me that he went to the Pennsylvania Company offices to see his old employees, and he didn't see their names in any of the windows, and he asked where they were, and they said, "Well, they're upstairs." They didn't want any Jewish names on the first floor. They were still working there, but they didn't want to show them at all.[30]

To outsiders this ruling class seemed arrogant and monolithic, if not pompous. Yet among themselves, Philadelphia's leading bankers felt free to let their hair down and acknowledge their human frailties. "In personality Edward T. Stotesbury was somewhat distant and reserved toward those who did not enjoy his confidence and friendship," his obituary observed. "To those who did, however, he was genial and sunny, a good raconteur, a keen and well-versed conversationalist, and an appreciative listener."[31] At a dinner party thrown in 1914 by Charles Harrison, the former provost of the University of Pennsylvania, Stotesbury told a self-deprecating story about his patronage of opera and opera singers. "I paid Mary Garden $1800 a night, and made an engagement to pay her $80,000 in the course of the winter," Stotesbury told the amused guests. "The newspapers accused me of spending too much time in her dressing room, while on the other hand she described me as 'such a timid little man.'"[32] Of Stacy Lloyd, president of the Philadelphia Saving Fund Society, it was joked within Philadelphia's banking fraternity that the initials "PSFS" stood for "Pretty Soft For Stacy."[33]

Within the context of this clubby and relatively closed circle, Joseph Wayne of the Philadelphia National Bank was regarded as a paradigm of the "new" Philadelphia banker. He was a large, ruddy bear of a man, so open and approachable that nearly everyone entering or leaving his bank hailed him as "Hello, Joe," to which he invariably replied, "Hello there." Wayne had come up the hard way, attending not a prep school but the Central Manual Training School—the same public high school that Albert Greenfield most likely attended—and he had filled numerous lowly positions before rising to the presidency of Girard National Bank in 1914 and then of Philadelphia National

Bank when the two banks merged in 1926.[34] Only by comparison to an outsider like Greenfield would Joe Wayne have seemed stuffy or conservative.

Of course, nothing examined up close is ever quite what it appears from a distance, and Philadelphia's banking circles were hardly as impenetrable as many immigrants assumed. The city's dominant banking house, Drexel & Co., had not been founded by Old Philadelphia Protestants at all but by an Austrian Catholic immigrant; and while its greatest banker, Anthony J. Drexel, had become an Episcopalian and married his children into some of Philadelphia's oldest Protestant families, Anthony's brother and equal partner remained a Catholic, and Anthony's niece became a celebrated nun and subsequently a saint.[35]

For that matter, Philadelphia's wealthiest and most formidable family in 1930—the Pews, of the Sun Oil Company—were neither Old Philadelphia Quakers nor Episcopalians but recently arrived Presbyterians from western Pennsylvania.[36] That outsiders like the Pews and Albert Greenfield could come so far so fast indicated that Philadelphia was hardly the closed and narrow society that many people supposed.

It also spoke well for Philadelphia that two such contrasting types as Greenfield and the Pews could do so well in the same place at the same time. The Pews were plain, introverted, publicity shy, and guided by a simple and rigid moral code; Greenfield was flamboyant, outgoing, complicated, and exulted in the limelight. Of J. Howard Pew it was said that most Philadelphians held him in awe, but of Greenfield it was said that most Philadelphians held him in both awe *and* contempt.[37]

The supposed titans of American finance were not as omnipotent as outsiders believed. J. P. (Jack) Morgan Jr., for all the reverence attached to his famous name, was, in fact, a shadow of his father, a figurehead who deserved neither the awe nor the fear that he was generally accorded.[38] Although as senior partner of J.P. Morgan & Co. he was technically E. T. Stotesbury's boss, in practice he deferred to Stotesbury's superior experience and acumen.[39] Such was Stotesbury's influence with Jack Morgan's father that after Anthony Drexel's death in 1893—when the New York partnership changed its name from Drexel, Morgan & Co. to J.P. Morgan & Co.—Stotesbury persuaded the elder Morgan to allow the Philadelphia house to keep its Drexel & Co. name and retain up to $10 million of its earnings.[40] Jack Morgan's saving grace as chief executive lay in his ability to surround himself with capable lieutenants like Thomas Lamont, Russell Leffingwell, and Dwight Morrow, all of them New Yorkers who, like the younger Morgan, tended to defer to Stotesbury in Philadelphia.[41]

Stotesbury did not pay much attention to Jack Morgan's social prejudices: Although Morgan loathed Jews—particularly the Kuhn, Loeb partner Otto Kahn, whom Morgan perceived as a German sympathizer during World War I—Stotesbury served as a pallbearer at Kahn's funeral in 1934.[42] Jack Morgan explicitly declined to serve alongside Jews on civic boards; Stotesbury served alongside Kahn on the Metropolitan Opera board and served with Greenfield himself on Philadelphia's first City Planning Commission, from 1928 to 1931.[43] In the course of building Wingwood House, their summer home in Bar Harbor, Maine, Stotesbury and his wife fired their society architect, Howard Major, and brought in a Jewish Philadelphian, Louis Magaziner, to redo the project completely.[44]

But in Philadelphia the greatest irony was this: Stotesbury, the city's leading banker and the man who epitomized Philadelphia's ruling class to those outside of it, was himself regarded as a parvenu and social climber to those within it.

Edward Townsend Stotesbury—known as Ned to his friends—was the eldest son of Thomas Stotesbury, a Philadelphia dry goods merchant who launched his business with money inherited from his father, a sea captain who had amassed (but later lost) a fortune in the molasses trade between Philadelphia, Jamaica, and Europe.[45] During the Civil War, Thomas prospered as a sugar broker, probably by provisioning the U.S. Army.[46] Ned's mother came from a well-known Philadelphia Quaker family, and Ned attended the private Friends Central School. In his teens he worked as a clerk at a wholesale grocer and then at his father's dry goods store.[47] But he was bored in his father's business and uninterested in attending university.[48]

In 1866, when Ned was seventeen, his father secured him a place as an office boy at Drexel & Co., at a starting salary of $200 a year. In his first years there Stotesbury demonstrated the same sort of diligent service that the young Albert Greenfield later performed for the lawyer J. Quincy Hunsicker. According to Stotesbury's biographer:

> He began by cleaning out inkwells, sweeping the office and doing errands or any job that needed to be done. He was always ready to offer his services; and before leaving in the afternoon, invariably asked Mr. Drexel if there were not something more he could do for him.[49]

Just as Greenfield learned conveyancing by writing up deeds and mortgages for Hunsicker, Stotesbury learned the intricacies of commercial paper by studying the balance sheets of Drexel's clients.[50] He rose swiftly through the ranks, but the death in childbirth of his wife, Frances Butcher Stotesbury, in 1881, when he was only thirty-two, so devastated Ned that he withdrew from Philadelphia society to immerse himself in his work and occasional travel abroad.[51] In 1883 he was made a partner at Drexel & Co., and by the mid-1890s he was second in the Drexel-Morgan partnership only to Pierpont Morgan himself, with a 14 percent share of what had become America's greatest investment bank.[52] As Drexel's resident senior partner in Philadelphia, Stotesbury became the main financing conduit for dozens of companies large and small, in Philadelphia and points west, and he served on the boards of major Philadelphia corporations like United Gas, the Baldwin Locomotive Works, the Reading Company, and five major banks.[53] In the process Stotesbury accumulated a fortune estimated at $200 million by the time of the crash of 1929.[54]

Yet the esteem in which he was held by Philadelphia's business leaders could not be transferred to Philadelphia society, in part because of Stotesbury's reclusive lifestyle. Without a wife by his side, Stotesbury developed into a man of supreme confidence in financial situations but awkward naïveté about social situations.[55]

That condition changed abruptly in 1912 when, after thirty-one years as a widower, Stotesbury married Lucretia Roberts Cromwell, a Washington socialite fifteen years his junior. Eva, as she was known, was determined to teach her new husband how to spend his money to overcome social obstacles.[56] Their wedding was attended by President William Howard Taft, among many other dignitaries,[57] and Ned's ultimate wedding present to his bride was Whitemarsh Hall, an enormous faux-Georgian chateau and estate that he built on three hundred acres just beyond Philadelphia's city limits north of Chestnut Hill.

This "Versailles of America," as it was called, consisted of six levels—three above ground—whose 100,000 square feet included 147 rooms, 28 bathrooms, and 24 fireplaces. The mansion, designed by Horace Trumbauer, took five years to construct and cost $3 million, as well as $3 to $5 million more for interior decorations. The grounds and English park-style atmosphere, including a mile-long drive to a statue-filled forecourt north of the main building, were designed by the famous landscape artist Jacques Gréber. In addition to the main house, the grounds housed twenty-two other buildings, including twelve dwellings, garages, greenhouses, stables, and gatehouses.[58] The estate's annual maintenance alone was said to cost $1 million.[59]

The grand opening of Whitemarsh Hall in 1921 was attended by eight hundred members of Philadelphia's high society, and the Stotesburys continued to entertain there for the rest of Ned's life, often hosting as many as six hundred guests at a time, among them U.S. presidents, European royalty, and iconic business figures like Henry Ford, who reportedly remarked after a visit, "It's a great experience to see how the rich live."[60]

Yet the Stotesburys occupied Whitemarsh Hall only in spring and fall. El Mirasol, their winter residence in Palm Beach, was designed (at least externally) as a reproduction of an old convent near Burgos, Spain. Its rooms, built around a patio with a fountain in its center, had ceilings twenty-five feet high, and its amenities included a complete motion-picture theater.[61] Wingwood House, their summer home in Bar Harbor, Maine, was a magnificent English colonial-style mansion overlooking Frenchman's Bay.[62] In all, Ned Stotesbury was said to have spent more than $50 million on Eva.[63]

Nevertheless, the Stotesburys' aggressive social-climbing tactics inevitably backfired in Philadelphia: They became the butt of jokes among the very people they hoped to impress, and Ned was never admitted to the Philadelphia Club—blackballed, it was rumored, by his own embarrassed son-in-law, Sidney Emlen Hutchinson.[64] In Palm Beach, with its more flamboyant social scene, the Stotesburys were said to cut a social swathe that they never quite managed in Philadelphia.[65] But at Bar Harbor in Maine, the Stotesburys' heavy-handed attempt to take over as social leaders drove most Old Philadelphians to Northeast Harbor, where they continued to summer into the twenty-first century.[66]

Ned Stotesbury's sudden and largely unsuccessful exposure to Philadelphia society seems to have engendered in him a prickly sensitivity that caused him to perceive personal slights where none existed. As a result of a misunderstanding in 1915 with George W. Norris, the city's director of wharves (and later governor of Philadelphia's Federal Reserve Bank), "we were not upon speaking terms for fifteen years afterwards," Norris later recalled, "until a reconciliation was effected through the good offices of his partner, Mr. Hopkinson."[67]

When Stotesbury was finally invited to the Assembly, it was said, he had the invitation framed under glass and enshrined, floodlit, in the front hall of Whitemarsh Hall.[68] Just as Albert Greenfield was perceived as moving too far too fast in commercial circles, so Ned Stotesbury was viewed in social circles. In the apprehension with which Philadelphia's Protestant Establishment viewed both Stotesbury and Greenfield, the two men shared more in common than either realized.

[8]

The Reckoning

In many respects William Fox made an odd choice to plead the case for Bankers Trust before Philadelphia's leading bankers. Only eight months earlier Fox had lost control of his film and theater companies after a long and bitter fight, during which he had frequently denounced the banking establishment. He had been a stockholder, creditor, and depositor of the precariously managed, Jewish-run Bank of United States, which Wall Street bankers had refused to rescue barely a week earlier.[1] Fox was a successful showman who naïvely believed in his ability to touch people's emotions, even those of cold-blooded bankers. He also believed, at least in December 1930, in the brotherhood of man—in the notion that people's shared humanity transcends ethnic or religious or class differences. But Fox lacked Greenfield's exquisite talent for sizing up the people he dealt with and charming them accordingly.

Fox was also, of course, a son of poor immigrants, a New Yorker and a Jew, and self-conscious about his outsider status to boot, so that he tended to perceive conspiracies even where none existed. His speech and appearance—the very traits Greenfield had so meticulously groomed for his own persona—were unlikely to inspire confidence among native-born Anglo-Saxon bankers. Fox's amanuensis, Upton Sinclair, noted that Fox had a "good Jewish nose," that he chain-smoked cigars, and that he wore sweaters and white socks to board meetings.[2] Beyond that, Sinclair added, "He is not always impeccable in his use of the English Language. Sometimes when he is not on his guard, he will say, 'I seen it,' or 'I done it,' and frequently he will mix a tense or declension."[3]

The very presence of such a man at Greenfield's side seemed likely to remind Philadelphia's most prominent bankers of their misgivings about Greenfield himself. But these shortcomings are evident only in retrospect. At the time Fox was simply trying to do whatever he could to help a friend and partner in trouble.

The same crisis that brought Fox to Philadelphia from New York on Thursday, December 18, 1930, also brought Pennsylvania's secretary of banking, Peter G. Cameron, from the state capital in Harrisburg. Barely a year earlier, the presence of such a state official would have provided a subtle reminder of Greenfield's seemingly unlimited power; now it merely served as a reminder of the impotence of state banking officials in a genuine financial crisis.

Like most of the Philadelphia bankers he supervised, Cameron was a Republican as well as an occasional recipient of Greenfield's personal favors (he had attended the 1926 Dempsey-Tunney fight as Greenfield's guest). Greenfield at this point was a member of the Republican State Committee as well as a friend of the Republican president, Herbert Hoover. But the Republican best positioned to help Greenfield with Philadelphia's bankers was Bill Vare, the city's Republican boss—a man closely tied to the city's railroads, industries, and banks—who routinely performed legislative favors for the party's major contributors. But Vare's support was now lost to Greenfield, thanks to Greenfield's reform efforts to sideline Vare in 1929.

Still, these considerations seemed minor as Fox and Cameron converged on Philadelphia. All the key players—Greenfield, Fox, Cameron, the eight members of the Clearing House Committee, the two dozen other Clearing House Association members, and indeed virtually all other Philadelphia bankers—agreed on the basic point: Bankers Trust Company had exhausted its cash resources;[4] its failure would trigger a chain reaction of similar runs on other Philadelphia banks and therefore must be avoided if at all possible.

The only real questions, it seemed, were how much would be required for the necessary relief, who would provide it, and what collateral would be required of Bankers Trust. Thus, Greenfield concluded that the Clearing House Association represented his only hope.[5]

Formally, the decision to rescue Bankers Trust would be made by the Clearing House Association, represented by the eight members of the Clearing House Committee headed by William Purves Gest.[6] In theory, the committee's pivotal figure was Joe Wayne of the Philadelphia National Bank, who was president of the Clearing House Association as well as president of a bank that, by this point, had loaned nearly $7 million to Bankers Trust.[7]

But in practice the Clearing House Committee would not act without the assent of Drexel & Co., the only Philadelphia banking house large enough to guarantee a bailout of such magnitude, and that approval could come only from a single man: Drexel's senior partner, Ned Stotesbury.

On that Friday and Saturday, December 19 and 20, Greenfield later recalled, "many urgent conferences were held."[8] But Greenfield was not present at all of them. One such meeting probably took place at the offices of Morgan, Lewis & Bockius, the patrician law firm that represented Drexel & Co., Joseph Wayne's Philadelphia National Bank, and William P. Gest's Fidelity-Philadelphia Trust Company—that is, the city's largest investment bank, its largest commercial bank, and its largest trust company. Since the first run on the Bankers Trust in late summer, the law firm's offices had become an informal meeting place where Wayne and Gest, often joined by Stevenson Newhall of the Pennsylvania Company, agonized over questions of policy—specifically, according to the law firm's history, "whether the stronger banks could and should prevent the weaker Philadelphia banks from folding."

It was here, apparently, that the law firm's banking team worked with Wayne and Newhall on December 19 to devise a plan to stake Bankers Trust. But Wayne and Newhall were far from certain of its success: While they desperately hoped to save a bank to which they were already on the hook for more than $7 million, they remained plagued by doubt as to whether Bankers Trust could be saved.[9]

Essentially, the Wayne/Stevenson rescue plan demanded that $10 million worth of Bankers Trust's dubious "book value" assets be replaced with cash—half from Greenfield and Fox personally, and half from the Clearing House Association—to be used as collateral for any loans made to Bankers Trust by the Clearing House. This requirement essentially reflected a lack of confidence in Greenfield, but Greenfield and Fox seized this opening and agreed to meet the bankers' demands.

On Saturday evening, the twentieth, Newhall presented the plan to the directors of Bankers Securities, which was the largest stockholder in Bankers Trust, having invested some $2.75 million.[10] (Newhall was not technically a member of the Clearing House Committee, but one of Newhall's subordinates at the Pennsylvania Company was, and in any case Newhall and Wayne had been the point men for the Bankers Trust rescue efforts since the summer.)

For the thirteen Bankers Securities directors, including Greenfield and Fox, who gathered in the Bankers Trust boardroom on Walnut Street,

Newhall reviewed the Bankers Trust takeover of the Bank of Philadelphia that summer, "with the approval of heads of the Pennsylvania Co. and the Philadelphia National Bank," according to the meeting's minutes—a reference that seems to support Greenfield's claim that he had entered the merger hesitantly (although, to be sure, these minutes were compiled by Greenfield's own corporate secretary). Newhall expressed the view that "everything possible should be done by the Clearing House Committee to serve Bankers Trust Company of Philadelphia and to protect its depositors."[11]

Under the plan being formulated, Newhall said, Bankers Securities would inject $4 million in cash in exchange for $4 million in book value of Bankers Trust's questionable paper assets—the specific assets to be chosen by the Clearing House Committee. In addition, William Fox would put up $1 million in cash in exchange for Bankers Trust's holdings of Bankers Securities common stock. In addition, Greenfield and Newhall told the directors, Bankers Trust would add "new elements of strength" to its board—that is, one or more directors who would represent the Clearing House Association.

In effect, the plan asked Greenfield and Fox—the two largest shareholders in Bankers Securities, which was in turn the largest shareholder in Bankers Trust—to guarantee $5 million of Bankers Trust assets. If those conditions were met, the Clearing House banks would advance "a substantial amount"—unspecified in the minutes, but contemplated at $5 million—to Bankers Trust. Thus, the total loan package would come to $10 million.[12]

As Greenfield put it nearly eight years later, this demand represented a "staggering commitment," to which he and Fox nevertheless acquiesced.[13] Before the seventy-five-minute meeting broke up at 7:15, the Bankers Securities board voted to approve the plan. (It also voted to purchase $2.5 million worth of insurance on Greenfield's life, apparently in response to death threats he had received from nervous depositors.)[14] Amid the mutual relief at the postponement of the crisis, apparently no one raised a critical question: Would $10 million suffice to keep Bankers Trust afloat?

All that remained, it seemed, was the formal but presumed routine approval of the transaction by the Clearing House Committee. Secretary of Banking Cameron, thinking the crisis over, returned to Harrisburg that Saturday night.[15]

The meeting to approve the rescue plan was called for the following evening—Sunday, the twenty-first—at the Merion home of William Purves Gest.[16] Wayne, Newhall, Stotesbury, and Gest, the host, were almost certainly present. Precisely who else attended—whether the eight members of the Clearing House Committee, or the heads of all thirty-four banks in the

Clearing House Association (as Greenfield contended), or a combination of prominent local bankers (as seems most likely)—is unclear; no minutes were taken, and no one present ever gave an account of what transpired.[17] What is certain is that neither Greenfield nor Fox nor anyone else representing Bankers Trust was invited, even though Bankers Trust, as a full member of the Clearing House Association, would technically have been entitled to attend a meeting of the full association.[18]

At that meeting, despite Greenfield's and Fox's assent to their conditions, the assembled bankers rejected the Wayne/Newhall plan and declined to offer further assistance, in effect dooming Bankers Trust. "Someone higher up gave adverse orders," Greenfield later speculated, "and the Bankers Trust Company's plea was turned down. We have never been told why but we have our own opinion."[19]

What exactly occurred at the home of William Purves Gest that night? Why did the Clearing House bankers renege on their agreement with Greenfield? If "someone higher up" gave them "adverse orders," as Greenfield claimed, who was it, and why?

In the absence of a firsthand account, for decades thereafter the bankers' last-minute rejection of Greenfield was widely blamed on E. T. Stotesbury and ascribed to the banking fraternity's innate anti-Semitism, or to its revulsion for Greenfield's rambunctious style, or both. "The Clearing House banks did not keep their word, apparently feeling that Mr. Greenfield had become too big, had tread on their toes, and here was a chance to check him," explained an article written about Greenfield for *Forbes* magazine in 1948.[20] To Greenfield's friend J. David Stern, the decision made by the bankers that Sunday night was "a dirty double-cross by his 'best friends' if ever there was one."[21] More than thirty years after Bankers Trust closed, Stern elaborated in his memoirs:

> The other Philadelphia bankers had resented the rapid growth of Al's bank. In the fall of 1929 [*sic*], they had persuaded him to take over and save from closing a string of suburban banks. They promised their support. When he needed it, they turned thumbs down.[22]

Greenfield, when he finally broke his own silence about the Bankers Trust crisis eight years later, went a step further: He suggested that he had been deliberately set up to fail when he was persuaded to acquire the Bank of Philadelphia in July 1930 and that the run on Bankers Trust that fall had been deliberately orchestrated. "It was evident a more or less concerted movement was at work to spread discontent among the depositors," he said. In the same speech, he referred to a "drive against the bank" that he described as "concentrated."[23]

Yet in the cold light of historical analysis, now that the players and their passions are removed from the scene, the notion that Philadelphia's leading bankers deliberately set Greenfield up to fail probably credits them with more ingenuity and deviousness than they possessed. It also flies in the face of logic and the available facts. Had Joseph Wayne and Stevenson Newhall conspired to destroy Bankers Trust from the outset, presumably they would not have loaned Bankers Trust more than $7 million on its way down. More to the point, Wayne and Newhall and their fellow bank chiefs were keenly aware that the failure of a large bank like Bankers Trust would likely lead to withdrawal stampedes at other banks, including their own.

Why, then, did they reverse themselves at the last minute and decline to rescue Bankers Trust? And who ultimately made that decision? Those questions can be answered only with the broadest sort of speculation.

The deciding voice was almost certainly that of E. T. Stotesbury, acting in his customary role as unofficial adviser to Philadelphia's banking fraternity. Stotesbury alone commanded the combination of resources, experience, and esteem capable of credibly questioning a decision that had seemed preordained. The Clearing House Association could not have acted without his approval.

Other circumstantial clues point to Stotesbury as well. Greenfield, who never bore grudges even against his bitterest rivals—and who maintained good relations thereafter with Wayne and Newhall as well as with Edward Hopkinson Jr., Stotesbury's successor as senior partner at Drexel—privately spoke disparagingly of Stotesbury even after Stotesbury's death in 1938.[24] (Greenfield may have learned what transpired at the meeting from his friend and fellow Bankers Securities director Addison Harris, who was a member of the Clearing House Committee.)[25]

Of Stotesbury it was said that if he did not like a deal, nothing could make him change his mind. Yet to the extent that it is possible to probe that mind, neither anti-Semitism nor personal animus toward Greenfield seems to have influenced his decision. Stotesbury may have had few Jewish friends, but he did have some—notably the New York banker Otto Kahn, at whose funeral Stotesbury served as a pallbearer. Furthermore, he was never known to express anti-Semitic sentiments, as Jack Morgan did. And while Stotesbury may have taken personal umbrage at the social slights accorded to him and his wife, he prided himself on his clinical approach to financial matters and on his refusal to let personal considerations influence his business judgments.

Ultimately, Stotesbury's objections to bailing out Greenfield's bank boiled down to an honest philosophical difference between two men of vastly different ages and business experiences. Greenfield, at forty-three, had spent his entire business career in the twentieth century; he had never experienced a financial depression, and as an immigrant he saw only what seemed to him the limitless upward possibilities of American enterprise. Stotesbury, conversely, was eighty-one and very much a creature of nineteenth-century America, with its recurrent cycle of financial panics in each generation. He had been centrally involved in alleviating the Panic of 1907, to such an extent that J. P. Morgan Sr. himself had visited Stotesbury in Philadelphia to discuss relief plans.[26] The stress caused by the Panic of 1893 may well have contributed to the death that year of Stotesbury's mentor, Anthony J. Drexel. Stotesbury was the only banker left in Philadelphia who remembered the Panic of 1873, when hundreds of American banks and eighteen thousand businesses (including more than half the nation's railroads) failed, half the nation's industrial workers were laid off, and federal troops had to be mobilized to contend with the strikes, lockouts, and riots that ensued.[27] It is even possible that, as an eight-year-old, Stotesbury witnessed the crowds of anxious depositors outside Philadelphia's Chestnut Street banks, just a few blocks from his home, during the Panic of 1857.[28]

Stotesbury's firsthand memory of the devastation caused by these previous panics left him averse to supporting any enterprise that was heavily dependent on illiquid assets, such as real estate, especially during a market downturn. Indeed, in anticipation of the property "bubble" he had foreseen, Stotesbury himself had been unloading Drexel's real estate investments (as well as his own) since the early 1920s—beginning, of course, with the Metropolitan Opera House that Greenfield had snapped up so eagerly in 1920.[29]

By contrast, Greenfield's faith in real estate—and specifically in his ability to visualize what might be done with a vacant lot or field—never faltered, even after the great crash of 1929. "Stocks and bonds are only claims on a wealth that may some day be produced, or the means of its production," he continued to insist even a generation later. "Real estate plus the creative labor of mind and hand are the only two sources of production and wealth."[30] In a very real sense, Greenfield was a visionary unencumbered by the lessons of the past; Stotesbury was a man of profound experience but incapable of perceiving that the future might be different. In his prime Stotesbury had demonstrated sufficient imagination to participate with Pierpont Morgan in the creation of U.S. Steel, the world's first billion-dollar corporation, in 1901. But as one Stotesbury biographer acknowledged, by 1930 "he showed a tendency more and more to exercise a veto power in business. The day of adventure for him was gone."[31]

It seems reasonable to conjecture that Stotesbury was not privy to the original decision by Wayne and Newhall to lend money to Bankers Trust during the run that fall. (Had Stotesbury been consulted then, the negotiations probably would not have proceeded as far as they did.) More likely, Stotesbury was not brought into the discussion until the eleventh hour—specifically, the Sunday night meeting at William P. Gest's home. The Clearing House bankers, having made demands that Greenfield and Fox had accepted on Saturday night, needed affirmation from a respected authority, and Stotesbury was the authority to whom they logically turned.

Stotesbury had often performed this function. He recognized the tendency of bankers to get carried away, sheep-like, by wishful thinking; at such moments he prided himself on his ability to cut to the heart of the matter with cold and independent judgment. The heart of the matter in this case, as Stotesbury probably saw it, was neither Greenfield's religion nor his character (nor William Fox's) but the dubious real estate collateral held by Bankers Trust. With a single cryptic but incisive question from Stotesbury—perhaps "Are you throwing good money after bad here?"—the entire mood in Gest's living room would have shifted.

It was now late Sunday evening, but the matter was not quite finished. When Greenfield and Fox learned of the decision that night (from whom, we do not know), Fox prevailed on a core group of prominent bankers to reassemble and hear him out. The bankers, still hoping to find some way to avoid a major bank failure in their city the next morning, reconvened late that night in the boardroom of Drexel & Co. downtown, this time with E. T. Stotesbury as host but again without Greenfield's presence.[32]

Here Fox found himself in Drexel's elegant new headquarters, a six-story stone building that the architect Charles Klauder had modeled in 1927 specifically after the Strozzi, Pitti, and Riccardi palaces of fifteenth-century Florence—an intimidating building whose thick teakwood doors, studded with wrought bronze nails, opened onto floors and corridors of marble, leading to executive offices paneled in oak from the Forest of Argonne in France.[33]

Fox's hyperbolic account of that meeting, as published by Upton Sinclair some two years later, is the only report we have:

At about 3 o'clock in the morning, I realized as clearly as it was possible that the destruction of Greenfield had to occur, and I made up my mind to test it to see whether I was right. I arose and made the most eloquent address of my life in behalf of Greenfield and the 125,000 poor depositors in the city of Philadelphia.[34] I said that if they permitted this bank to close its doors tomorrow, they would start a fire in the town. "You will have 125,000 depositors who are going to be upset. You will find your newspapers printing nothing else. You will find a run on every bank in Philadelphia. You might think you are out of range of this thing; I tell you that that is not so. I am not here merely because I want to help Greenfield; I am here in behalf of the men, women and children who have their money not only in this bank, but in every other bank in Philadelphia."

I pointed out what a terrible condition had arisen in New York when the Chase Bank and others decided the Bank of the United States [sic] must be closed; every bank in New York was affected. This would not only start a run in Philadelphia, but it would be a story for the whole state of Pennsylvania, and would start other runs.

I made the following proposal: "Gentlemen, you claim all this while that Greenfield has $4 million worth of bad debts on his books. I think you are wrong; I think a careful survey will show you that he probably has more. It will probably run to $5 million." They were sure that it was only $4 million that was more than sufficient to take care of those debts. I said I would loan $1 million of my personal money. I said: "I have just talked to Greenfield, and he says that when you liquidate his bank, if at that time there is any loss incurred by you, he personally will give you a guarantee for $1.5 million, and will collateralize that guarantee at this time. I have requested Greenfield to do that, to show his willingness to help the situation. After you have used up his one million and a half, you will have my million dollars, which you can have in cash or collateral."

While I was making this address, which I thought most eloquent, I noticed the president of the second largest bank in Philadelphia take his handkerchief out of his pocket, presumably wiping his face, and place it to the right hand side of his mouth and then grin and laugh and smile at the head of the largest bank, the Drexel Bank.[35]

Here Fox referred, apparently, to Joe Wayne and E. T. Stotesbury. He felt they were mocking his emotional rhetoric, and he may have been correct. Fox's speech was to some extent a virtual duplicate of the address that Joseph Broderick, the New York state superintendent of banks, had delivered barely a week earlier to Wall Street's leading bankers, urging them to rescue the

Bank of United States. Broderick's anguished words—"I warned them that they were making the most colossal banking mistake in the history of New York," Broderick later recalled—had fallen on similarly deaf ears.[36] The only difference was that Broderick, unlike Fox, was not perceived by his audience as a figure of ridicule.

More than eighty years later, what should a reader make of this account? What did Fox expect to achieve? More important, where was Greenfield during this last-ditch post-midnight appeal?

The likely answers provide some insight into the differences between these two friends and partners. Lacking Greenfield's acumen for sizing up people with whom he was dealing and for approaching them accordingly, Fox appealed to the bankers' sense of community and to their sympathy for the widows and orphans who had stored their pennies away in Bankers Trust. It is perhaps fair to say that Fox had watched too many of his own movies, and that the bankers in the room should have watched more of them.

Greenfield, for his part, probably realized by this point that the game was lost. (Fox's speech to the bankers mentioned Greenfield's reference to "*when* you liquidate his bank"—not "if.") As a man whose whole persona depended on his ability to cloak himself in an aura of success, Greenfield always preferred to operate from a position of strength, not weakness. Thus Greenfield would have instinctively avoided a situation where he would be cast in the role of a supplicant begging for help.

The prospect of a confrontation that pitted him and Fox against Philadelphia's Protestant Establishment would have been anathema to Greenfield in any case, for Greenfield believed himself a Philadelphia gentleman just like these bankers. In his own mind he was as much an heir to the tradition of his hero, Benjamin Franklin, as they were, if not more so. At some subconscious level, Greenfield hungered for their acceptance and shared their discomfort with Fox's populist comportment. The prospect of being rejected by men he saw as his fellow fraternity members may well have been more than Greenfield's psyche could bear, even at the risk of losing his bank.[37]

A t 4:20 A.M. that Monday, the twenty-second, an urgent telegram went out from Irland M. Beckman, secretary of the Bankers Trust board, to the homes of the bank's thirty-six directors, including Greenfield: "SPECIAL MEETING OF BOARD THIS MORNING DECEMBER 22ND AT EIGHT O'CLOCK. YOUR PRESENCE IMPERATIVE."[38]

Monday morning, December 22, 1930, dawned appropriately gloomy and rainy in Philadelphia.[39] At their 8:00 A.M. meeting—held an hour before the bank's doors were scheduled to open—the directors voted to voluntarily close Bankers Trust and temporarily turn its assets over to the Pennsylvania Department of Banking "to conserve assets for the protection of depositors and stockholders."[40]

Yet still Fox refused to throw in the towel. Now he decided to appeal directly to President Herbert Hoover. While the Bankers Trust directors assembled, as he later told it,

> I waited until about 8 o'clock . . . when I thought the President would be at his breakfast table. I called him on the 'phone; his secretary said he had instructions not to disturb him. I requested that the secretary give him my name at the breakfast table, and let the President say whether or not he wanted to be disturbed. A few minutes later the President came on the 'phone. I had in a brief way told him what was occurring to Greenfield. Since I had known of this since Thursday, he now severely criticized me for not coming to him promptly. By this time it was 8:15 and the Bankers Trust never opened. I learned later that President Hoover had made a strenuous effort to locate those who might be of help before 9 o'clock, but that the time was too short.[41]

At 9:00 A.M., just three days before Christmas, some 114,000 Philadelphians—representing about one of every five households in and around Philadelphia—experienced their first real taste of the Great Depression.[42] When the doors of Bankers Trust failed to open, crowds described as "fair-sized" gathered outside the locked doors of the bank's branches throughout the city. Some of the crowds grew as large as three hundred, most of them working-class women. At the main office downtown—one floor below Greenfield's own office—the dozen assigned police officers allowed onlookers to read the brief typewritten note on the door before telling them to move on.

A few women became hysterical, knocking on the doors and screaming at bank clerks they could see inside through the plate-glass window. One woman, who cried that she had deposited $1,100 on Friday, collapsed on the sidewalk outside a Bankers Trust branch at 713 Chestnut Street and was treated for shock at Jefferson Hospital. Another weeping woman said her husband was out of work and that they had counted on their savings of $3,000 to carry them through the winter. At the bank's South Philadelphia branch at Broad and Wharton Streets, several hundred men and women milled around the front door, trying to find a translator to decipher the typed note posted there because, as immigrants, they could not comprehend it themselves.[43]

At the *Philadelphia Record*, news of the Bankers Trust closing sent Greenfield's friend J. David Stern into shock. The *Record* had $350,000 on deposit there, all of it now frozen. Stern's paper had only $30,000 in other banks, and a $40,000 payroll to meet at the end of the week. As he later recalled, Stern told his secretary to cut off all his phone calls and visitors while "I sat in my back office, trying to figure out what to do. To be explicit, I sat in my private bathroom. My bowels were loose from fear." Stern's bathroom reverie was interrupted when his secretary, disregarding his order, announced the arrival of the *Record*'s paper supplier with the news that a $125,000 check from the *Record*, written on Bankers Trust, had bounced.[44]

Yet amid the turmoil throughout Philadelphia that day, one man seemed unperturbed: Greenfield himself. When Stern went to see Greenfield later that morning, he found him "cool, calm and master of the situation." When the movie mogul Louis B. Mayer wired Greenfield that day to ask, "What about my stock?" and to add, "Hope you are in no difficulties," Greenfield wired back, "In my opinion the maximum shrinkage in asset position of your stock [in Bankers Securities] due to bank closing will be less than 10%. Pleased to advise not in any personal difficulties. Regards. Albert."[45]

Greenfield, Stern later recalled, "acted as though nothing of importance had happened." In a matter-of-fact voice, Greenfield told Stern that he was $6 million in debt on personal guarantees of real estate mortgages and bonds. "In the last days," Stern later wrote, "he had poured into the Bankers Trust all the cash of his real estate business and other enterprises, as well as his personal accounts and those of his family." Yet he was already planning his comeback and seemed to relish the challenge.[46]

Greenfield actually may have had more than $400,000 personally on deposit at Bankers Trust, plus millions more indirectly through the deposits and stockholdings of Bankers Securities.[47] In all, Greenfield and his companies had some $3.5 million on deposit at Bankers Trust.[48] And his personal indebtedness at that moment may have exceeded $11 million.[49] He personally owed some $4 million to other banks, plus an additional $3 million in personal note guarantees, most related to the real estate syndicates he had assembled during the 1920s. These figures did not include his share of the debts owed by Bankers Securities. He had protected his home and farm and various other possessions by registering them in the names of his family members and business associates.[50]

Still, Greenfield's basic outline of his situation to Stern that morning was correct: He was the single largest victim of the Bankers Trust failure. Yet his unflappable demeanor, his refusal to seek sympathy for himself, his seeming inability to empathize with the bank's 114,000 smaller victims, his disingenuous insistence that he was merely one of thirty-six directors of Bankers Trust and held no other official position there—all this, together with his previous reputation as a master manipulator, fostered the widespread notion among the bank's depositors that *he* had victimized *them*, somehow deliberately orchestrating the bank's closing and making off with their money.[51]

Before the day was out Greenfield began receiving notes and phone calls—some pleading for his help, others offering to sell him their account value at a discount, others anonymously threatening violence against him. One letter written that day, signed only "A Groupe [*sic*] of Depositors," warned:

This is to advise you that if [you] do not arrange within the next few days to have all moneys paid out to the depositors of your Bankers Trust Co. I and a few more have sworn to it that we will kill you no matter where you may hide. You have without the slightest doubt deserved this and you shall get your reward. Remember: you shall pay with either your money if it takes your last dollar or with your life. The choice is yours.[52]

Wrote another:

Greenfield,
    Just a line to *warn you*! What sort of a creature are you anyway? All this bank trouble is at *your door*. . . . Think of the Xmas joys turned to sadness. Your dear friend Mitten took a boat ride. Many of the *Mastbaums have died*[,] and take it from me your turn will not be far off. You drew all your money from the bank before it closed its doors you *skunk. You are watched every move.* Make your peice [*sic*] *with God* is all I want to say. You will need *wings soon.*[53]

When Greenfield's children had a Christmas party at his Germantown home a few days later, their young guests noticed a policeman sitting in the kitchen with a gun on the table: Some angry Bankers Trust depositors, it was explained, had threatened to retaliate against Greenfield through his children.[54] "Greenfield will not die in bed," his former partner Louis Cahan remarked to an acquaintance.[55]

In an attempt to reassure the banking public, that Monday morning the Clearing House Committee issued a limp and unconvincing public announcement:

The Clearing House Committee regret the closing of the Bankers Trust Company, and advises that its closing does not involve any other institution in the city.

We believe that the financial situation in Philadelphia is sound, and there is no occasion for depositors to become alarmed on account of the closing of the Bankers Trust Company.[56]

This brief announcement made no mention of the committee's role in the closing of Bankers Trust; nor did it produce the desired effect. As Greenfield and Fox had warned, and as Wayne and Newhall had feared, the closing of Bankers Trust soon triggered withdrawal stampedes at other Philadelphia banks.

The immediate target that Monday was the Franklin Trust Company, headed by Greenfield's friend and business associate C. Addison Harris Jr., and widely perceived as a "Greenfield bank" even though Greenfield disingenuously insisted he had no connection to it.[57] The suspension of Bankers Trust inevitably generated rumors that Franklin Trust too was about to go under. But where the run on the Bankers Trust had involved some twenty-one thousand depositors who quietly closed their accounts over a period of four months at more than a dozen locations, the run on the Franklin Trust was an instant mob scene, the likes of which few Philadelphians had witnessed since the Panic of 1893.

Within a few hours, thousands of depositors besieged the Franklin Trust's central office as well as its four branches, demanding cash withdrawals of all their funds.[58] To replace the money that depositors hauled away, armored trucks delivered fresh currency to the beleaguered bank from its depositories as well as from other banks throughout the day and into the evening.[59]

The previous night, Philadelphia's leading bankers had imagined themselves under severe financial pressure, but that pressure was insignificant compared with the angry, vocal, potentially violent pressure that confronted them right now. Over the previous three days they had engaged in anxious but civil discussions of the pros and cons of rescuing Bankers Trust; now, with genuine mobs in the streets and no clear sense of where their anger might lead, the time for rational discussion had passed.

Again the Clearing House Committee members, as well as some other prominent bankers, hurriedly gathered at the office of Drexel & Co. Less than twenty-four hours had passed since their meeting at Gest's home in Merion, yet that meeting seemed light-years away. This time, E. T. Stotesbury was unavailable, and in his absence the meeting was hosted by his less forceful and incisive partner, H. Gates Lloyd. And this time, much like men being held up at gunpoint, the bankers hastily arranged to extend up to $20 million in credit to the Franklin Trust and quickly announced their decision in the hope of stemming the tide.

That is, the same bankers who on Saturday had hesitantly offered Greenfield's bank $5 million only if he put up an equal amount—and then on Sunday had reneged even on that offer—now hastily pledged $20 million to a bank run by a man who simultaneously worked as a vice president of one of Greenfield's companies, and they made that pledge without imposing any conditions. The night before, the bankers had decided the fate of Greenfield's bank without inviting him or any of his associates, but now Harris, president of the beleaguered bank as well as a member of the Clearing House Committee, was indeed present to make the case for rescuing the Franklin Trust.[60]

By the time that meeting broke up late Monday afternoon, some one thousand anxious depositors—including laborers and mechanics in work clothes as well as men and women in evening attire—were jammed into the Franklin Trust's main office at Fifteenth and Chestnut Streets. Joe Wayne—who had been up almost the entire previous night—strode in and mounted a table in the center of the lobby in a dramatic effort to stem the tide single-handedly, very much in a manner suitable to a William Fox movie.

He told the crowd:

Why all you people should be gathered here because of an idle rumor that something is wrong is beyond my comprehension.

We have looked over the balance sheet of this bank. The Philadelphia Clearing House Association is back of this institution 100 per cent. It is as safe as any bank in Philadelphia.

There is more money behind it than you could carry away. My advice to you is to go home, go to sleep, stop worrying and give these tired clerks a chance to get some rest.[61]

According to one newspaper report, the depositors applauded, and hundreds left the bank immediately.[62] Soon after, Wayne was joined by a chorus of confident voices consisting of Secretary of Banking Cameron (who insisted that the Franklin Trust was "absolutely sound") and even Mayor Mackey, who went so far as to deposit a thousand dollars in the Franklin Trust, adding, "This bank is as solid as the Rock of Gibraltar." In effect, the failure of the Bankers Trust had stampeded Philadelphia's bankers and public officials into issuing reassurances about the soundness of an institution whose reputation in banking circles was lower than that of the Bankers Trust that they had just permitted to expire. And those assurances, together with the Clearing House Committee's promised loan support, did stem the run on the Franklin Trust, at least for the time being.[63]

Yet another Philadelphia bank collapsed the next day. M. L. Blitzstein & Co., popularly known as the Blitzstein Bank, had been founded in 1891 to provide steamship ticket orders and foreign exchange services for immigrants; by 1930 it had evolved into a successful (albeit unregulated) private bank serving some six thousand immigrant depositors. Like most immigrant banks, Blitzstein & Co. had no real capital and little or no legal responsibility. Throughout Tuesday morning, December 23, amid news of the closing of a "real bank" downtown, desperate immigrants ran to withdraw their life's savings from Blitzstein's office at Fourth and Lombard Streets. By early afternoon the Blitzstein Bank too had exhausted its available funds and closed its doors, never again to reopen them.[64]

The following night, on Christmas Eve, Greenfield and Samuel Barker, the president of Bankers Trust, traveled to Washington to seek President Hoover's help in reviving their bank. But because Bankers Trust was a state-chartered bank, not a member of the Federal Reserve system, the federal government lacked jurisdiction over it. The best Hoover could do for Greenfield and Barker was to contact several banking officials, who helped allay tensions among some depositors. Andrew Mellon, Hoover's secretary of the Treasury and pillar of Pennsylvania's most prominent banking dynasty, might have helped Greenfield informally in this crisis, but Greenfield had alienated Mellon by opposing his presidential candidate at the Republican convention in 1928.[65]

Early in 1931, Bankers Trust laid off four hundred of its five hundred employees.[66] Within thirty days of the bank's closing, its assets paid off in full the $7.5 million advanced to it by Philadelphia National Bank and by the Pennsylvania Company.[67] But in May 1931, the Bankers Trust depositors' committee voted to exclude Greenfield from any official position if the bank reopened.[68] Greenfield nevertheless spent much of the next five months attempting to revive it, but that September the state ordered the bank liquidated.[69]

Over the next five years, as the bank's assets were liquidated, its depositors (including Greenfield) were paid off at 59 cents on the dollar—a higher proportion than Pennsylvania's Banking Department recovered from any of the state's other failed banks, and a sign that it might have survived in other circumstances. Still, Bankers Trust had lost 41 percent of its depositors' money and all of its capital. By those measures it was indeed technically insolvent, just as Stotesbury had surmised at the Sunday night meeting at William Gest's home in 1930.

In the wake of the Bankers Trust failure, thirty smaller Philadelphia banks and trust companies (out of eighty-nine in the city all told), as well as hundreds of building and loan associations, failed over the next two years. Across the nation, more than nine thousand banks—about 30 percent of all institutions—toppled like dominoes until the newly inaugurated president Franklin Delano Roosevelt imposed a bank moratorium in March 1933.[70] One of those dominoes was the Franklin Trust, which collapsed on October 6, 1931, less than ten months after Joe Wayne's reassuring speech in its lobby.[71] But Philadelphians pointed with pride to the cooperative efforts of the Clearing House, the principal banks, and Drexel & Co., which together saved about a dozen institutions through loans, cash deposits, and mergers.[72]

"The people of Philadelphia will never know how much they owe to these gentlemen and their associates," wrote George Norris, president of the Philadelphia Federal Reserve Bank.[73] Indeed, aside from the Bankers Trust, only one large Philadelphia bank, the Franklin Trust, was allowed to fold. Conspiratorial-minded observers were quick to note that both banks, and only those two banks, were connected with Greenfield. And they noted the remarkable parallel situation in New York, where that city's major bankers had also assembled a credit pool that had saved all the city's large banks with the exception of two—both owned by Jews.

Greenfield kept his thoughts on this issue to himself for nearly eight years—resolving, he said, "to bear in silence any blame that was wrongly placed on me"—until a new wave of political attacks in 1938 forced him to discuss the closing publicly and in detail.[74] "The closing of Bankers Trust was a wrong done to the people of Philadelphia," he insisted at that time. "It should never have been permitted. . . . It closed only because in 1930 a small, secret group of powerful men had the power of life and death over banks."[75]

Yet still the question persists: In retrospect, who was right about the condition of Bankers Trust—Albert Greenfield or E. T. Stotesbury?

Stotesbury's judgment concerning Greenfield's bank—"We'll let that one go," he supposedly said—may be open to question. He might reasonably be faulted for failing to perceive that the future might differ from the past, and for failing to recognize in Greenfield a man of sufficient imagination to surmount the historical patterns of America's past banking crises. But his motives seem beyond reproach.[76]

Had Stotesbury attended the Clearing House meeting about saving the Franklin Trust on Monday, December 22, no doubt he would have asked the same rhetorical question he probably raised the previous night about Bankers Trust—"Are you throwing good money after bad?"—and rightly so: The

Franklin Trust folded ten months later, despite its $20 million infusion from the Clearing House group.

More to the point, the rumors about the Bank of Philadelphia that triggered the run on Bankers Trust in the fall of 1930 were not baseless (as Greenfield contended) but well founded—as the embezzlement, conviction, and suicide of the Bank of Philadelphia's former president, Leon A. Lewis, subsequently confirmed.[77] Although Greenfield refused to acknowledge it, the blame for his acquisition of such an unstable bank lay primarily with his failure to perform adequate due diligence before buying it that summer.[78]

The Bankers Trust failure emboldened Greenfield's enemies to move against him on other fronts. Less than three months after the closing of Bankers Trust, he was summoned to testify before a state senate investigating committee as well as Philadelphia Common Pleas Court about his manipulations on behalf of his friend Thomas Mitten during the PRT's purchase of Quaker City Cab Company in 1928.

When the city filed suit in 1930 to nullify that sale, Greenfield at first denied that he had represented the PRT in its $1.4 million purchase of Quaker City Cab; he insisted that he had represented only the seller, Frank Sawyer of Boston. On another occasion, Greenfield maintained that he had not acted as an agent at all, but had bought Quaker City Cab himself from Sawyer and then sold it directly to the PRT. Finally, in March 1931, Greenfield admitted to the state senators that he had acted as agent for *both* the buyer and the seller in the Quaker City Cab deal, and that both had paid him a 5 percent commission, amounting to a total of about $180,000.[79]

But what had happened to the $1 million profit Greenfield had generated for his friend Mitten? Greenfield testified to the state senate investigating committee that on January 6, 1928, the day the PRT purchased Quaker City Cab, he made out a $250,000 check to "cash," which was then cashed and kept by Mitten. Five days later, Greenfield said, he gave Mitten another check made out to "cash," this one for $486,000. Both checks were made out at Mitten's request.

In his testimony to the investigating state senators, Greenfield professed to see nothing unusual about one of his clients wanting to receive $736,000 from the cab sale in cash. In theory, of course, Greenfield's client was not Mitten but Sawyer, who was the seller of the cab company. In practice, though, Sawyer was the straw man for Mitten, so the money might as well have gone to one man as to the other. The ensuing cross-examination was calculated to maximize Greenfield's embarrassment, which was not difficult to accomplish.

Q. Who cashed the check?

A. I don't recall.

Q. The check would show who cashed it.

A. Not necessarily. If I draw checks to cash, it would be cashed direct.

Q. Without endorsement?

A. Probably.

Q. What bank would hand out $250,000 in cash to a person without endorsing a check or without the person making the check going along to show it is okay?

A. I think any bank would.

Q. What bank was the check drawn on?

A. I think Bankers Trust Company.

Q. What bank would have $250,000 in cash lying around loose to pay to cash checks across the counter?

A. Any big bank. Bankers Trust Company would have several millions in cash on hand.

Q. Who asked you to draw the check to cash?

A. Mitten—or maybe it was Sawyer. It would be one or the other.[80]

There was, of course, good reason why Bankers Trust Company cashed Greenfield's checks without so much as a raised eyebrow. Bankers Trust was Greenfield's bank: He and his associates dominated its board of directors; his Bankers Securities Corporation—which owned about half of its stock— was its largest depositor; and Greenfield himself was its largest individual depositor.

Thus Greenfield had used his relationships with Quaker City, with Mitten, with the PRT, and with Bankers Trust to pyramid a $1 million profit for his friend Mitten. But what did Greenfield get from the deal, aside from his $180,000 in commissions?

The evidence suggests that Greenfield's manipulations in behalf of Mitten were in effect repayments for past favors. For one thing, by Greenfield's own estimate, his firm had received between $700,000 and $800,000 in fees from the PRT while it was under Mitten Management.[81] In addition, Mitten's ledgers eventually showed that in 1927, just before the Quaker City Cab deal was executed, Mitten had advanced Greenfield $1.5 million for unspecified purposes.[82]

The state's Public Service Commission refused to approve the sale of Quaker City Cab to the PRT. And a month later, in April 1931, Philadelphia Common Pleas Court Judge Harry McDevitt—coincidentally, the younger brother of Greenfield's early employer, John J. McDevitt—ruled that the "PRT has not even the right to own the Quaker City Cab Company, much less to pay Mitten Management a fee for managing it." His opinion called Greenfield's role "unconscionable" and ordered that Greenfield's commissions should be returned and the sale nullified.[83]

Two months later, the PRT severed its relationship with Greenfield, announcing that thereafter it would handle its own real estate transactions. Judge McDevitt's final judgment in November 1931 transferred substantially all the assets of Thomas Mitten's personal estate to the PRT.[84]

The crash of 1929 and the failure of the Bankers Trust wiped out Greenfield's fortune as well as the aura of success on which he depended. His real estate company, which had grossed as much as $130 million annually in the late 1920s, barely met its operating expenses in the early 1930s.[85] The depressed real estate market caused his real estate company to default on $4 million worth of debenture notes in November 1931.[86] The company's creditors could have seized its assets and divided them at once, but they concluded, as creditors often do in such situations, that they would probably get more money over the long run if they kept the company in the hands of its management rather than turn it over to a bankruptcy judge or a politically appointed trustee.

Thus, because of his real estate reputation, Greenfield was kept in the saddle at Albert M. Greenfield & Co., albeit with severe restrictions imposed to placate his creditors: His compensation was limited to 25 percent of the company's net profit after the payment of interest to its debt holders. As a result, Greenfield received no salary whatever from his real estate company for more than ten years beginning in 1931, or any dividends, interest, or other compensation.[87] For the six years from 1929 through 1934 Greenfield's total federal taxable income amounted to $154,448. Such was his plight that in 1932 he was forced to temporarily convey the title on his summer home in Ventnor, New Jersey, back to its original owner for failure to pay its property taxes.[88]

Yet Greenfield adamantly rejected his lawyers' repeated advice that he seek bankruptcy protection. "I have pride in my position in the business world," he later explained in a private letter, "so I refused the easy way."[89] Instead, he spent much of the 1930s persuading his creditors to work with him rather than force him into bankruptcy, typically by offering to pay off his debts over a twenty-year period, plus interest.[90]

Perhaps most remarkably, Bankers Securities remained afloat, even though it had had more than $2 million on deposit at Bankers Trust (of which it ultimately lost more than $800,000); even though it had invested $2.75 million in the stock of the failed bank (of which it lost everything); even though it had subscribed to nearly half of the $4 million bond issue on which Albert M. Greenfield & Co. defaulted; and even though its $8 million loan to City Stores in 1928 remained outstanding, with little likelihood that it would be paid off. In his annual report in February 1931, Greenfield insisted that Bankers Securities' capital "remains unimpaired" and "we have a surplus of over $1 million."[91] At Greenfield's own suggestion, the $100,000-a-year salary awarded to him by the Bankers Securities board after the Lit's deal in 1928 was reduced to $52,000 in February 1931 and again to $41,600 that September.[92] At about that time, the Bankers Trust Building, where Greenfield had his headquarters, received a new name: the Bankers Securities Building.[93]

(David Stern, too, survived by appealing to the good will of the *Record*'s paper supplier, as well as through advances from the newspaper's advertisers and Bankers Securities, which owned a large block of Record Company stock.)[94]

Greenfield's experience with Bankers Trust, one observer contended, "seems to illustrate a conclusion that was reached in the early '30s by a great many other Jews: that the Jews, as a commercial class, could never hope for better than second-best out of an alliance with the commercial and financial class of old family businessmen or with the political party that they dominated."[95] To others the Bankers Trust debacle recalled the words of Matthew Josephson, the chronicler of Wall Street's "robber barons" of the late nineteenth century: "In the life of every conquering soul there is a 'turning point.'"[96]

Yet even in his wounded state, Greenfield remained Philadelphia's indispensable man in many respects. In 1934, the PRT filed a bankruptcy petition. The subsequent reorganization proceedings were described by one of the lawyers as "a free-for-all" at which "people swarmed about the courtroom. Everyone was aggrieved, and it seemed that every lawyer in town had a client who wanted to intervene." To sort out this chaos, in 1936 the U.S. District Court appointed six men as trustees of the property. One of the six was Albert M. Greenfield; another was Edward Hopkinson Jr., the newly anointed senior partner at Drexel & Co., with whom Greenfield soon struck up the sort of friendship he never could have managed with Hopkinson's predecessor at Drexel, E. T. Stotesbury. The two men made the sort of odd couple that seemed to delight Greenfield: Hopkinson—tall, broad, shambling, self-effacing, former Spoon Man at Penn and captain of the swim team, scion of a family whose name had been synonymous with Philadelphia for more than two centuries—seemed everything that Greenfield was not.[97] But each man brought a complementary talent to their partnership: Hopkinson, control of Philadelphia's moneyed interests, and Greenfield, close friendships with labor leaders.[98]

The following year the court appointed three managers to supervise the PRT's reorganization; Greenfield and Hopkinson were two of the three. Moreover, Greenfield subsequently sat for twenty-six years on the board of the PRT and its successor, the Philadelphia Transportation Company (PTC), and served as chairman of the PTC for most of that time.[99] Whatever his conflicts, public officials explained, no one else possessed his uniquely savvy business acumen. It was Greenfield above all, remarked one lawyer, who "assumed a major role in engineering the emergence of the PTC from the ashes of the PRT."[100]

Optimism, as defined by the Mayo Clinic, "is the belief that good things will happen to you and that negative events are temporary setbacks to overcome."[101] Like most Americans, Greenfield emerged from the Depression chastened but wiser, aware for perhaps the first time of his own limitations and of the uncertainty of human nature. Yet this new insight rendered him stronger than ever. Now Greenfield's cheerful persistence in the face of overwhelming adversity became in some respects an even more impressive calling card than his dazzling deals of the 1920s.

Sometime in the early 1930s, Greenfield met with the city controller S. Davis Wilson—who as assistant city controller had spearheaded the city's suit against the PRT and Greenfield in 1931—and Wilson's press agent, Lou Wilgard. Another man who was present later described the conversation:

> I remember sitting in an office with S. Davis Wilson and Lou Wilgard and Mr. Greenfield, when Lou Wilgard told Mr. Greenfield, he said, "Greenfield, you're a *thief*!" And Greenfield sat there quietly and didn't twitch a muscle. And he said, "Wilgard, I'll be here long after you are gone!" And he smiled. . . . And he was![102]

"It amazed me, the people who relied on him for advice and solace," Greenfield's second-in-command at Bankers Securities, Gus Amsterdam, later reflected.

> Here was a man whose bank had failed just a few short years before. You might think he'd be depressed and would lack confidence. He was convinced the failure of the bank was a political, not a business,

failure. He was confident of his ability to do what he had to do. Always surrounded himself with young people. He never talked about why the bank failed. He didn't reminisce about things that didn't work out. He was the first to admit his mistakes but went ahead to his next success story.[103]

Greenfield's banking career was over.[104] But even as the Bankers Trust went under, a new idea was percolating in his mind. His eagerness to put his failures behind him may explain why he went to bed on Sunday night, December 21, rather than join Fox's pleadings in the Drexel boardroom. He would not merely vindicate himself with a new success; he would show the world how to create success out of failure.

Early in his career Greenfield wore a hat to conceal his baldness. He soon realized that his baldness reinforced his efforts to appear older and more substantial. *(Historical Society of Pennsylvania)*

Edna Florence Kraus was seven years younger than Greenfield, but he was instantly smitten with this walking vision of the good and beautiful life to which every immigrant aspired. *(Historical Society of Pennsylvania)*

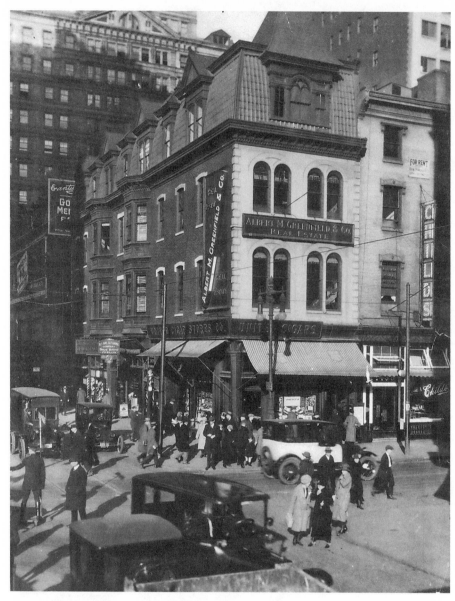

Greenfield understood the value of a high profile. In this photo, taken in November 1922, his name is splashed across his headquarters building at the corner of Fifteenth and Chestnut Streets in downtown Philadelphia. *(Albert M. Greenfield & Co.)*

Greenfield coveted the unfinished Bankers Trust Building on Walnut Street for its available bank charter. He bought the building before it was completed in 1923 and made it his permanent headquarters for more than forty years. The building's bay windows were added after this artist's conception was drawn. *(Historical Society of Pennsylvania)*

Greenfield's friendship with Dennis Cardinal Dougherty helped cement relationships between Philadelphia's Jews and Irish, two largely hostile ethnic groups. It also brought Greenfield the real estate business of the city's rapidly expanding Catholic archdiocese. The woman in this 1928 photo is Greenfield's wife, Edna. *(Historical Society of Pennsylvania)*

FACING PAGE:

A circle of Greenfield's friends gathered in 1928 to honor John Monaghan (front left, in light suit) upon his election as Philadelphia's district attorney. Greenfield stands just behind Monaghan in the center. Others in the picture include Lemuel Schofield, Philadelphia's director of public safety, as well as Greenfield's lawyer (front left), Mayor Harry Mackey (right of Schofield), Greenfield's early employer John J. McDevitt (second row, right, with arm draped over his shoulder), and Greenfield's associate Maurice Wurzel (light suit, directly behind Greenfield). To Wurzel's right, in the bow tie, is Daniel G. Murphy, a lawyer who publicly attacked Greenfield during Greenfield's feud with Moses Annenberg in 1938. *(Historical Society of Pennsylvania)*

1. Hon. John Monaghan
2. Mayor Harry A. Mackey
3. Lemuel Schofield
4. Murtha P. Quinn
5. A. M. Greenfield
6. John J. McDevitt
7. James J. White
8. Morris Brooks
9. Chas. H. Baruch
10. Furey Ellis
11. Maurice Wurzel
12. Paul Gottlieb
13. Wm. A. Carr
14. Daniel J. Murphy
15. P. J. McKewen
16. J. J. Fitzgerald
17. Father Jos. Sullivan
18. Coleman J. Joyce
19. Wm. Meenehan
20. J. A. Queeny
21. H. E. Purrington
22. Frank Boylan
23. George Huft

In the 1920s Greenfield seemed to loom over the Philadelphia landscape like some giant colossus, as suggested in this caricature by Charles E. Bell for the *Philadelphia Inquirer. (Albert M. Greenfield Foundation)*

The delicate and self-effacing Etelka J. Schamberg was the widow of a former associate. After her marriage to Greenfield in 1937 she blossomed into a talented portrait painter. (*Historical Society of Pennsylvania*)

Greenfield's five children were raised largely by nannies, maids, and butlers. This photo, taken about 1940, suggests their discomfort at growing up in their father's overwhelming shadow. From left are Carlotta, Elizabeth, Albert Jr., Gordon, and Patricia. (*Historical Society of Pennsylvania*)

Greenfield and his much younger third wife, Elizabeth Murphy (Bunny) Hallstrom, en route to Grace Kelly's wedding in Monaco in 1956. Bunny's pervasive influence softened Greenfield and smoothed his relationship with his children. *(Historical Society of Pennsylvania)*

Greenfield (right) developed a close friendship with his fellow extrovert, Philadelphia's reform mayor Richardson Dilworth (third from left). The man in the white dinner jacket is City Council president James Tate, who succeeded Dilworth as mayor in 1962. At left is state senator Israel Stiefel. *(Jay Stiefel)*

[PART IV]

COMEBACK

[9]

Merchant Prince

The largest single asset held by Bankers Securities in 1931 was the note for the $8 million that City Stores had borrowed in 1928 to acquire the controlling share of Lit Brothers. That loan had been secured by more than half of Lit's outstanding stock, and since the Lit's stock was pledged to cover the loan, in 1930 Greenfield had demanded and obtained a seat for himself on the Lit's board, "in order to look after the interests we had," as he later put it.[1]

Since the $8 million note represented more than two-fifths of Bankers Securities' assets, and since the City Stores chain was operating at a loss and had made no progress in reducing the loan principal in the depth of the Great Depression, conventional wisdom held that Bankers Securities was in a precarious position.[2] But where others saw impending disaster, Greenfield saw opportunity.

From his perspective on the Lit's board, Bankers Securities was not the holder of a note of dubious value; it was by far the largest creditor of City Stores, a chain that owned or controlled seven large department stores in six states, among them four of the finest and most established retailing names in the South, all of them at least as old as Greenfield himself: Maison Blanche of New Orleans, founded in 1887; Loveman, Joseph & Loeb of Birmingham, also founded in 1887; B. Lowenstein & Bros. of Memphis, founded in 1885; and Kaufman-Straus of Louisville, founded in 1879.[3] To Greenfield, City Stores was not a company tottering on the edge of bankruptcy at all; it was an empire generating $50 million in annual sales, with vast real estate parcels that he could manage through his real estate company. City Stores was the synergistic vehicle by which Albert M. Greenfield & Co. would return to profitability; it was also the vehicle by which Greenfield would shed his persona as a failed Philadelphia banker and reinvent himself as a merchant prince. The leverage he wielded through the $8 million note held by Bankers Securities was the wedge that he would use to launch his transformation.

Precisely when this notion first occurred to Greenfield is unclear; it may have trickled into the back of his mind even before Bankers Securities sold Lit's to City Stores in 1928. After Greenfield joined the Lit's board in 1930, the thought must surely have occurred to him—as it usually did in any business situation to which he was exposed—that he could do a better job of running the company than the existing management. But the existing management of City Stores would not go quietly, especially since it was run by a man cut from the same empire-building mold as Greenfield himself.

Rudolph J. Goerke was born in 1867 to parents who lived in the rear of their home furnishings store in Brooklyn.[4] As a young man working as a clerk there, he later claimed, he was so timid that he trembled to meet people. But one day (as a fawning Memphis newspaper profile put it early in 1931), Goerke "gave himself a good lecture and decided to bust loose and do things, come what might."[5]

Shortly thereafter, Goerke left his parents' shop to open a department store in downtown Brooklyn.[6] He liquidated that store in 1896, when he was twenty-nine, and used the proceeds to open a department store in downtown Newark, New Jersey. Over the next three decades, Goerke and his two sons operated department stores in Newark and Elizabeth, New Jersey, and Stamford, Connecticut. In 1925 he gained control of City Stores, which had been created just two years earlier.

Once in control, Goerke lost little time converting City Stores into his personal piggy bank. In June 1929 he arranged for City Stores to acquire Goerke's Newark department store for a price that was 50 percent higher than its actual value. He leveraged his title as a department store chain magnate into seats for himself on boards of banks in three cities where City Stores did business—including, after the Lit's purchase, Greenfield's Bankers Trust in Philadelphia as well as Greenfield's Bankers Bond & Mortgage Company.[7] In January 1930 Goerke persuaded the City Stores board to buy stock from a securities company he controlled. A real estate company owned by Goerke charged rent to City Stores units. When his company's department stores placed advertisements in newspapers, Goerke collected commissions from the stores. He also used his role as a potential advertiser to pressure newspaper publishers to buy City Stores shares that he owned, at higher-than-market prices.[8] Goerke paid himself inflated salaries from both City Stores and Lit Brothers—more than $170,000 even in the Depression year of 1931. He also continued to pay exorbitant salaries to his sons and various other relatives on his payrolls.[9] That is, Goerke engaged in many of the same synergistic pyramiding practices that Greenfield employed.

But where Greenfield had adjusted his corporate behavior and his personal compensation in response to the crash and its aftermath, Goerke resisted any adjustment to his lifestyle. By his own account, when he vacationed in Palm Beach early in 1931, "A Memphis banker told me I shouldn't have gone there this year in view of conditions, but I told him he's all wrong. I am going to live like I always live. People with money should spend as usual."[10] In 1931, when City Stores was $10 million in debt and operating at a loss, the company nevertheless paid out a total of $591,000 in salaries and rentals to Goerke family members and their interests.[11]

Like Greenfield, Goerke seems to have possessed a supreme confidence in his ability to achieve the impossible. "It's timidity that keeps people back," was one of his aphorisms. "Believe in yourself and go ahead."[12]

According to the same fawning newspaper profile:

> When things aren't going so well, Goerke believes in snapping out of it in some way or other. To see anyone just sit and "beef" irritates him. Not long ago when he visited one of the stores in another city, the millinery department wasn't doing so well. "Have all those mahogany fixtures done over in a cream color," he ordered.
>
> "Do you think that will help any?" the manager asked. "Danged if I know," Goerke replied, "but we'll be doing something to try to stimulate things."[13]

Greenfield was not so impressed by Goerke's leadership of either City Stores in general or Lit's in particular. Goerke, Greenfield told the SEC in 1941, "altogether did the kind of job in those days that was regarded as an improper one, and today would be considered as a criminal and illegal one."[14] As a Lit's director, Greenfield complained bitterly that Goerke was improperly draining assets from Lit Brothers to pay bills owed by City Stores.

In acquiring Lit Brothers in 1928, City Stores had assumed not only the $8 million debt to Bankers Securities (secured by Lit's stock) but also an unsecured $5 million debt to Halsey Stuart. With the national economy mired in the Depression in 1930, that investment house grew understandably nervous about recovering its $5 million principal and pressed Goerke to reduce the principal by $1 million. Over Greenfield's strenuous objections, Goerke responded by inducing the board of Lit's, which he controlled, to lend City Stores $1 million, which Goerke used to reduce the principal owed to Halsey Stuart. As Greenfield correctly pointed out, these actions jeopardized Bankers Securities, whose $8 million loan to City Stores was secured by Lit Brothers stock, whose value was being diluted by Goerke's actions. But Greenfield's concerns fell on deaf ears as long as Goerke controlled the Lit's board.

Like Greenfield in 1930, Goerke by 1931 was seriously overextended. Sales of Lit Brothers in that Depression year declined to $18 million, down from $30 million when City Stores acquired it in 1928. City Stores itself suffered an operating loss of $2.2 million in 1931.[15] In this situation, Goerke was preoccupied with stringing his creditors along until the economy recovered, in order to maintain his control of City Stores as well as Lit's and his various other enterprises.

One such gambit occurred on April 1, 1931, when Goerke visited Philadelphia. Greenfield's recollection of their dealings that day (as he recorded them in a memo to himself the next day) provides firsthand insight into two would-be titans jockeying with each other over matters large and petty, each searching for an advantage over the other. Goerke, wrote Greenfield, "called me on the phone and stated that he wished to have a talk with me. I told him I would be glad to see him if he would come up. He then invited me to lunch but I told him I was not going out but if he would come here I would have a sandwich for him too." At their 1:00 P.M. meeting, Goerke offered to pay Bankers Securities $800,000 toward the $8 million loan principal if Bankers Securities would extend the balance of $7.2 million for an additional three years. If Greenfield agreed to that plan, Goerke said, Halsey Stuart would agree to extend *its* loan to City Stores for another three years, thereby improving the likelihood that City Stores could pay off its loan to Bankers Securities down the road. Or, conversely, if Greenfield did not like that deal, Goerke said he could arrange for Halsey Stuart to pay $7 million for Bankers Securities' $8 million worth of City Stores notes right away. As Greenfield recalled, "I told Mr. Goerke that I was unable to recommend this proposition to my Board as it was a ridiculous proposition and therefore there was nothing to talk about."

At 1:30 both men went upstairs to the board meeting of Bankers Trust (which at that point was still technically a functioning corporation, even though its business had been suspended). Afterward, Greenfield invited Goerke back down to his office to discuss his proposal with Bankers Securities' president, Samuel Barker, and two other executives. Greenfield picks up the account again:

At about 3:15 P.M. the above gentlemen gathered in my office and Mr. Goerke stated that Halsey Stuart had a grudge against me personally and that he could get it straightened out if we would take $7 million for our notes.

I told him that I had no interest in Halsey Stuart's feeling against me and in any event would not pay $1 million or any money to change these feelings. I said to Mr. Goerke that I had no feeling against Halsey Stuart whatever and if a proposition could be had from them on a sane and profitable basis to Bankers Securities Corporation, I should be glad to discuss it with him further. In the meantime, he has submitted nothing that I could recommend to the board of the Securities Corporation.

If Bankers Securities declined to extent its loan to City Stores, Goerke warned (according to Greenfield),

> it would only result in litigation as he did not think the notes could be paid on December 1st, 1931 when due. I said to Mr. Goerke that I did not know of any litigation that would ensue and that I would consider the notes of City Stores Company backed by a majority of the Common and Preferred Stock of Lit Brothers good enough security to arrange to pay them when due.[16]

In this manner, Greenfield informed Goerke that in the event of a default he was ready and even eager to take possession of Lit Brothers, if not of City Stores itself.

By mid-1931 City Stores had reduced its debt to Halsey Stuart from $5 million to $2.8 million, but it still owed the full $8 million to Bankers Securities, and the principal remaining on both loans was due on December 1.[17] As Barker nervously put it in a memo to Greenfield in August, "The $8 million owing to us constitutes 41 percent of our assets. We are the big creditor of City Stores.... It is clearly impossible for City Stores to pay out of its present resources, and still live, anything like the $10.8 million becoming payable December 1."[18]

Barker urged Greenfield to accept a one-fifth payment of $1.6 million from City Stores by December 1 and extend the balance of $6.4 million for an additional four years. Taking over City Stores' money-losing business in lieu of a default, Barker argued, was something Bankers Securities neither wanted nor could afford. Besides, Barker added, "we owe special consideration as well as obligation to City Stores in that this debt owing us originated in a transaction by us and from which we realized large profit."[19]

Greenfield suffered no such trepidations or guilt pangs. He had other ideas, which he clearly had not shared with his president. "It is obvious that you are not acquainted with my efforts to date in this matter," he replied to Barker the next day. Goerke, he said, had already offered to pay at least $2 million "instead of $1.6 million suggested by you." Sounding like a man who was not at all troubled by the prospect of taking over a department store chain, Greenfield added:

> Naturally I am unwilling to recommend that our Board of Directors accept $2 million cash and renew the balance, even with additional securities pledged, until such time as I feel that Mr. Goerke has made every effort and every concession possible in order to secure the refinancing of the project elsewhere. This, in my opinion, he has not done as yet.
>
> While I am not familiar with merchandising methods and do not pass judgment on the operation of City Stores under Mr. Goerke, I am advised by people of experience in merchandising that his methods are not successful and that the record of Lit Brothers under his guidance has not been good.[20]

These memos—exchanged between men who worked on the same floor of the same building—reflected a widening gulf between Greenfield and Barker, who increasingly chafed at Greenfield's refusal to share power or even tell him what was going on. "Sam Barker did not like the position he was in," one of Greenfield's longtime lieutenants later recalled. "He was president of the bank, and president of Bankers Securities, but Albert ran the show, and Sam resented it."[21]

In a long letter to Greenfield on July 10, 1931, Barker unburdened himself:

> [Bankers Securities] has made very large profits, but it has also tied up its resources in considerable part in making the deal which resulted in the largest single profit realized during the life of the Corporation. At present its assets are largely frozen. . . . Stockholders are naturally restless and dissatisfied and will certainly become more so in the absence of dividends and with virtually no market for the stock.

Then Barker broached the difficult subject of Greenfield's one-man operating style: "I am sure we are not getting out of the organization the full value of what is in it. If not, it is my fault and yours. . . . No one man can do it. Nor can different officers sitting around at their desks and not keeping in close touch with what is going on."[22]

Greenfield replied five days later with a testy and reproving note that essentially refused to acknowledge Barker's concerns or Greenfield's own responsibility for them: "It is true that the assets are largely frozen, but the fact should not be lost sight of that we have approximately $5 million tied up in the Bankers Trust Company, of which you were president."[23]

Four months later, in discussing Bankers Securities' investment in a bond issue of Albert M. Greenfield & Co., Barker raised concerns about Greenfield's multiple conflicting roles:

I become more positively convinced, not only because our investment in these debentures is large, but because of your double position as president and chief stockholder of A.M. Greenfield & Company, also as guarantor of the $4 million issue, and as chairman of Bankers Securities Corporation, that the only right course will be at the board meeting Tuesday to refer the entire matter to a special committee instructed to ascertain all the facts. . . . For the fullest protection of Bankers Securities Corporation and your own best interests, and so that no one can ever doubt that this problem was given that special consideration which its importance and surrounding conditions make particularly necessary, the committee in this case should be appointed other than by you and consist of the most independent-minded men on the board.[24]

Greenfield's "Dear Sam" reply two days later suggests a man growing impatient with the restraints of technicalities devised by his lessers:

The matters contained in your letter we have discussed frequently and my thought was that these matters, together with any others which may come up in the same category, should be taken up when the final audit is made in December. Apparently from the contents of your letter, you think otherwise. After you have sent me today the sort of statement you think I should present at the meeting, I shall again discuss the subject with you in person and come to some decision with respect to bringing it before the meeting tomorrow.[25]

Meanwhile, with impending default looming over City Stores in November, Goerke grew increasingly desperate. To raise funds to reduce the company's debts, again he tried to milk Lit Brothers by declaring a 70-cent dividend on Lit's stock, more than half of which was still owned by City Stores.[26]

Then Goerke dispatched a New York lawyer named Robert Kast on a bizarre mission: Kast was to travel to Philadelphia under an assumed name and "by intimidation in voice and manner" frighten Greenfield into abandoning any attempt to remove Goerke from Lit's or City Stores. Instead, Kast—apparently having assessed the likely victor in the struggle—went to Greenfield and disclosed Goerke's scheme. Kast also appeared before a Bankers Securities board meeting on November 18 to propose a plan for the reorganization of City Stores that he had personally drafted.

"Confidentially, am I going to be taken care of?" Kast asked Greenfield afterward. "Will you be able to do anything for me?" Greenfield declined, just as he had declined Goerke's earlier (and equally dubious) offers.[27] Greenfield's interactions with Goerke and his emissaries appear to have reinforced Greenfield's doubts about Goerke's character and tactics—ironically, the same sort of doubts that the Clearing House Association bankers had harbored about Greenfield himself a year earlier.

A default on the two loans would have thrown City Stores into receivership, deposing Goerke from office and wiping out most of his investment. But when City Stores failed to repay the $8 million loan from Bankers Securities on December 1, 1931, Greenfield declined to exercise his right to the 501,000 Lit's shares as collateral. Instead, he left the $8 million debt on the City Stores books and, two days later, utilized his new leverage to elect five new directors to Lit's twelve-man board, all of them from his Bankers Securities organization.[28]

Greenfield's goal, it now developed, was not default but the *threat* of default: It was the tool by which he would drive Goerke from office. Once in charge of City Stores, Greenfield believed, he could recover that $8 million owed to Bankers Securities.

Goerke's strongest suit in this contest was Greenfield's lack of retailing experience, which Goerke emphasized in a letter to stockholders just ten days before the loan was due.[29] But by this point Halsey Stuart, to which City Stores still owed an unsecured $2.8 million, also believed that Greenfield was more likely than Goerke to pay off the debt. Thus emboldened, Greenfield approached Halsey Stuart and over several weeks devised a rescue plan for City Stores by which Goerke would surrender his voting stock to a voting trust chosen by Greenfield; Goerke and all his officers and directors would resign; Bankers Securities and Halsey Stuart would extend their loans to

City Stores for three more years; and City Stores would avoid being thrown into receivership.[30]

On the day the plan was presented—January 13, 1932—Goerke signed the agreement and sent his letter of resignation to City Stores, citing "a desire I have long had to be relieved of my responsibilities as president of your company, leaving to men younger than I the active management and direction of the company."[31] That same day, Greenfield and three of his associates were elected to the City Stores board, and Greenfield was elected chairman.

When City Stores failed to retire its $10 million debt by the new December 1934 deadline, Greenfield and Halsey Stuart worked out a new reorganization plan, under which Bankers Securities reduced City Stores' principal debt by $3.5 million in exchange for 58 percent of City Stores' outstanding stock. In effect, Bankers Securities paid $3.5 million for control of a corporation with assets exceeding $50 million.[32] And Greenfield, as a result of his high-stakes battle of nerves with Goerke, had transformed his securities firm into a merchandiser and himself from a financier into a department store magnate.

There remained the question of Greenfield's lack of retailing experience. He was above all a deal maker, not a manager or a merchant. His tendency to treat his executives as little more than errand boys invariably drove away capable men in favor of sycophants. Jack Cohen, president of Albert M. Greenfield & Co., resigned in July 1931 over what he called "irreconcilable differences" with Greenfield.[33] The long-suffering Samuel Barker, with whom Greenfield had created both Bankers Trust and Bankers Securities, departed the following year, submitting his resignation on April 22, 1932.[34]

City Stores reported some $3 million in operating losses from 1933 through 1935, when the company was being reorganized.[35] But after Bankers Securities firmly established control, City Stores gradually returned to profitability—assisted, to be sure, by new acquisitions (like the radio station WFIL) as well as the gradual recovery of the U.S. economy.[36] Lit Brothers, too, reported its first profit in fiscal 1935 after four years in the red and earned more than $1 million in the year ended January 31, 1937.[37]

The City Stores takeover defined Greenfield's operating style during the Depression. As properties (like City Stores) teetered on the brink of bankruptcy, Greenfield repeatedly appeared to snap them up for Bankers Securities at bargain prices and then pump new blood into them. He also went on the open market to acquire bonds on office buildings, often at 5 cents on the dollar, either through Bankers Securities or his Bankers Bond and

Mortgage Company. When he had acquired enough of the bonds in a given hotel, office building, or loft building to constitute control, he would demand that the building's management and insurance be turned over to his real estate company.[38] In this way Greenfield gained control of Philadelphia's Ben Franklin and Bellevue-Stratford hotels, the Steel Pier in Atlantic City, and any number of downtown Philadelphia office and loft buildings.[39]

In June 1933 Greenfield's name turned up on a list of favored clients of J.P. Morgan and Drexel & Co.—apparent evidence that he had returned to the good graces of Philadelphia's banking establishment.[40] That same year, in the process of acquiring a property management company in New York, Greenfield sought character references from Stevenson Newhall and Joe Wayne, and both of his presumed former adversaries complied enthusiastically—as well they might, since their loans to Bankers Trust had been repaid within a month after Bankers Trust shut its doors despite their refusal to offer it further assistance.

"I take pleasure in doing so," Wayne wrote, adding that Greenfield's "resourcefulness and industry are of the greatest value in this class of work and we ask for him your best consideration."[41] Newhall similarly gushed, "Through the difficult period of deflation, he has maintained his courage in an admirable way and displayed the same energy and close application to the solving of business problems which contributed to his success."[42]

Yet Greenfield's energy and courage were probably not as valuable as his encyclopedic connections. "He had a faculty for remembering just about everything told to him about a personal relationship," his second-in-command, Gus Amsterdam, later recalled. "He used his relationships to work out business deals—his ability to call up almost anybody—head of a bank or company—to find out if a property was available."[43]

Greenfield constantly peppered his associates with details of far-flung relationships that might be useful in closing a deal. One memo he sent in 1936 to Maurice Wurzel, president of Greenfield's Bankers Bond & Mortgage Company, suggests the extent of his prodigious memory:

In re: 2015 Chestnut Street
   Judge Harry E. Kalodner, when he was practicing law, represented an Estate or was Guardian for a one-eighth interest in mortgage [for] $72,000 secured on the above property. This mortgage I think was held by the Franklin Trust Co., and when it closed the Land Title and Trust became substituted trustee. Judge Kalodner's former client was Sophie Freberg, now represented by her brother-in-law, Morris E.

Kendall. Kendall, at the Judge's suggestion, told the Land Title he was glad to go along with the offer made by Bankers B. & M. to Land Title at $22,000. The Land Title advised Kendall that they have obtained an appraisal of the value of the property, indicating a value of $42,000 and they have advised the other parties interested in the mortgage that unless the $42,000 is paid, foreclosure proceedings will be commenced against Bankers B. & M. This is *confidential* information.

Judge Kalodner will be glad to discuss the matter with you at your convenience and he may be able to make some valuable suggestions. Please get in touch with him.

A.M.G.[44]

The critical element in his financial recovery, as Greenfield had recognized all along, was not money; but it also was not his steadfast faith in real estate. As his ancestors in Poland and Russia could have told him, it was what he carried around in his head.

In some respects the Great Depression was a more traumatic experience for rich families than for the poor, and more so for the totally dependent wives of the rich than for their husbands. But Edna Greenfield had already fallen apart well before her husband's bank collapsed, and in any case, Albert—whatever his deficiencies as a husband and father—was skilled at shielding his already dysfunctional family from the financial consequences. Such were the cold-comfort consolations of domestic life in the Greenfield household.

When the Bankers Trust closed, Greenfield's five children ranged in age from fifteen down to three. Because of Edna's germ phobia and her other apparently psychosomatic ailments—as well as her frequent travels to hospitals and institutions in New York, Europe, and elsewhere for therapy—the children continued to be raised by maids and butlers, although not as many as before. Gordon, as the oldest son, was shipped off to boarding school at Lawrenceville and then to Princeton—places that represented Albert's notion of the elite upper class to which he aspired but where Gordon unhappily found himself suspended in a kind of limbo between Jewish and gentile society, the sort of sphere where Greenfield himself flourished but his less confident children invariably suffered.

Albert and Edna rarely quarreled and seem to have never quite fallen out of love with each other. But between his preoccupation with his businesses and her preoccupation with her neuroses, both lacked the time and energy to tend to their relationship, not to mention each other's sexual needs. By the early 1930s Greenfield seems to have concluded that he could not give Edna the time and emotional support that she needed. In her role as a perpetual patient, Edna had become the one great challenge that Greenfield, for all his creativity, optimism, and energy, seemed incapable of solving. Consequently, he seems to have welcomed her absences as a way of avoiding his own emotional shortcomings.

February 1932 found Edna's secretary advising her friends and relatives that "she is spending a great deal of her time in New York now."[45] June found her at a private psychiatric facility in Ossining, New York, where a friend wrote to her, "Don't be dismayed or alarmed by the inevitable set-backs that are part of the experience at Stony Lodge"; Edna apparently remained there long enough to order stationery imprinted with her name and the institution's address.[46]

When Edna checked into Corey Hill Hospital in Brookline, Massachusetts, in late 1934 for consultation about a back problem, Greenfield typically encouraged her not to hurry back. "If you can ease the discomfort and pain you have in your back," he wrote, "that will go a great way towards enabling you to enjoy more your everyday activities. The short period of time you spend shut-up within the hospital is comparatively unimportant if Herr Professor succeeds in doing the job."[47]

Far from disturbing Greenfield, Edna's long absences liberated him to focus his energies on his work. But about this time Greenfield learned that Edna had taken a lover in New York, whom she apparently visited more or less every week. Greenfield appears to have reacted to this news with neither anger nor bitterness but with embarrassment. Edna's affair, he recognized, could potentially undermine one of his most valuable assets: his carefully crafted self-image. How, after all, would it look if a man known for his magnetic charm and his ability to master any situation was in fact being cuckolded by his own wife?[48]

For that reason, Greenfield in 1935 arranged for an amicable divorce in which, as one of his children put it, Edna relieved him of their marriage. The divorce was granted that October in Chihuahua, Mexico, on the grounds of incompatibility. That same day Edna married her lover, Charles Paine, and moved to New York permanently.[49]

Greenfield, who retained custody of the five children, appears to have been happy for Edna, even if he never deluded himself that Edna had "relieved" him of anything. Within less than a year, her marriage to Paine broke up, and Edna—now styling herself "Mrs. Kraus Paine"—returned to Philadelphia, albeit still dividing her time between an apartment on Rittenhouse Square and the Barclay Hotel in New York.[50]

"She ran away [from Albert] thinking that this great, big, handsome man would take care of her," Greenfield's daughter-in-law later summarized Edna's interlude with Paine. "But, of course, she realized afterwards that the only man who ever took care of her was Father."[51]

Edna was still the mother of Greenfield's children, of course, and for the rest of his life Greenfield voluntarily sent her a monthly support check for $800 and cheerfully made himself available when she asked for further help, as she often did.[52]

Shortly after her marriage to Paine fell apart, Edna resumed her therapeutic travels, journeying to Silver Hill in New Canaan, Connecticut, for a series of lectures by Dr. William Terhune on such subjects as "the nature of nervousness," "skill in living," and "the tranquil mind." She shared transcripts of the lectures with Greenfield and scribbled a note to him inside one of them: "I do and do not want to accept this new therapy. Am both hopeful and afraid that there might be something in it. . . . All these reasons for doubting the possibility of a cure through this kind of therapy—may be pure rationalization dictated by neurotic fear."[53]

The correspondence suggests a curious turn in their relationship. No longer legally bound to each other, Albert and Edna began to relate in a new atmosphere of maturity and mutual respect, in which Edna discovered that she did indeed have something to contribute: a keen understanding of the human frailties that Albert preferred to ignore, especially in himself. In effect, she became his good if slightly flaky old friend—more psychologically sophisticated than he was—and perhaps his only acquaintance (with the possible exception of J. David Stern) capable of bringing Albert down to earth when he grew too full of himself.

In one of Dr. Terhune's booklets that Edna sent Greenfield—"The Nature of Nervousness"—she underlined one paragraph in particular:

The maladjusted child or even adult has many feelings of discomfort which may give rise to misconduct. An otherwise good child may steal as the result of a subconscious conflict; similarly, people lie without reason, fight unnecessarily, give way to sexual irregularity when their lives have been otherwise blameless, and commit other anti-social acts. . . . Misconduct, then, is frequently the result of a neurosis, and such forms of misconduct can best be treated by curing the nervousness giving rise to it.

The phrase "sexual irregularity" was underlined by Edna and the word "Albert" scrawled in the margin nearby—perhaps Edna's way of calling Albert's attention to what she believed was her problem, or possibly his. In any case, their sexual relationship, which had long since ended, had become a matter that Edna now felt free to discuss candidly with him.[54]

Their otherwise amicable divorce did produce one collateral casualty: For all practical purposes, it ended Greenfield's friendship with Cardinal Dougherty, an implacable foe of divorce. Years later the Philadelphia builder Matthew McCloskey patched up the relationship, but by then Dougherty was near death.[55]

Another long-standing friendship fell by the wayside in 1936, when William Fox sought bankruptcy protection and Greenfield declined to rush to his rescue, as the two men had done for each other just a few years earlier. "I always felt that Fox's word was good for millions," Greenfield explained at one of Fox's bankruptcy hearings. "At one time I knew he was worth $25 to $30 million, but as he continued to speculate in the market I got the feeling toward 1935 that he had lost all or the greater part of his fortune. I decided that in the future any loans to him should be made on collateral only."[56]

On balance these personal losses seemed a small price to pay for the remarkable condition in which Greenfield found himself by the middle of 1936. His financial and family crises behind him, Greenfield had again clawed his way up to a plateau from which, it seemed, he could not be dislodged. "He has come back again with the same amazing agility that got him to the top in the first place," *Fortune* magazine marveled that June:

> Seated at his desk on the second floor of the Bankers Trust Building on Walnut Street under signed portraits of Herbert Hoover and Franklin D. Roosevelt, surrounded by pictures of the kiddies, George Washington, and Thomas Mitten, together with a document from the Pope announcing that he is a Papal Knight, a Chinese motto: "Be not disturbed at being misunderstood; be disturbed at not understanding," a grandfather clock, and a cuspidor, he reaches out into the city in diverse and mysterious ways. He has the ability to attach himself to all types and classes of people and make them do what he wants. And he can still raise cash quicker than almost anyone in the city."[57]

Fortune's reference to the signed portraits of both the sitting Democratic U.S. president and his Republican predecessor was a telling detail. For Greenfield had not merely transformed himself commercially; even more remarkably, within just a few years he had transformed himself politically as well.

[10]

New Deal Democrat

By the spring of 1932, as Greenfield's friend and hero Herbert Hoover prepared to seek reelection, one in every four working Americans was unemployed.[1] After three years of the most severe economic depression in American history, Hoover seemed likely to be turned out of the White House that fall, taking with him the entire business-oriented governing philosophy that had characterized Republican administrations since 1921.

The great crash as well as Greenfield's own business reversals had dashed whatever political ambitions he might once have harbored. His confrontation with Philadelphia's bankers had also soured him on the guiding Republican philosophy that society functions best when government leaves businessmen to their own devices.

Yet Greenfield's passion for politics persisted—partly out of his practical business need for friends in high places, partly out of his psychological need to be at the center of events, but mostly out of a genuine concern for the future of his adopted country—to which, as he saw it, he owed everything. Like most entrepreneurs, Greenfield had long bridled at government efforts to restrain or regulate business. But just as Greenfield possessed an uncanny sense of timing in his personal dealings, so he seemed to understand in the early 1930s—as most of his fellow Republicans did not—that the American system was malfunctioning and might require a thorough overhaul in order to survive.

The Democratic presidential favorite, the liberal New York governor Franklin D. Roosevelt, won an overwhelming majority of delegates on the first ballot at the party's convention in Chicago that June but failed to gain the necessary two-thirds majority in a field of ten candidates. His leading rival, the former New York governor Alfred E. Smith, drew formidable support from New York's Tammany Hall machine and many members of the Democratic National Committee, as well as the convention's host, Mayor Anton Cermak of Chicago, who packed Chicago Stadium with Smith supporters.

When word reached the *Philadelphia Record* that Roosevelt had finally been nominated on the fourth ballot, Greenfield's friend David Stern—the city's only Democratic newspaper publisher—spontaneously unlocked his pantry, liberated its stock of bootleg liquor, and launched a small celebration in his back office. As the night wore on, this office party expanded as friends dropped in to offer their congratulations.

"I was surprised," Stern later recalled, "to find how many men of affairs had been in secret accord with the *Record*'s editorial policy but had not dared to reveal their sympathy."

Stern was especially surprised to find Albert Greenfield among his visitors that night.

"Al, don't tell me you've come over to our camp?" Stern greeted him, according to Stern's later recollection.

"No, I won't say that yet," Greenfield replied. "It would give you a swelled head. I dropped in to congratulate you on picking the right horse. I admit I'm thinking it over. The Hoover Administration has us in an awfully tight fix. Perhaps your theory of spending our way out of the Depression is right."[2]

For a customarily decisive man, Greenfield had difficulty deciding whom to support in the 1932 election. Technically, he remained a registered Republican and a Hoover admirer. Through his political contacts that year, he secured several million dollars in government loans from Hoover's newly created Reconstruction Finance Corporation that saved his Bankers Bond & Mortgage Company from failure.[3] But almost from the moment Roosevelt was nominated, events—as well as his friend Stern—pushed Greenfield toward the Democrats.

The day after Stern's impromptu office party, Roosevelt broke with political tradition, dramatically flying to Chicago to accept the Democratic nomination in person for the first time at a national convention, where he pledged "a new deal for the American people." But in Pennsylvania—then the nation's second most populous state—his victory in November was by no means assured. The day after FDR's speech, the two leaders of the state Democratic Party, who had supported Al Smith, declared they would not work for "a Bolshevik candidate." John O'Donnell, chairman of Philadelphia's Democratic City Committee, explained to Stern that he could not campaign vigorously for Roosevelt, either, because the city's Republican boss, Bill Vare, was "an old friend" who had kept O'Donnell on the payroll for many years and had even paid the rent of Democratic headquarters as well, in order to maintain the public illusion of an opposition party.[4]

The state Democratic leaders shortly resigned and turned the Pennsylvania Democratic Committee over to Roosevelt men like the oil magnate Joseph Guffey and the Pittsburgh political reformer David Lawrence.[5] But they needed at least $100,000 to finance Roosevelt's statewide campaign, and, according to Stern, they had no idea where they could get it.

When the new state Democratic leaders met with Stern in his office, Stern told them he could not personally contribute more than $1,000. He did offer to print a million copies of a four-page campaign newspaper, which would save the party a $30,000 printing bill. But that help barely scratched the surface of the state campaign's funding needs.

On a hunch, Stern phoned Greenfield and told him what was transpiring in his office. Stern knew his friend well. "Al hated to be left out of anything," Stern later recalled. "He came over to tell us he would raise $25,000. By dinner time enthusiasm had replaced gloom."[6] In this manner Albert Greenfield took his first cautious step into the Democratic camp.

Still, that fall Greenfield bet one of his business associates $500 that Hoover would win the election. A week before Election Day he attended a Hoover rally at the Academy of Music and donated $25—no great display of enthusiasm, to be sure. He never publicly indicated which candidate he voted for in 1932 (although his close relatives said he voted for Roosevelt).[7]

Greenfield's divided loyalties notwithstanding, in January 1933, following Roosevelt's election, he and Stern were invited to meet with the president-elect. Their purpose was to argue against Roosevelt's plan to devalue the dollar by reducing its gold content, which Stern and Greenfield felt would fail to stop deflation. Roosevelt, of course, was less interested in their economic advice than in flattering two potentially influential supporters from the nation's third-largest city.[8]

Roosevelt himself was an immensely appealing figure to American Jews. His New Deal, with its emphasis on social welfare, cultural pluralism, and the rights of labor, spoke directly to the traditional Talmudic concerns of an excluded and long-persecuted minority group. In Roosevelt's administration, Jews became White House insiders in significant numbers for the first time: Roosevelt's "Brains Trust" included Treasury Secretary Henry Morgenthau Jr., the Harvard law professor Felix Frankfurter, the lawyers Benjamin V. Cohen and Samuel Rosenman, the financier Bernard Baruch, and the labor leader Sidney Hillman. It was no surprise, then, that whereas only 6.8 percent of Jews had voted Democratic in the 1924 presidential election, that percentage swelled to 77.3 percent by the time Roosevelt ran for reelection in 1936.[9]

Greenfield was hardly immune to these feelings. But switching sides in an overwhelmingly Republican city was a risky proposition for a man so heavily invested in Philadelphia. Consequently, Greenfield moved uncharacteristically slowly and obliquely while he made up his mind. By 1934, while still claiming allegiance to the Republican Party, Greenfield raised funds behind the scenes for the election of George H. Earle III and Joseph Guffey, helping them to become, respectively, Pennsylvania's first Democratic governor since 1890 and Pennsylvania's first Democratic U.S. senator since 1874.[10]

But Greenfield's gradual conversion to the Democratic Party also reflected his growing involvement with David Stern, whose aggressive and creative stewardship of the *Record* seemed to demonstrate that a liberal editorial philosophy made good business sense.

"Liberalism," Stern contended in a circular distributed to potential advertisers, "is an attitude of mind. It is intellectual independence. It strives to keep issues out in the open for open discussion. . . . Because the *Record* supplies the materials for thinking . . . it has made circulation gains unmatched in the standard size newspaper field."[11]

Under Stern, the *Record* became a newspaper that, as *Fortune* magazine put it, "irritates the 'real' Philadelphians no end."[12] When the City Council passed a wage tax in November 1932, Stern defiantly announced from the *Record*'s editorial page that he would refuse to collect it from his employees; the publisher, he wrote in the third person, "would rather serve six months in jail than submit to such tyranny." The chastened Council members subsequently repealed the tax. By successfully crusading for the repeal of Sunday "blue laws" (which among other hardships prohibited baseball games on Sundays) and the legalization of liquor sales in Pennsylvania, Stern won a loyal following that boosted the *Record*'s daily circulation from 114,000 when he acquired it in 1928 to 315,000 in 1936, overtaking its morning rival, the *Inquirer*. The *Record*'s Sunday circulation growth was even more dramatic: It rose from less than 100,000 to more than 400,000.[13]

Greenfield, as Stern's silent partner at the *Record*, often propped up the paper through rough financial periods by paying in advance for ads placed by Lit Brothers, Albert M. Greenfield & Co., and the Philadelphia Bonwit Teller department store. While Stern goaded Greenfield in new political directions, Greenfield pushed Stern to enter new businesses. When the publishing magnate Cyrus H. K. Curtis died in June 1933, the trustees of his estate put the *New York Post* up for sale and Greenfield urged Stern to buy it, just as he had urged Stern to buy the *Record* five years earlier.

The *Post* boasted a distinguished history: It was founded by Alexander Hamilton in 1801 and edited for fifty years by William Cullen Bryant, the first champion of trade unionism in the United States. But by 1933 the *Post* was also losing $1.25 million a year, or twice as much as the Curtis family's *Philadelphia Inquirer* was earning. Stern and most of his business associates feared that buying the *Post* would jeopardize their success with the *Record*. Greenfield and President Roosevelt were among the few who urged Stern to make the deal. ("The *Post* is an historic institution," Roosevelt told Stern. "You must preserve it.")

Stern's account of how Greenfield maneuvered him into buying the *Post* against his better judgment is a classic portrait of the irrational exuberance that infected anyone exposed to Greenfield's salesmanship.

After a raucous party in New York, Stern later wrote, "Al and I had spent what was left of the night at a New York hotel. Up at his usual time, indefatigable Al had called his office to say where he could be reached, and had been 'thoughtful' enough to tell his secretary to notify my office."

Greenfield awakened Stern with the news that Curtis Bok—Cyrus Curtis's idealistic grandson—was on the phone. Stern and Bok had become friends during the 1932 presidential campaign, when Bok had been one of the few young scions of wealthy Philadelphia families who joined the liberal camp. Alone among the trustees of the Curtis estate—who wanted to close the *Post* immediately to halt its losses—Bok desperately hoped to find a buyer for the *Post* rather than sully his grandfather's memory by folding it.

"Tell him I'll call him back," Stern mumbled.

"Here he is, Curtis," Greenfield said into the phone, shoving the receiver into Stern's hand.

"The *New York Post* closes today," Bok told Stern. "Dave, you still have time to save a great newspaper." No cash would be required, Bok said, and the property included a building worth $1 million.

But to Stern, Bok's offer was equivalent to leaving a dying baby on his doorstep.

"Sorry, Curtis," Stern replied. "The answer is still no."

Yet as he was hanging up, Stern later recalled, Greenfield stayed his hand.

"Do me a favor," Greenfield whispered. "Ask for half an hour to think it over and call back."

When Stern hung up the phone, Greenfield offered to raise $1 million that Stern could use to fund his operations at the *Post*.

"Not enough," Stern insisted. "To pull the *Post* out of the red will take at least $3 million. It's losing $25,000 a week."

"We'll raise $3 million," Greenfield insisted. It was never easy for even a fully awake businessman to say no to Greenfield, and Stern's resistance—already on edge from the previous night's carousing—was rapidly wearing down. The moment he hung up the phone, Stern later recalled,

> Al went to work on me. He is a consummate salesman. He painted the picture of a knight in shining armor, fighting for the New Deal, planting his standard on the pinnacle, New York. I was unmoved. Finally, in disgust, he said, "As for me, I would rather fall off the top rung than never climb the ladder." That taunt got me.

At three o'clock that afternoon, Stern and Greenfield met Jack Martin, Cyrus Curtis's stepson-in-law, at Greenfield's New York office. By five o'clock they had consummated the deal. On December 15, 1933, Stern became publisher of the *New York Post*.[14]

By 1935, Greenfield—still nominally a Republican—was nevertheless working aggressively with the building contractors John B. Kelly and Matthew McCloskey to transform Philadelphia's Democratic Party from an appendage of the Republican Vare machine into a viable opposition. Together they built a coalition of Jews and Irish Catholics in support of Kelly's candidacy for mayor that year. In a city that had never elected a Catholic mayor, Kelly drew more than 333,000 votes that fall, by far the largest Democratic vote in the city's history. Although Kelly lost to city controller S. Davis Wilson—a Democrat-turned-Republican who had spearheaded the city's suit against the PRT and Greenfield in 1931—the election firmly established a two-party system in Philadelphia for the first time.[15]

Wilson's campaign exploited widespread anti-Semitic fears that Jews were becoming too powerful (Wilson claimed that Bankers Securities was helping to finance the Democratic Party). But after the election Greenfield enlisted Wilson's support in a civic fund-raising campaign to induce the Democratic Party to hold its 1936 National Convention in Philadelphia. Such a gathering in a supposed Republican stronghold was the last thing Philadelphia's Old Guard wanted, but Greenfield—as chairman of what he dubbed the "All-Philadelphia Citizens Committee"—persuaded the city's overwhelmingly conservative Republican business leaders to rise above partisan politics and focus instead on the millions in economic benefits that a

convention would bring to Philadelphia (including, of course, his own hotels). The effort raised $200,000 for the Democrats and won their unanimous
approval of Philadelphia as their convention site.

Greenfield's rewards for this feat included the honor of delivering the
convention's concluding address, in which Greenfield, in effect, finally and
publicly announced his political conversion, as well as Philadelphia's. "Your
battalions may leave here tomorrow," he told the Democratic delegates,
with grandiloquent hyperbole that for once turned out to be prescient, "but
your invasion will leave indelible memories and influence on what we used
to describe as this Republican city. It is even possible your tremendous enthusiasm might cause future orators to refer to this old Quaker City as the
Democratic stronghold of Pennsylvania."[16]

As Greenfield had anticipated, his speech was condemned by Philadelphia Republicans who had supported his bipartisan convention drive and
now felt betrayed.[17] He was virtually ostracized by his fellow property owners for switching parties.[18] But there was no turning back.

During the convention week, Greenfield played host to Roosevelt himself
at Oak Crest Farm in Montgomeryville, and thereafter Greenfield made frequent trips to the White House to confer with FDR and his "Brains Trust."[19]
While politicians valued Greenfield above all for his fund-raising ability,
Roosevelt genuinely relied on Greenfield to keep him abreast of developments in what was rapidly becoming an important Democratic city, just as
Greenfield had predicted to the convention.[20]

Greenfield's newfound influence with FDR inevitably yielded unexpected benefits—psychological as well as financial. When the Philadelphia
Company for Guaranteeing Mortgages collapsed in 1936, Greenfield (as was
his custom) acquired many of its defaulted mortgages and bonds for a small
fraction of their original value. In the wake of its bankruptcy the federal government contemplated suing its board members for mismanagement. The
board members—many of them from the same social circle as the prominent
Philadelphia bankers who had rejected Greenfield six years earlier—now
turned to Greenfield for help. Greenfield, no doubt relishing the moment,
contacted his friend in the White House. Shortly thereafter, the government
dropped its plans to file a suit.[21]

Even after he switched parties, Greenfield kept a picture of Herbert
Hoover in his office, alongside a signed photo that Roosevelt had sent him.[22]
He had no quarrel with Hoover, he insisted, and continued to feel "the
warmest personal regard and friendship" for Hoover until the former president died in 1964.[23] But Roosevelt, he said years later, had saved the country
from economic revolution in 1932.[24]

Greenfield was well aware that many people saw him as a political op-
portunist. When the Republicans finally returned to power with Dwight D.
Eisenhower in 1952, he remarked privately, "Now everyone will expect me to
be a Republican again." Then he smiled as if to say, "No way."[25] His change to
the Democratic Party, he insisted in a private letter in 1959,

> was born of nothing other than a conviction, shared by countless
> other business and cultural leaders and others throughout this na-
> tion, that, in the national and worldwide social and economic crisis
> experienced by this country in the days of the Great Depression, the
> Democratic Party understood most clearly the problems and needs
> of our nation and possessed the program which would promote eco-
> nomic and social recovery for our people.[26]

Greenfield's *personal* feelings about Roosevelt were less sanguine. After a lunch with the president at the White House, one of Roosevelt's aides
brought in a large bowl of fruit and set it in front of the president. "We continued talking," Greenfield later recalled, "and he did not offer me one piece
of fruit the entire conversation." Here Greenfield waved his finger reprov-
ingly. "That's the real test of a man. I never liked FDR after that."[27]

In November 1936, a year after his divorce from Edna, Greenfield sold his
house in Germantown and moved a step up, into the former home of the
gas utilities tycoon Clarence H. Geist on Drexel Road, then the elite street in
Overbrook Farms, a leafy enclave of West Philadelphia that amounted to a
suburb within the city. Drexel Road's name was no coincidence: Overbrook
Farms was a planned community developed in the 1890s by two Drexel & Co.
partners, E. T. Stotesbury and Anthony Drexel's son-in-law James W. Paul.[28]
Stotesbury had sold his holdings there in the 1920s, and Geist, practicing the
gentile variation of upward real estate mobility, had moved across the city
line in 1933 to Philadelphia's Main Line suburbs—a place that Greenfield,
with his intense loyalty to the city, had despised even before his confrontation with Philadelphia's Main Line bankers in 1930.[29]

This capacious thirty-room showplace, built in 1904, came complete
with a broad veranda, a grand old winding staircase in the front hall, a baby
grand piano, a billiard room, and a bowling alley in the basement. Here
Greenfield installed himself with his three remaining school-age children
and six servants, as well as two "outservants," including a chauffeur for his
Rolls Royce.[30] All the mansion lacked was a woman's presence as mistress of
the household.

Greenfield's divorce from Edna in 1935 occurred less than two months before the death of Jesse Schamberg, a Philadelphia real estate broker who had worked for and with Greenfield and the Mastbaum brothers while intermittently operating in business for himself.[31] Schamberg's relationship with Greenfield was very much an off-and-on affair—in 1925 Schamberg claimed Greenfield owed him money for his interest in two settled properties, and in 1927 Schamberg accused Greenfield of disparaging his management of Greenfield's New York office.[32] But in 1921 the two men had been close enough to travel to Europe with their wives.[33]

Nevertheless, the two men were cut from very different molds. Where Greenfield modeled himself after Benjamin Franklin and Thomas Mitten, Schamberg appears to have preferred Beau Brummell. He was a fancy dresser who lived well above his means in a townhouse on Delancey Place, one of central Philadelphia's most elegant streets.[34]

Schamberg's pretentious personality contrasted with that of his wife, the former Etelka Joseph of Cincinnati, a delicate and self-effacing woman with a worldlier perspective than was usually found among ladies in Greenfield's circle. Etelka had attended Dr. Sachs's School for Girls in New York at a time when that institution was molding the daughters of New York's German Jewish upper class into formidable adults like the archaeologist Hetty Goldman and the *New York Times* matriarch Iphigene Ochs Sulzberger. Etelka had also spent five years studying art in France and Switzerland.[35] Among Jesse Schamberg's many detractors it was said that he had married Etelka so she could teach him how to dress.

When Schamberg died in December 1935 at the age of fifty-eight, Etelka was left with more debts than assets. She was forty-eight at the time—exactly the same age as Greenfield—and, of course, both of them were available. They were already well acquainted and ideally suited to each other's needs as well: Etelka needed a man to take care of her and her unmarried twenty-three-year-old daughter; Greenfield needed a woman who could smooth his remaining rough edges and guide him gracefully into a loftier social milieu.

Their marriage in October 1937 in many respects offered both Greenfield and Etelka the kind of moral and emotional support that neither of them had known with their first spouses.[36] For their honeymoon, Greenfield indulged Etelka's desire to travel to Mexico and meet Diego Rivera. Greenfield arranged the meeting with the legendary muralist and acquired, on the spot, *Nieves Orozco*, a gouache Rivera painting on a canvas-covered panel.[37]

Soon after their wedding, Etelka and her daughter, Yvonne, moved into the house on Drexel Road, and Greenfield began hosting the sort of large gatherings he would never have contemplated with Edna in Germantown.

After the first of these—Yvonne's wedding in December 1938—Greenfield began a tradition of throwing large New Year's Day parties, to which he invited scores of prominent figures in Philadelphia politics, the courts, the professions, business, and society.[38]

Etelka, for her part, now found the leisure and wherewithal to take up painting. One of her first subjects, painted some two years after remarrying, was Greenfield's Oak Crest Farm in Bucks County. Soon, instead of spending her days at home waiting for Greenfield to return from the city, she set up a studio at Oak Crest. Here she immersed herself in her new craft with much the same zeal that Greenfield applied to his business deals. Etelka also enlisted as her mentor Lazar Raditz, a Philadelphian well known for his portraits of various Rockefellers and DuPonts as well as prominent executives, doctors, and judges.[39]

To a large extent Etelka and Albert went their separate ways—she to her studio, he to his businesses. Often he was home without her while Etelka stayed at Oak Crest. But their separations seem only to have enhanced their mutual respect and affection.[40] Like Greenfield, but unlike Edna, Etelka possessed the confidence to seize opportunities on her own initiative—emboldened, to be sure, by the material security that Greenfield provided her. Before long, she had blossomed into a talented painter whose portraits, still lifes, and landscapes were exhibited at respected museums and galleries around the country, among them Philadelphia's fabled Pennsylvania Academy of the Fine Arts.

But one subject Etelka never painted was her husband. "She knows he smiles all the time," a magazine writer reported. "She couldn't do justice, she believes, to his 'toughness.'" That was one hint of Etelka's ability to observe her husband with a fresh pair of eyes and to cut to his essence. "He never asks" for things, Etelka told the writer. "He just expects."[41]

Unlike Edna—whose emotional needs seemed bottomless and consequently represented a constant reminder to Greenfield of his inadequacies as a husband—Etelka's needs were solely material and, consequently, reinforced Greenfield's preferred image of himself as the answer to a woman's prayers. With his stable new marriage, his new home in Overbrook Farms, his new political affiliation, his newly acquired department store empire, and his truce with his creditors from the 1920s, Greenfield by the late 1930s seemed to have assembled all the necessary pieces of a new identity. But he was about to discover that a man's past is not so easily discarded.

David Stern's elation over Roosevelt's renomination in July 1936 was compounded by good news on his northern publishing front: His gamble on the *New York Post*, which he had acquired at Greenfield's urging three years earlier, appeared to be paying off. Its circulation had climbed to 250,000. Its losses, once $25,000 a week, had been cut to $25,000 a month.[42] Stern had reason to believe that the *Post* might break even by the end of 1937.

But that August brought the news that the *Philadelphia Inquirer*, the morning competitor to Stern's *Record*, had been sold by the Curtis estate to Moses L. Annenberg, a shrewd, aggressive, and immensely wealthy publisher whose previous record in Chicago, Milwaukee, and Miami suggested a man determined to eliminate his competitors by fair means or foul.

Annenberg and his older brother Max were East Prussian Jews whose parents had immigrated to Chicago in the 1880s, when Max and Moe were small boys. Both brothers had come of age during Chicago's bloody newsstand wars that ensued after William Randolph Hearst invaded the Windy City in 1900 to challenge the dominant *Chicago Tribune*.[43] As circulation directors of Hearst's new morning and evening papers, the Annenberg brothers hired gangs of tough-fisted agents to intimidate dealers and newsboys into taking Hearst's papers and dropping the *Tribune*'s. The combat escalated from fistfights, broken bones, and wrecked newsstands to a shooting war in which five or six men were killed.[44]

By the time the actual shooting had started, Moe Annenberg had left the Hearst organization in 1906, following a quarrel with Max.[45] In their later years Moe and Max each claimed to have been a respectable businessman whose reputation was sullied by the public's confusion with his more violent brother. In any case, during their formative years the two Annenberg brothers had been paid obscenely large sums of money by Hearst to break the law and consort with known gangsters. When asked years later to explain how he had become a millionaire before he was thirty, Moses Annenberg had replied, "It is the difference between the well-fed house dog and the hungry wolf. I had a large family and I had to hunt or starve. I learned how to hunt and I kept it up."[46]

In the early 1920s, in partnership with a tough, beefy Chicago gambler named Jack Lynch, Moe had acquired two tip sheets for gamblers, the *Daily Racing Form* and the *Morning Telegraph*; then he had acquired the wire services that served bookmakers and horse parlors, so that he commanded a virtual monopoly on racetrack information.[47] To maintain that monopoly in what was, after all, an illegal activity, Moe Annenberg was said to pay an annual retainer to Chicago's Capone mob. Whenever a rival racetrack tip sheet was started, it was said, someone broke into the printing plant and wrecked the machinery.[48] Before his arrival in Philadelphia, Annenberg had used his Miami newspapers to launch a muckraking campaign against the city's mayor and police chief after they began raiding the bookie joints that paid Annenberg's wire services thousands every week.[49]

By the time he bought the *Inquirer* in 1936, Annenberg was said to be making between $6 million and $14 million a year, but his appetite seemed insatiable.[50] And where the Depression had driven Greenfield from the Republican Party into the Democrats' camp, it had produced the reverse effect on Annenberg, who saw Roosevelt's New Deal as the first step toward a socialist dictatorship.

Like Greenfield, Annenberg was a man of tremendous energy and ingenuity who yearned for social acceptance; unlike Greenfield, he was a dour and awkward soul. The *Inquirer* was to be the vehicle by which Annenberg shed his rough-and-tumble reputation and cloaked himself with new respectability that he planned to bequeath to his only son, Walter.[51] But his old habits died hard.

Five months earlier, the *Inquirer* had merged with its morning rival, the *Public Ledger*. Now Annenberg set out to eliminate his only remaining morning competitor: Stern's *Record*. Under Annenberg's ambitious plan, by removing Philadelphia's only Democratic voice he would stifle liberal ideology, destroy Pennsylvania's Democratic Party, and, in the process, ingratiate himself with what he perceived as Philadelphia's business establishment. The notion that Annenberg could spend his way to social acceptance in Philadelphia bore uneasy echoes of E. T. Stotesbury's similar attempt more than a decade earlier—echoes of which Annenberg as a newcomer was obviously unaware.

Greenfield and Stern were both, of course, highly competitive by their natures. But when Stern learned that Annenberg was coming to Philadelphia, he later confessed,

> I had a sinking feeling. This change of ownership threw a monkey wrench into my plans. The Curtis-Martin organization [at the *Inquirer*] was soft competition. My second team could deal with them. Now the opposing team was putting a Red Grange in the lineup. I ought to be in Philadelphia to meet this threat. But here I was tied up in New York.[52]

As was his practice, Annenberg assaulted the *Record* on multiple fronts simultaneously, combining lavish and creative circulation promotions with editorial attacks on Stern's friends and supporters. "I can lose five dollars to Stern's one dollar," he said, drawing on lessons he had learned from Hearst.[53] By 1937 Annenberg's heavy-spending game plan did indeed pull the *Inquirer* ahead of the *Record* in circulation while cutting the *Record*'s earnings by a third and the *Courier-Post*'s in half—earnings that Stern had counted on to offset the losses of his *New York Post*.[54] But Annenberg lacked Greenfield's instinctive ability to size up and win over his adversaries.

The very month he took charge, Annenberg abruptly canceled Lit Brothers' advertising in the *Inquirer* without giving any advance notice.[55] He apparently hoped that by denying valuable advertising space to a store controlled by Greenfield, he could pressure Greenfield into abandoning Stern. Annenberg had already neutralized one rising Philadelphia Democrat by hiring Richardson Dilworth as his corporate counsel; indeed, Dilworth later confided to Stern that he had delayed his political career and suppressed his liberal leanings because he could not afford to give up Annenberg's annual $50,000 retainer.[56] But Greenfield would not be so easily sidelined. In denying advertising space to Lit Brothers, Annenberg failed to reckon with Greenfield's love of a good fight, not to mention the fact that Lit's enjoyed advertising outlets at three other Philadelphia newspapers.[57]

Stern, who was hardly powerless, phoned the White House in fear that Annenberg was about to send strong-arm goons into Philadelphia to intimidate city newsstands. That call brought FBI agents to Philadelphia, as well as a squad of state police sent by Governor Earle—a Democrat like Stern—and a special detail of detectives to guard the city's newsstands, sent by Philadelphia's nominally Republican mayor, S. Davis Wilson.[58]

These mutual retaliations between Annenberg and Stern merely reinforced each man's fears about the other. Stern's phone call to the White House stoked Annenberg's paranoia about the New Deal's dictatorial powers. Precisely who was the aggrieved party in this power struggle—Annenberg with his millions and his goons, or Stern with his political friends in high places—is difficult to say. Suffice it to say that both men perceived themselves as threatened by the other. And both men believed, along with most of their fellow publishers, in using their newspapers to promote their commercial and political agendas.

Still, although Annenberg often announced his intention to "put Dave Stern out of business," he refrained from attacking Stern personally.

"He was more vulnerable in a mud-slinging contest than I was," Stern later remarked. "Instead of going after me, he pilloried my friends and supporters."[59]

Greenfield, the most vulnerable of Stern's friends because of his past wheelings and dealings, at first turned the other cheek to Annenberg, assiduously cultivating Annenberg's friendship just as he had done with Joe Wayne and Stevenson Newhall. When Annenberg's son, Walter, needed a place to live downtown, Greenfield found him an elegant bachelor suite on Rittenhouse Square.[60]

One Tuesday in the spring of 1937, while traveling by train to his New York office, Greenfield was startled by a stranger who extended his hand and introduced himself: Moses Annenberg. "You're a son of a bitch, Greenfield," Annenberg supposedly told him, "but you're my kind of son of a bitch and I wish you were with me and not with Stern." With that, Annenberg returned just as abruptly to his seat, leaving the bewildered Greenfield wondering whether to be flattered or annoyed.[61]

A few days later, having broken the ice, Annenberg invited Greenfield to lunch. But Greenfield, who always preferred to operate on his home court, instead invited Annenberg to take lunch with him and a few of his lieutenants in the Bankers Securities Building (just as he had done with Rudolf Goerke in 1931), and he went as far as to accommodate the menu to Annenberg's dietary needs.

At that lunch, according to Greenfield's later recollection, Annenberg "said to me that he admired me because of the manner in which I stood up and paid my debts and did not take the Bankruptcy Act as so many others did, and he told me in his own language that he thought it was a good job."[62] On parting, Annenberg told Greenfield, "I like you, Al. But you're financing David Stern. I've got to destroy you to destroy Dave Stern."[63]

Annenberg seems to have been disarmed by Greenfield's hospitality. Upon returning to his office, he made a clumsy attempt to reciprocate Greenfield's charm offensive:

> I again want to thank you for your thoughtfulness in going out of your way to provide me at your luncheon with black bread and boiled beef, to which I am more accustomed traditionally than to the fancy broiled squabs that you seem to enjoy.
>
> However, please be assured that no sarcasm is intended, but that little stunt of yours merely proves unusual ability in your efforts to properly and pleasantly entertain your guests."[64]

Annenberg subsequently invited Greenfield to be his guest at the 1937 Kentucky Derby in May, but Greenfield declined.[65] That was the last cordial interaction between them. That summer the *Inquirer* launched a series of articles that extensively rehashed the collapse of Greenfield's Bankers Trust Company and even went so far as to paint Greenfield as a radical leftist.[66] The *Inquirer*'s campaign against Greenfield, which continued for more than a year, constituted one piece of Annenberg's larger campaign to establish himself as a Republican power in Pennsylvania.

These attacks put Greenfield in an awkward position. On the one hand, he longed to be perceived as a Philadelphia gentleman, the sort who would never stoop to wrestling in the gutter with the likes of Annenberg. On the other hand, he hated to be perceived as a helpless punching bag; instinctively he longed to fight back.

Greenfield appears to have resolved this dilemma by venting his spleen in letters to Annenberg and other perceived enemies that he never mailed. In the unsent draft of one such letter to Annenberg in July 1938, for example, he wrote:

Ever since last October you have been having a lot of fun with me in your paper. . . . If that is what you have in mind, you can dish it out and I can take it. I hope you will be equally cheerful if the positions are reversed.

I am sure there is nothing personal in your attentions. It is purely business with you, as you explained to me last fall.[67]

Whether Greenfield actually intended to mail such missives or was just writing them as a form of anger therapy is unclear. What *is* clear is that Greenfield and Stern possessed more effective tools for retaliation, which they soon unleashed.

In the summer of 1938 a Pennsylvania legislative investigation, led by Greenfield's friend and lawyer Lemuel B. Schofield, concluded that Annenberg's racetrack wire was taking in $1 million daily. The result was passage of a law prohibiting telegraph services to bookie joints in Pennsylvania.[68]

Annenberg struck back in September when his preferred candidate for governor, the conservative Republican Arthur James, squared off against Greenfield's preferred candidate, the Democratic incumbent George Earle. Both morning papers resorted to the tactic of publishing news reports of speeches by their respective partisans, along with full texts of the speeches themselves. Thus, on September 20 the *Inquirer* headlined and reprinted a radio address by a Philadelphia lawyer, Daniel Murphy, claiming that Greenfield's businesses owed the failed Bankers Trust and Franklin Trust hundreds of thousands, perhaps millions of dollars—debts that Murphy said Governor Earle's administration had ignored. The *Inquirer* followed the next day with another front-page story, headlined "CLOSED BANK DEBTS UNPAID BY GREENFIELD."[69]

Greenfield responded that night with a long and detailed radio address, insisting that *he* was the prime victim of the Bankers Trust closing—it "knocked the props from under most of the enterprises in which I had investments," he said—and noting that the State Banking Department had refused to accept the settlements that he had worked out with all his other creditors.[70] But like Annenberg, Greenfield preferred to play offense. "Moses Hitler Annenberg," he added gratuitously, had a five-year plan to take over America and was like "a dog who had returned to its vomit."[71]

The *Inquirer* responded in kind the next day with an editorial masquerading as a news report:

Mr. A. Greenfield, who is a Russian by birth, is thoroughly familiar with the five-year plan, and perhaps knows more about it than anyone connected with the *Philadelphia Inquirer*. It is the same old story. He judges others by the ideas born in his own mind.

Since he is one of the bulwarks of the Democratic Party in Pennsylvania, it might be appropriate to point out that many of the Soviet Russian ideas, with which he is so familiar, are being tried out in the State under the direction of his good friends in Harrisburg.

The publisher of the *Inquirer* has no personal quarrel with Greenfield and cannot be responsible for the almost daily news developments concerning Greenfield's business conduct.[72]

As the quarrel escalated, Annenberg filed a libel suit against Greenfield shortly thereafter.[73] Three weeks after Greenfield's radio speech, with the election drawing near, an eight-column headline across the *Inquirer*'s front page reported another radio speech by the Republican lawyer Murphy: "GREENFIELD'S FIRM DREW $300,000 FROM BANKERS TRUST, LAWYER SAYS."

The article, accompanied by a photostat of a supposedly damning promissory note signed by Greenfield, contended that in 1930 Greenfield's personal holding company had drawn money from Bankers Trust five days before it closed and implied that Greenfield had done so knowing the bank was about to fold. The story neglected to mention that the transaction was merely a routine renewal of an old note that fell due that day and was promptly redeposited.[74]

For nearly eight years Greenfield had kept his silence about the closing of Bankers Trust—believing, as he put it, that "no good purpose would be served by telling the public what it was too late for them to know." But the *Inquirer* story finally forced his hand. Three days later, in a radio address he delivered over station WFIL (which Lit Brothers owned), Greenfield discussed what he called "The Wrong of 1930" in detail, concluding with this peroration:

> I am not complaining for myself, but the closing of Bankers Trust was a wrong done to the people of Philadelphia. . . . It closed only because in 1930 a small, secret group of powerful men had the power of life and death over banks. Today that has been corrected. A Democratic President and Congress have taken steps to place the control of the banking structure of the country where it belongs instead of in the hands of a few men in Wall Street and their satraps in the provinces.[75]

Then Greenfield announced that he had that day procured a warrant for Annenberg's arrest on a charge of criminal libel. In spite of Annenberg's "poisonous attacks," he insisted, "I am not active in the management of the Democratic Party. Much less am I one of its leaders. I am one of its followers because I believe in its principles." He urged Pennsylvanians of both parties to "show by their votes that politics in this state has no stomach for terrorism and intimidation, the methods of Moses Annenberg."[76]

The bitterness of the campaign seemed to have taken on a life of its own beyond either man's control. "A visitor to this city during the last week or two," the New York Times observed, "might have reached the conclusion, judging from radio addresses and newspaper accounts, that it was a campaign between Mr. Annenberg, the Inquirer's publisher, on the Republican ticket, and Albert M. Greenfield, Philadelphia real estate broker, as the Democratic nominee."[77]

In the midst of this feud, Annenberg, Greenfield, and Stern were approached by three Reform rabbis who feared that this unseemly public squabble among Jews was fanning the flames of anti-Semitism.[78] Annenberg assured the rabbis that he shared their concerns. But when his attacks on Greenfield continued, the rabbis turned to Greenfield.

Jews in the Midwest and Far West, wrote Rabbi Morris S. Goodblatt, president of the Philadelphia Board of Jewish Trustees,

> are alarmed at the effect which this personal controversy is having upon public opinion in regard to Jews in general. . . . We must once more appeal to your conscience and your sense of responsibility to

the Jewish people. We earnestly hope that the fear of God and the love of your people will cause you to heed this solemn warning.[79]

When he received Goodblatt's letter, Greenfield was incensed, both by its failure to condemn Annenberg and by what he felt was its implication that he was at fault. To Greenfield, the rabbis' implied message was: *What German Jew would stoop to quarrel with a Russian?*[80] "Why don't you go to Mr. Annenberg?" Greenfield snapped, according to his daughter. "*I've* been in this city for 40 years." His written response was only slightly more restrained: "If Jewry fails to denounce Annenberg as a traitor to its own ideals, Jewry must be prepared for whatever consequences follow."[81]

Political mudslinging customarily ends on Election Day, after which it serves no further purpose. But the bitterness between Annenberg and Greenfield festered even after the campaign ended with the victory of Annenberg's candidate, Arthur James. Both men's libel suits were still alive the following spring; early in May 1939, Greenfield's lawyers—including Schofield, who had investigated Annenberg for the Pennsylvania legislature—were preparing to bring in witnesses from Chicago and Florida to testify about Annenberg's gangster connections.[82]

The two libel suits were finally withdrawn that month with the signing of mutual public apologies. Yet more serious recriminations now arose on both sides of the quarrel. A federal investigation of Annenberg's racing wire operations came to a head on August 11, 1939, when a federal grand jury indicted Annenberg and his son, Walter, on ten counts of tax evasion. To spare Walter a prison sentence, Moses Annenberg agreed to plead guilty; he paid $9.5 million in back taxes and penalties and in July 1940 began a three-year prison sentence at the federal penitentiary in Lewisburg, Pennsylvania.[83]

Annenberg blamed Greenfield and Stern for his troubles. "I wrecked the New Deal in Pennsylvania to show people how to get back to sound business principles," he told his *Inquirer* colleagues, "and I'm going to be crucified for it. That's the kind of country we're living in."[84]

Greenfield's investigator Lemuel B. Schofield had indeed unearthed much damning evidence about Annenberg while preparing for the libel suits.[85] But Greenfield insisted he had had nothing to do with Annenberg's prosecution. According to Stern, the government's investigation had begun in 1933—three years before Annenberg had arrived in Philadelphia—when a Baltimore scandal sheet owned by Annenberg printed a scurrilous story about the FBI director, J. Edgar Hoover, a man notoriously prickly about personal criticism.[86] According to two of Roosevelt's cabinet members, the impetus for the Annenberg investigation had come from FDR himself, who said at one meeting, "I want Moe Annenberg for dinner."[87]

When Greenfield learned of Annenberg's conviction, he remarked to Stern, "He who digs a grave for his neighbor is apt to fall into it himself. Moe said he was going to destroy you and me. Now he's on his way to prison."[88] That private comment was all the satisfaction Greenfield took from his former adversary's downfall. Two years later, when Annenberg was diagnosed with a brain tumor, he was paroled, apparently with Greenfield's support. That humane gesture allowed Annenberg to die at home in July 1942.[89] "This ailment," Stern later generously suggested, "probably accounts for his eccentric conduct in Philadelphia."[90]

The change of administrations in Harrisburg in 1939 brought with it the dismissal of Greenfield's ally Irland Beckman as secretary of banking and his replacement by John C. Bell Jr., scion of a wealthy and distinguished Philadelphia family (his brother, Bert Bell, had helped create the National Football League in the 1920s). Bell was a hard-shell Republican, an anti–New Dealer closely connected to many of the "small secret group of powerful men" whom Greenfield had attacked during the campaign.[91] Once in office Bell moved, in his capacity as receiver of the Bankers Trust and Franklin Trust, to sue Greenfield for funds owed to both banks—the only creditors that had not settled privately with Greenfield.

"There have been so many rumors or reports of Greenfield's alleged hidden assets," Bell announced in June 1940, "that in fairness to all parties concerned a searching analysis and investigation of these alleged resources should and will be made in open court by my attorneys who will spare no effort to protect the interest of the depositors."[92]

Greenfield's obligations to the two closed banks consisted of endorsements and guarantees he had given in the 1920s for real estate transactions, secured mostly by properties whose value had been sharply reduced after the crash of 1929. But the prospect of a Republican fishing expedition into his personal finances forced Greenfield to do what his pride had prevented him from doing for nine years: The very month that Bell filed his suit, Greenfield sought bankruptcy protection from his remaining creditors—that is, from Bell—in federal court.[93] In effect, Greenfield chose to throw himself on the mercy of a Democratic U.S. District Court judge appointed by Roosevelt with Greenfield's support—fortuitously, Harry Kalodner, an old friend, a former reporter for Stern's *Record*, and himself a former debtor of Bankers Securities—rather than a Republican political appointee in Harrisburg.[94]

Greenfield's initial proposal to restructure his debts by paying them off in full over fifteen years, plus interest, was accepted by virtually all of his remaining creditors except Bell. Some of Greenfield's creditors would be dead by 1955, Bell said, and, consequently, he sought to force the immediate liquidation of Greenfield's assets.[95] (Greenfield, for his part, argued that it would be unfair to give Bell terms that were more favorable than those he had already reached privately with his other creditors.)[96]

For partisan political purposes, Bell managed to prolong Greenfield's bankruptcy proceedings through Pennsylvania's 1942 gubernatorial election and elicited Greenfield's admission that he had registered some of his real estate holdings and securities in other people's names. But Bell failed to substantiate the existence of any vast hidden Greenfield assets.[97] Following the Republican election victories in November 1942, Bell agreed to a settlement and Greenfield was dismissed from bankruptcy.[98]

Beckman, following his unceremonious replacement by Bell as secretary of banking, vented his bitterness to Greenfield shortly after leaving office in January 1939:

It still seems incredible to me that, as a career man in banking, I would receive but three hours' notice, after fifteen years with the Department, and that my laziest executive should be selected, in the face of strong support from banking and other interests. However, the sooner I can forget the ridiculousness of the situation, the better it will be for all concerned.[99]

Greenfield, in his reply to "Dear Beck," customarily saw Beckman's half-empty glass as half full:

It is true that in a democratic government there is very little appreciation for the services one renders, but one does have the great satisfaction of having the freedom that goes with this form of government, which makes up for all the lack of appreciation and the disappointments encountered.[100]

In this, as in all situations, Greenfield prided himself on his ability to grasp the big picture. That was the peg on which he had hung his willingness to settle his suit with Annenberg in May 1939. He wrote in his one-paragraph statement concerning that settlement:

In these days of tragedy for millions of the helpless abroad, with threats of war and turbulence in every edition of the news, I have decided to submerge my own feelings and spare the community the unseemly spectacle which trial of these actions would involve, even though the amends offered by the originator of a base and unfounded charge against me are so grudging and ungracious.[101]

It was Greenfield's way of acknowledging that the squabbles of two prideful men—two prideful *Jewish* men—were, after all, trivial next to the nightmare that was unfolding in Europe, especially for Jews, at that very moment.

[11]

Reluctant Zionist

A dolf Hitler's war against the Jews forced Greenfield (and, of course, many assimilated Jews throughout Europe and America alike) to confront his ambivalent feelings about his own Jewishness. In effect, it raised the question: Was Greenfield the second coming of Benjamin Franklin, as he sometimes liked to believe? Or was he above all a Jew, as Hitler preferred to believe?

Much of Greenfield's career had been characterized by his insistence that Jews were as American as anyone else, if not more so. "No people have a deeper understanding and appreciation of the American ideals of freedom in life and thought than the Jews," he declared in 1940.[1] And so he asserted his right to define himself above all as an American or a Jew or anything else, depending on the circumstances.

Thus, on the one hand, Greenfield had long cherished his status as a Jewish community leader. In his young adulthood Greenfield taught for many years with the Hebrew Sunday School Society and also developed an apparently genuine rapport with Joseph Krauskopf, the longtime rabbi of Philadelphia's Reform Congregation Keneseth Israel.[2] His prodigious fundraising efforts for Jewish causes after World War I were legendary. In the 1920s Greenfield quietly became a financial angel to the *Jewish World*, a Yiddish-language daily newspaper in Philadelphia; in 1940, to save the paper from folding, he acquired it outright for $15,300.[3]

Few prominent Americans had perceived the threat posed by Hitler as early as Greenfield did, or as forcefully. Precisely what accounted for his prescience is unclear. But when Hitler came to power in 1933, Greenfield was quick to advocate a boycott of German goods and services. "The danger to our brethren in Germany is much greater than any of us seem to realize," he wrote in a letter sent to his fellow Jewish businessmen, "and if the Hitlerites are permitted to go on as they are doing, we must face the fact that hundreds of thousands of Jews will either slowly starve or be driven to suicide in the very near future."[4] At Greenfield's urging, that year Lit Brothers removed German-produced merchandise from its shelves. But other large Jewish-controlled businesses, like the Macy's department store chain in New York, declined to boycott Germany, either out of reluctance to call attention to their Jewishness or fear of counter-boycotts against their businesses, or concern that anti-German pressure by American Jews would provoke even harsher Nazi measures against German Jews.[5]

On the eve of Rosh Hashanah in 1935, Greenfield issued a public statement comparing Hitler with a modern-day Haman—the villain of the Purim story in the Book of Esther—and calling on American Jews to unite in combating anti-Semitic propaganda, which he characterized as a global poison designed to "crush the Jew, to destroy his spirits."[6]

Greenfield similarly refused to support the Berlin Olympics in 1936. When the treasurer of the U.S. Olympic Fund solicited him for a contribution, Greenfield replied:

I cannot bring myself to believe any good purpose can be served by encouraging large numbers of American tourists to visit Germany this year. . . . There are times when for reasons of expediency one goes to parties in the homes of people one does not like; but this is one case when even to be seen there connotes an approval of the life and actions of the head of the house.

Jews, he noted, were hardly Hitler's only likely victims: "Not only Jews, but Catholics, liberals and other non-conformist minorities are subjected to mental and physical barbarity by the legal measures the present German government is enforcing."[7]

After the Nazis vandalized synagogues through Germany in the Kristallnacht riots of November 1938, Greenfield urged President Roosevelt to sever diplomatic and commercial relations with Germany.[8] He also lobbied Roosevelt to loosen U.S. immigration laws in order to provide refuge for persecuted European Jews. And he prevailed on his estranged friend Cardinal Dougherty to urge the president to provide humanitarian assistance to

Jewish refugees in Palestine.[9] None of these efforts succeeded in altering U.S. government policy, but they suggest the extent of Greenfield's willingness to speak out about the ominous situation in Europe.

Yet since his earliest days as a real estate broker Greenfield had consciously sought to differentiate himself from other Jews in the eyes of gentile society. He was never an observant Jew in the religious sense. He maintained an interest in Jewish culture and history, supported the Reform Congregation Keneseth Israel, and occasionally attended services there, but he never attached much importance to Judaism as a religion.[10] Deep down, Greenfield probably shared the low regard for all religions professed by his older brother William, who believed that all clergy, rabbis included, were corrupt. But unlike William, Albert kept such opinions to himself rather than jeopardize his standing in either the Jewish or gentile community.[11]

As was the case when he flouted Ashkenazic Jewish tradition by naming his son after himself, Greenfield repeatedly asserted his right to define Judaism on his own terms. His home—first with Edna and then with Etelka—was very much a secular household, where gifts were distributed to the children for Christmas, not Hanukah.[12] He staffed his household with German help, following what he believed was the practice of the Protestant upper class. (Only when he discovered, in the early 1930s, that his faithful German servants were taking young Albert Jr. to Nazi Bund meetings did Greenfield replace them with an Irish staff headed by a devoted Irish butler.)[13]

Greenfield's children received little or no Jewish instruction, and he sought to enroll them at some of the prestigious boarding schools that had sprung up between 1880 and 1910 to accommodate the desire of America's then newly rich Protestant industrial barons to mold their children into a national upper class.[14] Greenfield, a newly rich baron of a later generation, similarly perceived the private school tie as a vehicle to attach his family to America's upper class, but he outdid the nineteenth-century tycoons by sending his sons, Gordon and Albert Jr., to schools of even more venerable lineage: Lawrenceville in New Jersey (founded in 1810) and the Quaker-operated William Penn Charter in Philadelphia (founded by Penn himself in 1689).

In the lower grades, Greenfield's children attended the secular (but predominantly Jewish) Oak Lane Country Day School only because he failed to enroll them at private schools favored by upper class Protestants, to his great frustration.[15] When his fourteen-year-old daughter Carlotta was in her final year at Oak Lane in 1934, Greenfield tried to enroll her at Baldwin, an exclusive private girls' school in the suburb of Bryn Mawr. He wrote to Edna in Paris:

I have received another letter from Miss Johnson which seems to be just a polite stall. I have given up hope of getting Carlie into this school and am giving consideration to other schools but have not yet determined where I want to make application. The next time, we must make certain in advance that she will be accepted. It is increasingly difficult to get a Jewish girl into a first class boarding school unless the child has an exceptional record, and such a record Carlie, as you know, has not made.[16]

Not until two years later did Greenfield's persistence finally pay off with Carlotta's admission to Baldwin.[17]

Two years after that struggle, Greenfield's fourth child, Patsy, was similarly finishing up at Oak Lane. Greenfield applied on her behalf to Rosemary Hall, a prestigious girls' boarding school in Connecticut. But Patsy was rejected because, as Greenfield explained to Edna, "their quota of Jewish girls is filled. At least, so they claim."[18]

Above all, Greenfield balked at the limitations that a "Jewish" label implied. His personal heroes were neither Moses nor the Maccabees, nor even the Rothschilds or Jacob Schiff, but Benjamin Franklin and Napoleon.

He was especially sensitive about being lumped with other Jews as a group. When the supporters of Robin Hood Dell, Philadelphia's summer music venue in Fairmount Park, sent out a fund-raising letter signed by twenty-five prominent supporters, Greenfield was quick to notice that his name had been bunched together with the other four Jewish names on the list. "I regard this as a mistake," he wrote in a memo to his vice president, Samuel Rosenbaum, who was a leader of the campaign, "and hope you can change same by scattering them."[19]

Similarly, Greenfield complained to his newspaper publisher friend David Stern about what he considered the excessive number of Jewish names in the *Philadelphia Record*'s chatty "Round the Town" gossip column. "I have for several months spoken to Tommy [Stern's son] about so many names of our own group being mentioned in this column," Greenfield wrote. "It reads more like a column in the *Jewish Exponent* or the *Jewish World* than a column in a metropolitan newspaper where our own people are less than 13% of the population."[20]

When he suffered the slings and arrows of anti-Semitism—as inevitably happened to any Jew who ventured with such alacrity into gentile circles—Greenfield's preferred response was to ignore it, at least for public consumption, no matter how much it may have rankled him privately. His campaigns against anti-Semitism in behalf of European Jews under Hitler were never accompanied by any suggestion that he himself had suffered from anti-Semitism. Although Greenfield privately blamed the failure of the Bankers Trust on the anti-Semitism of his fellow bankers, he took pains to avoid such an assertion in public.[21] His preferred posture toward anti-Semitism, as in all matters concerning himself, was to accentuate the positive, ignore the negative, and avoid painting himself as a victim.

While Greenfield downplayed his Jewish identity for public consumption, he was quick to respond when his credentials as an American were questioned. In 1937 Governor Earle appointed Greenfield to the largely ceremonial post of chairman of the Pennsylvania Commission for the U.S. Constitution Sesquicentennial. It was the sort of honor Greenfield savored, linking him as it did to his adopted country's Founding Fathers. But a nativist group called the Patriotic Order Sons of America attacked Earle for appointing an immigrant to such a role—a choice that, the Sons of America said, slighted the 75 percent of Americans who were native-born.

"The celebration of the 150th anniversary of the Constitution of the United States," the group declared in its telegram to Earle, "calls for a man of American birth and background." It was unfair, the group insisted, "to select a man said to be born in Russia who is known purely for his commercial and political enterprise to head such an important American celebration."[22]

Greenfield responded to this challenge as if he had been preparing for it all his life—which in a sense he had. "It is true that I was born on a spot outside the United States," he declared. "My parents did not consult me about the matter. As they brought me to Philadelphia when I was about three years old, I confess I have no recollection of any country as my home except America."[23]

Whether Greenfield was three when he came to America or—as seems more likely—between four and six, his point had been made. Governor Earle, like Greenfield, refused to budge, and the Patriotic Order said nothing more on the issue.

W hen Hitler invaded Poland in September 1939, Greenfield was fifty-two years old and seemingly at the peak of his financial and political powers. In less than ten years he had overcome a bank failure and a mountain of debt, he had reinvented himself as a department store magnate as well as a nationally influential Democrat, and he had survived a bitter proxy fight with Rudolph Goerke and an equally bitter political feud with Moses Annenberg.

Yet these personal triumphs seemed trivial amid the global existential challenge posed by Nazi Germany. World War II, like the Great Depression before it, shaped and changed virtually every member of Albert Greenfield's generation. The war took the lives of as many as 70 million people and shattered many times that number; it threatened the very survival of democracy as a viable form of human governance; and, of course, it specifically threatened the survival of Hitler's special target, the Jewish people, more than 5 million of whom were exterminated by the Nazi regime for no crime other than their Jewish lineage.[24]

Yet when Hitler finally went to war against Poland, France, and Great Britain in 1939—in effect confirming Greenfield's grim warnings of the past six years—Greenfield himself seemed to fade into the background. In early June 1940, as the world watched in shock while the German army advanced toward Paris, Greenfield was preoccupied not only with his recently filed personal bankruptcy but also with digesting and reorganizing the Loft Candy Corporation, a vast (albeit mismanaged) confectioner and retailer that Greenfield acquired that month—not with his own money (for he was technically bankrupt) but through a syndicate comprising his companies and his friends.[25] At the time, Loft's was losing nearly $200,000 annually, but it appealed to Greenfield because its 161 retail shops in New York, New Jersey, Pennsylvania, and Connecticut spent more than $1.5 million annually on leases suitable for management by Greenfield's real estate company.[26]

After the United States finally entered the war in December 1941, many prominent executives suspended their business activities to devote themselves full-time to America's war effort. William Knudsen, president of General Motors, persuaded corporate innovators to give up their salaries and perquisites to join him as "dollar-a-year men" in Washington. The construction and shipbuilding magnate Henry J. Kaiser recruited executives from blue-chip companies like Lockheed, Chrysler, Boeing, and General Electric—again, for a dollar a year—to produce everything from dams to tanks to ships to steel.[27] The banker C. Jared Ingersoll, scion of an Old Philadelphia family, temporarily stepped down as president of a railroad holding company to become coordinator of national defense industries in the Philadelphia area.[28] The Chicago sand-and-gravel magnate Henry Crown—like Greenfield a Jewish immigrant from Eastern Europe—became a colonel in the U.S. Army Corps of Engineers, where he supervised the production of inflatable decoy landing barges that subsequently were credited with saving hundreds of lives in the Allied invasions of France and the Philippines.[29]

Amid this national emergency—which he, more than most others, had foreseen—Greenfield too contemplated volunteering his services to the government. But his business, political, and legal concerns monopolized his time to such an extent that he seems to have made no serious attempt to join the war effort, and no government agency tried to recruit him.[30]

Of course, the financial challenges that Greenfield faced—assimilating new acquisitions, mollifying investors, reducing debts—were common to all big businesses. The difference between Greenfield and the "dollar-a-year men" like Bunky Knudsen and Henry Kaiser was that they ran large, structured bureaucracies in which no individual was indispensable, not even the chief executive. Greenfield, by contrast, continued to manage his far-flung operations as a one-man band, even as his City Stores chain expanded to employ thirty thousand workers in seven states. His top executives, many of them quite capable in their own right, were paid to carry out his orders, not to make decisions on their own (as Samuel Barker, among others, had learned to his regret). Greenfield's enterprises simply could not function without him.

In any case, it seems to have been recognized—by both the White House and Greenfield himself—that Greenfield was a unique executive who functioned best when running his own team rather than as a player on someone else's and that even as a leader, Greenfield's skills could not easily be transferred to some operation other than his own.[31]

Thus, in Greenfield's case, the most striking thing about World War II is how little this global catastrophe affected his own life. Confronted with an existential threat to his nation as well as to his people, this master organizer—this seemingly inexhaustible font of energy, this Jewish community leader who prided himself on his vision and his patriotism—somehow assumed the role of spectator.

"I am very proud of my associates who have gone into the Service in aid of our country," Greenfield explained in a 1943 letter to his right-hand man, Gus Amsterdam, then a captain with the U.S. Army Air Corps in Texas.

> At the same time I am very much over-worked, trying to carry not only my own load, which you know is quite heavy, but also of those who have gone. However, it will be over some day and, if I survive, I shall have the satisfaction of being associated with men who have made their contribution to our country in this emergency.... We are busier than ever at the office, business being good—in fact, too good because of the absence of some of my associates and the shortage of good help, making it necessary for me to spend long and tedious hours at my desk. I suppose I can put that down as my contribution to the situation.[32]

This was a startling confession from a man who claimed to regard work as "the supreme luxury of life." It suggests the frustration of a mover and shaker who thrived at the center of things but in this case had manipulated himself to the sidelines.

As a prominent figure of reputed great wealth, Greenfield was accustomed to fielding pleas for help—some from worthy causes, some from impoverished Philadelphians, some from Bankers Trust depositors, some from Europeans claiming to be his relatives—which he customarily handled on an ad hoc basis. But cries for help from a new source—European Jews desperate to escape Hitler's grasp—escalated in 1938 as Nazi Germany intensified its anti-Semitic policies and Hitler's domain expanded into Austria and the Czech Sudetenland. In 1939 Greenfield's own brother-in-law and attorney, Gilbert Kraus—whose office was located in Greenfield's Bankers Securities Building—seized the moment by traveling surreptitiously to Austria and organizing an undercover mission that rescued some twelve hundred Austrian Jewish children from Hitler's reach.[33] Yet Greenfield's response to this new avalanche of despair remained haphazard.

In one case beginning in 1939, Greenfield spent a year and wired $500 in a seemingly futile effort to extricate a Polish Jewish woman named Ghesa Szalet and her father from Berlin to a safe refuge in Norway or England. Then, in what Greenfield described as "a welcome and astonishing piece of news," in February 1941 the young woman informed him that she had arrived safely in New York.[34]

In another case, a twenty-eight-year-old Czech Jew named Paul Fantl—fired from his position with an insurance company in April 1939 because of new anti-Jewish laws promulgated after the Nazi occupation there—sought an affidavit from Greenfield that would enable him to emigrate to America. "My only hope is to go to America," the young man wrote, adding, "You must not believe that I lost the courage, that I fear to fight, but what can a man do if he is deprived of the possibility to fight, because he is a Jew?" In response, Greenfield's secretary, Lillian Maeder, advised Fantl, "Mr. Greenfield . . . regrets that he is already so deeply committed in connection with numerous similar affidavits, that he finds himself unable to do anything further at this time along the lines you indicate."[35]

Greenfield also seemed unable or unwilling to exploit his political connections in behalf of European Jews. During the first two years of the war, before the United States joined the fight, his friend and lawyer Lemuel B. Schofield served as head of the U.S. Immigration and Naturalization Service as well as a special assistant to the U.S. Attorney General, but there is no evidence that Schofield liberated any European Jews. At Greenfield's prodding, Senator Joseph Guffey of Pennsylvania managed to rescue one Jew from Germany in 1941.[36] For once in his career, Greenfield appears to have been so overwhelmed by his own commercial preoccupations that the thought of creating an agency to address these mounting requests in some systematic fashion, or referring them to some other appropriate agency, did not occur to him.

Greenfield was hardly alone in this respect: Most American Jews in the 1930s did little or nothing to save European Jewry. But Greenfield had promoted himself as a man who relished impossible challenges and huge risks. Even before Kristallnacht and the Munich Pact in the fall of 1938, which painfully clarified Hitler's designs on both the Jews and the rest of Europe, Greenfield's ex-wife, Edna, urged him to take the lead in rescuing Jewish refugees from Nazi Germany. Greenfield, who in most circumstances cheerfully accommodated Edna's requests, in this case declined. "I have gone my limit to help the victims of the Nazis," he replied but added that there was "nothing additional that I can undertake to do."[37]

Indeed, Greenfield seems to have responded to Hitler's systematic campaign against European Jewry much as he had responded to his wife's neuroses during their marriage—that is, the magnitude of the problem exceeded his capacity and, consequently, was best left to others.

Greenfield's response to the Jewish Zionist movement was similarly ambivalent. Theodor Herzl's dream of a Jewish homeland in Palestine, first proposed in Basel, Switzerland, in 1897, gained little traction among American Jews for decades thereafter. The Reform Jews with whom Greenfield had nominally affiliated—and who had largely set the agenda for American Jewry since the Civil War—tended to define Judaism solely as a religion and to reject the idea that Jews constituted a "nation."[38] As early as 1923 Greenfield's Sunday School principal, Judge Horace Stern (later chief justice of Pennsylvania), invited Greenfield to his home to meet the Russian-born British Zionist Chaim Weizmann (later the first president of the State of Israel)—not, as Judge Stern described it, in order to hear Weizmann's views but "to enable him to learn the view of those of us who, while sympathetic with the cause of Palestinian colonization, are indifferent or hostile to Zionism."[39]

These Jews, mostly of German descent, considered the United States their new promised land and feared that Jewish support for another country might undermine their hard-earned status as loyal Americans—a view with which Greenfield, in his patriotic enthusiasm, entirely concurred. Jews,

Greenfield wrote in a letter in 1924, are "adherents to an all-impelling faith, and that faith, and not any nationalistic ambitions, should be the principal consideration of Jewish communities, particularly in this country where our people really have attained the freedom of worship for which they have suffered for centuries."[40]

When a long-lost uncle wrote to Greenfield from Palestine in 1929, seeking funds with which to buy land and seeds for an orange plantation, Greenfield quickly set him straight: "Contrary to your belief, I am not an ardent Zionist," he replied. "However, that does not matter. You need some help and I am very glad to be able to enclose a draft to your order."[41]

Yet the growth of Jewish colonies in Palestine, coupled with Hitler's existential threat to the Jews, made it increasingly difficult for any American Jew of good will—least of all one like Greenfield, who prized his place in the Jewish mainstream—to avoid supporting Zionist causes. Although Greenfield refused to fund Zionist political organizations, in 1926 he donated $2,500 to the Hebrew University in Jerusalem, citing it as "a source of pride to every Jew—Zionist or non-Zionist."[42] Greenfield also served as treasurer of the Palestine Emergency Fund, which solicited funds to relieve Jewish victims of the anti-Semitic Arab riots of 1929 in Palestine.[43]

America's entry into World War II, coupled with the growing awareness of Hitler's extermination program in the early 1940s, raised a basic philosophical question for anti-Zionists like Greenfield: If America was indeed the new Zion for the world's Jews, but America refused to admit the millions of Jews trapped within Hitler's Third Reich, where else were European Jews to go?

The lack of an adequate answer to that question lay behind the phenomenally rapid growth of support for Zionism among Americans. In 1941 the Central Conference of American Rabbis, long a bastion of anti-Zionist sentiment, elected the Zionist Rabbi James G. Heller as its president; seven months later that organization adopted a resolution calling for the formation of a "Jewish army" in Palestine.[44] Anti-Zionist Reform rabbis, stunned and resentful at being marginalized in a forum they had long dominated, assembled in Atlantic City in June 1942 to consider their options. There they created the first and only American Jewish organization ever founded specifically for the purpose of opposing a Jewish state in Palestine.

The American Council for Judaism, as it was called, was essentially a Philadelphia-based movement, and its leaders included several Reform rabbis and laymen with close ties to Greenfield, including the Sears Roebuck patriarch Lessing Rosenwald and William Fineshriber, Greenfield's rabbi at Congregation Keneseth Israel.[45] Its initial Statement of Principles decried "growing secularism"—a euphemism for Zionism—in American life and called for devotion to "the central prophetic principles of life and thought, principles through which alone Judaism and the Jew can hope to endure and bear witness to the universal God."[46]

The creation of the council seemed to leave little room for compromise between ardent Zionists and anti-Zionists. It produced painful divisions not only within the Jewish community but also within the Reform Jewish community. (The prominent German Jewish Philadelphia lawyer Morris Wolf and his Zionist son, the author and librarian Edwin Wolf, simply agreed not to discuss the issue.)[47] Greenfield did what he could to keep a foot in both camps. He did not join the American Council for Judaism; nor did he join any Zionist organization. Without identifying himself as a Zionist, in 1943 he financially supported the "We Shall Never Die!" tour sponsored by the Committee for a Jewish Army, a radical Zionist organization that raised money to rescue European Jews.[48] But gradually he evolved into a Zionist in much the way he had evolved into a Democrat: out of his conviction that it was right, as well as his reluctance to be left on the sidelines at a critical moment in history.

"There seems to be nothing to do but carry on," Greenfield wrote to Gus Amsterdam in France in February 1945, three months before the war in Europe ended, "and what is equally important[,] to carry on after the war is over and victory is achieved. Everything must be done and such a peace made that your children and my grandchildren do not have to go thru [sic] the same thing."[49]

The end of the war brought with it a new president in the White House whom Greenfield quickly embraced as a kindred spirit. Although Greenfield ranked Roosevelt second only to Jefferson in his pantheon of great Americans, he was one of the first to perceive a quality about Harry S. Truman that other Americans appreciated only much later: "The man who governs our country must govern with his heart as well as his head," Greenfield remarked about Truman to a reporter. "One is no good without the other."[50]

Roosevelt may have welcomed Jews into his inner circle in unprecedented numbers, but Truman numbered Jews among his close personal friends. One of those friends, Edward Jacobson, had met Truman in the Army during World War I, and the two men had operated a haberdashery in Kansas City afterward.[51] As Truman rose from a U.S. senator to vice president to president upon Roosevelt's death in 1945, Jacobson had often lobbied him about the plight of European Jews. Soon Greenfield found himself performing a similar role—even though, in 1947, he voluntarily abandoned one of the primary sources of his influence.

David Stern's *Philadelphia Record* was not only Philadelphia's sole Democratic newspaper but also a faithful champion of labor unions. Nevertheless, in November 1946 the *Record*'s own newsroom union, the Newspaper Guild, went on strike for nearly three months. Greenfield, Stern's not-so-silent partner at the *Record* as well as an instinctive fighter, in this case counseled surrender with all the persuasive salesmanship he could muster. Stern recalled the conversation in his memoirs:

In the third month of the strike, Al Greenfield walked into my office. He brought an offer from the *Bulletin* to buy me out for $12 million. Al had figured that, after paying all debts, minority stockholders and capital gains tax, I would have enough left to make me comfortable in old age.

"Old age? Where do you get that stuff?" I snorted.

"You're sixty-one," Al replied. "At the pace you're going, drinking a quart of whiskey a day and chain smoking those Winston Churchill cigars, I don't give you many years. You nearly kicked the bucket last fall when you had pneumonia."

"I've got a job to do," I snapped. I was thinking of the editorials I had to write before press time. Al took another meaning from my words.

"Dave, you have been doing a great job, for the working man and the underdog. You were the first publisher to recognize the Guild. And what has it got you? The people you fought for are trying to cut your throat!"

"Only one crazy, Commie-controlled union. All the other unions are backing us up loyally."

"I'm sure you're going to win," Al said as he rose to leave. "The whole city is for you and your men. Maybe you can keep it up for a few more years and then Tom [Stern's son] can take over. But when you retire, it will be with less money than the *Bulletin* is offering you now. Dave, you've worked hard for forty years. I know you haven't saved a cent. If anything happened to you and your newspapers, Jill would receive a little insurance money. You owe it to your wife and children to grab this chance to get out on easy street."

Al had touched my Achilles heel. I had no savings. For twenty years I had been drawing a large salary but had laid nothing aside.[52]

As both men well understood, the *Bulletin* intended to close the *Record* in order to eliminate a competing paper.

Eighteen years earlier, Greenfield had goaded Stern into buying the *Record*, stressing the need for a Democratic voice in Philadelphia and declaring, "I would rather fall off the top rung than never climb the ladder." Now he was urging Stern to make personal security his highest priority, even though doing so would deprive the city of a Democratic voice, not to mention depriving Stern of a purpose in life—as Greenfield well understood. While selling the *Record* would leave Stern "entirely comfortable financially," Greenfield wrote to Etelka (then vacationing in Florida) shortly before the sale, "I am sure he will never be happy away from the smell of newsprint and ink. It gets in the blood, as I am sure you know from your experience as an artist."[53]

No doubt Greenfield believed he was looking after Stern's best interests (although closing a business—an admission of failure—was an action Greenfield would not have taken himself). Stern was embittered by what he saw as the betrayal of his unions and also exhausted by his competition with Walter Annenberg's formidable *Inquirer*; Greenfield's offer effectively provided him a graceful way out of his difficulties.[54] But in this transaction, as in so many others, Greenfield was hardly a disinterested adviser: His 6 percent commission for brokering the *Record*'s sale would come to $720,000.[55] And even if the *Record* closed, he would continue to enjoy some subtle access to Philadelphia's surviving newspapers by virtue of the advertising placed by his retailing companies: Lit Brothers, Bonwit Teller, and Loft Candy. (Greenfield shortly earned an additional commission by brokering the sale of Stern's Camden papers on behalf of the *Bulletin*.)[56]

To be sure, Stern was an adult, capable of making his own decisions. He might have sold the *Record* even without Greenfield's arguments.[57] But why would Greenfield urge such a course of action on his friend—especially when another embattled friend, President Truman, needed the *Record*'s support in the coming election? Ultimately, a mystified observer must conclude that the deciding factor sprang from nothing more than Greenfield's inability to resist a deal, and from his instinctive preference for change as opposed to the status quo.

On February 1, 1947, Stern published his final issue of the *Record*. His farewell statement was his last written work as a newspaperman. The *Bulletin* promptly closed the paper, leaving Walter Annenberg's *Inquirer* as Philadelphia's only remaining morning newspaper.[58]

As the 1948 presidential election approached, Greenfield emerged as an important Democratic fund-raiser—treasurer of the Democratic Party's Campaign Committee—as well as a confidant of President Truman.

Greenfield's remarkable fund-raising success as head of a bipartisan Philadelphia citizens' committee attracted both the Democratic and Republican national conventions to Philadelphia in 1948, reinforcing his reputation as the sort of miracle maker that Truman's campaign desperately needed.[59] (At the 1948 Democratic National Convention Greenfield was introduced to the nation as "a man who can very properly be called Mr. Philadelphia . . . because no movement takes place in this great metropolitan city for the interest of the community and humanity in general, that does not find our next speaker heading one of the important committees.")[60] In the process he was inevitably pulled into the Zionist cause.

In the summer of 1947, when Lawrence Horowitz of the Zionist Organization of America asked Greenfield to urge the president's full cooperation with the United Nations plan for separate Arab and Jewish states in Palestine, Greenfield readily complied. With Truman's support, the UN partition plan for Palestine passed in the General Assembly that November, paving the way for the creation of the State of Israel the following spring.

When the State of Israel was born in May 1948, Truman saw to it that the United States became the first nation to grant Israel diplomatic recognition. His quick response required great courage at a time when Western governments were preoccupied with preventing the spread of communism in Europe and Asia. In the midst of the first major crisis of the Cold War—the Soviet Union's blockade of Western access to Berlin, which began in June 1948—the United States needed to maintain its ties to the oil-rich Arab nations that viewed Israel as their enemy. For that reason, Truman's recognition of Israel was strenuously opposed by leading members of his administration, most notably Secretary of State George C. Marshall.[61]

The birth of Israel failed to silence the opposition of the American Council for Judaism, which by this time had attracted fourteen thousand members. "Israel is a foreign state and can in no way represent those of Jewish faith of other nations," the council declared days later.[62] In addition, Israel's survival was not assured: The day after its birth, the armies of six Arab countries invaded the new nation, plunging the Middle East into a war that dragged on for a year.[63]

Throughout the 1948 presidential campaign—played out against the backdrop of Israel's War of Independence—all three major polling organizations predicted a landslide victory for Truman's opponent, Governor Thomas E. Dewey of New York. The Democratic Party "might as well immediately concede the election to Dewey and save the wear-and-tear of campaigning," wrote the *New York Times*. *Life* magazine published a cover portrait of Dewey with the caption, "The Next President of the United States."[64]

Later it was said that only Truman himself believed he would win, but Greenfield similarly refused to entertain the prospect of the president's defeat. At one point in the campaign, according to some accounts, Truman's prospects were so dubious that some Midwest radio stations demanded payment in advance for his advertisements. Truman telephoned Greenfield and asked him to raise at least $100,000 within forty-eight hours lest he lose vital airtime, and Greenfield assured the president that the necessary sums would be delivered.[65]

When Truman campaigned with his wife, Bess, in Philadelphia early in October, the Greenfields acted as hosts.[66] About that time the embattled president sent Greenfield a note:

I have heard of the generous way in which you have expressed confidence in my leadership and want you to know of my heartfelt appreciation. I am more grateful than I can say.

The Democratic Party must go forward with progress, and your continuing support gives me strength and courage to carry on the fight in the weeks and days ahead.[67]

Truman's campaign also enjoyed backing from other wealthy Jews who were grateful for his support of Israel. But as long as Israel's future remained uncertain, Truman faced resistance about Israel from his secretary of state, George C. Marshall, and other advisers who feared that U.S. support of Israel would push Arab countries into the Soviet orbit. In September, to the dismay of Zionists, the United Nations mediator Folke Bernadotte proposed a compromise peace plan that allowed for only a tiny Jewish state and called for the internationalization of Jerusalem. Bernadotte was assassinated the next day by a self-proclaimed Jewish terror group, but his plan was supported by Marshall.[68]

In an effort to exploit this division within Truman's administration, in late October Governor Dewey issued a statement reiterating his support for Israel and questioning the sincerity of the Truman administration's backing. To most observers this ploy seemed likely to drive the final nail into the Truman campaign's coffin.

At this point—Friday, October 22, less than two weeks before the election—Greenfield took matters into his own hands. Truman, he decided, must issue a clear statement reaffirming his commitment to Israel—not for the sake of Israel or the Jews but for the benefit of America's future, which, as Greenfield saw it, depended on Truman's reelection.

That day Greenfield phoned Judge Louis E. Levinthal, a prominent Philadelphia Zionist then serving General Lucius Clay as special adviser on Jewish affairs in Germany and Austria. If he could arrange an appointment with Truman the next day, Greenfield asked, would Levinthal accompany him to Washington?[69] As Levinthal later recalled, "I told him I would go whenever he wished me to." A half-hour later Greenfield phoned back to tell Levinthal he had made an appointment to see Truman at the White House at 5:00 P.M. the next day. The two men met at the Philadelphia airport and flew down to Washington in Greenfield's private plane.

At the White House, Greenfield and Levinthal met with Truman for about forty-five minutes. According to Levinthal's later recollection, based on notes he took at the meeting:

[Truman] manifested his regret that the Palestine question was being made a partisan issue in the political campaign. He told us that he had thought that since both party platforms had clearly indicated support of Israel, it was improper for the Republican candidate to have issued his statement of support for Israel ten days before the election was to take place. Mr. Greenfield told the President that he was not speaking as a Zionist, for he had never been a member of the Zionist Organization, nor was he speaking as a Jew, but rather as an American citizen and a loyal supporter of the Democratic Party and its candidates. (Of course, it was not necessary for Mr. Greenfield to remind the President that he was serving as the treasurer or chairman of the Finance Committee of the Democratic campaign.) Mr. Greenfield pointed out that in view of the position taken by the Secretary of State with regard to the Bernadotte plan, continued silence on the part of the president might be misconstrued as agreement by the chief of state with his Secretary of State. . . .

The President told us that he would like to issue a clarifying statement as he had been urged to do so by many of his friends and supporters, but that Secretary Marshall had strongly opposed the idea. The President then suddenly broke off his conversation and turning to me said: "Young man, if you will prepare a draft of the sort of statement you think it would be proper and advisable for me to issue, I will consider it, but I make no promises. I would want Secretary Marshall's complete approval of the statement I would issue." Then, as we were leaving, he turned to Mr. Greenfield and said with a smile, "See that the statement is one that the President of the United States, not the president of the Zionist Organization of America, may appropriately make."[70]

Truman told Greenfield and Levinthal to leave three copies of their draft at the White House no later than midnight that evening, apparently so Truman could discuss it with Secretary Marshall the next morning. Greenfield and Levinthal promptly checked into a nearby hotel, where they spent several hours working on a draft statement for Truman, which was typed for them by a stenographer furnished by one of Levinthal's Washington lawyer friends.

They also sought help from Eliahu Epstein, the representative of Israel's provisional government. But Epstein expressed the view that as a foreign diplomat he would be wise to avoid getting involved. The two men labored on alone.

Greenfield delivered copies of their draft to the White House shortly before midnight Saturday, as Truman had requested, and he and Levinthal flew back to Philadelphia in Greenfield's plane. "When he left me at my apartment," Levinthal later recalled, "neither of us knew whether or when or in what form the statement would be issued."

But Monday morning Greenfield excitedly phoned Levinthal with remarkable news: A front-page story in the *New York Times*, headlined "Truman Reaffirms Stand on Israel," carried the full text of a statement Truman had issued on Sunday. The statement conformed word-for-word with the draft that Greenfield and Levinthal had submitted Saturday night.

In the critical passage, Truman declared:

On May 14, 1948, this country recognized the existence of the independent State of Israel. I was informed by the Honorable Eliahu Epstein that a provisional government had been established in Israel. This country recognized the provisional government as the *de facto* authority of the new State of Israel. When a permanent government is elected in Israel it will promptly be given *de jure* recognition.

The Democratic platform states that we approve the claim of Israel to the boundaries set forth in the United Nations resolution of November 29, 1947, and consider that modification thereof should be made only if fully acceptable to the State of Israel.

This has been and is now my position.[71]

In view of Truman's slim margin of victory the following week, Levinthal later wrote, "I believe it is reasonable to assume that the timely issuance of the statement on Palestine helped substantially to achieve the victory of the Democratic ticket."[72] That timeliness, of course, was made feasible by Greenfield's initiative and his access to Truman as well as his persuasiveness, not to mention his possession of a private plane. But more important than the election result was Truman's commitment, at Greenfield's urging, to grant de jure recognition to the Israeli government. At the close of the day, this secular Jew who had consistently distanced himself from the Zionist cause had nevertheless played a significant role in the birth of the State of Israel.

When Truman was sworn in for a second term the following January, Greenfield was among the dignitaries seated behind the president on the U.S. Capitol portico.[73] In gratitude for his help, Truman offered Greenfield a cabinet post or an ambassadorship—even, Truman suggested, to the Soviet Union. Greenfield demurred, on the ground that such a sensitive post should properly be filled by a career diplomat. Besides, as Greenfield's assistant later put it, "he knew his work was here in Philadelphia."[74]

[12]

Godfather

The Israel Philharmonic was coming to the Academy of Music for a benefit concert, to be followed by a fund-raising dinner for a Jewish cause at the Bellevue-Stratford Hotel. The dinner's organizers had tried to negotiate with the hotel manager in hopes that the hotel would give them the meal and the facilities at cost or perhaps donate the entire affair altogether. But the manager refused to budge from the Bellevue's regular posted rates.

The disappointed dinner organizers took their complaint to Greenfield, whose Bankers Securities owned and operated the Bellevue. For some fifteen minutes they buttered him up, praising his civic achievements and good works. For a while Greenfield basked in their praise and made no effort to stop them. Finally he said, "I'm enjoying this so much. But tell me, why are you here?" as if he did not already know.

When they told him, Greenfield assumed his preferred didactic posture. "You must understand," he intoned, "that the Bellevue-Stratford is a business. I hold the manager responsible for turning a profit. So if he's taking a hard line with you, I'm glad to hear it. If you wish a personal contribution from me, you may ask for one. But not for a discount from one of my businesses."[1]

Within Greenfield's complicated psyche, two conflicting personas constantly struggled. One was the benevolent elder statesman who dispensed favors and advice to grateful supplicants like the organizers of the Israel Philharmonic concert. This was the Greenfield who often invoked the need to maintain standards, not only in business but also in dress, manners, and lifestyle. "There's a certain fitness of things," this Greenfield liked to say: Things not only had to be right, they had to *look* right.[2]

The other Greenfield was the street hustler, constantly driven to scramble for the best deal as if his life depended on it. This was the Greenfield who, in 1946, began acquiring stock in the Hoving Corporation of New York, a holding company created by a tall, thin, patrician retailer named Walter Hoving. Over the next ten years, Greenfield gained control of the Hoving Corporation, which in turn gained control of such prestigious retailers as Tiffany & Co., the upscale jeweler, and the chic Bonwit Teller women's specialty stores in New York, Boston, and Chicago, whose clientele included such celebrated customers as Rose Kennedy, Marlene Dietrich, and Mary Martin.[3]

At one point in these adventures, Greenfield assembled a deal to acquire yet another store for Hoving to manage. But when he and Hoving arrived for the formal closing of the sale, Greenfield could not resist the temptation to bargain some more. The other side, outraged, walked out.

"Well," Greenfield remarked afterward to Hoving, as the two partners commiserated over lunch, "I guess I tried to trade that deal once too often."

"Yes, you did," Hoving replied, according to his later recollection.

"But you don't understand, Walter," Greenfield shrugged. "I would rather bargain on a deal than have an orgasm."[4]

The social critic Thorstein Veblen once observed that admission into the upper class depends not on manners but on money, which can only be obtained ruthlessly. Once you have gained entry, *then* you can behave politely, and so can your children and their children.[5]

So it was with Greenfield. In the evening of his life he sought to suppress the hustler within in favor of the gentleman, albeit with only limited success. After he acquired Lansburgh's, Washington's oldest department store, in 1951, a *Washington Post* feature writer who visited his home on Drexel Road marveled at his "meticulously cut suits and pastel waistcoats, elegantly spanned by a heavy gold key chain," as well as his "library lined with first editions of Dickens, Audubon and Fielding and hung with original paintings by Whistler and Sir Joshua Reynolds."[6] Greenfield had always dressed fastidiously, even in those early days at Cahan's print shop, but now he took to carrying a narrow walking cane, in the fashion of wealthy German Jews. He became a man of manners, fond of old-fashioned social appurtenances and aphorisms. Although his native tongue had been Yiddish, he liked to toss German expressions into his conversations.[7]

His style was classical, a throwback to his own romanticized conception of nineteenth-century European gentry rather than twentieth-century

notions of propriety. He and Etelka slept in separate bedrooms, in the style
of the British upper class. His wardrobe was huge, but only because he never
threw his suits out, continuing to wear them proudly when they were twenty
or thirty years old. The notion of being seen at the "right table" in a restaurant or staying in the "right suite" at a hotel was as foreign to him as it would
be to a king or a pope (although Greenfield would not attend a civic banquet
unless he was seated at the head table).[8]

People who had known him for many years suddenly discovered that
Greenfield was a man of culture and learning who could quote the classics
and name all the states in Germany. This was no pose: He had always been
an avid reader, especially of biographies and history. He had simply never
needed to impress anyone with this knowledge. Now he did.

With almost anyone beyond his immediate household, Greenfield displayed an innate social sensitivity that enabled him to zero in on the thoughts
of others. During a snowstorm in the late 1940s, Greenfield's niece, Grace
Fried, had dinner with Greenfield and Etelka at their mansion on Drexel
Road. When Grace left afterward, Greenfield asked her to telephone him
when she got home. As Greenfield had feared, Grace's car was marooned
in a snowdrift en route. But rather than trouble her uncle, she ducked into a
drugstore and called him from a pay phone.

"You told me to call when I got home," Grace said.

"And *are* you home, my dear?" Greenfield replied, perceiving her ruse
through the phone wires. When Grace confessed that she was not, Greenfield sent his car and chauffeur to complete her journey.[9]

Increasingly, he relished his role as a communal godfather. The poor and
helpless who had once turned to political ward leaders for help now often
found Greenfield a more useful alternative. He always read his own mail,
and if someone touched his imagination, he would put everything else aside,
spend hours with the petitioner, and then overwhelm his new friend with
financial or moral support, even while he kept more important people waiting.[10] When acquaintances or employees sent their children to Greenfield
for jobs or for help in gaining entrance to medical school, Greenfield would
interview them himself before forwarding the request, in effect screening
out the unqualified for the benefit of admissions departments or his own
personnel managers.[11] Decades later Philadelphia abounded in people who
were directly touched by Greenfield in such a manner: an African American boy who sought his help in getting into West Point; the son of a police
officer who had once held a door for Greenfield; a young advertising salesman who called on Greenfield and wound up spending the day with him;

a "sloppy neighborhood kid"—the son of one of Greenfield's nephew's law clients—who flourished for decades as a Philadelphia internist after Green-field interviewed him and then recommended him to Hahnemann Univer-sity Medical School.[12] When Philadelphia banks refused—perhaps because of anti-Semitism—to lend money to the four Shanken brothers for their plan to commercially develop their farm in suburban Willow Grove, Greenfield arranged for the financing, helped them lease the shops that became the suc-cessful Willow Grove Mall, and continued to mentor them thereafter.[13]

In much the same way, once he had reached the peak of respectability Greenfield extended a benevolent hand to African Americans whose pres-ence had sometimes discomfited him back in the days when he was scram-bling toward the top. As a young real estate broker, Greenfield had adhered to the common practice of redlining—that is, excluding black homebuyers—in certain neighborhoods.[14] Before the Ben Franklin Hotel opened in 1925, he instructed the manager to avoid using "colored service in the Hotel" be-cause "in Philadelphia the highest class of hotels have only white service."[15] In 1921, he sent a complaining note to the leasing agent of his office building:

We beg to advise you that there is considerable lounging on the ground floor of the N.E. Cor. 15th & Chestnut Sts., occupied by us.

It seems as if the elevator operators, as well as the janitors, have considerable colored friends who hang around the hall a great deal of the time.

We shall thank you if you will kindly issue instructions to these employees, prohibiting such lounging.[16]

Yet even then Greenfield appears to have begun to perceive a common bond between African Americans and his own marginalized minority group. As early as 1925 he made a donation to the all-black Tuskegee Insti-tute in Alabama.[17] In 1924, with his support, Edna Greenfield sponsored a series of summer concerts at Bryn Mawr College, one of which included a black soloist: the young and then largely unknown Philadelphia contralto Marian Anderson, singing "Negro Spirituals."[18]

By the post–World War II years the world had changed, and so, of course, had Greenfield. Now he emerged as a leading crusader against racial preju-dice and segregation. In 1951 he opened what may have been Philadelphia's first racially integrated apartment building.[19] Under his chairmanship, the PTC began hiring black bus drivers. His hotels became the first in Philadel-phia to rent rooms to blacks; in the early 1950s, when all other Philadelphia hotels declined to host the National Urban League, an organization devoted to promoting black self-reliance, Greenfield offered the League convention facilities at the Bellevue-Stratford.[20]

For that matter, Greenfield's enthusiasm for Harry Truman may have been based less on Truman's support for Israel than on Truman's order, during the summer of 1948, to desegregate the U.S. Armed Forces: Greenfield was so impressed by Truman's decision, he told an acquaintance, that he volunteered to campaign for him.[21] After Truman's election, Greenfield quietly and successfully urged Truman to appoint the first black judge to the U.S. Court of Appeals: William Hastie, who took office in 1949. And when the newly appointed Judge Hastie was unable to find a house in Philadelphia, Greenfield interceded, persuading his brother William to sell his house in the city's Oak Lane neighborhood to Hastie over the objections of William's white neighbors.[22]

Greenfield's racial attitudes were affected by his contacts with people in low places as well as high. One day in the early 1950s Greenfield was lunching with one of his vice presidents at Horn & Hardart, a downtown Philadelphia restaurant whose two-person tables were bunched closely together. The adjoining table was occupied by a single dowdy, middle-aged black woman. When Greenfield noticed that the woman was quietly crying, he leaned over to her and asked what was the matter.

"They're not going to serve me," the woman replied. "You came in after I did, and you were served."

In some subconscious manner Greenfield may have seen in the woman's mistreatment an echo of his own past painful exclusion as a Jew. He summoned the waitress. "You haven't taken her order," he said—and the waitress complied.

"You see?" Greenfield told the woman after the waitress scurried off. "She was just too busy to take care of you."[23]

In 1951 Greenfield gave $1 million to the University of Pennsylvania for an ambitious and unprecedented project: the Albert M. Greenfield Center for Human Relations, the nation's first institution specifically designed to train students to promote interfaith and interracial relations.

"Fear and prejudice, which go hand in hand, are divisive and destructive," he declared at its opening.

> Medical science has eliminated many ancient scourges. . . . We can have faith that centers for the study of human relations will produce as great triumphs in the battle against malignant fears. In so doing, they will liberate vast reserves of human energy for creative service to those great tasks that the ideal of brotherhood sets before us.[24]

By 1961, when the civil rights leader Martin Luther King Jr. spoke at Philadelphia's Academy of Music, Greenfield was the local luminary chosen to introduce him. "He has become an inspiration to countless thousands of people," Greenfield said of the young preacher whose successful boycott of segregated buses in Montgomery, Alabama, had electrified the nation in 1955—"not just Negroes, not just whites, but to people the length and breadth of the world who are learning anew through him a new respect for the individual—a new regard for the dignity of man."[25]

Greenfield was similarly well ahead of his time in his treatment of women.[26] He appointed Mildred Custin president of Bonwit Teller's Philadelphia operation at a time when virtually no other department store company was headed by a woman, and she subsequently became president of Bonwit's in New York. "I know it's chic or at least popular to badmouth him," Custin said later, "and I know he usually loved to get the best of every bargain. But he taught me a lot and I always thought I owed him a lot."[27]

At a dinner meeting in the mid-1950s of the all-male board of Philadelphia's Albert Einstein Medical Center, the secretary read a letter from the women's auxiliary asking for representation on the board. The request was greeted with rolled eyes and furtive grins; one man waved his cigar and suggested, "File it," and then joined in the hearty laughter that he had provoked. Only Greenfield remained unamused. "Wait a minute," he told the group:

This is no matter for facetiousness. We are, I presume, civilized men—too civilized, I should expect, to deal in such an offhand manner with a request that is completely proper and legitimate. . . . After all, there is not a man here at this table who has not been raised by a woman, and who among you would argue that in his case she did a bad job? . . . I think it should be voted here that it is the board's consensus that there is no reason why women should be deprived of the opportunity to serve on this board.[28]

It was not so voted then and there, but shortly thereafter women were indeed admitted to the hospital's board.

To his business associates and his employees, Greenfield in his seventh decade became increasingly patriarchal. He would take good care of you, yes, but only if you let him run the show and make the decisions. He rewarded his closest business associates by making them presidents and directors of his various companies; they reciprocated with undying loyalty, even when, as was often the case, his business decisions seemed to defy logic. He was a demanding boss who kept a tight rein on his help and expected his executives to match his own long hours and make themselves available at all times, even on vacation. In one typical memo he advised a staffer, "The office opens for business at 9 o'clock. The record shows you have been late six times from Sept. 1 to Sept. 25. Please make an effort to be here on time daily."[29]

But his loyal old hands at Bankers Securities and Albert M. Greenfield & Co. perceived, if only subconsciously, that Greenfield's apparent bullheadedness was merely a screen behind which he weighed and sifted all viewpoints that confronted him. He was, said one of his executives, a man with "a very hard crust and a very soft center."[30] His greatest asset, they instinctively understood, was his ability to gain people's confidence. By seeming to act at all times on instinct, Greenfield reinforced his self-assured persona. Had he used standard analytical processes to arrive at his decisions, he might have appeared so weak and indecisive that his image of supreme self-confidence—a fragile commodity to begin with—might have evaporated. Consequently, his devoted colleagues were only too happy to bask in his glow.

"If Greenfield told you to jump off the Ledger Building because you could fly, you'd give it serious thought," George Johnson Jr., the president of Albert M. Greenfield & Co., once recalled to a new associate. "He was that inspirational."[31]

As Greenfield himself liked to point out at gatherings of his twenty-five-year club, in his companies, "Few die and no one resigns."[32] In 1951 Greenfield created a forty-year club that included, among other veteran employees, his first office boy, his first secretary, and his first clerk, all of whom had since been promoted to positions of high-level responsibility.[33] His secretary, Lillian Maeder, had been with him since 1927; his office attendant and coat holder, Conlius Bond, since 1921; one of his real estate agents, John J. Cree, had started as Greenfield's first office boy in 1910.[34] The rare Greenfield executives who did die or retire—like Maurice Wurzel, George Johnson Sr., and Walter Grosscup—were often succeeded by their own sons.

The result was a family-like atmosphere at Greenfield's Walnut Street headquarters as well as an ability to move quickly (since Greenfield made all the big decisions) and, consequently, profitably. By 1949, when Greenfield gained control of the nine Franklin Simon specialty shops in Manhattan, his City Stores chain had expanded its domain from five department stores when Greenfield took charge in 1932 to twenty-two, its revenues had grown from $33 million to $168 million, and its profits hit a record of $5 million.[35] Bankers Securities, which controlled City Stores, celebrated its twenty-fifth anniversary in 1953 by reporting a sixfold increase in its assets during that period.[36]

But the downside of Greenfield's loyalty to his old-timers was his reluctance to prune executive deadwood. Even a loyal acolyte like George Johnson

Jr. once acknowledged that, in any given situation, "Greenfield would rather hire the cheaper person, even if he's a moron."[37] And much like his real estate and banking syndicates in the 1920s, many of Greenfield's operations after World War II constituted exercises in smoke and mirrors.

City Stores, for example, owed most of its glowing sales and earnings figures not to any real internal growth but to Greenfield's relentless acquisitions, as well as the nation's general economic recovery during and after World War II. Greenfield's dogged loyalty to Center City, his contempt for the suburbs, and his refusal to recruit expensive but creative executive talent rendered him helpless to respond creatively as postwar American consumers migrated from the old urban centers to newer suburban shopping malls.[38]

Bankers Securities, for all its increase in assets since 1928, paid no dividends to its common stockholders—and hardly any to its preferred stockholders—from 1932 through 1949.[39] Its Philadelphia hotels were distinguished mostly by their dreariness, largely a result of Greenfield's reluctance to spend money on improvements. As late as 1961, the Bellevue-Stratford— the company's most elegant hotel—lacked air conditioning for more than one-third of its rooms.[40] At the Ben Franklin, the company's largest hotel, the general manager reported to Greenfield that occupancy had slipped in 1958 because of soiled wallpaper, old furniture, and faded draperies in the guest rooms. "It is difficult to believe," he added, "that toilets could not be flushed without holding the flushometer handle down for a long period, and guests had to run the water twenty minutes before they could get hot water in the basins or showers."[41]

Greenfield's executives rarely challenged their boss's chintziness. When George Frederick, president of Greenfield's Loft Candy operation, retired to Florida in 1957, he remained on Loft's board at Greenfield's request; but when Frederick asked to be reimbursed for his travel expenses, Greenfield replied, "Absolutely not. If he wants to be on the board, he pays his own way." Yet Frederick accepted Greenfield's decision and remained on the board at his own expense.[42]

Similarly, Greenfield objected when Frederick's successor, Leonard Wurzel, attempted to automate Loft's outmoded eight-story, 400,000-square-foot factory on Long Island. New machines then being installed by Loft's competitors would have eliminated much of the manual labor involved in placing individual pieces of candy in boxes. But the machinery required a large initial capital outlay. "I wasn't allowed to spend more than $5,000 without the board's approval," Wurzel later recalled. "I was too new at that time, and I was too young to impress all these old guys that I knew what I was talking about."[43]

Because he was essentially a deal maker, Greenfield's management decisions often seemed inscrutable. At some point in the 1950s, for example, he installed Irving D. Rossheim, a former film executive with First National Pictures, as a vice president at Loft Candy Corporation on Long Island. Rossheim's immediate boss, Leonard Wurzel, found him intelligent, effective, and capable. Then one year Rossheim took a vacation cruise with his wife. As was the custom at the time, reporters hungry for gossip gathered at the ship to interview the departing passengers, and the next day one New York newspaper erroneously identified Rossheim as the president of Loft Candy. The following day, as Wurzel later recalled it, Greenfield called him.

"I want you to fire Irving," Greenfield said.

"Fire Irving? Why?"

"Did you read the newspaper?"

"Yes."

"Well, he said he was president," Greenfield said. "*You're* the president. He's not the president."

"Well, he made a mistake," Wurzel said.

"No, no," Greenfield replied. "He didn't make a mistake. Get rid of him."

Wurzel was flabbergasted but followed Greenfield's order. He was further mystified when, upon returning from his cruise, Rossheim accepted his dismissal without complaint. Years later Wurzel remained puzzled by the incident. The best he could figure was that Greenfield had hired Rossheim to repay some sort of obligation—either financial or social—but had dropped Rossheim once he considered the debt satisfied.[44]

Greenfield's absentee management of his department stores defied conventional retailing wisdom, which held that only a hands-on proprietor could keep abreast of inventories, customer tastes, and changing fashions. To a large extent Greenfield's management of his subsidiaries consisted of telephoning each of his dozen or so presidents at the beginning of every business day with a single question. As one of those presidents—Leonard Wurzel of Loft Candy—later recalled, the conversation invariably went like this:

"Good morning, Leonard. How are you?"

"Okay. How are you?"

"Good. What's your cash balance?"[45]

This question was not merely intended to keep his presidents on their toes; to Greenfield, a company's balance of cash on hand was its most important yardstick—far more significant than, say, its return on investment or its long-term growth prospects. He understood that as long as his stores, hotels, and office buildings maintained sufficient cash balances to pay commissions and fees to his real estate and insurance management companies, his overall enterprise would succeed.

Greenfield's preoccupation with real estate explained why, for example, Loft Candy operated more than three hundred retail outlets in the 1950s—a time when other candy makers were selling their products through wholesalers to supermarkets and specialty stores, in order to save on their overhead costs and gain broader access to customers. Greenfield, by contrast, was only too happy to see Loft's paying higher rents at all its stores, even as the stores suffered declining volume because customers were increasingly buying their candy elsewhere. Whether Loft's or any of his other companies made a profit or were doomed to failure was secondary in his mind. As Greenfield well understood, no business lasts forever, and, in any case, he had failed before and survived, exuberantly, to tell the tale.

Indeed, the old, driven Greenfield—the bargain hunter who lived from one deal to the next and improvised his business plan as he went along—was never far beneath his new mellow surface. Some of his biggest mistakes occurred because, rather than heed his more cautious associates, he persisted in the delusion that he could rescue any troubled company. In 1949 Greenfield acquired Hearn's, a 122-year-old department store on lower Fifth Avenue in New York, only to see it close six years later.[46] In 1951, against the advice of his longtime aide, Alfred Blasband, Greenfield purchased Snellenburg's, a fading seventy-eight-year-old retailer that then ranked last among Philadelphia's five downtown department stores.[47]

"I pleaded with him not to buy it," Blasband later recalled. "I said, 'Mr. Greenfield, you've got Lit Brothers on Market Street—a hard-hitting department store. You'll be competing with yourself.'" Greenfield bought Snellenburg's anyway. "He was on a roll," Blasband explained. "His ego was all the way up to here. That was one of his weaknesses—his ego. When he developed an ego, you couldn't stop the man."

Greenfield directed Blasband to find a new president to revamp Snellenburg's. After Greenfield interviewed and rejected six candidates for the presidency, as Blasband recalled,

he called me up to his office and said, "Alfred, I want you to take over."

I said, "Mr. Greenfield, I'm not an operating man. This place needs an operating man."

He said, "I think you can do it."

Four times I turned him down. The fifth time I accepted. I knew I had to, or look for another job.[48]

In 1954 Greenfield stubbornly clung to his plan to open a Lit Brothers department store in already decaying downtown Camden. "All my associates think I'm crazy, but we're doing it anyway," he told a friend, sounding very much like the old Greenfield who had bragged about his fondness for risk thirty years earlier. The store was a disaster from its opening day.[49] But, of course, Lit's bottom line differed from Greenfield's.

It should come as no surprise, then, that Greenfield's preferred new benevolent self-image never gained universal acceptance. As late as 1954 one bitter (and presumably envious) competitor described him as "a kind of Chinese war lord, operating in the wrong country and the wrong century."[50] Many rival East Coast department store owners referred to him (as one of them put it) as "a hyena, a snake, a vulture, the Bag and Bones Man, the Angel of Death."[51] In 1948 Philadelphia's leading business and civic executives created the Greater Philadelphia Movement, a new organization dedicated to demonstrating, as one civic leader put it, that "businessmen can still lead the parade"; Greenfield was pointedly excluded from its membership.[52] "Though many prominent Old Philadelphians admire him," one chronicler of the city's upper class observed, "he has been described by others as the kind of man, rather like Stotesbury, who would give himself a testimonial dinner and then clap at the speeches."[53]

But most businessmen kept their misgivings about Greenfield to themselves, for fear of his retribution. One of the few exceptions—a longtime Philadelphia merchant named J. J. Cabrey—sent Greenfield an unsolicited three-page typed letter in 1951 that emphasized the fear generated by Greenfield's "fierce monopolistic spirit":

> I am in trade myself and I know the things that men say. Greenfield will reward you if you are on the mark, but he will crush you if you fail. The *Daily Trade Record* said some such thing about you this week. Another man said this morning, when I suggested that he buy the Bailey Building that you had for sale . . . that to deal with Greenfield is to invite the hand of death. I don't believe any such thing, but I do know numerous men who are afraid of you (the middle-aged who have long worked for concerns you have purchased) and I can't say that they don't need to be afraid.
>
> Where will the whole thing end and is it truly pleasing to God?[54]

Greenfield—who read and responded to virtually all his mail, and who cherished his reputation—replied with a long letter of his own that sought to square his personal actions with his ideals:

I have always lived under the assumption that our only hope of salvation, in this life and in the hereafter, depended upon our living decently and with dignity, doing the best kind of job which our talents made possible and lending a helping hand whenever possible to those less able or less fortunate.

The charge that he was a monopolist, Greenfield said, especially rankled:

That is so far from the reality that I cannot believe that you have had any real knowledge of my business background. My dislike of monopoly and my refusal to become part of a group which dominated many of Philadelphia's largest business enterprises, as well as its politics, for years, resulted in my losing practically everything I had built up in a financial way during my long business career. That experience occurred in the not too distant past and is far too vivid in my mind for me ever to be guilty of similar practices.[55]

Here lay the essence of Greenfield's perception problem: While many people viewed him as a monopolist systematically crushing his competitors, Greenfield perceived himself as an underdog, perpetually struggling in behalf of all outsiders against an entrenched and bigoted power elite. The problem lay in his failure to recognize that he himself was such an intimidating force of nature that few people, least of all cautious Philadelphians (Cabrey aside), were willing to confront him.

He had no use, for example, for anyone who complained that America was no longer a land of opportunity. "Nonsense," Greenfield told a reporter who raised that question in 1953. "There are greater opportunities now than ever before. The whole *world* is your opportunity. It's for a man to determine how much he can contribute to it."[56]

Ironically, it was Greenfield's perpetually anxious ex-wife, Edna, who probably came closest to defining the essence of his problem. In 1950, when Edna was so troubled by her germ phobia that she had stopped eating and was losing weight, she traveled to Europe to explore the possibility of undergoing a partial lobotomy to relieve her anxieties—a procedure that she underwent the following year, with some success.[57] Before returning from France, Edna sent Greenfield a letter asking him to arrange the "courtesy of the port, or the next best thing" for her when her ship docked in New York—"anything to avoid standing around in the cold and having some disagreeable officer pull your belongings inside out," she explained. "This is a procedure which I dread." To this request Edna gratuitously appended an insightful perception:

"The world is in a mess and it takes a stout heart to face life with cheer and courage. You my dear Albert are among the well-equipped. Be grateful—and not too hard on those less fortunate."[58] Greenfield, who instinctively shrank from Edna's psychoanalyzing, refused to be drawn into the discussion. "Request granted," he replied by cable. "Regards, Albert."[59]

The more effective the corporate leader, it is sometimes said, the less effective the family leader. Within his own home, Greenfield demonstrated little of the affectionate charm that he utilized so successfully to finalize business deals and transform enemies into friends. "In our family, to say you 'loved' someone was considered unduly sentimental," his youngest son, Albert Jr., later recalled.[60] Greenfield's dealings with his children seem characterized to a large extent by a remarkable tone-deafness toward their feelings. When his oldest son, Gordon, was a sixteen-year-old boarding student at Lawrenceville, Greenfield sent him a letter that mentioned Gordon's cousin Robert Greenfield, who was also sixteen: "Your Uncle Bill showed to me Bob's school report and it is so good that I took it away from him for the purpose of sending it along to you as I knew you would be interested in the splendid record Bob is making." In the process he fostered a resentment that Gordon harbored toward his unsuspecting cousin Bob for the rest of his life.[61]

All five of Greenfield's children bridled under the burden of his all-encompassing shadow—not to mention his biting sarcasm and arbitrary mannerisms, which for some of them led in adulthood to alcoholism, emotional problems, and broken marriages. "None of his children measured up in his mind," recalled Greenfield's nephew Robert Greenfield, on whom Greenfield lavished more attention—legal connections, club memberships, investment opportunities—than on his own children.[62]

Some of Greenfield's children worshipped him, some resented him, but none succeeded in standing up to him. Gordon—the eldest, and the only child to be held by Edna—related more to his mother and distanced himself from his father (while remaining employed by one of his father's companies); he subsequently moved to New York and embraced conservative Republican politics, as did his sister Patsy. Betty, the second child, became a teenage rebel against conformity and prejudice, openly embracing the Democratic Party several years before her father did; rather than be given away as a bride by her father, she eloped in 1938.[63] Carlotta, the middle child, adored her father (and ardently embraced his politics) and detested her mother.

In lieu of personal attention, Greenfield constantly showered his children with gifts, shares of stock, and other material kindnesses that merely exacerbated their struggles to break out of his orbit.

"We are not a family of many written words," Greenfield's daughter Carlotta wrote him in 1947, when she was twenty-seven and trying to carve out a business career for herself at Greenfield's Maison Blanche store in New Orleans, "so I always find it rather difficult to fully thank you for your presents. That they are always very generous makes me feel like a little girl who has been given a great big piece of chocolate candy, when actually she has done nothing to deserve same."[64]

Four years later, when Carlotta was on her fourth marriage and pregnant, she made another pitch for her father's attention after receiving yet another unsolicited gift from him:

In trying to express my appreciation for your usual generosity, I am, in this instance, in the peculiar position of being very grateful for your assistance, but at the same time wishing your insistence had not made your help necessary. I know you understand what I mean when I express this seeming contradiction. There is something honest and satisfying in getting recompensed for work put forth. You always made the assertion that to work and work hard was a privilege. Few people understand you and even fewer agree with you. I am not among these—I feel the most tremendous unrest when my mind is not occupied with something beyond my personal affairs and problems. . . . Some day, when we have the opportunity for some small talk, I shall attempt to persuade you that having a baby is not an occasion for going into a state of decline.[65]

Greenfield's inadvertent tendency to kill his family with kindness extended to his eagerness to provide jobs in his various companies not only for his children but for his children's friends, his siblings, his relatives, his in-laws, and even his ex-in-laws. During World War II, when Carlotta broke off her marriage to Robert Sturgeon while Sturgeon was fighting with the U.S. Marines on Iwo Jima, Greenfield instinctively took his son-in-law's side. "You're my son, and you will be my son forever," he wrote to Sturgeon.[66] When Sturgeon returned from the war in 1945, Greenfield hired him at his real estate company and kept him employed in some capacity thereafter; when Sturgeon remarried in 1950, Greenfield sent the newlyweds a china piece as a wedding gift; and when Greenfield's own son and namesake, Albert Jr., applied to become a commissioned officer in the Marine Reserves, Sturgeon was one of the five people he cited as a reference.[67]

Of Greenfield's five children, Carlotta came closest to inheriting the drive and ambition of the father she worshipped. During World War II, when she was in her early twenties, Carlotta was a fighter pilot, said to have flown twenty-three missions, including the first flight over Japan by a woman in U.S. Navy history.[68] After leaving the Navy with the rank of admiral, Carlotta set out to establish her own business career, although (like her brothers and brothers-in-law) she usually found it most convenient to work at her father's companies—as a training director at Maison Blanche in New Orleans, for example, or as a junior sportswear buyer at Oppenheim Collins in New York. Before finally settling down with an entrepreneur named Allen Howard in 1953, when she was thirty-two, Carlotta divorced four husbands within a period of eleven years—because, it was said, she could not find a man who measured up to her father.[69]

That impression was reinforced by an unsolicited letter that one of her employers sent to Greenfield in 1949. Harry Serwer, a merchandising consultant in New York who did business with Greenfield's stores, wrote:

> Carlotta and I have decided to part company because I could not afford to lose an assistant for so many weeks. I liked the girl very much. She has unusual integrity, is frank and direct in her approach to a problem. More than that . . . much more, she has a rare intelligence. Given the time and continued presence, she would have made a top assistant. . . . Her great commercial fault was her great moral asset: She has such a love for her father, such a great regard for him as a man, that it transcended everything she did. At times, watching her and listening to her, I wondered if the umbilical cord had ever been cut. . . .
>
> Here was a girl from a rich family. She could have socked into the family purse. But she gave every evidence of desiring to earn her own way. . . . She wanted to make a go of it. She, I suspect, did it less for her pride than for a spiritual obligation to her father. . . .
>
> Also, when I compare her expressed intelligence with some of the retail executives I've met in my career—and I met and hobnobbed with hundreds—I believe she would be a natural for one of your retail operations. Personally, I don't think she could ever be loyal to anyone but her father. I guess I resented that more than anything else.[70]

The most frustrated of Greenfield's children was the one who bore his name: his youngest, Albert Jr., who tried repeatedly to wriggle out from under his father's thumb, without success. As a young man, Albert Jr. loved animals and hoped to become a veterinarian, but his father declared that such a career was not suitable and refused to permit it.[71] Albert Jr. then rebelled by enlisting in the Navy when he turned eighteen, in 1945. Although he was discharged five months later with the end of World War II, in 1947 young Albert enlisted again, this time in the Marines.[72] There, far from his father's reach—or so he thought—he found in the comradeship of his fellow enlisted men the closest thing to a family he had known. "The Marine Corps was his father," Albert Jr.'s son later remarked.[73]

In June 1950, as Albert Jr. was preparing to be married—in a match virtually arranged by his father—his Marine unit was recalled to active duty with the onset of the Korean War.[74] His unit, the 15-Millimeter Howitzer Battalion, flew to Seattle and from there boarded a huge troop ship bound across the Pacific for Korea. But the ship had steamed only about two hundred miles from shore when a helicopter flew overhead and landed on the deck. Minutes later, Albert Jr. heard his name summoned over the loudspeaker. When he appeared on deck, he found himself confronting a Navy admiral. "Sergeant Greenfield," the admiral informed him, "I have an Executive Order from the Commander-in-Chief for you to get on that helicopter. You're going Stateside. It's your lucky day. *Who do you know?*"[75] The elder Greenfield had tapped the highest of all his connections—the president of the United States—to reach across the continent and into the Pacific to pluck his son out of harm's way.[76]

The humiliated Albert Jr. spent the duration of the Korean conflict at Parris Island in South Carolina and on other domestic Marine bases while his battalion comrades fought and died in Korea. He remained bitter toward his father for years afterward—but not so bitter that he did not return to work for his father's real estate firm.[77] Eventually, young Albert left to form his own real estate company, which developed projects in Arizona, Florida, and the Caribbean—sometimes in competition with his father—and he moved to a 260-acre farm in distant suburban Chester County. Here, perhaps in reaction to his own childhood experiences, he raised four children, who later described him as an "intensely affectionate" father.[78]

When Greenfield's children were adults with children of their own, he rarely visited their homes, even as he and Etelka periodically traveled to Europe. Instead, the five children and their children were expected to surround him at Thanksgiving and Christmas—partly, to be sure, because he genuinely enjoyed small children, but most likely because his ego demanded homage.

Still, Greenfield was far more successful as a grandfather than as a parent. Whereas his children resented the attention he seemed to lavish on everyone but them, his grandchildren relished the prospect of dropping into his house to find Greenfield lounging in his library with the likes of Harry Truman, the two men drinking scotch and sodas and laughing over political stories. Years later Greenfield's oldest granddaughter, Janet Guth, recalled what it was like:

> I remember at three sitting in that big house in Overbrook in the library, watching him when he read a newspaper or talked on the telephone. I had a little kid's kind of bench that I could sit on—practically at his feet—and I would just be wide-eyed with all the different people who would come in and out. Every time I showed up, whatever he was doing, he stopped for me, and if he had company in the dining room, I was invited in, and I would be introduced in this formal way to every single person that would enter the room: "Now, this is my granddaughter Janet." I knew that there was something special about all this, about riding around in that Rolls Royce. I felt like I was in a fairy tale when I was with him and living his life for a couple days, sitting at a huge dining room table, always with finger bowls and crystal and little silver nut dishes, one for each place setting.[79]

Greenfield liked to amuse his grandchildren by spontaneously crawling about on his hands and knees, barking like a hound dog in his raspy high-pitched voice, or standing on his head—even into his sixties—or crinkling up his eyes and wrinkling his nose into what he called a "rabbit face" in order to make children laugh. His humor was never subtle, but children loved it.[80] Often he joined his grandchildren in watching episodes of *Mr. Ed*, his favorite television program. "He thought this talking horse was very funny," Janet Guth recalled.[81]

"To be a Greenfield grandchild in that era was awe-inspiring," recalled another granddaughter, Priscilla Luce. "We knew that he was being shared with the rest of the world and that we were part of his world clearly, and he loved us and cared about us, but we were certainly not his sole priority in life."[82]

Much of the balm in Greenfield's family life throughout the 1940s was provided by Etelka, who welcomed Greenfield's children and grandchildren alike—not so much to her home as to her studio at his farm, where she spent much of her time. Greenfield's granddaughter Janet Guth, herself a painter, attributed her interest in color and painting to Etelka.[83] When President Truman visited Philadelphia, it was Etelka who entertained Mrs. Truman.[84]

Etelka customarily spent a winter month at a spa or resort, usually in Florida.[85] Her descriptive letters to Greenfield from there reflect her aesthetic eye ("great trees and heavy jungle fringe the banks, with masses of moss swaying like weighty pennants") but also the tenderness of her feeling for him:

I do regret your overwork and the consequent colds you contract. . . . You are a constant source of worry to me, believe it or not, and though I can't conceive that you need me for a minute, I am much concerned that you work all hours at night, and that by doing, you are undermining your resistance. . . . Well now, there's only a little space for a lot of love from Etelka.[86]

In April 1949, believing she was suffering from nervous exhaustion, Etelka returned to Florida in the hope of recovering her strength. When she failed to recover, Greenfield joined her in Florida, where he accompanied her back to Philadelphia, taking Etelka directly from the train to the University of Pennsylvania Hospital. There she was operated on by the noted Philadelphia surgeon I. S. Ravdin, who discovered a cancer. Whether Greenfield was specifically told of her condition is unclear; in any case his replies to well-wishers in the weeks that followed suggest his customary refusal to accept bad news.

"Etelka's condition has indeed improved over the weekend and I am hopeful she has turned the corner," he wrote in one letter.[87] In another, he remarked, "Etelka's general condition is improved, although the past two days have not been good."[88] To Louis Johnson, secretary of defense in Washington, he wrote in May, "My little wife has been very ill, and although her spirit and courage are magnificent, her progress has been slow. However, I am hoping that from here on her improvement will be more marked."[89] But Etelka's cancer was one adversary that Greenfield's sheer optimism alone could not defeat. She died eighteen days later, at the age of sixty-one.[90]

When Etelka died, Greenfield was sixty-one and still vigorous, as his grandchildren who watched him stand on his head could attest. By the fall of 1949 he was seeing other women again, although whether the attraction was romantic or commercial is unclear (and may well have been unclear to Greenfield and the women he dated as well). His pursuit of an old friend, Mary Roebling, for example, paired Greenfield with a female equivalent of himself: a vivacious, ambitious former secretary who had nearly quintupled the assets of the Trenton Trust Company after assuming its presidency upon her husband's sudden death in 1936. Mary was, she claimed, the only woman president of a major bank in the East.[91]

Through the middle of 1950, in what appears to have been a courtship dance but might merely have been a business pursuit, Greenfield began showering Mary Roebling with American Beauty roses, orchids, chocolates, and books of poetry as well as gourmet snacks for Mary's consumption when she traveled to Argentina to meet Eva Perón. Mary, for her part, reciprocated by sending Greenfield poinsettia plants and flowers as well as thank-you notes of faint protest. ("You know you should not do all these things. You are too good to so many people; but I do thank you any way. Affectionately, Mary.")[92] When Greenfield threw a reception for Paul-Henri Spaak, president of the UN General Assembly early in 1950, Mary served as his hostess for the event.[93]

On one hand, marriage to Mary Roebling would have aligned Greenfield not only with an influential and high-profile banker but also with one of America's legendary industrial families: Mary's late second husband, Siegfried Roebling, was the grandson and great-grandson of the men who built the Brooklyn Bridge.[94] On the other hand, Mary was eighteen years younger than Greenfield and, at five-foot-seven, towered over Greenfield (who was also five-foot-seven) when she wore her customary heels.[95]

Greenfield's dalliance with Mary Roebling lasted into 1951.[96] But by the summer of 1950 whatever urgent need he might have felt for a female consort had been abated by the arrival in his home of Albert Jr.'s new nineteen-year-old bride, the former Barbara Littman of London. When Albert Jr. was called up to the Marines that summer, Barbara moved into Greenfield's mansion while she commuted to classes at Penn and prepared for the birth of her first child. In that odd arrangement, Greenfield found himself living in his own home for two years with a lovely and adoring young daughter-in-law who was unburdened by his own children's emotional baggage. In the process, Barbara developed a closer relationship with Greenfield than any of his own children had known. Amid this satisfactory if temporary housekeeping arrangement, Greenfield's quest for a wife receded to a back burner.

According to Western custom, a man chooses a bride and proposes to her; but in practice, the woman often creates the opportunity for the man to choose *her*. In Greenfield's case it was not so much a woman as a confluence of political events that conspired to bring a new bride into his life.

For Philadelphia's endlessly frustrated political reformers, the years after World War II brought an astonishing realization: The holy grail that they and their ancestors had vainly sought since the Civil War—genuine reform of the city's antiquated political system—might finally be within their grasp. A new generation of "Young Turks"—sons of the city's privileged business elite, Depression-era graduates of Ivy League schools, New Dealers at heart regardless of their party affiliation—had come of age and begun fomenting a serious revolution. The Young Turks gathered in two new civic organizations: the liberals in the local chapter of Americans for Democratic Action, the Republicans in the Greater Philadelphia Movement.[97] Their standard-bearers were a pair of patrician WASPs who had rebelled against their conservative backgrounds: the aloof but highly principled Joseph Sill Clark and the passionate extrovert Richardson Dilworth.

Unlike previous generations of idealistic but ineffective reformers, these pragmatic Young Turks knew better than to tackle City Hall by themselves. They sought out older, more powerful allies and found them not only within the city's long-excluded ethnic groups but also within the ranks of Old Philadelphians, many of whom had long stewed in silent resentment of the city's corrupt political leadership.[98]

One of the Young Turks' early recruits was Edward Hopkinson Jr., E. T. Stotesbury's successor as senior partner at Drexel & Co., with whom Greenfield had developed a friendship during their years on the board of the PRT and its successor, the PTC. Hopkinson, in turn, recruited Greenfield for "the Renaissance," as the reform movement came to be known. Greenfield soon became one of the movement's leading fund-raisers.[99]

Although Dilworth ran for mayor and lost in 1947, he received an impressive 44 percent of the vote, and by 1949 the Renaissance could no longer be denied.[100] That year this coalition succeeded in persuading Pennsylvania's legislature to grant Philadelphia, for the first time, the basic right to choose its own form of government.[101] Later that year the movement tasted an even more giddy victory when Clark and Dilworth were elected city controller and treasurer, respectively—the first Democrats elected to citywide office in Philadelphia in the twentieth century. When Clark and Dilworth discovered, upon taking office, that the tools for municipal government at their disposal were obsolete, they launched a new crusade for a "Home Rule Charter" that would replace political patronage with a strong civil service system and reorganize the city's useless agencies so that they could actually function.[102]

The exhilaration of this Renaissance threw Greenfield into close contact with a whole new generation of local movers and shakers who represented a refreshing change from the older men with whom he dealt in his business life. One such civic leader was Elizabeth Murphy Hallstrom, a vivacious career woman who had led the Philadelphia chapter of the League of Women

Voters and then advanced to the top position at a succession of other local civic groups.

Greenfield had first known "Bunny" Hallstrom, as her friends called her, as the daughter-in-law of A. L. Hallstrom, a president of the Philadelphia Chamber of Commerce, which Greenfield himself headed in 1951.[103] He probably first dealt with her in 1947, when Bunny was executive secretary of Philadelphia's Foreign Policy Association and Greenfield led an ambitious but ultimately unsuccessful campaign to locate the United Nations Building in Philadelphia.[104] At that point Bunny was thirty-three and recently divorced, with two young children: a rare high-level career woman making her way in a largely all-male environment.

Although Bunny was twenty-five years younger than Greenfield—younger even than Mary Roebling—she and Greenfield shared much in common.[105] Like Greenfield, Elizabeth exuded a combination of charm, intellect, and personal confidence that enabled her to deal as an equal with powerful men, much as Greenfield had dealt with powerful gentiles. Also like Greenfield, she was self-made—raised in poverty in Camden—and defied easy categorization: She was a Unitarian who had grown up in a family of Irish Methodists.

When the Foreign Policy Association merged with Philadelphia's United Nations Council to become the World Affairs Council in 1948, Elizabeth remained as the new group's executive director and Greenfield joined her board as its treasurer. Their first meeting there was hardly auspicious: Greenfield felt that the council should be run as a business and keep its programs within the limits of its budget; Elizabeth felt, as she put it, that "the organization must do what needs to be done, then find money to do it."[106]

By the end of 1950, Philadelphia's proposed new Home Rule Charter was drafted and ready for voter approval.[107] Greenfield led the effort to raise funds to promote the charter (although some of the funds he raised were used, at Greenfield's insistence, to pay for his own TV appearances in behalf of the cause).[108] A rally in support of the charter, with Greenfield as master of ceremonies, attracted thirty-three hundred Philadelphians to the Academy of Music in March 1951.[109] The following month, Greenfield delivered a radio address urging his fellow Philadelphians to "decide at the polls tomorrow whether we shall go forward under a modern charter of our own choosing or whether we shall retain the straitjacket imposed upon us by the State Legislature more than thirty-two years ago."[110]

After Philadelphia voters approved the new charter the next day, the exuberant reformers set their sights on the ultimate prize: City Hall, with Joseph

Clark as the Democratic candidate for mayor and Dilworth running for district attorney.

On Election Day that November, after a long day of poll-watching, some of the reformers—Bunny Hallstrom among them—retired to Greenfield's home to watch the returns on Greenfield's large (by 1951 standards) television set in the comfort of Greenfield's library, a dark, paneled room with a Persian rug covering Mercer tile. At some point that evening, Greenfield's daughter-in-law, Barbara, went upstairs to do her Penn homework and tend to her new baby, and the other guests drifted away as well. When Barbara came downstairs later to check on the returns, she found Greenfield and Elizabeth sitting alone on the sofa. Elizabeth—footsore and exhausted from standing at the polls all day—had propped her feet in Greenfield's lap, and he was massaging her toes. They looked, Barbara later remembered thinking, like a comfortable old married couple.[111]

They were married two months later, less than two weeks after Clark took office as Philadelphia's first Democratic mayor of the twentieth century. Greenfield was sixty-four; Elizabeth was thirty-nine and very different from his previous wives. Where Edna had been dependent and Etelka self-reliant, Bunny was both self-reliant and totally invested in her new relationship. She resigned her post with the World Affairs Council to devote herself to softening her new husband's rough edges, gathering in his family, and doing for Greenfield what Eva Roberts Cromwell had done for E. T. Stotesbury: persuade a workaholic husband for the first time to spend and enjoy his money.[112]

To put his past life behind him, Bunny persuaded Greenfield to sell the mansion in Overbrook Farms and move to an even more impressive estate: Sugar Loaf, an ornate eighteen-room stone house at the top of Chestnut Hill, Philadelphia's upper-class enclave in the city's northwest corner. Like the Main Line, Chestnut Hill was a creation of the Pennsylvania Railroad—specifically, of the Pennsy director Henry Howard Houston, who in the 1880s built a rail line there, bought most of the land west of the tracks, and then built a family church, a summer hotel, and a country club to enhance his investment. Unlike the Main Line, Chestnut Hill remained within Philadelphia's city limits and so appealed to members of the upper class with a sense of civic involvement.[113]

Sugar Loaf's five acres put Greenfield next door to Henry Houston and just a few blocks from his patrician friend Edward Hopkinson Jr.—who had lived in the same house on Montgomery Avenue since his marriage in

1911—and from Mayor Joseph Clark and Congressman Hugh Scott. Philadelphia's grandest old man, U.S. Senator George Wharton Pepper, had actually once lived on the grounds of Sugar Loaf, in a tiny gardener's cottage as a boy in 1873.[114]

With Elizabeth's encouragement, Greenfield hired the noted architect Edward Durrell Stone to completely renovate Sugar Loaf's building and grounds. Stone ripped the house apart, replacing cramped rooms and narrow windows with glass bay windows two stories high and clear glass skylights, developing what *Town and Country* magazine called "a new architectural concept within its solid stone walls for the requirements of modern living."[115] The master portion of the house had nine rooms, most with fireplaces; on the second floor, the separate bedrooms for Bunny and Albert were connected by a sitting room where they liked to gather. Stone also designed outdoor terraces for cocktails or dining, a tiled flower room, a third-floor playroom, an electric elevator, an imposing entrance hall with Italian sculpture and a specially woven carpet, and—inexplicably, given Greenfield's lack of interest in religion—two kitchens, one of them kosher.[116] From Henry Houston's estate next door, Greenfield purchased an additional fourteen and a half acres and added a guesthouse as well as a pool house equipped with dressing rooms and a complete kitchen. The grounds were landscaped with beautiful trees, gardens, and views of the distant downtown from a commanding site.[117]

Elizabeth was no artist like Etelka, but she possessed an artistic eye. Under her tutelage, Greenfield became something of a patron of the arts, with an eclectic collection at Sugar Loaf that included works by Rembrandt. One of Monet's original "water lily" paintings hung in their front hallway, the dining room housed an extensive collection of works by Willem de Kooning, and a hand sculpture by Rodin sat on a desk.[118]

In this showplace, Bunny and Albert threw large, elaborate Thanksgiving and Christmas meals for his children and their families, impeccably presented by the servants. They also hosted receptions for public figures like the French premier Pierre Mendès-France and Vice President Lyndon Johnson, as well as New Year's Day receptions attended by as many as seven hundred people.[119]

A few of Greenfield's relatives resented Elizabeth as a gold digger. But most held her in much the same affectionate awe that they had previously reserved for Greenfield alone. "Elizabeth Hallstrom brought into Albert's life a warmth and youthfulness that was remarkable," recalled his granddaughter Priscilla Luce, who was four when Greenfield married Elizabeth.

Into my grandfather's life comes this young, vibrant, lovely woman who is making him incredibly happy. Any idiot could see that. Even

I could see it as a child. He softened after their marriage. Her influence was pervasive. She brought the family together, even these warring siblings who had been pitted against each other in many ways by their parents and who had had this terribly traumatic upbringing. Those family dinners I think were largely her inspiration. She made sure everybody was well treated. Gifts were given on time, birthday gifts were given—she took charge of all of that. In essence, she was the wife that, if he had had her when his kids were little, it would've been an entirely different story.[120]

Years earlier, when Greenfield was hiring a chauffeur, the applicant had asked what his hours would be. "That's simple," Greenfield had replied. "When I sleep, you sleep." The chauffeur later estimated that he had averaged about five hours' sleep a night.[121] Elizabeth's combination of management skills and loving affection changed all that. At a dinner party one night at Sugar Loaf, when Elizabeth sent the butler to bed, Albert sputtered, "Why should he go to bed? *I'm* still up." "Yes, dear," Elizabeth replied, "but he's working." Greenfield said no more.[122]

Greenfield himself was incapable of articulating or acknowledging how his remarkable new wife had changed him. Introspection was never his strong suit. When his aging male business associates expressed curiosity about his May–December marriage, Greenfield tended to retreat behind locker-room banter. Shortly after his marriage to Bunny, at one of his board meetings, his fellow directors asked how he liked his new wife. "Oh, *she's* fine," Greenfield quipped. "But *I* need a new *putz*. I can't screw anymore."[123]

Yet for all his macho protestation, there was no denying the remarkable thing that had happened to him. This master of reinvention, who throughout his life had fancied himself the agent of change in any given situation, had tried and failed to reinvent himself as a benevolent godfather, only to find someone else who had done the job for him. In the process, Greenfield the self-styled miracle maker had somehow stumbled into a miracle he had never imagined in his wildest dreams: He had found the fountain of youth.

[PART V]

LEGACY

[13]

Civic Savior

For all his triumphs, one stain still tarnished Greenfield's record: Despite his lifetime of civic cheerleading, his adopted city remained a national embarrassment. Philadelphia after World War II resembled a doughnut: a vast metropolis built up around a hollow center. Center City's streets, many of them still illuminated by gaslight, were all but deserted at night. Only a few decent residential blocks remained, mostly around elegant Rittenhouse Square. The rest of the downtown, and even Independence Hall, was engulfed in slums.[1]

Almost everything about the city seemed old, tired, and constrained. The Pennsylvania Railroad's "Chinese Wall" still effectively choked off the downtown's northern limit at Market Street. New hotels and restaurants were deterred by Pennsylvania's antiquated blue laws, which banned the sale of alcoholic drinks on Sundays. New buildings were still restrained by the tradition that no structure could rise higher than William Penn's hat atop City Hall. While the world's two tallest buildings—the 102-story Empire State Building and the 77-story Chrysler Building—had risen in New York, not a single new office or luxury apartment building or hotel had been built in Philadelphia since the 30-story Philadelphia Saving Fund Society's tower had been launched in 1930.

The smell of burning garbage, still carted to open dumps by horse-drawn wagons, permeated Philadelphia's dirty streets. The city's sewage-polluted water required so much chlorination to render it safe for drinking that a glass of Philadelphia water was known as a "chlorine cocktail."

Even industries were beginning to flee Philadelphia because of the city's crushing tax burden. The old vaudeville joke—"Last week I went to Philadelphia, but it was closed"—remained as valid as when W. C. Fields (himself a Philadelphia native) had first uttered it early in the twentieth century.

Greenfield's holdings were still concentrated in the eastern half of Philadelphia's "doughnut hole": the old downtown historic district along the Delaware River, with its narrow streets and cozy but cramped buildings. Until 1800 or so, this community had been known as Society Hill, after the Free Society of Traders that helped William Penn promote and settle the city.[2] But the name had long since fallen into disuse, along with the neighborhood's handsome eighteenth- and nineteenth-century homes, now converted into lofts and rooming houses disfigured by grime and stucco. Dock Street, the city's obsolete and unsanitary 175-year-old produce and meat market, sprawled over several blocks of this district, creating a health hazard as well as appalling traffic jams.[3]

The cause of this blight was clear enough. For the first half of the twentieth century, Philadelphia's city government was by most accounts the most wasteful and ineffective in the United States. The city's WASP business leaders tolerated this status quo because they lived in the suburbs and did not have to drink the city's tainted water, walk its mean streets, or breathe its polluted air.[4]

The passage of Philadelphia's Home Rule Charter in 1951, coupled with the election of the Clark-Dilworth ticket later that year, brought new hope that William Penn's idealized "greene country towne" might yet be saved. But it also served to remind Greenfield that he had yet to leave a permanent imprint on his adopted city.

Since the 1940s Greenfield had led a quixotic crusade to save America's cities through massive government urban renewal programs. In 1943 he had become chairman of the Urban Land Institute, a national urban real estate organization. "Year after year," he lamented in a speech then, "we have seen our substantial citizens follow each other to the open spaces surrounding our city, and the establishment of newer and newer suburban centers, and in the process continually draining away the civic health and economic vitality of the older districts."

To Greenfield, the crux of the problem was that cities built for another day could not compete with new suburban areas "built expressly for modern living." Yet cities were still worth saving, he insisted: "I have yet to meet a man who really enjoys battling traffic for five, ten or fifteen miles at the end of his business day. Nor do I believe that there is any real pleasure in hanging from a strap for an hour or two a day." The solution, as Greenfield saw it, was to create the "superior environment" of the suburbs in urban locations that were more convenient to people's workplaces.[5]

The challenge was actually more severe than Greenfield realized. He failed to foresee that, over the next generation or two, the nuisance of commuting from the suburbs to the city would be eliminated—not by suburbanites moving back to cities but by companies moving their city offices and plants to the suburbs. Greenfield also failed to acknowledge that his own dominant presence might have contributed to Philadelphia's downtown decay: During the postwar years, ambitious commercial developers like the Tishmans of New York—then expanding their operations to Chicago, Detroit, and other cities—were said to have avoided Philadelphia because they perceived that Greenfield had the local market sewn up.

Yet Greenfield was correct in perceiving that central cities—the incubators for all the world's creative solutions for at least two millennia—would die without some massive overhaul. As early as 1912 Philadelphia's City Council had sought to address this issue by creating a planning board, only to disband it seven years later as the city's budget shrank.[6] The concept was revived in 1928 with a city planning commission, whose board included Greenfield and E. T. Stotesbury, among other local notables. That same year a regional planning federation was also created, with a similar blue-ribbon executive committee that included Greenfield, Stotesbury, William Purves Gest, and Stotesbury's Drexel partners Thomas S. Gates and H. Gates Lloyd.[7] But these groups lacked professional staffs or real power to influence policy, and both efforts withered in the face of the crash of 1929 and the Great Depression that followed.[8]

Yet another planning commission was created by the City Council in 1942 amid a power vacuum caused by the sudden death of Mayor Robert Lamberton. Its first chairman was Edward Hopkinson Jr., the Drexel & Co. senior partner with whom Greenfield had developed a friendship in the 1930s. Hopkinson brought Edmund Bacon—at that time one of the few American city planning executives trained in urban design—onto the planning commission's staff in 1946 and made him its executive director three years later.[9] To whet Philadelphians' appetites for change, in 1947 Hopkinson raised $340,000 to mount a spectacular exhibition called "Better Philadelphia" in Gimbels department store downtown. This stunning display used scale models, dioramas, moving objects, and flashing lights to dramatize for 385,000 previously pessimistic Philadelphians what their city's decaying center could look like in thirty years if the commission's proposed projects were carried out.[10]

But the planning commission lacked the power to implement its ambitious visions. The Young Turk leader Richardson Dilworth, in his unsuccessful 1947 campaign for mayor, had charged that the commission was "sabotaged" by the old Republican organization; Hopkinson was one of the "nine old men" he singled out for criticism. In 1952, with Clark and Dilworth installed as mayor and district attorney, Hopkinson remained on the planning commission partly because Greenfield interceded when the new administration tried to remove him. The city, Greenfield said publicly, owed Hopkinson "a debt of gratitude for unselfish public service."[11] Yet for all his denials, Greenfield was hungry to succeed his friend, if only because revitalizing the blighted neighborhood around Independence Hall—his primary domain—was a subject close to both his heart and his wallet.[12]

Other Philadelphians, most notably Ed Bacon, were wrestling with the same challenge, without much success. As early as 1946, Bacon urged the city to use federal funds to help restore the colonial district as a residential community.[13] In 1947 Bacon first proposed the concept of pedestrian walkways that would enable residents and visitors to experience the historic district in a new and exciting way.[14] When he became executive director of Philadelphia's City Planning Commission in 1949, Bacon personally championed the concept of downtown living by moving his family to a townhouse near Rittenhouse Square.[15] Other prominent Philadelphians tried to do likewise. The banker C. Jared Ingersoll, scion of an Old Philadelphia family, moved into an abandoned house in the historic district.[16] (When the Ingersolls first visited the house, they found a drunk asleep in the front hall. In the best stiff-upper-lip tradition of her class, Agnes Ingersoll simply stepped over the unfortunate man and continued her inspection.)[17]

But these symbolic gestures were pebbles cast in an ocean. After the Philadelphia Redevelopment Authority failed to find builders or bankers who would invest in such an obviously deteriorated area, the agency declined even to put the restoration project up for bid. "Everyone thought the idea was screwy," Bacon later recalled. "Most respectable people had moved away."[18]

The conquest of City Hall by Clark and Dilworth, whom Greenfield had supported and financed, seemed an opportunity to expand his involvement. But that would require his parsing the relationship between Clark and Dilworth, which was more complicated than people realized.

To most Philadelphians, Clark and Dilworth were two peas in a pod— "Damon and Pythias," as one national magazine called them.[19] Both men were idealistic liberals born into wealthy, upper-class families that summered on the beaches of Southampton, Long Island; both had graduated from New England prep schools and Ivy League colleges and law schools; and both had rebelled against their conservative family backgrounds. Yet beneath the surface their differences outweighed their similarities.

Clark was a man of deep convictions and an almost scholarly interest in the workings of municipal government, but he was aloof, arrogant, and openly contemptuous of professional politicians—the sort of idealist who, as one observer described him, "loved humanity but couldn't stand people."

Dilworth, by contrast, was a passionate extrovert with a genuine empathy for people from all walks of life.[20] Where Clark seemed uncomfortable among ethnic minorities, Dilworth as district attorney made an explicit point of hiring Jews, Catholics, African Americans, and women in an office previously monopolized by white Protestant males like himself. As one of Clark's aides later put it, Clark left people "with the impression that you were bothering him, while Dilworth made you feel that he had been waiting all his life to meet you."[21]

Nothing quite epitomized the two men's differences as their posture toward Greenfield. Much like the bankers who had rejected Greenfield in 1930, Clark seemed immune to Greenfield's celebrated charm. At a conference in 1955 to discuss the future of the city's antiquated Dock Street food market, Greenfield's opening remarks went on too long to suit Clark. "Albert," he shouted, "for God's sake be quiet and let someone else talk for a minute." Clark apologized after the meeting, and those familiar with Clark knew that he treated everybody this way. But Greenfield took Clark's reaction personally. "He wounded me," Greenfield told a friend. "He wounded me."[22]

Having created the city's merit hiring system, Clark was preoccupied with avoiding any appointment that smacked of patronage.[23] A loose cannon like Greenfield, accustomed to playing by his own rules and buying influence through his campaign contributions, was anathema to Clark. Clark also subscribed to the long-standing philosophy of the local Citizens' Council on City Planning, which believed that real estate operators should be kept far from planning commissions, lest they unfairly exploit their access to confidential information about the city's prospective land purchases.[24]

So although Greenfield had been one of Clark's heaviest supporters in the 1951 election, Clark went out of his way to keep him at arm's length.[25] He reappointed the Republican Hopkinson as the planning commission's chairman. To Greenfield he offered only a seat on the Philadelphia Redevelopment Authority, then widely perceived as a weak link in the city's urban renewal plans, with a small and ineffective staff.[26]

As mayor, Clark quickly demonstrated to a tired and cynical city what government could accomplish with inspired leadership. He replaced the city's sidewalk gas lamps with electric lights, instituted street cleanings on a regular basis, launched a new sewage treatment system, and replaced the city's horse-drawn garbage wagons with modern sanitation trucks. Modern fire stations and playgrounds sprang up around the city.[27] But Clark had promised to serve only one term as mayor, and in 1956 he left office in favor of Dilworth.[28]

Like Clark, Dilworth had experienced his share of quarrels with Greenfield. In 1954 Greenfield had dashed Dilworth's hopes of running for governor by withholding his support on the ground that Dilworth could not win.[29] And, of course, this was the same Richardson Dilworth who, as the *Inquirer*'s general counsel, had represented Moses Annenberg so tenaciously against Greenfield and David Stern during their bitter feud in 1938.

Privately, Dilworth described Greenfield as "the most selfish son of a bitch who ever lived. . . . God, he was absolutely ruthless. He was only interested in making money. Very little else interested him. Oh, at times he could make gestures that were sincere. You know, nobody is completely avaricious. And there were times when he would do decent and generous things. But by and large his one interest was financial power."[30]

However, Dilworth—much like Greenfield—was never one to nurse old resentments, especially against someone he found useful. Greenfield, Dilworth reflected years after leaving office, "knew every facet of the city. He knew virtually every figure in it. He was enormously resourceful and he was not only a very attractive man, he was tremendously well read and very funny. A hell of a conversationalist. He was up on everything."[31]

By the time Dilworth became mayor, Greenfield's financial support of Dilworth's political career had ripened into the sort of chummy relationship that delighted both men. When Dilworth vacationed, he habitually sent Greenfield breezy postcards like this one from southern California:

> Dear A.M.,
>   Weather here is marvelous, but I had hoped to find Marilyn Monroe and Jayne Mansfield at the Racquet Club here. Instead find only such bags as Mary Pickford & Marion Davies. They are the youngest things here.
>   Sincerely, Dick.[32]

It was impossible to imagine Joe Clark sending such a card, to Greenfield or anyone else.

Dilworth took office not long after the Pennsylvania Railroad finally honored its twenty-eight-year-old pledge to vacate its little-used Broad

Street Station next to City Hall. This momentous decision opened up the possibility that the station building and the tracks leading from it—the infamous "Chinese Wall" that divided Center City—could be removed, and four new downtown blocks could be redeveloped in some exciting fashion as "Penn Center."[33]

Dilworth was impatient to replace Hopkinson with someone who could translate the planning commission's maps and models into bricks and mortar—especially, to make Penn Center "a model for the greater cities of the U.S." and to develop the historic area around Independence Hall.[34] Those tasks required someone capable of harnessing the city's business community to work with the city's planners—as Dilworth put it, "a person of proven standing in the community, preferably a practical man of business, capable of translating the plans into reality."[35]

The news of Greenfield's appointment as chairman of the planning commission produced a furious reaction. The banker C. Jared Ingersoll resigned in protest because, he said, "No real estate man should be placed in a political position where he had so much to do with the value of individual pieces of real estate."[36] Ed Bacon, the planning commission's executive director, also contemplated resigning.[37] To Bacon, putting Greenfield in charge of the planning commission was tantamount to putting the fox in charge of the chicken coop. Greenfield had already been rejected as a developer of Penn Center because city planners feared that he wanted to overbuild, and also because his relentless haggling alienated the railroad's officials.[38] Who knew how he would commandeer the city's resources in his own backyard east of Broad Street?

Once again Greenfield, by his sheer personal presence, had crystallized an old civic debate: Is a community best served by detached and impartial public servants or by experienced players with money at stake? And once again this debate was clouded by concerns, however subconscious, that the city's WASP power structure—in this case represented by Hopkinson, Ingersoll, Bacon, and John Phillips of the Citizens' Council on City Planning—was being nudged aside by Eastern European Jewish immigrants like Greenfield, city solicitor Abraham Freedman, city representative Frederic Mann, and Dilworth's development coordinator, William Rafsky.[39]

Nevertheless, Dilworth refused to back away from Greenfield. "No one knows the city as he does," the mayor told reporters.[40] For years Dilworth had complained that Philadelphia's City Planning Commission was all plans and no action; now, he said, Greenfield would supply the action. Privately, Dilworth suggested another reason: His sometime-friend, sometime-adversary Greenfield would be easier to control inside his administration than outside of it.[41]

To placate his critics, Greenfield took the extraordinary step of resigning from his original real estate firm, Albert M. Greenfield & Co., and selling his controlling stake to its employees. His interest from that moment on, Greenfield announced, would be "a sentimental one, not of material interest."[42] But, of course, it was impossible to completely separate Albert Greenfield from the firm that he had nurtured for a half-century and that still bore his name. He did not vacate his headquarters in the Bankers Securities Building on Walnut Street; instead, he merely moved his office one flight upstairs. He retained ownership of three other personal real estate companies. And Greenfield remained chairman of Bankers Securities, which still controlled downtown office buildings, department stores, hotels, and apartment complexes.[43] Divorcing Greenfield from Philadelphia real estate was like trying to separate a tortoise from its shell.[44]

On January 4, 1956, just days after Dilworth's inauguration, Greenfield was unanimously elected chairman of the commission.[45] Those who expected him to operate differently from his predecessor did not have to wait long to confirm their hopes (or fears). Drawing on his clout as a past and potential political fund-raiser, Greenfield persuaded the City Council—most of whose members were regular Democrats hostile to Dilworth—to increase the planning department's annual budget by more than half, to more than $500,000, and to allot $4 million more for urban renewal.[46]

In later years, 1956 would be recalled in Philadelphia as the year Center City finally began to reverse its long decline. Upon assuming office, Greenfield focused his attention not on the Penn Center space west of Broad Street but on the area he knew best: the historic district east of Broad Street. Here he approached the challenge like a developer rather than a bureaucrat.

The city's future, he theorized, depended on building up its tax base, which in turn depended on attracting affluent people to live nearby and spend their money in its department stores, hotels, and restaurants. Like Ed Bacon, Greenfield recognized that the Georgian homes in the historic district, now largely abandoned or converted to dingy rooming houses, offered the potential cachet that could entice affluent homeowners back to the neighborhood—if the general area improved. But to Greenfield, a piecemeal, house-by-house approach to reviving downtown living was doomed to failure. "The reason nothing is moving and nobody has bought down there," he argued, "is because nobody has been given a guarantee that his investment will be protected and the climate of the whole area improved."[47]

Greenfield's solution was to draw up a detailed revitalization plan that would qualify the entire thousand-acre tract southeast of Independence

Hall—an area that comprised one-quarter of downtown Philadelphia—for urban renewal under the Federal Housing Act of 1954. In effect, the city would condemn all properties within the project's boundaries; but instead of leveling everything and rebuilding from scratch, as other cities were doing, Philadelphia would offer every existing homeowner the opportunity to keep his or her property by restoring its exterior to its original period—and the city would provide low-cost loans to do the job, as well. At the same time, vacant houses and lots would be offered to newcomers at bargain prices, again with the stipulation that façades be restored according to the plan's rigid specifications.[48]

To create confidence among homebuyers, the plan called for realizing some of Bacon's visions, like installing new brick sidewalks and imitation gas lanterns, creating green walkways that connected Society Hill to Independence National Historical Park, and building a major addition to the neighborhood's McCall public elementary school.

This was a unique surgical approach to urban renewal—what one observer called "an attempt to salvage what is good of the old, add what is needed of the new, and in general transform that part of the city into a sort of urban residential paradise without making a museum-fossil out of it."[49] It was also a radical departure from Greenfield's previous seat-of-the-pants approach to urban development.

In a city previously accustomed to old money and slow movement, here was the most complex and demanding urban project ever attempted—in Philadelphia or anywhere else. In effect, Bacon's vision and Greenfield's plan both sought to reverse the process that the Pennsylvania Railroad had begun eighty years earlier—that is, it would draw Philadelphia's upper and upper-middle classes back into the heart of the city, much as the railroad had lured them to the Main Line in the nineteenth century.

That the plan would benefit Greenfield's own nearby hotels, department stores, and office buildings was obvious but also beside the point. In this case Greenfield's great strength lay in his *lack* of objectivity: Precisely because he had huge investments in the historic district, he enjoyed widespread credibility.

Greenfield objected to reviving "Society Hill" as the name for this district because he felt it connoted snobbishness and exclusivity. But when his own preferred title—"Old City Urban Renewal Area"—failed (for obvious reasons) to generate any discernible excitement, "Society Hill" was resurrected after an absence of more than 150 years.[50]

The first enthusiastic convert to his plan was perhaps also the most important: Dilworth's first public act as mayor was a directive to proceed with

Greenfield's proposed plan. Shortly after, Dilworth announced that he would personally build himself an eighteenth-century-style townhouse on Washington Square, at Society Hill's western edge.[51] No such townhouse had been built anywhere in Philadelphia since the turn of the twentieth century. Dilworth clearly intended it as what one observer called "a straw in a change of wind, a wind of change blowing for the first time in Philadelphia's history from west to east, rather than from east to west."[52]

But new residents could not be induced to invest in Society Hill unless government and private developers invested millions as well. Fitting together all the public and private elements of the Society Hill project, it soon became apparent, exceeded the scope of any public agency. Greenfield's solution was to create a nonprofit public-private partnership between the city and business leaders who had a stake in the downtown. Forming this new civic body—possibly the first of its kind anywhere—became Greenfield's primary mission.

That spring he spoke at length to virtually every leading industrialist, banker, and merchant to drum up financial support. The business leaders he buttonholed soon discovered what homebuyers and shopkeepers had learned fifty years earlier: Greenfield had an answer for every objection. He could wax lyrical about Society Hill—"this plot of one thousand acres that combines all that civilization has to offer." But he could also get down to hard economic facts and figures, pointing out that retail sales on Market Street had declined by 15 percent in the past eight years, even while sales in the greater Philadelphia region had grown. He reminded the banks and insurance companies holding mortgages on stores and buildings in the area that they would be the long-run losers if the downtown withered. When skeptics asked if people would really live downtown, Greenfield could reassure them not as a detached urban planner or economist but as a lifelong developer who had put his money where his mouth was.[53] "He understood the history, he understood the economics, he understood the politics, and then he understood how to sell it to a broad citizenry of the city that would have to support it on a continuing basis," Philadelphia's redevelopment director Walter D'Alessio later recalled.[54]

One nagging personal obstacle remained. Mayor Dilworth believed that the perfect organization for reviving the historic district already existed. The Greater Philadelphia Movement (GPM), the new civic voice of the city's business community, had recently taken the lead in building a new food distribution center to replace the obsolete Dock Street Market on Society Hill's eastern end. But the GPM represented the same fraternity of Republican bankers who had abandoned Greenfield in 1930, and Greenfield had been pointedly excluded when the GPM was formed in 1948. Only a few months earlier, the GPM had suspended its plans to build a new food distribution center in South Philadelphia because of alleged interference by Greenfield, whom the GPM accused of exercising a "personal veto" over the City Council. Greenfield had responded by calling GPM's statement "a violent attack upon me personally."[55] He was not eager to cast his lot with them.

The impasse was not solved until Dilworth sat down with Greenfield and the advertising executive Harry Batten, a founder of the GPM, at the Bellevue-Stratford Hotel and persuaded them to join forces for the good of developing Society Hill.[56] The Old Philadelphia Development Corporation (OPDC), as it was called, was formed in May 1956, with $2 million in capital, an annual budget of $100,000, and a board that included city officials, business and labor leaders, and two university presidents. William Day, chairman of the First Pennsylvania Bank—one of the city's oldest, and the successor to Stevenson Newhall's Pennsylvania Company—was "dragged in" by friends, as he put it, to serve as the new organization's chairman.[57]

Since the Philadelphia Redevelopment Authority lacked experience with marketing and selling individual homes, this new OPDC was tasked with finding and securing homebuyers and bringing them to the closing table, even though it never actually took title to any properties. Instead, the OPDC served as the intermediary between the Philadelphia Redevelopment Authority and individual homebuyers without assuming any of the liabilities of ownership. Whether Greenfield came up with this ingenious structure is unclear, but it was difficult to imagine anyone else conceiving it.[58]

To lead this new partnership, Greenfield courted John P. Robin, who had overseen downtown Pittsburgh's pioneering Gateway Center development. Robin was initially reluctant to leave a fast-moving, free-spending city like Pittsburgh for a cautious, parsimonious place like Philadelphia, but Greenfield won him over by offering an annual salary of $35,000—more than any Philadelphia official received.[59] Over lunch on Robin's first visit to Philadelphia, Greenfield painted a rapturous picture of Philadelphia's future and of Robin's "unique opportunity" to make a contribution to his time in a much larger city. But Robin remained skeptical.

"Are you all together?" Robin asked, referring to Philadelphia's business leaders. "Because the reason I was able to work it out in Pittsburgh was because the Mellons were behind me, and once the Mellons said yes to anything in Pittsburgh, that meant that everybody was for it. . . . Do you have anything like that in this community?"

"Well, that's exactly what we're putting together in OPDC," Greenfield eagerly replied. "We're putting together a vehicle where the total community can get behind a project that's worthwhile."[60]

To the planning commission's meetings, as in all his other dealings, Greenfield brought his exquisite sense of timing and human relations. As one observer recalled, he would let a discussion flow freely until he sensed that people were repeating themselves. Then he would bring things together quickly. "Now, gentlemen," he would typically say, "I'd like to express myself. I do not have a monopoly on wisdom. However . . ."[61]

Greenfield also brought to the job an array of resources rarely found in a public official. One evening in the summer of 1956, members of Mayor Dilworth's staff were preparing a mailing to five hundred prominent Philadelphians, inviting them to a meeting at which plans for Society Hill would be unveiled. The invitations had to be mailed that night, but City Hall was already closed and the postage was not available. A Dilworth assistant telephoned John O'Shea, Greenfield's public relations assistant at Bankers Securities, and O'Shea arranged for Dilworth's staff to use the postage machine at the Bellevue-Stratford Hotel that night so the mailing could go out on time.[62]

If Greenfield wanted something badly enough, Philadelphia's development coordinator, William Rafsky, noted admiringly, he could usually get it done.[63] In one instance, Philadelphia's city planners objected to an architectural design that the General Services Administration (GSA) had devised for a federal courthouse on the proposed Independence Mall, but the GSA refused to budge from its original plans. When the Philadelphians gathered to plot their next step, Greenfield astonished the roomful of professional planners and commission members by reaching for the phone and placing a call to the White House.

"Inside of twenty minutes," one board member later recalled, "he had on the telephone, personally, the White House, the Governor, the Mayor, and the two United States Senators. . . . It left the leading businessmen and citizens present with mouths open in awe and wonderment and respect." The result was a conference to discuss the issue, after which the federal agency modified the design to suit the Philadelphians' objections.[64] That sort of clout was impossible to replicate. "Philadelphia's Greenfield," noted *Architectural Forum*, "is the kind of planning commissioner few cities can afford."[65]

From the outset, Greenfield's expertise dazzled the bankers, academics, and civic leaders on the planning commission. "I've never seen a man know so much about . . . real estate and know every parcel that came up for question," marveled his fellow commissioner G. Holmes Perkins, dean of the School of Fine Arts at the University of Pennsylvania.[66]

Dilworth too professed himself amazed. "It is extraordinary the way in which you put direction into the work of the staff of the Commission, pinpointed the projects which should be concentrated upon, and on which work should be commenced," Dilworth wrote Greenfield early in 1957. "The result is that in a little over a year more plans have been translated into projects than ever before.[67]

Greenfield's chairmanship created another of the "Odd Couple" relationships that delighted him but often discomfited others—in this case pairing a Jewish entrepreneur with Ed Bacon, a professional city planner of long-standing Quaker lineage.[68] At first, almost everything about Greenfield's free-wheeling operating style rubbed Bacon the wrong way, from Greenfield's resistance to new high-rise buildings ("He feared they'd draw tenants away from his own buildings," Bacon later remarked) to the arbitrary way he ran meetings ("He would take command firmly and speak at great length, but he was not a good listener") to his hunger for recognition ("If I gave a speech and didn't mention him prominently, I would hear about it the next day"). Periodically, Greenfield would summon Bacon to his office in the Bankers Securities Building, where, Bacon recalled, "He sat me in a chair like an elementary school student. I was in the presence of the master."[69]

Nevertheless, Bacon ultimately perceived that Greenfield's operating style was critical to translating Bacon's plans from paper into reality, and by both men's subsequent accounts they worked together efficiently. Bacon later recalled:

Albert Greenfield was a very difficult chairman, and I found it quite painful to serve under him but nonetheless managed to do it. He was very bull-headed, and of course he was very much tied up with vested interests. However, it is true that he did back the idea—although it was difficult for him to do so—of our doing the comprehensive plan, and he had that much influence with Council that he was able to get funds necessary for it. In fact, I have a strong suspicion he was the only person who would have been able to do that. And although he certainly messed with the detailed zoning cases and made our lives miserable in that regard, he never interfered with our comprehensive plan in any way, and I certainly give him credit for that.[70]

Within a year of Greenfield's arrival at the planning commission, a private developer (with public funding) demolished the decrepit Dock Street Market to make way for what became the neighborhood's primary anchor: Society Hill Towers, a residential complex of three 31-story apartment buildings as well as low-rise houses, all designed by the noted architect I. M. Pei.[71] Society Hill was subsequently reborn as an upper-middle-class enclave of more than six thousand residents, many of them living in restored colonial homes, just as Greenfield and Bacon had envisioned.[72] It was the envy of cities everywhere.

Society Hill's renewal triggered the subsequent reinvention of downtown Philadelphia as a center of arts and culture, gourmet restaurants, upscale hotels, and gleaming high-rise office buildings that towered well above William Penn's statue on City Hall. In 1980 a U.S. census study concluded that no downtown neighborhood in America could match Philadelphia's Center City for its combination of population, household income level, education level, and number of people who both lived and worked in the same neighborhood. While the population of Philadelphia declined by nearly one-quarter between 1960 and 2000, the downtown population grew by more than half. By the end of the twentieth century, nearly eighty thousand people were living within the boundaries of William Penn's original town—far more than resided in any downtown outside New York or Chicago.[73] "Of all the big cities," the urban affairs journalist Jeanne R. Lowe wrote in *Cities in a Race with Time*, a book on urban renewal published in 1967, "Philadelphia has come closest to a comprehensive approach to the complex challenges confronting our urban centers."[74]

Success has many parents, of course. The resurrection of Society Hill was subsequently attributed variously to Dilworth, Bacon, Greenfield, Rafsky, Robin, Perkins, D'Alessio, and several others. When Rafsky was interviewed years later, he cited Bacon, Greenfield, and himself as the prime movers. Greenfield, he added, "claimed all of the credit, which is all right with me."[75]

In June 1956, while Greenfield was busy launching the OPDC, a notable Philadelphia property fell into his hands. For $650,000, Bankers Securities took title to the former Drexel & Co. headquarters at Fifteenth and Walnut Streets—the very same Florentine-style palazzo where, in 1930, E. T. Stotesbury had sealed the fate of Greenfield's bank with the humiliation of Greenfield's friend William Fox.

In the aftermath of this sale, a curious urban legend arose: Upon taking possession of the building, it was said, Greenfield had entered with several police officers, stalked through the six stories from roof to basement, and personally fired everyone, from the chief executive down to the janitor. Then he had locked the front door, urinated against the outside wall, and abandoned the vacant building to rot, as a demonstration of the fate that awaited anyone who might cross him.

It was the sort of delicious revenge fantasy that many a businessman might dream for himself and presumably imagined for Greenfield. But it was totally spurious and surely out of character for Greenfield, who had never seen the benefit in bearing grudges. The myth also did not make any sense: Greenfield would hardly have alienated his friend Edward Hopkinson—still Drexel's senior partner—with such a gratuitously crude and vindictive gesture; nor would he have offended the WASP bankers whose support he was then courting so solicitously for the renewal of Society Hill. More to the point, Drexel & Co. had already vacated the building fourteen years earlier.[76]

To the extent that Greenfield exacted any sort of "revenge" on Stotesbury, it had already occurred after Stotesbury's death in 1938, when the grand old banker's cash-strapped executors put his three-hundred-acre Whitemarsh Hall estate up for sale. They found no buyer until, after World War II, Greenfield acquired it and entered into a joint venture to develop the land with the builder Matthew McCloskey. Together they demolished Stotesbury's massive Georgian chateau and replaced it with Whitemarsh Village, a community of some 546 individual homes priced to appeal to servicemen returning home from the war. It was Greenfield's only major foray into suburban housing, but it was immensely profitable: His companies provided the financing and insurance for the project as well as mortgages for the homebuyers. But if Greenfield took any special pleasure in disposing of Stotesbury's estate, he kept it to himself.[77]

When the Drexel Building downtown was sold in 1956, Bankers Securities initially announced that it would move its executive and administrative offices there. But even this symbolic gesture may have discomfited Greenfield, and the plan was dropped. Nevertheless, the myth that Greenfield had urinated on the building persisted (in another version, he urinated on Stotesbury's desk), if only because, as Greenfield's detractors pointed out, at least one piece of it was true: The old Drexel Building did indeed stand vacant for more than twenty years thereafter.[78]

Barely a year after his appointment to Philadelphia's City Planning Commission, Greenfield submitted his resignation to Dilworth, effective no later than mid-1957. He cited the pressure of his various business interests, apparently an allusion to a management crisis at his department store chain, City Stores Company.[79] "We both understood that once the blueprint was set and the wheels set in motion," he wrote to Dilworth, "I was free to address myself to my prior commitments."[80] At Dilworth's urging, Greenfield stayed on at the planning commission until January 1958.[81]

After Greenfield left the planning commission, Dilworth continued to turn to him for informal advice. In one case Dilworth asked Greenfield how he felt about the city's acquiring the site of the Pennsylvania Railroad's Broad Street Station, across from City Hall, to create a park or plaza there. Greenfield's reply provides a good sample of the savvy chumminess with which the two men related. In his memo, Greenfield said he had examined the site and "find no precious stones in the basement."

> Two and a half million dollars, Dick, is about one million more than the lot is worth, but if you want the city to buy it in order to create another rendezvous for the idle and the drifters as already exists at Reyburn Plaza, as far as I am concerned I shall make no effort to stop you from indulging your whim with reference to this property.[82]

The summer after Greenfield left the planning commission, he and Bunny flew to Geneva to attend a global peace conference. Dilworth—left behind in City Hall to wrangle with the city's Democratic boss, William J. Green—sent them a bon voyage telegram:

> If there is anyone who can convince Khrushchev and Nasser that it is better to be wise than smart, it is yourself. Hope you have a fine and productive session and that after establishing world brotherhood you can do the same for Willie Green and myself.
>   Dick Dilworth.[83]

[14]

Lion in Winter

I n the spring of 1959, when he was seventy-one, Greenfield retired as chairman of Bankers Securities, the holding company he had created and run since 1928.[1] A month later he also stepped down as chairman of Bankers Securities' largest subsidiary, City Stores Company, which he had chaired since 1932.[2] By 1962 he had resigned as well from Bankers Bond & Mortgage (which he had founded in 1924) and from the PTC's board (where he had served since 1936).[3]

His new purpose, Greenfield announced, was to spend his last years re-paying his success through "a debt of never-ending work and effort" to his fellow man. In doing so he flouted the time-honored Philadelphia Quaker business tradition of "doing good by doing well"—the notion that a man should focus on making money, the better to enrich his community, rather than dissipate his energies in philanthropy. But, of course, Greenfield's hero Benjamin Franklin had flouted that notion too: "Do well by doing good," Franklin had insisted.

Greenfield does not seem to have given much thought to the question of precisely how he would wean himself from businesses he had nurtured (and been supported by) for decades. In this case, as in so many others through-out his life, he seems to have been driven not so much by logic as by his in-stinctive preference for change over the status quo.

Although he remained on the boards of his various businesses, in each case Greenfield turned the chairmanship over to his longtime right-hand man. Gustave G. Amsterdam had served Greenfield loyally and capably since his arrival at Bankers Securities in 1935. For a generation the two men had complemented each other perfectly: Where Greenfield was short and stocky, Amsterdam was tall and imposing. Where Greenfield operated on instinct and seat-of-the-pants acumen, Amsterdam was analytical and cautious. Where Greenfield was brash and outspoken, Amsterdam was owlish, polite, even-tempered, and patient to a fault. Where Greenfield was egotistical, Amsterdam was self-effacing. Where Greenfield radiated charisma, Amsterdam was dour and professorial. (Once, on their way to a party, Amsterdam's vivacious wife, Valla, was overheard telling him, "Smile, Gus! Pretend you're at the office!")[4]

Perhaps most important, where Greenfield had provided the perfect foil for Old Philadelphians by fulfilling their stereotype of the pushy Jew-on-the-make who gave no quarter and asked none in return, Amsterdam had made a conscious (and largely successful) effort to gain acceptance for his own company and for Jews in general within Philadelphia's business establishment.

In theory, Amsterdam was ideally suited to implement the plans of a rambunctious genius like Greenfield. The fact remained that Bankers Securities was ultimately a one-man organization, and the flamboyance and the brilliance of that one man could not be replicated by anyone, least of all Amsterdam.

When Greenfield resigned from Bankers Securities, that company's nationwide net assets were valued at slightly more than $80 million.[5] Greenfield personally owned slightly more than one-third of the stock, and through his personal foundation he controlled an additional one-fifth.[6] To the chagrin of his children, Greenfield sold his controlling one-third interest to his loyal executives, a group that included Amsterdam; Greenfield's nephews, Bruce Greenfield (who became president) and Robert Greenfield; and a few others. The price was only $9.1 million, and even this paltry sum was financed by Greenfield over a twenty-year period at the low interest rate of 4 percent. In effect, the sale of Bankers Securities was an early example of what later became known as a "leveraged buyout": The acquiring executives gained control of the company while investing hardly any of their own money, and they could repay their debt out of the dividends they would declare for themselves over the next twenty years.[7] "It was a ridiculous deal on my father's part," Greenfield's eldest son, Gordon, later complained.[8]

The arrangement, however, spared Greenfield the bother of selling his stock to outside investors, and it enabled him to maintain his ties with an organization that had become, in many respects, more of a family to him than his own family. And as Amsterdam later observed, however generous

Greenfield may have seemed in selling Bankers Securities to his employees for a bargain price, no one else had made him a better offer.[9] The market probably understood—as Greenfield most likely recognized as well—that most of the value of Bankers Securities existed within Greenfield's own head and could not easily be transferred.

To bolster Amsterdam's leadership position as chairman, Greenfield created two ten-year voting trusts that gave Amsterdam absolute control of Greenfield's voting stock as well as control of the Bankers Securities stock owned by Greenfield's foundation.[10] In theory this arrangement would insulate Amsterdam from the petty pressures of the marketplace. The flaw in that theory is that the pressure of the marketplace is what drives corporate performance.

But, of course, corporate performance had never been Greenfield's paramount concern. In this case, as in so many others, he sought to reward his colleagues in the only way he knew: through material gifts. "It does not seem possible for the Bankers Securities Corporation to exist without you at its head," William Fox's widow, Eva—who still owned 23 percent of Banker Securities stock—wrote to Greenfield when he announced his retirement. In a conclusion that was more prescient than she realized, Eva Fox added, "The Fox family will be the loser, but I want you to know that all of us extend to you our very best wishes."[11]

Greenfield's desire to serve his community in this closing stage of his life was surely sincere, but it also represented a final attempt to salvage his public reputation for posterity. Much of his energy in the years that followed was devoted to improving interfaith and interracial relations, especially through his work for the National Conference of Christians and Jews and for his Greenfield Center for Human Relations at Penn. In the fall of 1964, Greenfield's long support of Catholic institutions won him audiences with Archbishop John Krol of Philadelphia and Francis Cardinal Spellman of New York; those meetings were said to have influenced the Vatican Council's subsequent decision to officially repudiate the belief in the Jews' collective guilt for the crucifixion of Jesus.[12]

As the 1960 presidential campaign approached, all the major Democratic candidates—including the ultimate victor, John F. Kennedy—solicited Greenfield's support. At first Greenfield leaned toward Adlai Stevenson, the Democrats' unsuccessful candidate in 1952 and 1956. But in June 1960, shortly before the Democratic National Convention, Greenfield stunned his fellow Pennsylvania delegates by affixing his name to a full-page ad in several major newspapers in support of the Senate majority leader, Lyndon Johnson of Texas.[13]

The precise reasons for Greenfield's enthusiasm remain puzzling; it may have been related to Johnson's relative empathy toward businessmen like himself.[14] At the Pennsylvania delegates' caucus, Kennedy received sixty-four votes and Stevenson eight; Greenfield was the only delegate voting for Johnson. (Unlike most of the delegates, who were beholden for their jobs to Pennsylvania's governor, David Lawrence, or to Philadelphia's Democratic boss, Congressman William J. Green, Greenfield could flout the party line without fear of recrimination.)[15]

Johnson, a man of huge ego and equally huge insecurities, was inordinately touched by Greenfield's gesture. "Seldom does one have the opportunity to see his friends stand up and be counted," Johnson wrote to Greenfield after securing the vice presidential nomination. "I will not forget you and your expression of confidence as long as I live."[16]

When Kennedy won the nomination, Greenfield supported the ticket wholeheartedly, contributing $10,000 and lending his personal public relations assistant, John O'Shea, to the Democratic National Committee. But even after Kennedy won the election and moved into the White House, Greenfield continued to cultivate his odd relationship with Johnson. In 1961, at Greenfield's invitation, Johnson addressed the World Affairs Council of Philadelphia, Bunny Greenfield's former organization.[17]

This remarkable demonstration of loyalty came at a time when Johnson's political career seemed to have hit a dead end: Having surrendered his Senate leadership position for the vice presidency, Johnson now found himself shut out by the Kennedys and mocked by their glamorous Camelot courtiers as "Uncle Cornpone."[18] Yet Greenfield—the confidant of Hoover, Roosevelt, and Truman—continued to treat Johnson as a figure worthy of respect and admiration. Among political observers as well as Greenfield's friends, the question persisted: Why would a political operator like Greenfield, who thrived on being at the center of things, attach himself to a player who had been relegated to the sidelines? What was the old kingmaker's game?

Greenfield's motives for supporting Johnson remain obscure, but it is at least possible that he had no game at all. Greenfield's motives were always more complicated than most people realized; not everything he did was prompted by an expectation of a payoff. He may have stood by Johnson out of sheer loyalty and sympathy—just as he had stood by his executives and employees through good times and bad; just as he had stood by his son-in-law Bob Sturgeon when Carlotta divorced him; and just as he had intervened for that forlorn black woman awaiting service in the Horn & Hardart restaurant. Or perhaps Greenfield saw, in Johnson's rejection by the Kennedy crowd, a mirror image of the rising Jewish real estate developer whose hopes of becoming a Philadelphia banker had been dashed by another crowd of establishment courtiers more than thirty years earlier.

In retirement Greenfield continued to operate from his office in the Bankers Securities Building, an arrangement that fostered the widespread impression that he had not retired at all, much to the confusion of employees and clients and also much to Gus Amsterdam's annoyance. When a group of managers at Loft Candy Corporation tried to buy their company from Bankers Securities in 1964, its president, Leonard Wurzel, first approached Greenfield, not Amsterdam. As Wurzel later recalled:

> Greenfield and I got in a conversation one day about my buying control of Loft's, which I thought was a great idea. At that moment Greenfield said to me, "OK, Leonard, I'll help you buy it." Greenfield wrote on a little piece of paper what he wanted me to produce in terms of money—$4 or $5 million. So we canvassed Wall Street to try to get somebody to raise the money for us and we had a pretty good deal arranged. . . .
>
> I went to see Greenfield and I said, "OK, here's the deal." He said, "Well, look, I'm not the boss any more. You gotta go see Gus Amsterdam." . . .
>
> I knew Gus Amsterdam for years and went down to see him, and I said, "Mr. Greenfield told me to show this proposal to you." He looked at it and he said, "Well, Albert may want that, but I'm not buying it." And that was the end of the deal.[19]

Most of the Loft managers, including Wurzel, quit in disgust soon afterward, and thereafter Loft's lost money every year until it went bankrupt with a $6 million accumulated deficit.[20]

Elizabeth had hoped to persuade Greenfield to travel in retirement, and in the summer of 1962 the Greenfields did spend two months hop-scotching the world from Japan to Turkey, Greece, and Italy. Their journey was eased by the former Democratic governor of New York, Averell Harriman, then assistant secretary of state for Far Eastern affairs, who arranged for Greenfield to receive diplomatic courtesies as a visiting U.S. statesman. At the Vatican, the Greenfields had an audience with Pope John XXIII—Greenfield's first papal audience since Pope Pius XI had made him a papal knight in 1930.[21]

Upon their return in August, Greenfield took his annual physical examination. When the tests detected a duodenal ulcer, he entered the University of Pennsylvania Hospital the following month for surgery. The surgeon, again, was I. S. Ravdin—the same doctor who had operated on Etelka during her terminal illness in 1949. After a stay of nineteen days, Greenfield was released in October, only to return eleven days later for a second operation to repair bleeding in the ulcer and then a third operation six days after that.

In the process, Ravdin discovered a slow-growing but inoperable cancer. And so Ravdin and Elizabeth Greenfield confronted a quandary: How would an irrepressible optimist like Greenfield respond upon learning that he had at last come face to face with an adversary that brains, spirit, or courage could not overcome? Fearing that the news would destroy Greenfield's morale, Ravdin and Elizabeth initially agreed to conceal the diagnosis from him.

Greenfield was not released from the hospital until December 8 and did not return to his office until February 25, 1963.[22] By then, one suspects, he had deduced the truth of his condition for himself. But as anyone who recalled him during the Bankers Trust crisis of 1930 could attest, Greenfield could not bear to be seen as an object of pity. So for his own benefit, as well as that of Elizabeth and Ravdin and everyone he dealt with, he appears to have maintained, at least for a while, the charade that the surgery had succeeded and he was on the road to recovery.

As Greenfield grappled with his mortality, he suffered the further indignity of watching the dissolution of his empire. The John Bartram Hotel was closed in 1962. The Philadelphia Bonwit Teller store was sold the following year.[23] Bonwit's, at least, continued to operate under a new owner. But on the afternoon of February 15, 1963, several hundred bewildered shoppers at Snellenburg's were suddenly told by the public address system to leave the premises at once: The ninety-year-old department store was closing as of that moment.[24] The Yellow Cab Company too was sold the following year.[25]

Greenfield's last hurrah occurred on the Fourth of July, 1963, when Vice President Johnson spoke at Independence Hall. Later that afternoon Greenfield and Elizabeth hosted a reception at Sugar Loaf that presented Johnson and his wife and older daughter to more than two hundred prominent Philadelphians, Republicans as well as Democrats, ranging from Old Philadelphia names like Edward Hopkinson, Sturgis Ingersoll, and Thomas S. Gates to politicians like Senator Hugh Scott and New Jersey Governor Richard Hughes to German Jewish figures like Lessing Rosenwald and Hays Solis-Cohen to old friends like Mary Roebling to erstwhile enemies like Walter Annenberg. Even the archbishop of Philadelphia, John Krol, made an appearance.

For this two-hour event, the Greenfields spared no expense. As guests approached the main house along the winding driveway, they were greeted not only by American flags but also by the thirteen-star original flag of 1776, as well as the state flag of Texas. Waiters carried trays of champagne and caviar. The society bandleader Mark Davis led his orchestra on the terrace, where the vice president danced with Elizabeth Greenfield as well as Greenfield's daughter-in-law Barbara Greenfield, among many others. "Tell Albert that he gives a party Texas-style," Johnson remarked to a reporter as he left.[26]

Less than five months later, President Kennedy was cut down by an assassin's bullet and Johnson succeeded him. For the fourth time in Greenfield's career, the White House was occupied by a president who owed him a large debt of gratitude. In his own uncanny way, Greenfield had once again bet on the right horse—a longer shot, even, than Hoover or Truman.

But, of course, by then it was too late for the connection to do Greenfield much good, even had he expected anything in return. He took his reward in small favors from Johnson: a ride in a presidential motorcade, a seat on a presidential advisory committee on how best to implement the new civil rights laws of 1964 and 1965, and an appointment to the federal Appeals Court bench for his friend Abraham Freedman.[27]

During Greenfield's long and difficult illness, his weight fell from 170 pounds to 92. He tried to continue conducting business but grew so frail that when he took lunch at the Bankers Securities dining room he had to be propped up in his chair by pillows.[28] The cancer inevitably weakened his immune system, leaving him vulnerable to other ailments: In the summer of 1965 he suffered a viral infection.[29]

By 1966 Greenfield had begun, in his customarily methodical fashion, to put his affairs in order. At every gift-giving opportunity, he distributed stock in his various enterprises to his children, grandchildren, and siblings—always with the stipulation that the shares not be sold until after his death, thus enabling him to maintain control while he lived.[30] He assigned a $70,000 insurance policy on his life to assure the continued support of his ex-wife, Edna. "The income from this fund, together with other arrangements that I have made for you," he wrote to her, "will provide you with sufficient income so that I trust you will be comfortable as long as you live."[31] He prepared personal letters to be delivered to friends and associates after his death.[32] He summoned Mildred Custin, his former president at the Bonwit Teller shop in Philadelphia, from her job as president of Bonwit's in New York to his home at Sugar Loaf and handed her an envelope. "I want to give you this $25,000," he told her. "You did a great deal for Bonwit's and for me."[33]

When J. David Stern visited Greenfield in July, he found his old friend no more perturbed by the imminent prospect of death than he had been by the prospect of imminent financial ruin in December 1930. "Al told me what to expect—in as matter-of-fact and impersonal a manner as though he was discussing the weather," Stern later recalled. "He was the most courageous character I have ever known."[34]

That last summer also brought Greenfield a note of appreciation from Edna. "Sometimes it is good to follow an impulse & I am doing just that in writing you this little note," she said. "You are often in my thoughts, and particularly now as June 18th approaches. I need not remind you of what happened on that date in 1914"—a reference to their wedding. Then, in an apparent reference to the loss of Greenfield's second wife, Etelka, seventeen years earlier, Edna added:

> Strange how sometimes the most tragic events turn out well in some ways. You are so lucky to have Elizabeth as a wife. Her dedication to you during that long illness was unswerving & she had the capacity to carry on under the terrific strain. Few could have done it— certainly not I.[35]

Toward the close of 1966, barely two months before he died, Greenfield's devoted secretary of many years gave birth to her first child. Betty Morris Reese was a stylish and attractive woman, but through most of her long employment with Greenfield she had seemed destined for spinsterhood— so much so that even after her mid-life marriage everyone in the office, including Greenfield and even Betty Reese herself, continued to refer to her as "Miss Morris."[36] By 1966 she was well into her forties, and her pregnancy and motherhood came as a surprise to her friends and, indeed, to Betty Reese herself.[37]

On her way home from the hospital it occurred to Betty Reese that someone else had also surprised the world even though, like her, he had been counted out in his early forties. So instead of driving straight home, she directed her husband to proceed to 9230 Germantown Avenue in Chestnut Hill. There, in the living room at Sugar Loaf, she placed her newborn daughter, ever so gently, in Albert Greenfield's lap.[38]

[15]

House of Cards

G reenfield was buried on January 8, 1967—a cold, wet Sunday very much like the rainy Monday morning when the Bankers Trust had closed thirty-six years earlier. Some fourteen hundred mourners at Keneseth Israel—among them the governor-elect of Pennsylvania, the mayor of Philadelphia, the former Philadelphia mayors Joseph Clark (now a U.S. senator) and Richardson Dilworth, and the planning commission director Ed Bacon—heard Greenfield eulogized by Rabbi Bertram Korn as "a thoroughly unique figure in the drama of contemporary American life."[1]

He was laid to rest at Adath Jeshurun Cemetery in the family plot he had purchased for his parents in 1928, where he had subsequently provided gravesites for four other relatives who had predeceased him: his eldest sister, Molly Newton, and her husband; his second wife, Etelka; and Etelka's daughter, Yvonne Schamberg Straus. The plot's idiosyncratic arrangement, apparently of his own design, set Greenfield's grave conspicuously apart from the others, who were buried together in a single row below him.[2]

In its obituary, the *New York Times* estimated Greenfield's personal fortune at between $25 million and $100 million and described him as one of America's wealthiest men.[3] But, in fact, Greenfield's influence had always exceeded his wealth. When his estate was inventoried, it was found to be worth just $14.9 million.[4] And because he had done little estate planning, much of that was consumed by taxes.[5] In his lifetime Greenfield had donated some $6 million to charitable causes—a substantial amount, to be sure, but minuscule beside the more than $20 million that the Pew family's foundations then disbursed each year.

In accordance with Pennsylvania law, Greenfield left one-third of his estate to his widow, Elizabeth. His will also established a trust for his first wife, Edna, that would maintain the $800 monthly payments he had sent her since their divorce in 1935 for the rest of her life—which, as things turned out, continued for another nineteen years.[6] He also created residuary trusts to generate income for each of his children.[7]

To administer these trusts as well as the other provisions of his will, Greenfield appointed his wife, four of his five children—all but Gordon— and his two closest associates at Bankers Securities: his successor, Gus Amsterdam, and his nephew, Bruce Greenfield. Each trustee's tenure, the will stipulated, was "dependent on his or her maintaining a cordial and satisfactory relationship at all times with my wife"; it gave Elizabeth the power to dismiss any trustee on those grounds—a hint that all was still not entirely copasetic between Greenfield's children and his wife.[8]

Greenfield's five children—all very different from each other—mirrored their father in one important respect: All rejected the path that their father had taken, just as Greenfield himself had rejected *his* father's path. None of the children lived in Philadelphia when Greenfield died, and none was actively involved in Albert's businesses. Gordon, the eldest, held a seat on the Bankers Securities board (as did Greenfield's widow, Elizabeth), but he had long since moved to New York and embraced conservative Republican politics to boot. Three of Greenfield's children had relocated to the suburbs he had despised. Two of them—Betty Zeidman in Bucks County and Albert Jr. in Chester County—like their father, courageously raised the Democratic Party's banner in hostile Republican strongholds.

Greenfield's strained relationship with his oldest son, Gordon—the only one of the five children to have been held by their mother and perhaps, consequently, the only one to relate more closely to Edna than to Albert—persisted into his will, where Greenfield inserted an awkward personal message to Gordon, explaining why he had been bypassed as a trustee:

> You must know that I have the same deep and abiding affection and love for you as I have for your sisters and brother. In addition, I have a rare respect for your business abilities. I have not, however, appointed you an Executor or Trustee. You have neither roots nor business in Philadelphia any more and I concluded it would be best not to appoint you as one of the fiduciaries of my Will. I hope and pray that this decision of mine will not make any real lasting difference to you and that you will still hold me in blessed memory even though you may be momentarily disappointed by this action of mine.[9]

But, of course, Greenfield's strength lay not in family management but in business management, or so it was commonly assumed. When Greenfield died, Bankers Securities was still widely perceived much the way Greenfield had been regarded—as a mysterious and manipulative octopus whose tentacles extended into every conceivable corner of Philadelphia and far beyond. Gus Amsterdam, who had inherited Greenfield's corporate titles as well as many of his civic board memberships, was considered one of the city's most powerful men—even more powerful than Greenfield, for Amsterdam had been welcomed into the same Philadelphia business establishment that had largely rejected Greenfield. This perception presumed that Amsterdam had inherited Greenfield's acumen along with his titles.

In fact, Greenfield had left his successors a house of cards: a wildly disparate empire of real estate, department stores, hotels, a candy company, a mortgage banking company, and assorted other businesses whose primary connecting thread was Greenfield's interest in them.[10] Its fabled Philadelphia properties, like the Ben Franklin and Bellevue-Stratford Hotels, shared a common characteristic with many of its department store chains, like Lit Brothers, Franklin Simon, W. & J. Sloane, Lansburgh's in Washington, and Richard's in Miami: All were businesses coasting on their past glory. City Stores, which accounted for more than half of Bankers Securities' assets when Greenfield died, lost money in all but one of the dozen years after his death.[11]

In his active days Greenfield had managed to put a good face on even the worst of his holdings. Each of his businesses involved bringing people together in some manner—a skill for which Greenfield had no equal. Amsterdam, by contrast, had spent three decades marinating in the real estate business, one of the few fields in which an owner can make money by doing nothing.

It was not his fault that the decade after Greenfield retired brought race riots as well as civil rights and antiwar protest demonstrations to America's major cities, including downtown Philadelphia, where many Bankers Securities properties were located. But Amsterdam failed to recognize that times had changed. So as his company's hotels and department stores gradually went to seed, Amsterdam chose to sit on them and wait for better times, or sell them, rather than improve them. And often, because he lacked Greenfield's sense of timing, he waited too long to sell—until he had no choice but to close and liquidate a property.

The decline had begun even before Greenfield's death, with the closing of Snellenburg's and the John Bartram Hotel in the 1960s. After Greenfield died, the process accelerated. Bankers Securities closed Kline's Apparel

Stores of Kansas City as well as the Lit Brothers store in Camden in 1970, sold the bankrupt Loft Candy Corporation in 1971, and closed Lansburgh's, the venerable Washington department store, in 1973. Of its sixty-five Franklin Simon women's specialty stores, twenty-five were sold in 1977.[12] The company's flagship hotels, the Bellevue-Stratford and the Ben Franklin, began losing money in 1974; the Ben Franklin's occupancy rate over the next few years hovered barely above 20 percent—the lowest in the United States, it was said.[13]

In July 1976, when a pneumonia epidemic that killed twenty-nine visiting American Legionnaires was traced to a rare bacteria that had seeped through the air conditioning ducts at the Bellevue-Stratford, a former Bankers Securities executive remarked, "You just knew it had to be a Bankers Securities hotel—BSC would never spend the money to repair the air conditioning."[14] The Bellevue—the "crossroads of the city" since 1904—closed that year.[15] And in 1977 the Lit Brothers chain, which during the 1930s and 1940s had led all Philadelphia department stores in sales volume, closed as well after ten consecutive years of losses.

Despite these dismaying results, when Amsterdam's ten-year voting trust expired in 1969, the partners in his investment group agreed to extend it for ten more years.[16] By the mid-1970s Bankers Securities itself was losing millions of dollars each year and recording sharp declines in its net assets as well as its stockholder equity.[17] Yet for most of the time since Amsterdam's accession, his group of investors continued to award themselves dividends in order to repay the debt they had incurred when Greenfield sold them the company in 1959. In effect, Amsterdam was bleeding Bankers Securities *and* shrinking its asset base at the same time.[18]

Increasingly, Greenfield's relatives came to view the Albert M. Greenfield Foundation, not the companies, as Greenfield's true legacy. By the mid-1970s, family members were frustrated with the poor performance of Bankers Securities stock, which was adversely impacting the foundation (since stock in Bankers Securities was the foundation's primary asset).[19] Greenfield's widow and two of his children occupied three of the foundation's five board seats, but here too Amsterdam, as president, enjoyed legal control through a voting trust.[20] When the family members tried to vote the foundation's shares to elect an anti-Amsterdam slate at Bankers Securities' 1974 annual meeting, Amsterdam ruled them out of order and voted the foundation's shares himself.[21] When family members tried to nominate Albert Greenfield's outspoken daughter Carlotta Howard as their representative on the Bankers Securities board, Amsterdam reduced the number of board seats, adopted staggered terms, and then voted Carlotta down when she was finally nominated in 1976.[22] In any given situation Amsterdam seemed brilliantly inventive at protecting himself from accountability but clueless about improving his company's earnings.

Into this quandary in 1977 ventured a Philadelphia accountant-turned-investor named Jack Farber, then in his mid-forties, who specialized, as he put it, in "cleaning up the corporate messes left by other executives."[23] By then Greenfield had been dead for ten years, City Stores was losing $25 million a year, and the company had closed four of its divisions. Its collection had dwindled to five department store groups, a women's specialty chain, a discount store, and the W. & J. Sloane chain of fifty home furnishings stores.

More troubling to Farber than the numbers was the universally low regard in which City Stores operations seemed to be held by consumers, suppliers, and competitors alike. In the course of his due diligence investigation Farber asked a friend—the chief executive of a women's sportswear business—where he thought City Stores' Richards chain ranked among the three department store chains in southern Florida. "They're probably fifth," the friend replied. Nevertheless, Farber was intrigued by the underlying value in City Stores' assets, which he believed amply exceeded the low price at which City Stores stock was then trading.

In late 1977 and early 1978 Farber acquired a 15 percent stake in City Stores and set about trying to leverage a position for himself on the City Stores board, where he hoped to become an agent of constructive change. Achieving that goal would also inevitably require his playing a similar role at Bankers Securities, which controlled City Stores and whose management was largely identical to that of City Stores, and equally entrenched.

At first Farber found Gus Amsterdam cordial, polite, and receptive to his overtures. As Farber later realized, Amsterdam had nothing to lose by letting Farber poke his nose around the City Stores operation, since Greenfield's voting trust assured Amsterdam of control, no matter what Farber found.

What Farber discovered at virtually every store he visited was medieval management, incapable of answering even the most basic retailing questions, such as: How do you control inventory? And how do you keep track of inventories by store? "In all my experience with managements good and bad," Farber later wrote, "I had never seen one quite this backward, and at such a large scale." The problem, Farber concluded, was an inbred culture of denial. "Managers of the operating companies perceived that their first priority was to tell City Stores corporate management whatever they believed that corporate management wanted to hear," he recalled. Like Samuel Barker years earlier, Farber had inadvertently put his finger on the essential problem with Albert Greenfield's management style, which had persisted long after Greenfield was gone.

Farber's predicament gradually became clear. He had invested more than $2 million for a minority stake in a moribund company that could not be salvaged without a change of management. Yet under the terms of the voting trust, Gus Amsterdam could not be removed, either from the chairmanship of City Stores or of its parent, Bankers Securities.

Years earlier, in a remarkably similar situation, Albert Greenfield had successfully resisted the notion that Rudolph Goerke's control of City Stores was invincible. Now Farber adopted the same attitude toward Gus Amsterdam.

He found support among some of Albert Greenfield's children, who were equally disgruntled with Amsterdam's performance. Greenfield's nephews, Bruce Greenfield and Robert Greenfield, remained dependent on Amsterdam—Bruce as president of Bankers Securities (and, consequently, Amsterdam's right-hand man), and Robert as outside counsel as well as a director of Bankers. But Albert Greenfield's oldest son, Gordon, had been abruptly removed from the Bankers Securities board by Amsterdam in 1973 after some thirty years as a director. To Farber, Gordon vented his bitterness. Not only was Amsterdam incompetent, he said, but Amsterdam had stolen Gordon's birthright by dissipating the value of the Greenfield family's most important legacy: its foundation.

Although Gordon no longer worked in the company, he and two of his sisters were directors of the Greenfield Foundation, which owned more than one-fifth of the stock of Bankers Securities (which in turn owned 51 percent of City Stores). The three siblings were eager to sell the foundation's plummeting stock in Bankers Securities so they could use the proceeds to fund the foundation's good works. Gordon and his sisters lacked the legal means to replace Amsterdam as the foundation's president, but as a majority of the foundation's five-person board they possessed the power to sell the foundation's assets. And so they did: In October 1978, over Amsterdam's livid objections, the Greenfield Foundation voted to sell its stock in Bankers Securities to Jack Farber.

Amsterdam still exercised legal control over both City Stores and Bankers Securities, of course. But Farber's growing position in both companies—he now owned about 25 percent of City Stores and 24 percent of Bankers Securities—made it increasingly difficult for Amsterdam to ignore Farber's complaints. It also emboldened Farber to speak up more forcefully at City Stores board meetings.

In mid-1979, with $10 million in past due bills and only $3 million cash on hand, City Stores sought protection from its creditors under Chapter XI of the Federal Bankruptcy Act.[24] Ordinarily, a corporate bankruptcy filing represents, at the very least, a reflection on the quality of a company's management. Yet still Amsterdam refused to resign or to sell his Bankers Securities stock to Farber.

Now Farber enlisted the support of William Fox's daughters, Mona and Belle Fox, who had inherited their father's 23 percent stake in Bankers Securities and were as chagrined by the decline in the stock's value as Greenfield's children were. Still Amsterdam refused to resign or sell.

By August 1979 the market value of Bankers Securities stock had shrunk to about $8 million, a small fraction of its value when Albert Greenfield had sold control to its employees twenty years earlier. That month Farber received a confidential visit from Albert Greenfield's nephew, Robert Greenfield, who was outside counsel to Bankers Securities as well as one of its directors and principal shareholders: Bob and his brother Bruce between them owned 10 percent of Bankers Securities stock.

Bob Greenfield had previously struck Farber as a solid, pragmatic lawyer, but now Farber found him nervous and frightened. Bob told Farber that he had lost confidence in Amsterdam's ability to save either Bankers Securities or City Stores. To the extent that he possessed personal wealth, Bob said, the great bulk of it was tied up in his Bankers Securities stock. As City Stores went down the drain, there seemed a good chance that Bob and his brother Bruce would wind up with nothing. "I've been poor, and I've been reasonably rich," Bob told Farber. "I don't want to be poor again."

Bob asked Farber if Philadelphia Industries would buy his Bankers Securities common stock and perhaps his brother Bruce's stock as well. Such a purchase would put more than half of the voting shares in the hands of Farber and the Fox sisters, who were committed to Amsterdam's removal. But, of course, such a benchmark was meaningless because, under the voting trust, Amsterdam enjoyed legal control regardless of who owned the Greenfield brothers' stock.

Still, Farber saw in the Greenfield brothers' desperation a psychological wedge to induce Gus Amsterdam to quit: "If he got the message that his stubborn defense of his own narrow personal interests was hurting his close friends and colleagues," Farber later recalled thinking, "perhaps that would get his attention."

Ultimately, Farber offered Bob and Bruce Greenfield a $300,000 bonus above the value of their shares if they could persuade Amsterdam to sell his stock and terminate the voting trust. When the brothers presented Farber's proposal to Amsterdam, he was at first incensed that his longtime supporters had turned against him. But finally he realized that the game was up.

On November 26, 1979, following a City Stores board meeting in New York, Farber met with Amsterdam and Bruce and Bob Greenfield in a small adjoining room to sign the agreement.[25]

Farber asked Amsterdam if he was ready to participate.

"Yes," Amsterdam replied.

Farber asked if Amsterdam had any questions.

"No," Amsterdam said.

"Do you want to discuss anything about continuity, or whatever?" Farber asked.

"No," Amsterdam repeated. Then he signed the agreement, left the room without another word, and Bankers Securities Corporation vanished into history.[26]

Albert Greenfield's far-flung empire had survived him by less than thirteen years. Yet in retrospect the remarkable thing about its demise was not that it collapsed so soon after his death, but that Greenfield's successors managed to keep it afloat as long as they did. Bankers Securities may well have been the world's largest one-man corporation, but ultimately it was, after all, only a one-man corporation. Albert Greenfield alone had created his empire and, by his death, had sown the seeds for its demise. If he had left an enduring legacy, anyone looking for it would have to search elsewhere.

Epilogue

Merion Station, December 1930

ut let us return to the twenty-first of December 1930 and the Main
Line home of William Purves Gest. The Philadelphia bankers who
gathered there that night—Joe Wayne, Stevenson Newhall, E. T.
Stotesbury, and the rest—have vanished, just as their clubby world has
largely disappeared.[1] In their place, *you* must decide whether to risk millions
of dollars to rescue Albert Greenfield's bank.

With the benefit of hindsight, you know several things that those bankers in 1930 did not. You know, for one thing, that the Bankers Trust Company was relatively sound, just as Greenfield insisted it was. You know that
within a few years the Great Depression will end and prosperity will return.

You also know that it is unwise to judge Greenfield in an ethnic or cultural context; he simply defies any convenient stereotype. You know that it
is futile to try to destroy Greenfield. You know that, over the next thirty-six
years, Greenfield's resourcefulness on many fronts will produce great benefits for Philadelphia, and very likely for you as well. You know that after his
death, the decline of Greenfield's bold and feisty spirit will cause one Pennsylvania governor to write an entire book decrying his fellow Americans as
"a nation of wusses."[2]

You also know that Greenfield will help transform Philadelphia, and indeed America, from an exclusive oligarchy based largely on bloodlines into
an inclusive meritocracy. You know that, in the face of this upheaval, the
WASP establishment will relinquish its leadership role in almost every facet
of American life and indeed in the world, from multinational corporations

to Ivy League universities to Congress and the Supreme Court and even the White House.[3]

But you also know that the meritocracy ushered in by people like Greenfield will prove a mixed blessing. You know that public trust in government, business, and the not-for-profit sector has declined since the old WASP establishment stepped down. You know that, beginning in the 1980s, the stodgy bankers in this room, with their quaint "3-6-3 rule" for conducting business, will be succeeded by a new breed of creative financiers, very much in the mold of Albert Greenfield, who will devise financial vehicles of such ingenious complexity that the entire banking community will lose sight of the basic principles of risk evaluation, causing the collapse of America's housing market as well as a global stock market crash in 2008. You know that such calamities might have been avoided had bankers been a little less brilliant and a little more boring.

You also know that certain questions about how Greenfield amassed and maintained his fortune have never been adequately answered. You know that not everything he did was entirely proper. You know that it is unhealthy to let one individual accumulate too much power. You know that, come the twenty-first century, business psychologists will conclude that the best executives are not extroverts like Greenfield but introverts who take more careful risks and let proactive employees run with their own ideas.[4]

Finally, while you know that those Philadelphia bankers were wrong to let Bankers Trust die in 1930, in some corner of your mind lurks the same nagging doubt about Greenfield that plagued Joe Wayne and Stevenson Newhall.

Well, what is your decision? Make it soon, because life must go on. Millions of decisions are made every day in any large city, and while most of them lack the scope or urgency of the Bankers Trust crisis, very few are resolved solely on rational grounds. The accumulated total of such decisions over months and years answers the ultimate question: What sort of community will this become?

In the last analysis, Albert Greenfield's contribution cannot be found in his real estate deals, his buildings, his department stores, his financial companies, his civic activities, his political maneuvers, or his philanthropy—for the glory of all these was ephemeral. His greatest legacy lay in his ability to throw into focus, by virtue of his oversized personality, issues of broad civic and national concern.

Many of the age-old obstacles to human progress that Greenfield challenged—pessimism, timidity, prejudice, fear of immigrants, resistance to change—still persist. Following the global stock market crash of 2008, public opinion polls consistently found Americans doubtful about the nation's ability to recover. In one survey, 25 percent of non-Jewish Americans blamed Jews for the ensuing financial crisis.[5] Notwithstanding the conclusions of most economists, in 2010 a poll found that 74 percent of Americans believed illegal immigrants weakened the nation's economy.[6]

To his admirers and detractors alike, Greenfield brought a very different message: The way things are is not the way things have to be. Individually, you possess the power to define yourself. Collectively, you can change the world. So what sort of world do you want? And how will you achieve it?

Albert Greenfield is no longer here to ask those questions. But the questions, now and forever, remain.

Acknowledgments

T his book evolved out of an article I wrote about Albert Greenfield for *Philadelphia* magazine in May 1976. In 1983—by which time Greenfield's voluminous papers were beginning to be made public—I updated that article as a chapter in *Jewish Life in Philadelphia, 1830–1940*, a book edited by the late Murray Friedman.

So I thank, first, my editor at *Philadelphia*, the late Alan Halpern, and its publisher, D. Herbert Lipson, for supporting and encouraging my initial interest in this complex figure. Similarly, I thank Murray Friedman for enabling me to probe my subject further as new material became available.

The author's advance provided to me by Temple University Press, while generous by academic publishing standards, would not have enabled me to devote most of the past three years to the final researching and writing of this book. That support was provided through generous research grants from the Albert M. Greenfield Foundation, Jack Farber, and the Feinstein Center for American Jewish History at Temple University. Although the first two of these funders are interested parties in Albert Greenfield's career (Farber's company, CSS Industries, took over much of Greenfield's empire), both of them readily foreswore any control over the contents of this book or even the opportunity to review its contents prior to publication. So I am especially grateful not only for their financial generosity but also for their moral support of the principle of independent intellectual inquiry.

Much of my research involved several months of examining Albert M. Greenfield's personal papers at the Historical Society of Pennsylvania. No single individual could peruse these one thousand-plus boxes of material, and indeed I did not. But I was especially fortunate that three other writer/researchers had previously immersed themselves in the Greenfield papers and published their findings, thus enabling me to explore other areas of Greenfield's papers with a minimum of redundancy.

Peter Binzen published his research in a privately commissioned study of Bankers Securities Corporation that appeared in 1985. Andrew Harrison's extensively researched doctoral thesis about Greenfield appeared in 1997. Serena Shanken Skwersky, a Philadelphia psychologist whose family built the Willow Grove Mall that Greenfield financed in the 1940s, spent much of the past decade combing through Greenfield's papers, photographing more than a thousand documents, largely as a labor of love, and compiled her own privately printed book about Greenfield in 2012.

All three of these individuals selflessly shared their findings with me. Andrew Harrison descended to the basement of his home to retrieve several specific documents at my request. When I asked Peter Binzen if I could peruse his Greenfield files, he invited me to come to his home and haul them away, which I did—a whole file cabinet's worth. Those files included, among their many pearls, notes of interviews that Peter conducted in 1985 with people I had overlooked in 1975, as well as copies of Bankers Securities board minutes whose originals, as far as I can determine, have since been destroyed.

I owe a special note of gratitude to Serena Skwersky, who in many respects functioned almost as a de facto research associate—responding promptly to my frequent e-mail questions, furnishing digital copies of photos and documents from her extensive stock, and sometimes pointing me in research directions that had not occurred to me. In our joint (albeit futile) pursuit of Greenfield's birth records in Ukraine, she also enlisted a genealogical researcher there and shared the cost of his services with me.

My task was also greatly expedited by the Historical Society's masterful job of organizing and cataloging the Greenfield papers. I am especially grateful to the Historical Society's librarians, who cheerfully accommodated my requests right up until closing time on many nights. These include the library's senior director, Lee Arnold, as well as Dan Rolph, Sarah Heim, Steve Smith, David Haugaard, Ron Medford, Matthew Lyons, Willhem Echevarria, Matt Shoemaker, Margaret Maxey, and Amanda Dean. My thanks go also to Dana Dorman, Faith Charlton, and Allison Chomet of the Historical Society, who kept me abreast of the Greenfield materials that they continue to digitize even as I write this.

Of Greenfield's friends, colleagues, relatives, acquaintances, and rivals whom I interviewed at length in 1975 and 1976, only two survive at this writing. Nevertheless, I thank them all, living and dead, for their time and insights. In alphabetical order, they are Gustave G. Amsterdam, E. Digby

Baltzell, Boyd Barnard, Alfred Blasband, Clifford Brenner, John Bunting, Chester Cincotta, Bruce Greenfield, William Greenfield, John Guinther, Bernard Guth, W. Carlton Harris, Thomas LaBrum, D. Herbert Lipson, John O'Shea, Elizabeth Greenfield Petrie, Irwin Solomon, Rabbi Malcolm Stern, Emily Sunstein, and Elizabeth Greenfield Zeidman.

My thanks, similarly, go to those who granted me interviews since my research resumed in 2010: Judge Arlin Adams, Albert M. Greenfield III, Barbara Greenfield, Robert Greenfield, Janet Guth, Priscilla M. Luce, Bob Olson, Juliet Six, and Leonard Wurzel. I also thank Deborah Szumachowski, who transcribed my tapes of many of these interviews.

In addition to providing their memories, Barbara Greenfield and Priscilla Luce—Albert Greenfield's daughter-in-law and granddaughter, respectively—spent a full day accompanying me as I visited Albert's former homes and offices. Since Barbara Greenfield was herself one of Philadelphia's most experienced real estate brokers, her presence on these visits was doubly valuable. Her son, Albert Greenfield III, also provided me with a large carton's worth of his own father's papers, many of which proved useful.

Most notably, Albert Greenfield's nephew and attorney, Robert Greenfield—who remained in full possession of his faculties and memories right up to his death in December 2012 at the age of ninety-seven—provided insightful responses to my frequent telephone and e-mail inquiries over several years. In the last two months of his life he read a rough draft of my manuscript and gave me valuable feedback; our last conversation took place just a month before he died.

Others who graciously permitted me to pick their brains about their fields of expertise include Hasia Diner of New York University, Rebecca Kobrin of Columbia University, and Lila Berman of Temple University (on Jewish immigration); Elaine Kolinsky (on the Lozovata region of Russia); Miriam Weiner (on Jewish genealogy); Matthew Meisel and Linda Serody (on the Serody family genealogy); Vanda Krefft (on William Fox); Wayne Willcox (on E. T. Stotesbury); Richard Sylla of New York University, Gary Richardson of the University of California at Irvine, and Jeffrey Slemrod (on financial history); Jonathan Stern and David Loeb (on J. David Stern); John Rossi of LaSalle University (on Philadelphia politics in the 1930s); Thomas Kolsky of Montgomery County Community College (on Zionism in the 1940s); G. Terry Madonna of Franklin and Marshall College (on Philadelphia's charter reform movement); and Walter D'Alessio, Paul Levy, G. Craig Schelter, and Gregory Heller (on Philadelphia urban renewal in the 1950s).

In particular, Vanda Krefft and Wayne Willcox have spent years researching forthcoming biographies of William Fox and E. T. Stotesbury, respectively, and, consequently, my dealings with them often became the equivalent of interviewing Fox and Stotesbury themselves, although both subjects have been dead for more than half a century.

Of the preceding experts, I am especially grateful to eight who reviewed chapters of this book and provided valuable responses. Vanda Krefft reviewed five chapters; Lila Berman reviewed three; and Dana Dorman, Gregory Heller, Thomas Kolsky, Paul Levy, Richard Sylla, and Wayne Willcox each reviewed one.

Librarians, archivists, and officials I contacted at various institutions went out of their way to help, even to the extent of performing some of my research, mailing me materials, and discussing their findings with me in lengthy phone calls and e-mail exchanges. For this help, my thanks go to Maxine Croul and David Kahn of the Central High School archives; Claire Schweriner and Phyllis Sichel of the archives at Congregation Keneseth Israel; Max Buten of the Lower Merion Historical Society; Joseph Newby and Maureen Kelly of the Lower Merion Township Building and Planning Department; Jessica Lydon, Sarah Sherman, Weckea Lilly, Ann Mosher, and Carol Ann Harris of Temple University Library's Special Collections Department; Nancy Isserman of Temple's Feinstein Center; and John Gibson, caretaker of Adath Jeshurun Cemetery in Philadelphia, home to the Greenfield family plot.

Remarkably, nearly all of Albert Greenfield's former homes and offices in Philadelphia still stand at this writing. When I visited these buildings, their current occupants and owners were uniformly gracious and generous with their time and attention. For this, I thank Dorothy "Pat" Simmons of Children's Services (at Greenfield's former office on Walnut Street); John M. Haas and Tara Capizzi of the National Catholic Bioethics Center (at Greenfield's former home in Overbrook Farms), Jeffrey M. Taylor, principal of Philadelphia Electrical & Technology Charter School (in the former Crozer Building, where Greenfield worked as an office boy); Marc Wiser, rental agent for the Avenue of the Arts Building (the former Real Estate Trust Building, where Greenfield had an early office); Josh McNally and Mark McGrath of Chestnut Hill College's Sugar Loaf facility (at Greenfield's last home); and Dr. Vincent Tisa and his receptionist, Denise Brotnitsky (whose podiatry office occupies Greenfield's former home in South Philadelphia).

Others who provided insights and/or directed me to useful resources include Robert Baxter, Frank Binswanger Jr., Joseph Daughen, Tildy Davidson, Bill Greenfield, Jim Greenfield, Melanie and John Harris, Don Harrison, David Horwitz, Mary Hurtig, Sam Katz, Colette Kleitz, Caryl Levin, Faith Lewis, Howard Magen, Alice Martell, Helen McGowen, Carol LeFaivre

Rochester, Edward Rosen, Carole Shanis, Jay Stiefel, Roberta Tanenbaum, Rabbi Avi Winokur, and Renee Zuritsky.

Because my research took place over a span of more than thirty-five years, my work also necessarily involved seeking advice on a rarely confronted question of journalistic ethics (see Author's Disclosure). The respected ethicists whom I consulted gave serious consideration to my question and provided useful guidelines. For that I thank Kelly McBride of the Poynter Institute and Kevin Smith, Elizabeth Donald, Hagit Limor, and Jim Pumarlo of the Society of Professional Journalists.

And, of course, I thank Micah Kleit, executive editor of Temple University Press, for proposing this book and for the professional manner in which he shepherded it through to publication. Other key people behind the scenes at Temple included Charles Ault, director of production; Joan Vidal, senior production editor; and Kate Nichols, who supervised the jacket design. I am especially grateful to Kathleen Deselle, the book's wonderfully persnickety copy editor; to her supervisor, Rebecca Logan; and to John Hulse, who prepared the index. I also thank my agent, Linda Langton of Langtons International in New York, for nailing down the details of the contract.

Finally, I would be remiss if I failed to express my deep gratitude to my wife for her patient and loving support through long periods when I was preoccupied with Albert Greenfield to her exclusion. If it is true that writers, like actors, tend to take on the characteristics of their subjects, I shudder to think what it must have been like to put up with me while I immersed myself in the psyche of a whirling dervish who wore down three wives during his tempestuous lifetime. To Barbara I say: Thank you for sticking with me— before, during, and, I hope, long after my sojourn with Albert M. Greenfield.

Principal Characters

Amsterdam, Gustave G. (1908–2001). Associated with Albert Greenfield from 1935. Elected vice president of Bankers Securities in 1946 and executive vice president in 1951. Succeeded Greenfield as chairman of Bankers Securities and City Stores, 1959–1979.

Annenberg, Moses (1878–1942). Publisher of *Philadelphia Inquirer*, 1936–1940. Feuded with Albert Greenfield during Pennsylvania gubernatorial campaign in 1938.

Bacon, Edmund (1910–2005). Urban planner and architect who was executive director of Philadelphia's City Planning Commission when Albert Greenfield became its chairman in 1956. Joined commission in 1946 and was executive director 1949–1970.

Barker, Samuel H. (1872–1939). President of Bankers Trust and Bankers Securities under Albert Greenfield, 1928–1932. Financial editor of Philadelphia *North American* from 1907 to 1925, when he quit to go into business for himself.

Beckman, Irland McKnight (1897–1982). Hired by Albert Greenfield as comptroller of Bankers Trust in 1929. Pennsylvania state banking examiner, 1923–1929, and rejoined state's Department of Banking in 1930. Appointed Pennsylvania Secretary of Banking by Governor George Earle in 1938 and supervised payments to depositors of Bankers Trust. Replaced by new governor Arthur James in January 1939.

Bell, John C., Jr. (1892–1974). Pennsylvania Secretary of Banking, 1939–1942, and receiver of Bankers Trust and Franklin Trust Co. Sued and investigated Albert Greenfield between 1940 and 1942.

Blasband, Alfred (1905–1996). Longtime Albert Greenfield aide; hired as clerk in 1929 and remained with Bankers Securities for more than forty years. Bankers Securities director from 1939. Headed Snellenburg's department store under Greenfield, 1951–1960, and Yellow Cab Co.

Bortin, David (1885–1971). Lawyer who represented Albert Greenfield in his bankruptcy, 1940. Childhood pal of Albert from South Philadelphia.

Cahan, Louis H. (1876–1971). Philadelphia printer; Albert Greenfield's early partner in Cahan, Grossman and Co. and then Cahan, Greenfield and Co., 1905–1911. Later real estate developer; did some deals with Greenfield until dispute in 1934.

Cameron, Peter G. (1876–1944). Pennsylvania Secretary of Banking involved in meetings to save Albert Greenfield's Bankers Trust in December 1930; supervised liquidation of Bankers Trust. Forced to resign February 28, 1931, perhaps at Greenfield's instigation.

Cincotta, Chester J. (1893–1987). Head of Albert M. Greenfield and Co. leasing department as of 1945, among other titles in long career dating from 1920s into 1970s. Said to have saved Greenfield by tackling would-be assassin.

Clark, Joseph S., Jr. (1901–1990). Reform Democratic mayor of Philadelphia, 1952–1956; U.S. senator from Pennsylvania, 1957–1969.

Clarke, Harley Lyman (1881–1955). Chicago utilities magnate who bought Fox's voting shares of Fox Film Corp. in 1930 in deal brokered by Albert Greenfield. Succeeded Fox as president of Fox Film and Fox Theatres in 1930. President of Utilities Power and Light Corp. until 1936 and a partner of Samuel Insull.

Custin, Mildred (1906–1997). Hired by Albert Greenfield as president of Bonwit Teller in Philadelphia in 1958; president of Bonwit's in New York, 1965–1970.

Dilworth, Richardson (1898–1974). Mayor of Philadelphia, 1956–1962; appointed Albert Greenfield chairman of Philadelphia's City Planning Commission in 1956.

Dougherty, Dennis (Cardinal) (1865–1951). Archbishop of Philadelphia, 1918–1951; made cardinal in 1921. Made Albert Greenfield exclusive real estate agent for Archdiocese of Philadelphia.

Earle, George H., III (1890–1974). First Democratic governor of Pennsylvania since 1890; elected in 1934 with Albert Greenfield's support.

Fleisher, Alfred (1878–1928). Principal in Mastbaum Brothers & Fleisher, Philadelphia real estate firm that acquired land with Albert Greenfield on Fifty-Second Street in 1910. Became president in 1926 on death of Jules Mastbaum.

Fox, William (1878–1952). Film producer and partner of Albert Greenfield. Born Vilmos Fuchs in Hungary; came to United States at age nine. Started in movie business in 1904; founded Fox Film Corp. (now 20th Century-Fox) in 1915 and sold it in bankruptcy in 1936. Greenfield's silent partner in creation of Bankers Securities in 1928; on its board from 1928 to 1941 as well as on board of Greenfield's Banker Bond & Mortgage Co.

Gest, William Purves (1861–1939). Head of Philadelphia Clearing House Committee, which allowed Bankers Trust to fail in 1930. Joined Fidelity Trust Co. in 1889; president from 1915.

Goerke, Rudolph J. (1867–1938). President of City Stores from 1925 and of Lit Brothers from 1929 until Albert Greenfield displaced him in 1932. Opened Goerke's department store in Newark in 1896; also opened stores in Plainfield, Elizabeth, and elsewhere.

Gordon, William D. (1892–1961). Pennsylvania Secretary of Banking who was appointed February 1931, possibly at Albert Greenfield's behest, to supervise Bankers Trust; ordered its liquidation in fall 1931. Later vice president and treasurer of Greenfield's City Stores for seventeen years.

Greenfield, Albert M. (1887–1967). Born Avrum Moishe Grunfeld in Lozovata, Ukraine, on August 4, 1887. Came to United States in 1892. Founded Albert M. Greenfield & Co. in 1905, Bankers Bond & Mortgage Co. in 1924, and Bankers Securities in 1928. Married Edna F. Kraus on June 18, 1914; they divorced in October 1935. Married Etelka J. Schamberg on October 1, 1937 (she died in 1949). Married Elizabeth Murphy Hallstrom on January 14, 1952. Died in Philadelphia on January 5, 1967.

Greenfield, Bruce H. (1917–2005). Nephew of Albert Greenfield; son of William Greenfield. Joined Bankers Securities in 1953; president from 1970 to 1982. Also director of City Stores.

Greenfield, Esther Vita Serody (1858–1928). Albert Greenfield's mother. Born in Lozovata, Ukraine; married Jacob Grunfeld ca. 1876. Came to United States in 1892 and to Philadelphia in 1896.

Greenfield, Etelka Joseph Schamberg (1887–1949). Albert Greenfield's second wife. Born in Cincinnati and raised in New York. Married Jesse J. Schamberg in 1911 (he died in 1935). Married Albert on October 1, 1937.

Greenfield, Jacob (ca. 1854–1928). Albert Greenfield's father. Born Jacob Grunfeld in Nemirov, Russia (now Ukraine). Married Esther Vita Serody ca. 1876. Came to New York ca. 1891 and to Philadelphia in 1896. Opened small chain of groceries; later operated furniture store in Strawberry Mansion section of Philadelphia.

Greenfield, Robert K. (1915–2012). Nephew of Albert Greenfield; son of William Greenfield; brother of Bruce Greenfield. Lawyer, outside counsel, and director of Bankers Securities; also Greenfield's personal lawyer.

Greenfield, William I. (1882–1978). Albert Greenfield's older brother; father of Robert and Bruce Greenfield. Born Isidor Grunfeld in Russia on January 1, 1882; came to United States in 1896. In 1920s, president of Almar Stores, a chain of more than one hundred food markets in Philadelphia area.

Grosscup, Walter T. (1884–1950). Albert Greenfield executive and ally; joined him in 1929. Elected to City Stores board on Greenfield's slate in January 1932; succeeded Samuel Barker as president of Bankers Securities in April 1932. Left Bankers Securities to become chairman of Pennsylvania Liquor Control Board in 1935. In that role, accused of steering liquor board business to Albert M. Greenfield & Co. and to J. David Stern's *Record*.

Grossman, Israel (1873–?). Insurance broker who served as president of Cahan, Grossman & Co. (Albert Greenfield was the third partner) in 1905. Sold his interest that same year, and the firm became Cahan & Greenfield.

Guffey, Joseph F. (1870–1959). Liberal head of Pennsylvania Democratic Party. Elected U.S. senator with Albert Greenfield's support in 1934; state's first Democratic senator in sixty years. Served two terms, 1935–1947.

Hadley, Will B. (1883–?). Philadelphia city controller who sued the PRT and Mitten Management in 1931, alleging that Mitten purposely overpaid Albert Greenfield $1 million for real estate.

Harris, C. Addison, Jr. (1882–?). President of Franklin Trust Co. up to its closing in 1931. A founding director of Albert Greenfield's Bankers Securities in 1928; also on board of Greenfield's Bankers Bond & Mortgage Co.

Hopkinson, Edward, Jr. (1885–1966). Old Philadelphian who partnered with Albert Greenfield in reorganizing the PRT and its successor, the PTC. Lawyer; joined Drexel & Co. banking house in 1926 and succeeded E. T. Stotesbury as senior partner in 1938. First chairman of Philadelphia's City Planning Commission from 1943 to 1955; encouraged Greenfield to succeed him there in 1955.

Hunsicker, J. Quincy (1844–?). Philadelphia real estate lawyer; Albert Greenfield's first employer, ca. 1901–1902. Employed lawyer John J. McDevitt, who took Greenfield with him when McDevitt left Hunsicker.

Ingersoll, C. Jared (1894–1988). Old Philadelphian who resigned from Philadelphia's City Planning Commission in protest of Albert Greenfield's appointment as chairman in 1956.

Isman, Felix (1873–?). Real estate broker who acquired land on Fifty-Second Street in 1910 with Albert Greenfield and Mastbaum Brothers & Fleisher. Moved to New York about 1918.

Johnson, George H., Jr. (1916–2008). President of Albert M. Greenfield & Co. and director of Bankers Securities and City Stores through 1970s. Joined Albert M. Greenfield & Co. in 1939; vice president in 1952 and president from 1968 to 1980.

Johnson, George H., Sr. (1886–1960). President of Lit Brothers under Albert Greenfield from 1933 through mid-1940s. Director of City Stores from 1932 and Bankers Securities from 1940 to 1960.

Kalodner, Harry E. (1896–1977). U.S. District Court judge and longtime friend of Albert Greenfield who presided over Greenfield's bankruptcy case in 1940. As reporter for J. David Stern's *Record*, covered Bankers Trust closing in 1930. Secretary to Governor George Earle from 1935 to 1939, appointed to federal bench by Roosevelt in 1938, and made Appeals Court judge by Truman in 1946.

Kelly, John B. (1889–1960). Philadelphia contractor and ally of Albert Greenfield in reviving Philadelphia Democratic Party after 1933.

Kraus, Gilbert J. (1898–1975). Albert Greenfield's brother-in-law and lawyer. Instrumental in rescue of "B'rith Sholom children" from Hitler's Austria in 1939.

Kraus, Solomon C. (1866–1928). Albert Greenfield's father-in-law; real estate broker. Started in coal business and entered real estate in North Philadelphia; also became "father of building and loan associations in South Philadelphia." Joined Albert M.

Greenfield & Co. in 1920 as first vice president; retired in 1925. Vice president of American Jewish Congress; grand master of B'rith Sholom Lodge. Left family an estate believed to be worth close to $1 million.

Krauskopf, Joseph (1858–1923). Rabbi of Keneseth Israel Reform (German Jewish) congregation, Philadelphia, which Albert Greenfield joined in 1914. Humanitarian who helped shape Greenfield's views on social justice issues. Born in Prussia.

Kunze, Earl (?–?). Philadelphia paperhanger who was briefly Albert Greenfield's partner in his first real estate business in 1904.

Leech, Edward T. (1892–1949). Editor of *Pittsburgh Press*, 1931–1949. Conducted mudslinging campaign against Albert Greenfield in 1941.

Levinthal, Louis E. (1892–1976). Common Pleas Court judge in Philadelphia, 1937–1959; president of the Zionist Organization of America, 1941–1943.

Lewis, Leon A. (1885–1934). President of Bank of Philadelphia & Trust Co., taken over by Albert Greenfield's Bankers Trust in July 1930; in takeover, made vice president and director of Bankers Trust and resigned August 20, 1930. Indicted December 1931 for allegedly embezzling $100,000; convicted May 1933 of taking lesser amounts and sentenced to two years. Committed suicide August 29, 1934, while appealing case.

Mackey, Harry A. (1869–1938). Won Philadelphia mayoral election in 1927 with Albert Greenfield's support; served from 1928 to 1932.

Mastbaum, Jules E. (1872–1926). Principal in Mastbaum Brothers & Fleisher, Philadelphia real estate firm that acquired land with Albert Greenfield on Fifty-Second Street in 1910. Brother of Stanley.

Mastbaum, Stanley V. (ca. 1881–1918). Principal in Mastbaum Brothers & Fleisher, real estate firm that acquired land with Albert Greenfield on Fifty-Second Street in 1910. Brother of Jules.

McCloskey, Matthew B. (1893–1973). Philadelphia contractor and ally of Albert Greenfield in reviving Philadelphia Democratic Party in 1930s.

McDevitt, Harry S. (1885–1950). Philadelphia Common Pleas Court judge who ordered Albert Greenfield's commissions returned for sale of Quaker City Cab to the PRT in April 1931. Brother of Greenfield's early employer, John J. McDevitt. Known as "Hanging Harry."

McDevitt, John J., Jr. (1879–1945). Lawyer whom Albert Greenfield met in Hunsicker's office in ca. 1902 and followed when McDevitt went into practice on his own. Brother of Judge Harry McDevitt.

Mitten, Thomas (1864–1929). Albert Greenfield's friend and business associate. President of Mitten Management, which operated the PRT in 1920s. Born in Brighton, England. Drowned in possible suicide at his Poconos estate October 1, 1929.

Monaghan, John (1870–?). Childhood friend of Albert Greenfield. Philadelphia Common Pleas Court judge, 1916–1927; Greenfield successfully supported him for district attorney in 1927; served one term, 1928–1932. Greenfield donated four large manual organs to St. Charles Borromeo Seminary in his honor in 1928.

Newhall, C. Stevenson (1877–1950). As executive vice president of Pennsylvania Co. (later First Pennsylvania Bank), led futile efforts to rescue Albert Greenfield's Bankers Trust in 1930. Joined Pennsylvania Co. in 1896; elected president in 1948.

O'Shea, John J. (1919–1990). Public relations man; Albert Greenfield's personal assistant, 1955–1963.

Paine, Edna Florence Kraus Greenfield (1894–1987). Albert Greenfield's first wife and mother of his five children. Married Albert on June 18, 1914. Divorced Albert in Mexico in October 1935 and immediately married Charles Paine there; divorced Paine in 1936.

Petrie, Elizabeth Murphy Hallstrom Greenfield (1912–2003). Albert Greenfield's third wife; married Albert on January 14, 1952. Executive director of World Affairs Council of Philadelphia, 1947–1952. Married to John L. Hallstrom from 1933 until their divorce in 1946; after Albert died, married Donald A. Petrie, Washington attorney, in 1973.

Roebling, Mary G. (1905–1994). Chairwoman of Trenton Trust Co. and longtime friend of Albert Greenfield. Widow of Siegfried Roebling, her second husband. Linked to Albert romantically from 1949 to 1951, between his second and third marriages.

Rosenbaum, Samuel R. (1888–1972). Joined Bankers Securities as assistant to Albert Greenfield in 1930; made vice president in 1931. Later vice president of Greenfield's Bankers Bond & Mortgage Co., president of radio station WFIL, vice president of Bankers Securities and Albert M. Greenfield & Co., and director of Lit Brothers, Bellevue-Stratford Hotel, and other Greenfield concerns. Second wife was harpist Edna Phillips (1907–2003), who was first female member of Philadelphia Orchestra in 1930.

Schamberg, Jesse J. (1877–1935). Philadelphia real estate broker; intermittently vice president of Albert M. Greenfield & Co. in 1920s. In 1911 married Etelka Joseph, who married Albert after Schamberg died.

Schofield, Lemuel B. (1892–1955). Philadelphia lawyer and ally of Albert Greenfield from 1920s; hired by Greenfield in 1938 to investigate Moses Annenberg. Bankers Securities director, 1943–1955. As Philadelphia Director of Public Safety in 1929, raided private clubs to confiscate liquor. U.S. Commissioner of Immigration and Naturalization from 1940 to 1942.

Simon, David E. (1869–?). Early real estate mentor (ca. 1901–1902) to Albert Greenfield, who may have worked in Simon's office. Client of John J. McDevitt, lawyer for whom Greenfield worked.

Stern, Horace (1878–1969). Supervisor of Hebrew Sunday School Society, where Albert Greenfield taught, beginning ca. 1916. Cofounder of Stern & Wolf, 1903–1920, law firm that represented Greenfield in his early years. Philadelphia Common Pleas Court judge, 1920–1935; elected Pennsylvania Supreme Court justice in 1935, with Greenfield's support; and chief justice, 1952–1956. Republican, but Greenfield supported him for state supreme court in 1935.

Stern, J. David (1886–1971). Albert Greenfield's friend and fighting liberal publisher of *Philadelphia Record*, which he bought in 1928 with Greenfield's support. Met Greenfield in Cahan's print shop in 1905 while editor of *YMHA Review*, another Cahan client. Bought *Camden Courier-Post* in 1920 and bought *New York Post* in 1933, both with Greenfield's support. Sold *Record* in 1947 to *Bulletin*, which promptly closed it.

Stotesbury, Edward T. (1849–1938). Banker; senior partner of Drexel & Co., 1904–1938, and key figure in Philadelphia bankers' refusal to rescue Albert Greenfield's Bankers Trust in 1930. Joined Drexel & Co. in 1866; made partner in 1883 and senior partner in 1904.

Vare, William S. (1867–1934). Youngest of three brothers who dominated Philadelphia politics as Republican bosses from 1890s to 1930. U.S. congressman, 1915–1927. Became head of Philadelphia Republican organization on death of brother Edwin in October 1922. Elected U.S. senator 1926 with Albert Greenfield's support but denied Senate seat for excessive campaign spending. Suffered stroke in August 1928; broke with Greenfield in 1929 over Greenfield's reform efforts.

Wayne, Joseph, Jr. (1873–1942). As president of Philadelphia National Bank from 1926, led futile effort to rescue Albert Greenfield's Bankers Trust in 1930. President of Philadelphia Clearing House Association, 1930–1941, from which Greenfield sought aid in 1930 Bankers Trust crisis. Worked his way up from office boy to president of Girard National Bank in 1914; became president after its merger with Philadelphia National Bank in 1926.

Wilson, S. Davis (1881–1939). Republican mayor of Philadelphia, 1936–1939. Teamed up with Albert Greenfield to bring Democratic National Convention to Philadelphia in 1936. But alienated Greenfield and Democrats, was charged with corruption, resigned in 1939, and died a week later.

Wolf, Morris (1883–1978). Founder of Stern & Wolf, later Wolf, Block, Schorr and Solis-Cohen, Philadelphia's first major Jewish law firm. Legal counsel to Albert Greenfield on many deals.

Wurzel, Leonard (1918–2013). President of Loft Candy under Albert Greenfield and successors, 1957–1964, after working there since 1946. Son of Maurice Wurzel.

Wurzel, Maurice L. (1888–1949). President of Peoples Bank & Trust Co. in the 1920s. President of Albert Greenfield's Bankers Bond & Mortgage Co. through the 1930s. Director of Bankers Securities in 1930. Installed by Greenfield as president of Loft Candy in 1940. Father of Leonard Wurzel.

Notes

PROLOGUE

1. U.S. Weather Bureau report for Philadelphia for December 21, 1930, *Philadelphia Bulletin*, December 22, 1930.

2. Gest was born February 27, 1861. See Gest's biographical entry in Stafford, *Who's Who in Philadelphia in Wartime*. Further details were provided to the author by the Lower Merion Historical Society.

3. Gest's father, the lawyer and financier John Barnard Gest, became president of the Fidelity Trust Co. in 1891, at which time William became assistant to the president. See William P. Gest biographical materials, binder 5, call no. PHE-5-GES03, Lower Merion Historical Society, Bala Cynwyd, PA. The 1900 U.S. census shows John Barnard Gest, age seventy-six, still living in Philadelphia; it also lists William P. Gest as assistant to the president of Fidelity Trust.

4. The term "Main Line" is actually derived from the "Main Line of Public Works," the complex of rails, canals, and inclined planes created by the state in the mid-nineteenth century to connect Philadelphia and Pittsburgh. Burt, *Perennial Philadelphians*, 196.

5. Fisher, *Diary of Sidney George Fisher*, quoted in Burt, *Perennial Philadelphians*, 532.

6. Burt, *Perennial Philadelphians*, 196. The Welsh Tract is described on page 59.

7. See "Pennsylvania Railroad History" at http://www.prrho.com/prr.htm; see also Daughen and Binzen, *The Wreck of the Penn Central*, 17, citing the London *Economist*.

8. The 1900 U.S. census lists Gest in the house with his wife, Isabel; daughters Isabel and Lillian; and five servants. By 1930 they are down to four servants: a cook, chauffeur, maid, and charwoman.

9. Burt, *Perennial Philadelphians*, 533.

10. Gest's house valuation appears in the 1930 U.S. census.

11. Catherine Drinker Bowen (Henry Drinker's sister), in *Family Portrait* (122, 131), says that Edward Drinker was born on Christmas Eve in 1680—two years before William Penn arrived—and that he lived in a cave above the Delaware River and had four wives and eighteen children.

12. Burt, *Perennial Philadelphians*, 491; Bowen, *Family Portrait*, 176.

13. See "History," *Merion Tribute House*, http://www.tributehouse.com/history.asp. The quotation is from Eldridge Johnson, founder of the Victor Talking Machine Company (in 1891), who offered to demolish the house on his Merion property to build a tribute house there.

14. C. Stevenson Newhall obituary, *Philadelphia Inquirer*, December 16, 1950.

15. Wayne (president of the Clearing House Association, a consortium of leading Philadelphia banks), Newhall, Stotesbury, and the host, Gest (chairman of the Clearing House Committee, charged with resolving the Bankers Trust crisis), were almost certainly present. Precisely who else attended—whether the eight members of the Clearing House Committee, or the heads of all thirty-four banks in the Clearing House Association (as Greenfield contended), or a combination of prominent local bankers (as seems most likely)—is unclear; no minutes were taken, and no one present ever gave an account of what transpired.

CHAPTER 1

1. Cave and Coulson, *Source Book for Medieval Economic History*, 101–102. Also see T.P., "Taking the Skeleton out of Jewish History's Closet."

2. Actually, Jews rarely predominated in royal financial affairs, and then only for brief periods of time. See Michael Walzer, "Imaginary Jews," *New York Review of Books*, March 20, 2014, pp. 31–33.

3. Josephus, *Contra apionem*, 1:12, quoted in *Jewish Encyclopedia*, 4:188.

4. This subject is explored in Biale, *Power and Powerlessness in Jewish History*.

5. MacDonogh, *Frederick the Great*, 347.

6. Thorndike, *The Very Rich*, 126.

7. See, for example, the Schumpeter column in the *Economist*, January 7, 2012, p. 60.

8. In 1569 Poland annexed the Grand Duchy of Lithuania, a huge state whose territory extended from the Baltic to the Black Sea, covering most of what later became western Russia.

9. "Commerce," in *Jewish Encyclopedia*, 4:192.

10. William Greenfield, interview by the author, October 17, 1975. My sole source of the names of Jacob and Hannah Serody is the death certificate of their daughter, Esther Vita Serody Greenfield, who died August 15, 1928, at Atlantic City, New Jersey. A Serody family tree lists four children of Jacob and Hannah Serody, three of whom came to the United States. There may have been others as well.

11. A Russian vierst is roughly equivalent to a kilometer—that is, five-eighths of a mile.

12. The Jewish population in 1897 was 5,287, or 59 percent of the total. See "Nemirov," in Berenbaum and Skolnik, *Encyclopedia Judaica*, 15:68–69. According to William Greenfield (in our interview), the Jews there were "all storekeepers."

13. Robert Greenfield, interview by the author, October 5, 2011. He added that when Albert Greenfield was dying in 1966, he heard Albert in his hospital room rambling to himself in Yiddish—a suggestion that Yiddish may have been Albert's first language. The parents of Jacob Grunfeld are listed as "not known" on Jacob's death certificate (Philadelphia birth records, April 27, 1928, No. 34759), and there is no Hebrew inscription on Jacob's gravestone, a common source of the names of the deceased's parents. The sole source of Jacob's father's name as "Moshe" is an October 1962 letter to Albert from Rabbi Mortimer J. Cohen that jocularly addresses him as "Rebbe Abba Yaakov b. Mosheh." See Skwersky, *Knight of Philadelphia*, 15.

14. Albert Greenfield once told an interviewer that his parents were married for fifty-two years; see Sidney Fields, "Albert M. Greenfield: Credo for Achievement," *New York Daily News*, February 16, 1953, Historical Society of Pennsylvania (HSP), box 565, folder 2. Both Jacob and Esther Greenfield died in 1928; hence the deduction of 1876 as the year of their marriage. Esther's gravestone says she was born in 1859; her death certificate, dated August 15, 1928, gives the birth date as August 25, 1858. Jacob Greenfield's naturalization petition, dated January 9, 1915, gives his birth date as April 10, 1855, but much of the information in that petition is incorrect.

15. Robert Greenfield, interview by the author, July 25, 2011.

16. Birth records and other reliable documents for the Grunfeld/Greenfield family are almost nonexistent, and family members often fudged dates and ages on their official papers. Andrew Harrison, in "Mr. Philadelphia" (2), says that Molly, the eldest sibling, was born in 1880 but provides no attribution. Molly's gravestone at Adath Jeshurun Cemetery, Philadel-

phia, says she was born in 1881. Since the next child, William (born Isador), was born January 1, 1882, 1880 seems a more likely birth date for Molly. Jacob's naturalization petition of January 9, 1915, gives Molly's birth date as May 21, 1880, but many other dates and even the sequence of his children are inaccurate in that petition. William said his sister Rose was five years younger than he (that is, born about 1886) and in various interviews said Albert was six or seven years younger than he; if Albert was born in August 1887, the difference between the two brothers would be five years and seven months, which is more or less consistent with William's recollection. Both William (in 1901) and Albert (in 1906) raised their ages to apply early for citizenship, Albert claiming August 4, 1884, as his birth date. See Albert Greenfield petition for citizenship, filed February 14, 1906, admitted May 14, 1906, U.S. District Court, Eastern District of Pennsylvania, No. 11707. Albert continued to claim 1884 and, later, 1885 and 1886 as his birth date until, in the 1930s, it was more convenient for him to claim the younger (and probably more accurate) birth year of 1887. For example, his World War I draft registration card (1917–1918) says he was born August 4, 1884, but his World War II draft registration card (1942) says he was born August 4, 1887. His father, Jacob Greenfield, further muddied the issue on *his* citizenship application (filed April 30, 1915) when, presumably to accommodate his sons' falsified ages, he listed Albert as his third child rather than his fourth and said he was born September 8, 1886. Contradictorily, the ship's passenger manifest for the liner *Coblenz*, which left Hamburg for Glasgow on December 18, 1891, lists Esther Grunfeld's son Abraham as age six years, seven months, which would put Albert's birth at May 1885.

17. Albert's Hebrew name was provided in a memo by his brother William, October 2, 1962, HSP, box 884, folder 1. The name had other variations depending on whether one spoke Yiddish, German, or Ukrainian. Barbara Greenfield said Albert was called "Abishe Moishe"; see Greenfield, "Albert M. Greenfield," 2. Others have identified Albert's original name as "Avrum Moishe."

18. William Greenfield, interview by the author.

19. Binzen, Daughen, and Friedman, *Rise and Fall of the House of Greenfield*, 9.

20. Greenfield, "Albert M. Greenfield," 2.

21. William Greenfield, in our interview, mentioned that Jacob was buying grain in Lozovata in competition with a rival, so that one of them had to leave.

22. The 1891 date is consistent with the recollection of Jacob's son William Greenfield (born January 1882) that he was "about ten" when his father left for America; William Greenfield, interview by the author. It is also consistent with a ship's manifest listing Jacob Grünfield, age thirty-four, as arriving in New York on June 25, 1891, aboard the ship *Lahn* from Bremen (this Jacob Grünfield is identified as German and a laborer by occupation, possibly reflecting Russian Jews' common practice of working their way through Germany before boarding ship for America). Jacob's own petition for naturalization, dated January 9, 1915, says he emigrated from Hamburg (not Bremen) in mid-December 1892 and arrived in New York on December 31, 1892; it does not list the name of the ship. This petition strikes me as unreliable because many other dates on it are mistaken; indeed, it seems possible that the petition was filled out for Jacob by someone else who made up specific dates when Jacob could not supply them. (An earlier manifest for the ship *Servia*, which arrived in New York from Liverpool on February 20, 1889, lists a passenger named Jakob Grunfeld, age twenty-nine, "Austrian laborer"; but this is probably not our Jacob, if only because our Jacob Grunfeld fathered a daughter, Anna, born in Russia probably in late 1891.)

23. *Trow's New York City Directory* for 1893 through 1896 lists a Jacob Greenfield, grocer, at 135 Suffolk Street on the Lower East Side. This is consistent with Jacob's arrival in and departure from New York and also with his subsequent occupation as a grocer in Philadelphia. However, Jacob's son William said that Jacob got a job in a factory in New York; William Greenfield, interview by the author. Like many immigrants, Jacob may have worked in a New York factory while also selling groceries on the side. The birth certificate of Jacob's daughter Rebecca, born April 13, 1896, lists the address as 154 Orchard Street and lists Jacob's occupation as "shirt ironer"; Jacob might have moved to Orchard Street by then. (City directories are

usually accurate for the year preceding their cover date.) See New York City Record of Birth, 1896, No. 16382.

24. Two ship's passenger manifests record the journey of five Grunfelds who appear to be Esther Grunfeld and three of her children and perhaps an older male relative. They are listed as boarding the ship *Coblenz* on December 18, 1891, at Hamburg, bound for Glasgow, Scotland, where they transferred to the *Devonia*, arriving in New York on January 6, 1892. The party includes an Esther (mistakenly spelled "Ester") Grunfeld, age thirty-three years, eight months, and three children: Abram/Abraham (age six years, seven months), Rachel (age one year, eight months), and Mordche, an infant son (age four months). Also listed is a Moses Grunfeld, age fifty-three years, six months, who may have been unrelated or may have been a distant relative (he was born in Focsani, Romania—about five hundred kilometers southwest of Nemirov—and died in Switzerland in 1917). The age given for this Esther Grunfeld places her birth at April 1858, which is very close to the birth date of August 25, 1858, that appears on Esther Greenfield's death certificate (dated August 15, 1928). I surmise that this "Ester" is probably Jacob Greenfield's wife, and her son Abram/Abraham might well be Abishe, or later Albert. To be sure, this entry fails several important tests. Albert's older brother William Greenfield told me in our interview that Jacob left Russia for America when William was about ten (i.e., about 1892) and was in the United States by himself for about four years. That recollection is more or less consistent with Barbara Greenfield's account at Albert's seventy-fifth birthday party in 1962 (and she says she got this information from Albert himself); see Greenfield, "Albert M. Greenfield." Barbara Greenfield's story has Esther arriving in 1895 with her baby Anna, and the other siblings—Molly, William, Rose, and Abishe (Albert)—arriving in the spring of 1896. (Esther must have arrived by mid-1895 because she delivered a daughter in New York on April 13, 1896.) But it is possible that when William (who was ninety-three when I interviewed him) said Jacob was alone in New York for four years, he meant four years until the whole family was reunited in New York in 1896. The 1891–1892 ship's passenger records for the *Coblenz* and *Devonia* fail to account for Anna, who was definitely born in Russia, probably in late 1891 or 1892, but I speculate that the four-month-old male infant brought by Esther in December 1891 may actually have been a baby girl—Anna—since such records were often inaccurate. Also, the *Coblenz* register inexplicably says that this Grunfeld family came from Riga, Russia. These inconsistencies notwithstanding, this seems the most likely record of Albert's arrival in America with his mother, especially since no other record of Esther's arrival in America (or Albert's) has been found.

25. The journey from Lozovata to Hamburg was described by William Greenfield in our interview. He did not say who specifically was in the group or where the boat took them. Albert's daughter-in-law Barbara Greenfield, in a paper prepared for Albert's seventy-fifth birthday in 1962, said Esther and the baby (Anna) joined Jacob in New York three years after Jacob left and that the remaining children traveled alone through Bremen (not Hamburg) and Liverpool. See Greenfield, "Albert M. Greenfield," 2. The *Coblenz* and *Devonia* ship's passenger manifests list Abram/Abraham Grunfeld as age six years, seven months, but other evidence suggests he was more likely four.

26. Albert told a reporter in 1955 that the family, including his parents, had spent two years in England before proceeding to America. See Brecht, "The Greenfield Story." But Albert is an unreliable source; like many immigrants, he constantly altered the narrative of his migration to suit his purposes in his adopted land. Barbara Greenfield, in "Albert M. Greenfield" (2), implies that Albert was among the latter group of siblings who came to America via England in 1895–1896. Albert's daughter Elizabeth Zeidman said in our October 19, 1975, interview that she found a book inscribed "Abraham Moses Greenfield"; the surname had been changed in England, she said, but the book itself was not necessarily from England. I surmise that Albert conflated the story of his siblings' passage through England with his own story as a way of Anglicizing his past.

27. Greenfield, "Albert M. Greenfield," 2; see also Harrison, "Mr. Philadelphia," 4, citing his interviews with Elizabeth Zeidman and Albert Greenfield Jr. in 1994. Who this man was, whether he was Jewish, or whether he existed at all is unclear.

28. Albert M. Greenfield III, interview by the author, April 5, 2012. He said his source was his father, Albert M. Greenfield Jr. The ship's record would provide the captain's name, but I have found no ship's record for the arrival of Molly, William (then Isador), and Rose Grunfeld/Greenfield in America.

29. Molly Greenfield Newton's second child and first son, Albert Greenfield Newton, was born in 1901. Since Albert Greenfield was only fourteen at the time, Molly presumably named her son after someone else.

30. Greenfield, "Albert M. Greenfield," 2. William Greenfield, in our interview, said that the siblings arrived in New York on "the second day of Shavuot," which would be May 19, 1896, according to a perpetual Hebrew calendar. William's son Robert Greenfield, in our September 15, 2011, interview, said that Molly came to America on her own with two younger siblings and that he thought William was one of them; presumably the third in the group was the third eldest sibling, Rose, who would have been not quite ten in the spring of 1896. Rebecca Greenfield's birth on April 13, 1896, is recorded in New York City birth certificate no. 16382. It lists Rebecca as the tenth child born to Jacob and Esther and the sixth to survive. Jacob's naturalization petition of 1915, less reliably, says that Rebecca was born March 25, 1896. Barbara Greenfield's 1962 account says Rebecca had a twin sister who died shortly after, but there is no record of such a birth.

31. Albert Greenfield, "What America Means to Me," undated radio address (ca. January 1951), HSP, box 508, folder 14.

32. "Populist Party Platform," July 1892, available at http://www.wwnorton.com/college/history/eamerica/media/ch22/resources/documents/populist.htm.

CHAPTER 2

1. William Greenfield, interview by the author, October 17, 1975. The friend's name may have been Freiberg. In 1930 Albert Greenfield received a letter from a Joseph Freiberg of Philadelphia saying, "About 37 years ago my father loaned your father money to come to Philadelphia from New York City. . . . He took care of him for a while and got him a job as a shirt ironer." Letter from Joseph Freiberg to Albert Greenfield, January 15, 1930, Historical Society of Pennsylvania (HSP), box 147, folder 6. Jacob Greenfield first appears in *Gopsill's Philadelphia City Directory* in 1899, listed as an ironer; in 1900 he is listed as a laborer and in 1901 again as an ironer.

2. Andrew Harrison says that Jacob and his family initially stayed in Clifton Heights, Pennsylvania, a Delaware County town southwest of Philadelphia. See Harrison, "Mr. Philadelphia," 5. His apparent source is an interview with Albert Greenfield's son Albert Jr. on November 25, 1994. Jacob Greenfield's naturalization petition, dated January 9, 1915, says he took up residence in Pennsylvania on September 20, 1896. The petition is unreliable on many facts, but this date seems about right.

3. William Greenfield, interview by the author.

4. "Greenfield Willing to Be Civic Leader of New Type Unlike the Old-Time 'Boss,'" *Evening Public Ledger*, January 22, 1929, HSP, box 900, folder 8. When the reporter asked Greenfield to recount his early struggles, he replied, "I can tell you no such story, as it would not be the facts. . . . I wouldn't say that all this was such a hard struggle. My father made a comfortable income of from $3,000 to $4,000 a year and sent all of us to high school and two of us to college."

5. Harrison, "Mr. Philadelphia," 5.

6. See Weigley, *Philadelphia*, 481, for employment statistics as of 1904. Philip B. Scranton, in *Workshop of the World*, says that at the turn of the twentieth century, roughly seven hundred separate Philadelphia companies operated in textiles alone, employing some sixty thousand people. See also Harrison, "Mr. Philadelphia," 5.

7. Guinther, *Philadelphia*, 114.

8. Hodos, *Second Cities*.

9. Binzen, Daughen, and Friedman, *Rise and Fall of the House of Greenfield*, 9–10.

10. Steffens, "Philadelphia." This was the fifth in a series of articles exposing urban corruption, later published in book form as *The Shame of the Cities* (1904). "All our municipal governments are more or less bad," Steffens wrote. "Philadelphia is simply the most corrupt and the most contented" (195).

11. Harrison, "Mr. Philadelphia," 6, citing Tabak, "The Transformation of Jewish Identity," 32, 43, 59. See also Whiteman, "Philadelphia's Jewish Neighborhoods," 246.

12. Jacob makes his first appearance in *Gopsill's Philadelphia City Directory* in 1899 at 1019 S. Sixth Street; in 1900 he is listed at 529 Christian; in 1901 at 1156 S. Ninth Street; in 1903 at 1245 S. Fifth Street; in 1904–1906 at 1849 S. Twelfth Street; in 1907 at 1833 S. Twelfth Street; in 1908 at 2300 S. Twelfth Street; and in 1909 at 523 Tasker Street.

13. Binzen, "They Came, They Saw and They Built Empire." William says here that he was about six years older than Albert.

14. William Greenfield, interview by the author.

15. Greenfield, "Albert M. Greenfield," 2–3.

16. Skwersky, *Knight of Philadelphia*, 18.

17. Ibid., 18–19. Horace Binney (1780–1875) practiced law in Philadelphia from 1800 and served as a Whig member of Congress during Andrew Jackson's presidency.

18. The school's history is noted in a talk given by Albert at a reunion in 1926. See Albert Greenfield talk to Binney School alumni dinner, 1926, HSP, box 73, folder 6. A third floor was added in 1900, after Albert graduated.

19. Albert Greenfield talk to Binney School alumni dinner. "Miss Emma" is not identified beyond her given name.

20. Greenfield, "Albert M. Greenfield," 4.

21. Binzen, "They Came, They Saw and They Built Empire."

22. Greenfield talk to Binney School alumni dinner.

23. Albert may have sold newspapers outside the Drexel Building at Fifth and Chestnut Streets. An unnamed banker claimed that Albert told him that he used to watch the Drexel partner E. T. Stotesbury—Albert's subsequent nemesis—go in and out of the building. See Fisher, "Sugarloaf."

24. Records of the Binney School appear to have been destroyed. In an uncharacteristically precise recollection, Albert told an interviewer in 1929 that he graduated from the Binney School "at the age of 11 years and ten months," which would be June 1899. "Greenfield Willing to Be Civic Leader."

25. The four were Central, Girls High, Northeast, and Central Manual Training School. See "Men and Things" column, *Philadelphia Bulletin*, November 1933, Cheesman Herrick file, Temple University Urban Archives (TUUA).

26. From 1854 to 1900, Central High School was located on the east side of Broad Street at Green. In September 1900, the school moved to a larger building in a lot across Broad Street bounded by Broad, Green, Fifteenth, and Brandywine Streets. Manual Training School opened in 1883 at Seventeenth and Wood Streets and was renamed Central Manual Training School well before Albert would have attended; it remained there (about a half-mile from Central High) until 1912. See "A Short History of Old Manual and the Class of 1901," TUUA. Central High School's commercial program, launched in 1898, was apparently housed in the school's previous building and may have drawn on some of the programs at (or become confused with) Central Manual Training; see Cheesman Herrick obituary, *Philadelphia Bulletin*, February 27, 1956. Central High School's enrollment book, which lists every student who attended the school from its opening in 1837, contains no record that Albert ever enrolled, attended, or graduated. David Kahn and Maxine Croul (Central High School archivists), e-mail correspondence with and interviews by the author, January 13, 19, 23, 24, 2012. Albert claimed in some interviews to have attended Central High, but in most interviews he was vague about the identity of his high school; by contrast, he always referred specifically to the Binney School and attended at least one of its reunions. In 1951 Albert received a letter from John Paul Call of New York, who claimed to have attended Central High with Albert, but there is no evidence that Call attended the school either. Letters from John P. Call to Albert Greenfield, August 13,

1951, and August 30, 1951, HSP, box 495, folder 13. In November 1950, Cheesman Herrick, a former Central High teacher, wrote to Albert claiming to have taught him at Central High. Herrick created and directed Central High's "commercial department," which offered business courses, from 1898 to 1909; it is perhaps possible that students from Central Manual (some six blocks from Central High) attended some of those classes or that Herrick scouted Central Manual for ideas for his department. It is also possible that, when he wrote the letter at age eighty-four, Herrick was merely trying to attach himself to Albert Greenfield's legacy. Letters from Cheesman Herrick to Albert Greenfield, 1950 and 1951, HSP, box 495, folder 14. It is also worth noting that Albert never received Central High School's Alumni Award of Merit—the sort of honor he would surely have lobbied for (and deservedly so) had he attended that school; David Kahn, e-mail correspondence with the author, November 14–15, 2012.

27. In a typed transcript of an interview in 1924, Albert said, "I attended classes at the Horace Binney School; and had a year or two of high school." He did not identify the high school. HSP, box 49, folder 9.

28. Elizabeth Petrie, interview by the author, October 15, 1975.

29. Robert Greenfield, interview by the author, October 5, 2011. Two of Albert's childhood friends were David Bortin (born 1885) and the much older John P. Monaghan (born 1870), respectively Jewish and Irish. Both became influential lawyers.

30. Greenfield, "Albert M. Greenfield," 6. Also Robert Greenfield, interview by the author, October 5, 2011.

31. Harrison, "Mr. Philadelphia," 81.

32. Albert Greenfield address to Young Men's Hebrew Association (YMHA), Philadelphia, April 2, 1922, HSP, box 30, folder 7. A profile of Greenfield in the *Evening Public Ledger* on January 22, 1929, remarks, "The study of Napoleon Bonaparte is his hobby." See "Greenfield Willing to Be Civic Leader." See also Harrison, "Mr. Philadelphia," 8.

33. Lois Brunner, "Mr. Albert M. Greenfield," *Philadelphia*, March 1951, pp. 5–6, HSP, box 503, folder 5.

34. Wanamaker's is characterized as such in Hendrickson, *Grand Emporiums*, 78.

35. Greenfield, "Albert M. Greenfield," 5. When Greenfield was honored by the Philadelphia Press Association in 1963, he referred to his past as a reporter for the *Public Ledger* and read excerpts from newspapers (but not articles he had written) of May 1904, when he said he was a reporter. See "Press Group Hails Old Newsie Greenfield."

36. Hunsicker was born in 1844, according to the 1880 and 1900 U.S. censuses. His office was located in Room 711 of the Crozer Building at 1420 Chestnut Street (later known as the American Baptist Publication Society Building). The description is taken from Hunsicker, *Genealogical History of the Hunsicker Family*, 79–81.

37. Brecht, "The Greenfield Story"; Greenfield, "Albert M. Greenfield," 5.

38. Valentine Hunsicker settled in Germantown, to the northwest of Philadelphia, in search of religious freedom; see Hunsicker, *Genealogical History*, 79–81.

39. John J. McDevitt Jr. (1879–1945) graduated from the University of Pennsylvania Law School in 1900. Because he was not yet twenty-one, he had to wait several months to be admitted to the bar. John J. McDevitt Jr. obituary, *Philadelphia Bulletin*, November 15, 1945. Nochem Winnet describes McDevitt (as of 1924) as "physically a very big man" who "weighed about 300 pounds." See Winnet, *Vignettes of a Lucky Life*, 37.

40. Drexel's will, probated in 1893, quoted in Rottenberg, *The Man Who Made Wall Street*, 142.

41. Marc Weiss, *Rise of the Community Builders*, 5, 18–26, cited in Harrison, "Mr. Philadelphia," 12. California began licensing real estate brokers around this time; the first professional organization, the National Association of Real Estate Boards, was created in 1908.

42. See, for example, "The Rise of Felix Isman."

43. Rottenberg, *Wolf, Block Schorr and Solis-Cohen*, 16.

44. Drinker's talk to the American Bar Association's Section on Legal Education and Admission to the Bar, Memphis, Tennessee, October 22, 1929, cited in Stevens, *Law School*, 184. See also Putnam, "Mr. Drinker's Desk," 29–33. Drinker's comments have been unfairly

excerpted to suggest he was anti-Semitic; see, for example, Auerbach, *Unequal Justice*, 126–127. In fact, Drinker was arguing for the need to require more extensive and rigorous legal education. A similar condescending attitude toward immigrants was expressed privately in the 1930s by no less a figure than Franklin D. Roosevelt. After a meeting with Ambassador Joseph P. Kennedy, a grandson of Irish immigrants, Roosevelt told his son-in-law that all Kennedy cared about deep down was preserving his fortune, and FDR added, "Sometimes I think I am 200 years older than he is." See Buckley, "Family Guy," 212.

45. William Greenfield, interview by the author. Albert said he spent two years in Hunsicker's office while attending the University of Pennsylvania Law School. See "Greenfield Willing to Be Civic Leader." But in the Penn Law School's catalog for the fall 1903 semester, Albert listed his address as 403 Land Title Building—that is, McDevitt's office.

46. Law School Student Records, 1894–1915, University of Pennsylvania archives, UPB 6.71, box 6. The University of Pennsylvania Catalogue, Fall 1903, p. 516, lists Albert's address as 403 Land Title Bldg. McDevitt was listed in the 1904 City Directory at 402 Land Title Bldg., presumably having moved there from Hunsicker's Crozer Building office in 1903. (Albert is listed in 1904 as "assistant secretary" in McDevitt's office.)

47. At a testimonial dinner for then-Common Pleas Court Judge Monaghan in 1926, Albert said he was "a mere boy" when a law student named Dave Phillips introduced him to Monaghan, who was then a young barrister, and "we three came to be fast friends." Untitled typed manuscript, HSP box 73, folder 6.

48. Harrison, "Mr. Philadelphia," 11.

49. Brecht, "The Greenfield Story," 5. Also Barbara Greenfield, interview by the author, March 30, 2011.

50. Harrison, "Mr. Philadelphia," 11.

51. Brecht, "The Greenfield Story," quotes Albert: "I conceived the notion to go into the real estate business, and into the real estate business I went" (34).

52. *Gopsill's Philadelphia City Directory* for 1900, 1902, and 1903 lists Finberg as an insurance broker at 218 S. Fourth Street; beginning in 1904 he is listed as "real estate" at 635 Walnut. Cahan, the printer, is listed from 1900 through 1903 at 310 Chestnut and thereafter at 218 S. Fourth Street.

53. Earl Cahan, interview by Peter Binzen, 1985. He said his father, Louis Cahan, was born in 1876 and had been brought to the United States at age eight or nine.

54. J. David Stern later described Albert's office in Cahan's building as a cubicle. See Greenfield, "Albert M. Greenfield," 11.

55. The only source that mentions Kunze is Greenfield, "Albert M. Greenfield," 5.

56. The description of the mustache and attire is taken from Greenfield, "Albert M. Greenfield," 5.

57. *Gopsill's Philadelphia City Directory* lists Jacob as a grocer (rather than an ironer or laborer) for the first time in 1904; the address is 1849 South Twelfth Street, listed as both his business and home address. Albert is also listed at this address in 1904 and 1905. Albert, in a January 22, 1929, *Evening Public Ledger* interview, said his father was a grocer "first at Fifth and Wharton Streets and then at 12th and Wolf." Greenfield's "Albert M. Greenfield" (2) says Jacob opened his first grocery store at 342 Christian Street and "then, in quick succession, and often concurrently, 516 Christian, Second and Thompson, Fifth and Wharton, 12th and Mifflin, 12th and Wolf, Sixth and Allegheny, Emerald St., Second and Morris, and the largest at 52nd and Vine. Finally, in approximately 1908, the family was able to 'go private,' as the saying went, and they moved to 523 Tasker St., a private home removed from the business."

58. "Greenfield Willing to Be Civic Leader." See also Harrison, "Mr. Philadelphia," 7. The average worker's annual wage in 1897, according to a U.S. Labor Department study, was $451; see Binzen, Daughen, and Friedman, *Rise and Fall of the House of Greenfield*, 12.

59. Brecht, "The Greenfield Story."

60. Harrison, "Mr. Philadelphia" (10), says Albert was confirmed at the Reform Congregation Keneseth Israel (which he joined in 1914), but Albert's name does not appear in the congregation's complete record of its confirmants. Keneseth Israel archivist Claire Schweriner

said confirmation would have been at age sixteen and only after attending Sunday school; Claire Schweriner, interview by the author, April 17, 2012. Jacob's High Holidays escapades are described in Greenfield, "Albert M. Greenfield," 3.

61. William Greenfield, interview by the author; Robert Greenfield, interview by the author, July 15, 2011. Rabbi Bertram Korn of Keneseth Israel, with whom Albert often spoke of his mother, made this point in his eulogy for Albert in January 1967. He added that Albert "always spoke with profound tenderness and reverence" about her. HSP, box 898, folder 4.

62. William Greenfield, interview by the author; also Robert Greenfield, interview by the author, July 25, 2011. In many interviews Albert ascribed the $500 to his mother and never mentioned William. But William said he and his mother had each loaned $500 to Albert. "I think he'll do all right," William says he told their mother.

63. Brecht, "The Greenfield Story."

64. *Gopsill's Philadelphia City Directory* for 1905 lists Albert as a "secretary" employed at 218 S. Fourth Street—Cahan's address. This suggests that Albert was there in 1904, when the directory information would have been compiled. Barbara Greenfield, in "Albert M. Greenfield," is less reliable about dates, but she too says Albert formed his partnership with Kunze in 1904 (see page 5).

65. A file card for Albert Greenfield (card #593) in the University of Pennsylvania Law School archives lists him as a member of the class of 1906 but says he last attended in 1905.

66. Greenfield, "Albert M. Greenfield," 5.

67. Earl Cahan, interview by Peter Binzen; William Greenfield, interview by the author.

68. Letter from J. David Stern to Albert Greenfield, August 1962, quoted in Greenfield, "Albert M. Greenfield," 11–12.

69. See, for example, Binzen, Daughen, and Friedman, *Rise and Fall of the House of Greenfield*, 15; "Changing Philadelphia's Skyline," 1947, HSP, box 394, folder 16.

70. Elizabeth Zeidman, interview by the author, October 19, 1975. The house was at 523 Tasker Street. It appears in *Gopsill's Philadelphia City Directory* of 1910 as the home of both Jacob and Albert, suggesting that they moved there in 1908 or 1909. Greenfield, in "Albert M. Greenfield," says they moved to 523 Tasker Street "in approximately 1907" (2).

CHAPTER 3

1. William Greenfield, interview by the author, October 17, 1975.

2. Ibid.

3. Albert Greenfield speech to young Jewish professionals group at Philadelphia YMHA, April 2, 1922, Historical Society of Pennsylvania (HSP), box 30, folder 7.

4. Ibid.

5. Irwin Solomon, interview by the author, October 15, 1975.

6. Brecht, "The Greenfield Story"; see also Albert Greenfield obituary, *Philadelphia Bulletin*, January 5, 1967. The average national income figures are taken from Zipser, "Along the Highways and Byways of Finance," cited in Skwersky, *Knight of Philadelphia*, 22.

7. Albert Greenfield petition for citizenship, filed February 14, 1906, admitted May 14, 1906, U.S. District Court, Eastern District of Pennsylvania, No. 11707. It lists his age as twenty-one years, four months (that is, born January 1885). Robert Greenfield, interviews by the author, July 25, 2011; September 15, 2011.

8. Many people claimed credit for "inventing" the movies. By 1890 an obscure (and Jewish) Philadelphia optician named Siegmund Lubin was advertising himself as "the world's largest manufacturer of life motion picture machines and films." See Eckhardt and Kowall, "The Movies' First Mogul," 103.

9. See, for example, ibid., 100–101.

10. William Greenfield, interview by the author.

11. Brecht, "The Greenfield Story." But in the January 22, 1929, *Evening Public Ledger* profile of Greenfield, Greenfield refers to the Fifty-Second and Sixtieth Street syndicates and says his largest transaction in 1910 was $1.8 million, without specifying which deal he meant.

See "Greenfield Willing to Be Civic Leader of New Type Unlike the Old-Time 'Boss,'" HSP, box 900, folder 8. Albert in 1955 may have conflated the two deals, but clearly the Fifty-Second Street syndicate of 1909–1910 and the Sixtieth Street syndicate of 1910–1911 were separate and each very large deals. In 1924 Albert denied he had cleared $1 million in a single deal; see Harrison, "Mr. Philadelphia," 18n. The origins of the Mastbaum firm are unclear. A history of Albert M. Greenfield & Co. says Mastbaum Brothers & Fleisher was formed in 1912; presumably the Mastbaum brothers operated without Fleisher before then. Letter from Albert M. Greenfield & Co. to Cassatt & Co., January 23, 1929, HSP, box 125, folder 4.

12. "Greenfield Willing to Be Civic Leader." Also, Brecht, "The Greenfield Story," says that the Sixtieth Street operation was completed in 1911.

13. Earl Cahan, interview by Peter Binzen, 1985.

14. For the first time, *Gopsill's Philadelphia City Directory* for 1908 lists Albert's real estate office at 230 S. Fourth and Cahan's at 218 S. Fourth. Presumably the move occurred in 1907.

15. Cahan, interview by Binzen. *Boyd's Philadelphia City Directory* for 1912 lists Albert at the Real Estate Trust Building, southeast corner of Chestnut and Broad. Presumably he was operating there in 1911. The Real Estate Trust Building was built in 1898; it is known as the Avenue of the Arts Building as of this writing.

16. William is listed as secretary and treasurer in *Boyd's Philadelphia Business Directory* for 1915. By then the operation had moved to Thirteenth and Chestnut Streets.

17. Brecht, "The Greenfield Story"; see also Harrison, "Mr. Philadelphia," 19.

18. Brecht, "The Greenfield Story"; see also Harrison, "Mr. Philadelphia," 20.

19. *Boyd's Philadelphia City Directory* for 1910 lists Cahan's home address as 2001 N. Thirty-Third Street and Kraus's as 2213 N. Thirty-Third Street.

20. Gordon Greenfield eulogy at funeral of Edna Kraus Paine, June 7, 1987; see also Solomon Kraus obituary, *New York Times*, July 30, 1928.

21. William Greenfield, interview by the author.

22. Elizabeth Zeidman, interview by the author, October 19, 1975.

23. Gordon Greenfield eulogy at funeral of Edna Kraus Paine; Barbara Greenfield, interview by the author, July 18, 2011; Robert Greenfield, interview by the author, November 28, 2011. Edna was born August 3, 1894, according to her marriage certificate. She attended Bryn Mawr for one year in 1911–1912, according to Bryn Mawr College alumnae records.

24. Harrison, "Mr. Philadelphia," 15–16. By 1913 the Russian percentage was surely higher.

25. Winnet, *Vignettes of a Lucky Life*, 253.

26. Albert formally joined Keneseth Israel on September 1, 1914, according to the congregation's archives; Claire Schweriner, interview by the author, April 17, 2012.

27. Barbara Greenfield, interview by the author.

28. Juliet Six (Albert's granddaughter), interview by the author, September 7, 2011.

29. Albert and Edna were married June 18, 1914. He joined Keneseth Israel September 1, 1914; Claire Schweriner, interview by the author.

30. Precisely where these classes took place is unclear. The Hebrew Sunday School Society of Philadelphia, the first such Jewish society in America, was founded in 1838 by Rebecca Gratz, who served as its president until 1864. It was modeled after the networks of church schools, mostly Protestant, that sprang up after 1827, when Massachusetts banned religious instruction in the public schools. See Diane A. King, "Jewish Education in Philadelphia," in Friedman, *Jewish Life in Philadelphia*, 239. Horace Stern (later a Pennsylvania Supreme Court justice) is listed as a delegate from Keneseth Israel to the council of the Union of American Hebrew Congregations, New York, January 22, 1923. Stern's original law partner, the prominent Philadelphian Morris Wolf, in a January 6, 1967, condolence note to Elizabeth Greenfield, wrote, "I think that with one exception Horace Stern and I are the only persons extant who have been continuously in touch with Albert since he taught in the Sunday school of which Horace was the principal—one half century ago"—that is, about 1916. HSP, box 899, folder 9. Morris Wolf was a lifelong member of Rodeph Shalom, Philadelphia's other leading Reform congregation; Mary Hurtig (Wolf's granddaughter), interview by the author, August 18, 2012.

31. Harrison, "Mr. Philadelphia," 21. The St. James, then located at 1226–1232 Walnut Street, still stands at this writing and is known as the Walnut Square Apartments.

32. See Harrison, "Mr. Philadelphia," 21. Gordon Greenfield was born June 16, 1915. The address of the house was 2401 S. Broad Street, at Ritner; it is still standing at this writing. The author's visit there in July 2012 found the Greenfields' front living room—now a doctor's waiting room—largely preserved intact since Albert lived there, with the original fireplaces, moldings, chandelier, glass light fixtures, and parquet floors.

33. The namesake of Albert's first son is largely speculation among Albert's grandchildren, including Albert M Greenfield III and Juliet Six, daughter of Gordon Greenfield.

34. Albert M. Greenfield III, interview by the author, September 22, 2011. Gordon's daughter Juliet Six identified Judge Gordon as the namesake; Juliet Six, e-mail message to the author, April 9, 2012.

35. Elizabeth was born March 9, 1917; see Skwersky, *Knight of Philadelphia*, 114.

36. Priscilla Luce, interview by the author, July 20, 2011; Janet Guth, interview by the author, October 26, 2011; Albert M. Greenfield III, interview by the author.

37. Brecht, "The Greenfield Story." The exact price was $2,040,000.

38. Harrison, "Mr. Philadelphia," 18–19; *Boyd's Philadelphia City Directory*, 1915. As late as December 14, 1918, Albert received a letter at Thirteenth and Chestnut. His letterhead as of March 26, 1921, lists his office at the northeast corner of Fifteenth and Chestnut. HSP, box 1, folder 1; box 2, folder 4. Presumably, he moved to the latter address in 1919 or 1920. The nameplate appears in a photo of the latter building taken in November 1922.

39. Brecht, "The Greenfield Story." See also Harrison, "Mr. Philadelphia," 23. Albert is the sole source of this information. Neither the defaulting client nor the amount in question has ever been identified.

40. This phenomenon is discussed in Reichley, *The Art of Government*, 104–105.

41. McCaffery, *When Bosses Ruled Philadelphia*, 102.

42. Ibid., 101.

43. Vare, *My Forty Years in Politics*, 133.

44. Greenfield, "Albert M. Greenfield," 11.

45. "The Residence of Mr. and Mrs. Albert M. Greenfield," 52. The renovations cost $9,404.

46. The new house was located at 310 W. Johnson Street. Harrison, "Mr. Philadelphia" (22), says Albert purchased the house "months prior" to a fire at his South Broad Street home in late November 1918.

47. *Philadelphia Bulletin*, November 25, 1918, p. 7. The servants are identified as Gertrude Bradley ("colored"), the maid, and Marie Cottman, the cook.

48. Greenfield, "Albert M. Greenfield." The nanny is described only as "Hedwig." Presumably this is Hedwig Lehmann, listed in Albert's household in the 1920 census as a "nursemaid," age twenty-seven.

49. Weigley, *Philadelphia*, 561–564.

50. Sidney Fields, "Albert M. Greenfield: Credo for Achievement," *New York Daily News*, February 16, 1953, HSP, box 565, folder 2. In the same article, Albert claimed that he had defeated "a well-entrenched incumbent" by "a surprising majority." He also claimed that he had been reelected for a second term but had resigned. I found no evidence to support either of these claims.

51. Harrison, "Mr. Philadelphia," 57.

52. See, for example, postcard from William Vare to Albert Greenfield, August 27, 1924, HSP, box 54, folder 2.

53. Harrison, "Mr. Philadelphia," 24.

54. Rosen, "German Jews vs. Russian Jews," 206.

55. Harrison, "Mr. Philadelphia," 24. That drive was a forerunner of the Allied Jewish Appeal, created in 1938, mostly by Philadelphia's Russian Jewish community, out of concern about anti-Semitism in Europe. See Rottenberg, "The Rise of Albert M. Greenfield," 219; "Albert M. Greenfield Named Chairman of Leaders Dinner," *Jewish Exponent*, April 5, 1946, HSP, box 368, folder 5.

56. See Rosen, "German Jews vs. Russian Jews," 193, 206–207. In 1925, for example, prominent Sephardic and German Jews like the Rosenbachs, Sterns, Rosenwalds, Fels, Fleishers, and Adlers gave a combined total of $52,775 to the Federation; Greenfield alone gave $31,000. See list of annual Federation subscribers, July 15, 1925, cited in Baltzell, *An American Business Aristocracy*, 493.

57. Harrison, "Mr. Philadelphia," 74. Adler (1863–1940) was a founder of the Jewish Welfare Board, an editor of the *Jewish Encyclopedia*, and a participant in the Paris Peace Conference of 1919.

58. Letter from Alfred Klein to Albert Greenfield, ca. 1923, HSP, box 37, folder 2. A capital campaign headed by Albert in 1922 raised $4 million; see "Albert M. Greenfield Named Chairman of Leaders Dinner." The Federation's annual fund drive of 1923, also led by Albert, raised $1,325,000. See Harrison, "Mr. Philadelphia," 78.

59. *Polk's Philadelphia Blue Book, Elite Directory and Club List*, 1924, 624, cited in Baltzell, *An American Business Aristocracy*, 324.

60. Solomon Kraus obituary, *New York Times*, July 30, 1928. The merger occurred in 1921, according to Harrison, "Mr. Philadelphia," 26.

61. Letter from Albert Greenfield to Solomon C. Kraus, November 12, 1921, HSP, box 10, folder 10.

62. Davenport, "Philadelphia," 186.

63. "A Message of Thrift," 1922, HSP, box 42, folder 2.

64. Many biographies of Fox erroneously list his birth name as Fried. His original first name may have been Vilmos, although no documentary support for that name exists; Vanda Krefft (Fox's biographer), interviews by the author, November 2011–September 2013.

65. William Fox obituary, *New York Times*, May 9, 1952, HSP box 524, folder 6; Vanda Krefft, correspondence with the author, November 2011–September 2013.

66. A Greenfield & Co. memo of May 19, 1941 (from Peter Binzen's private collection), details terms of the 1921 lease, suggesting that Albert arranged it.

67. "Fox-Stanley Pact," 1. Vanda Krefft also shared her insights on this; correspondence with the author, November 2011–September 2013.

68. "Activities of Day in Real Estate." See also Quirk and Haas, "Fox Theatre."

69. Greenfield was doing about $127 million a year by 1920. Davenport, "Philadelphia," 186.

70. Maher, *Twilight of Splendor*, 27, cited in Dilks, *Morgan, Lewis and Bockius*, 88.

71. Lippincott, "Edward T. Stotesbury," 9–10.

72. The sale of the Met is described in detail in "Syndicate Seek[s] Philadelphia Academy." Also see *Philadelphia Bulletin*, April 28, 1920.

73. Albert Greenfield interview transcript, ca. 1924, HSP, box 9, folder 9.

74. Harrison, "Mr. Philadelphia," 27; Marion, *Within These Walls*, 199.

CHAPTER 4

1. Albert Greenfield's speech to the Chestnut Street Association, April 8, 1929, cited in Harrison, "Mr. Philadelphia," 30.

2. Ibid., 27.

3. Binzen, Daughen, and Friedman, *Rise and Fall of the House of Greenfield*, 21.

4. The phrase was coined by University of Pennsylvania sociologist E. Digby Baltzell. See Rottenberg, "A Breakthrough against City's 'Anti-leadership' Disease?"

5. Letter from Albert Greenfield to Harry Sundheim, April 9, 1921, Historical Society of Pennsylvania (HSP), box 6, folder 15. According to the letter, Greenfield's syndicate acquired six hundred of the Philadelphia Bonwit's one thousand shares for a price not to exceed $300,000. The sellers were Paul J. Bonwit, Hartzfeld, Seigel, and others.

6. Albert Greenfield & Co. press release, December 19, 1921, HSP, box 8, folder 2. See also Harrison, "Mr. Philadelphia," 28–29. The building still stands at the southwest corner of Fifteenth and Chestnut as of this writing.

7. Harrison, "Mr. Philadelphia," 29.

8. Ibid., 27.

9. Shortly after launching his Greenfield Building project, Greenfield bought an interest in the Pennsylvania Building, a seventeen-story office complex across Chestnut Street; as of 2014 it still stands on the northwest corner. In 1924, on behalf of a client, Greenfield acquired that building for $3.6 million while retaining his own stake in it and negotiating his company's appointment as the building's rental agent; Harrison, "Mr. Philadelphia," 30. With the Mastbaum brothers, Greenfield acquired several properties on Locust Street for $1.4 million, developing them into a theater and office complex that they sold for $2 million; Harrison, "Mr. Philadelphia," 3. In March 1923 Greenfield headed a syndicate that purchased the Walton Hotel at Broad and Locust Streets, a red-brick structure resembling a castle that had been the city's most elegant hotel on its opening in 1896.

10. Binzen, Daughen, and Friedman, *Rise and Fall of the House of Greenfield*, 22. See also Earl Cahan, interview by Peter Binzen, 1985; Harry E. Kalodner, "Bankers Trust Building Sold to Local Syndicate," 1923, HSP, box 37, folder 2.

11. Binzen, Daughen, and Friedman, *Rise and Fall of the House of Greenfield*, 22; Earl Cahan, interview by Peter Binzen; 1923–1924 newspaper clippings, HSP, box 37, folder 2. The building opened January 1, 1924; see Albert M. Greenfield & Co. press release, HSP, box 51, folder 14. Albert moved into the Bankers Trust Building on September 1, 1924; see Albert M. Greenfield & Co. press release, HSP, box 46, folder 15. The building, renamed the Philadelphia Building in 2006, still stood at this writing.

12. Samuel Rosenman, quoted by Boyd Barnard, interview by the author, October 20, 1975.

13. Cincotta told this story to Bob Olson when Olson was corporate secretary of Greenfield's Bankers Securities between 1971 and 1973; Bob Olson, interview by the author, September 28, 2011. Curiously, Cincotta did not mention this incident when I interviewed him in 1975.

14. Binzen, Daughen, and Friedman, *Rise and Fall of the House of Greenfield*, 23.

15. Press release, February 21, 1923, HSP, box 32, folder 14. Also see Binzen, Daughen, and Friedman, *Rise and Fall of the House of Greenfield*, 23–24.

16. Harrison, "Mr. Philadelphia," 31.

17. Letter from Samuel Freeman to Albert Greenfield, October 29, 1925, quoted in Harrison, "Mr. Philadelphia," 31.

18. Letter from David Phillips to Albert Greenfield, February 21, 1927, quoted in Harrison, "Mr. Philadelphia," 29.

19. Barbara Greenfield, "Albert M. Greenfield," 5–6. The party was hosted (and the song sung) by Alex Lieberman, a real estate and insurance broker as well as a fellow member with Albert of the Chestnut Street Association, September 22, 1926.

20. *Philadelphia Bulletin*, December 1, 1926.

21. Robert Greenfield, interview by the author, November 21, 2012; he recalled seeing Albert wearing his pince-nez in the mid-1920s.

22. See *Country Home*, June–July 1921, HSP, box 2, folder 4.

23. Unidentified newspaper profile of Albert Greenfield, 1924, HSP box 49, folder 9. A. J. Drexel's horseback rides are described in the *New York Press*, October 30, 1973, cited in Rottenberg, *The Man Who Made Wall Street*, 4.

24. Harrison, "Mr. Philadelphia," 80.

25. Letter from Albert Greenfield to Edna Greenfield, April 29, 1926, HSP, box 73, folder 2. See also Harrison, "Mr. Philadelphia," 80.

26. Philip Klein, interview by Walter Phillips, February 26, 1980, p. 6, Walter Phillips Oral History Project (WPP), Temple University Urban Archives (TUUA). The other members of the "awards clique" mentioned by Klein were Horace Liversidge, president of the Philadelphia Electric Company; Revelle Brown, president of the Reading Railroad; John Dimond; and Albert Nesbitt.

27. Harrison, "Mr. Philadelphia," 74. See Oak Lane tuition invoice for Gordon, Elizabeth, and Carlotta, September 22, 1926, HSP, box 75, folder 10. Oak Lane was a progressive private elementary school in Cheltenham Township, just north of Philadelphia, founded in 1916 by wealthy Jewish parents like Albert whose private school options were limited by Jewish quotas at other private schools. Albert was one of Oak Lane's early trustees, along with other prominent Jews like Judge Horace Stern, Lessing Rosenwald, Maurice Fleisher, Samuel Fels, and Joseph Snellenburg. Oak Lane's parents included Leopold Stokowski, and its alumni included the linguist and political activist Noam Chomsky. The school moved to the suburb of Blue Bell, Pennsylvania, in 1965 and closed in 2010.

28. Harrison, "Mr. Philadelphia," 55–58.

29. Ibid., 67–68.

30. Ibid., 70.

31. Ibid., 67–68.

32. Ibid., 30–31.

33. Ibid., 69.

34. Ibid., 35.

35. Ibid., 32.

36. Ibid., 39.

37. Davenport, "Philadelphia," 186. The figure given is for 1925.

38. Harrison, "Mr. Philadelphia," 39–40.

39. Ibid., 42.

40. Binzen, Daughen, and Friedman, *Rise and Fall of the House of Greenfield*, 23.

41. Boyd Barnard, interview by the author; Robert Greenfield, interview by the author, November 21, 2012. Barnard said Albert was "the only broker then" who was simultaneously operating as a broker and taking positions in real estate. Robert Greenfield, Albert's nephew and lawyer, said, "Only later was it seen as unethical."

42. Albert M. Greenfield obituary, *Philadelphia Bulletin*, January 5, 1967.

43. Letter from Dennis Dougherty to Albert Greenfield, November 28, 1921, HSP, box 8, folder 6.

44. For a description of Dougherty, see Morris, *American Catholic*, 170.

45. Morris, *American Catholic*, 166–167. Dougherty pronounced his ban on movies in 1934.

46. Dennis Cardinal Dougherty obituary, *New York Times*, June 1, 1951. See also Morris, *American Catholic*, 170.

47. Harrison, "Mr. Philadelphia," 34.

48. Gus Amsterdam, interview by Peter Binzen, 1985.

49. Elizabeth Zeidman, interview by the author, October 19, 1975.

50. "Honored by Pope," unidentified Philadelphia newspaper clipping, April 11, 1930, available at http://thealbertmgreenfieldfoundation.org/ourarchives/photos/category/5 -philanthropy.

51. John O'Shea, interview by the author, October 15, 1975, p. 3.

52. E. Digby Baltzell, interview by the author, October 16, 1975.

53. For more on Mitten's background, see Hagley Museum and Library, "Philadelphia Transportation Company Agency History Record," available at http://research.frick.org/di rectoryweb/browserecord2.php?-action=browse&-recid=6878. See also Shaw, "The Life of Thomas Eugene Mitten."

54. Shaw, "The Life of Thomas Eugene Mitten," 558.

55. Letter from Albert Greenfield to Thomas E. Mitten, September 15, 1926, HSP, box 75, folder 4.

56. Shaw, "The Life of Thomas Eugene Mitten," 558–559.

57. Albert Greenfield, testifying in 1931, fixed his first dealings with the PRT at "around 1917"; see *Philadelphia Bulletin*, March 12, 1931.

58. Elizabeth Zeidman, interview by the author.

59. Thank-you note from T. E. Mitten to Albert Greenfield, January 6, 1927, HSP, box 88, folder 8.

60. Shaw, "The Life of Thomas Eugene Mitten," 44–45.

61. *Philadelphia Bulletin*, May 25, 1925.

62. In memos of November 15 and 17, 1926, Greenfield acknowledges that the 178 shares owned by his secretary, Miss Wiggins, are actually his (HSP, box 75, folder 4). See also Harrison, "Mr. Philadelphia," 42.

63. *Philadelphia Bulletin*, March 12 and 13, 1931. Both articles concern Albert Greenfield's testimony in Harrisburg.

64. *Philadelphia Bulletin*, October 19, 1925.

65. *Philadelphia Bulletin*, May 25, 1925. Albert Greenfield was appointed receiver of the Producers & Consumers Bank by Common Pleas Court on May 4, 1925, and made permanent receiver on May 26. See Greenfield's petition to Common Pleas Court for leave to sell assets of P&C Bank, ca. March 1926, HSP, box 77, folder 1.

66. Earl Cahan, interview by Peter Binzen, 1985; see also Binzen, Daughen, and Friedman, *Rise and Fall of the House of Greenfield*, 22.

67. Harrison, "Mr. Philadelphia," 42–43.

68. Agreement between Albert Greenfield and T. E. Mitten, February 1, 1926, HSP, box 77, folder 1.

69. A letter of July 26, 1926, notifies Greenfield of a directors' meeting; see HSP, box 75, folder 4. A letter from a depositor to Greenfield from July 1, 1926, refers to him as a director of the Mitten Bank; see HSP, box 77, folder 1.

70. Letter from T. E. Mitten to "The people of Philadelphia," June 3, 1927, HSP, box 76, folder 6.

71. Harrison, "Mr. Philadelphia," 41. Pennsylvania seized the seventeen institutions on July 14, 1925.

72. *Philadelphia Bulletin*, August 25, 1925.

73. Greenfield, "Albert M. Greenfield," 6.

74. Robert Greenfield, interview by the author, August 17, 2011; Barbara Greenfield, interview by the author, July 18, 2011. Both were citing impressions they got from Albert's children.

75. Priscilla Luce, interview by the author, July 20, 2011; Janet Guth, interview by the author, October 26, 2011; Albert Greenfield III, interview by the author, September 22, 2011.

76. Robert Greenfield, interview by the author, August 17, 2011; Barbara Greenfield, interview by the author.

77. Letter from Berta Rantz to Edna Greenfield, November 2, 1924, HSP, box 52, folder 5. Miss Rantz apparently taught at the Walden School in New York.

78. Letter from Albert Greenfield to Berta Rantz, December 8, 1924, HSP, box 52, folder 5.

79. Letter from Albert Greenfield to Jacob Greenfield, January 21, 1925, HSP, box 58, folder 10.

80. Robert Greenfield, interviews by the author, July 25 and August 17, 2011.

81. Albert Greenfield Jr. was born June 18, 1927. Jacob Greenfield died April 27, 1928; Sol Kraus died July 29, 1928; Esther Greenfield died August 15, 1928.

82. Priscilla Luce, interview by the author; Janet Guth, interview by the author; Albert Greenfield III, interview by the author; Juliet Six, interview by the author, September 7, 2011.

83. Harrison, "Mr. Philadelphia," 38.

84. Philadelphia had thirteen general circulation newspapers in 1895, of which eight remained in 1913. Emery and Smith, *The Press and America* (527–528), says Philadelphia had five morning and three evening papers but mentions only seven: the *Inquirer*, *Public Ledger*, *Record*, and *North American* in the morning, and the *Bulletin*, *Evening Public Ledger* (founded 1914), and *Daily News* (founded 1926) in the evening.

85. "Stern Suspends Three Papers," *Editor and Publisher*, February 8, 1947, p. 7, HSP, box 401, folder 2.

86. J.S.K., unidentified newspaper column, 1947, HSP, box 401, folder 2.

87. Stern's wife, Juliet (Jill) Lit, was the niece of Samuel D. Lit and Jacob D. Lit, who owned Lit Brothers. See Stern, *Memoirs of a Maverick Publisher*, 127.

88. "Stern Suspends Three Papers," 7.

89. Stern, *Memoirs of a Maverick Publisher*, 169.

90. Letter from David Riesman to Thomas E. Mitten, June 12, 1926, HSP, box 75, folder 4. The writer was the father of the sociologist David Riesman.

91. Harrison, "Mr. Philadelphia," 38. Greenfield owned fifty shares in the *Camden Courier-Post*, worth $5,000.

92. Stern, *Memoirs of a Maverick Publisher*, 169. The *Record* had been acquired at public bankruptcy auction in 1905 by Tom Wanamaker, son of the merchant John Wanamaker. After Tom died in 1915, his brother Rodman Wanamaker ran it (albeit unprofitably) until his own death on March 9, 1928. See Stern, *Memoirs of a Maverick Publisher*, 170–171. Harrison, "Mr. Philadelphia," 38, says that with Stern out of the picture, Greenfield represented Curtis-Martin Newspapers, a Curtis family partnership, which bought the *Record* for $2.5 million shortly after. But Stern said he bought the *Record* the following year from the Wanamaker estate; see Stern, *Memoirs of a Maverick Publisher*, 170–171.

93. Harrison, "Mr. Philadelphia," 41–42. Although Greenfield was subsequently faulted for other activities in the 1920s, investigations in the 1930s and 1940s found no malfeasance in his reorganization of the building and loan associations.

CHAPTER 5

1. The Bank & Trust Co. of West Philadelphia was located at Fifty-Second and Market Streets; see Binzen, Daughen, and Friedman, *Rise and Fall of the House of Greenfield*, 56. The Philadelphia National Bank merged with Girard National Bank (not to be confused with Girard Trust) on April 1, 1926; at the time of their merger, those two banks had deposits of $140 million and $73 million, respectively. At the end of 1926, the combined bank had deposits of $200 million. See Wainwright, *History of the Philadelphia National Bank, 1803–1953*, 193–195.

2. Letter from Albert Greenfield to T. E. Mitten, June 14, 1927, quoted in Harrison, "Mr. Philadelphia," 43.

3. Peter Temin, *The Jacksonian Economy*, cited in Rottenberg, *The Man Who Made Wall Street*, 28.

4. Bankers Trust Company held its first board meeting December 28, 1926; see Harrison, "Mr. Philadelphia," 43. The bank moved downtown on March 5 or 6, 1927; *Philadelphia Bulletin*, December 22, 1930.

5. Greenfield called for a moratorium in a speech before the Philadelphia Real Estate Board on October 13, 1927. The Market Street National Bank Building opened in 1929. See Harrison, "Mr. Philadelphia," 37–38.

6. In the ten-year period beginning in 1926, 144,400 houses in Philadelphia were auctioned off by the sheriff, of which 99 percent were against mortgages. See Davenport, "Philadelphia," 186.

7. Letter from Peter Cameron to Albert Greenfield, August 31, 1926, Historical Society of Pennsylvania (HSP), box 158, folder 11; letter from Albert Greenfield to Peter Cameron, September 1, 1926, HSP, box 158, folder 11.

8. The bank's statement of condition as of April 11, 1927, lists seventeen directors. HSP, box 82, folder 7. The number of directors in 1930 was "several dozen"; see Albert Greenfield, "The Closing of Bankers Trust," WFIL radio address, October 17, 1938, HSP, box 238, folder 10.

9. For Barker's background, see Binzen, Daughen, and Friedman, *Rise and Fall of the House of Greenfield*, 56; Harrison, "Mr. Philadelphia," 45; Skwersky, *Knight of Philadelphia*, 98.

10. "Business: Philadelphia Failure"; see also Harrison, "Mr. Philadelphia," 45; Binzen, Daughen, and Friedman, *Rise and Fall of the House of Greenfield*, 56.

11. Alfred Blasband, interview by Peter Binzen, 1985.

12. Binzen, Daughen, and Friedman, *Rise and Fall of the House of Greenfield*, 57. The late closing hour was outlandish but not unique. The Franklin Trust Company started midnight banking in 1914; see Wainwright, *History of the Philadelphia National Bank*, 203. In the late 1920s Greenfield became a large depositor and creditor of this bank as well.

13. Harrison, "Mr. Philadelphia," 44. One source cites a May 1, 1929, letter from Barker to Bankers Trust employees that says Bankers Trust had $23 million in deposits—"ten times what it was January 1, 1927." See Binzen, Daughen, and Friedman, *Rise and Fall of the House of Greenfield*, 58.

14. Binzen, Daughen, and Friedman, *Rise and Fall of the House of Greenfield*, 58.

15. Letter from Samuel Barker to Albert Greenfield, June 11, 1927, HSP, box 82, folder 6.

16. Letter from Samuel Barker to Bankers Trust directors, November 29, 1927, HSP, box 82, folder 6.

17. Fox purchased the stock in July 1928. Harrison, "Mr. Philadelphia," 44.

18. See, for example, Barker's early letter to Bankers Securities directors on the origins of the company, cited in Binzen, Daughen, and Friedman, *Rise and Fall of the House of Greenfield*, 32.

19. Greenfield, in an April 1, 1959, letter to Fox's widow, Eva, said, "This company [Bankers Securities] was organized very largely with the help of your late husband. In fact, it was he who originally suggested that I should undertake the organization of a securities company." HSP, box 738, folder 2. For his discussion of bank-owned securities companies in Philadelphia, see Wainwright, *History of the Philadelphia National Bank*, 203.

20. Letters from Samuel Barker to Albert Greenfield, June 11, 1927; July 8, 1927; October 28, 1927, HSP, box 82, folder 6.

21. List of Bankers Securities shareholders in chronological order, March 14, 1930, HSP, box 140, folder 4.

22. Binzen, Daughen, and Friedman, *Rise and Fall of the House of Greenfield*, 32-34; also Gustave G. Amsterdam, interview by the author, September 25, 1975.

23. Wainwright, *History of the Philadelphia National Bank*, 203.

24. Binzen, Daughen, and Friedman, *Rise and Fall of the House of Greenfield*, 5.

25. Ibid., 34.

26. Ibid.

27. Undated list of Bankers Securities shareholders, possibly 1930, HSP, box 140, folder 4. All the listed shareholders invested in April 1928; Greenfield and Fox were first, investing on April 4, 1928.

28. Binzen, Daughen, and Friedman, *Rise and Fall of the House of Greenfield*, 34. See also list of Bankers Securities shareholders in chronological order. In an August 27, 1931, letter to David S. Malis, Esq., Greenfield said, "As you probably know, Bankers Securities Corp. owned a very substantial block of stock of Bankers Trust Company and for this reason it always carried a large deposit with Bankers Trust Company." HSP, box 155, folder 2.

29. Barker, in a December 21, 1928, letter to Bankers Trust shareholders, describes the syndicate. HSP, box 93, folder 9. Harold Saylor, deputy Pennsylvania attorney general, writing to Greenfield's lawyer, Stanley Folz, on July 29, 1930, notes that Bankers Trust loaned the syndicate more than the legal limit of 10 percent of its capital. HSP, box 152, folder 26.

30. Letter from Samuel Barker to Albert Greenfield, February 25, 1928, HSP, box 93, folder 9.

31. Letter from Samuel Barker to Bankers Securities shareholders, May 19, 1928, HSP, box 93, folder 9.

32. Samuel Lit's death date is surmised from a eulogy in the *Philadelphia Jewish Times*, February or early March 1929, HSP, box 128, folder 15.

33. Binzen, Daughen, and Friedman, *Rise and Fall of the House of Greenfield*, 38-39; Hendrickson, *Grand Emporiums*, 423-424. Rachel Lit Wedell, later Rachel Arnold, died in 1919; Samuel D. Lit died in 1929; and Jacob D. Lit died in 1950. Some accounts say the original store was a hat shop.

34. See, for example, Albert Greenfield's speech on "The Trend of Real Estate in a War Economy," January 22, 1942, cited in Harrison, "Mr. Philadelphia," 25.

35. Letter from Albert Greenfield to Thomas Mitten, September 4, 1928, HSP, box 105, folder 11.

36. Tribute to Samuel D. Lit, *Philadelphia Jewish Times*, February or early March 1929, HSP, box 128, folder 15.

37. The reported price at the time was $10.5 million, or $21 per share for 501,000 shares; see *Philadelphia Bulletin*, October 18, 1928. Greenfield, testifying before the Securities and Exchange Commission (SEC) in 1941, said he offered Colonel Lit $20.50, "and I think that is what we paid him for the stock, not $21." See Binzen, Daughen, and Friedman, *Rise and Fall of the House of Greenfield*, 39. In that case, the total price would have been $10,270,500, not $10.5 million.

38. Binzen, Daughen, and Friedman, *Rise and Fall of the House of Greenfield*, 39–40. See also City Stores Co. letterhead, May 24, 1929, HSP, box 128, folder 15. It is possible that Greenfield may have whetted Goerke's appetite for Lit's by first offering Goerke a contract to manage the store.

39. Binzen, Daughen, and Friedman, *Rise and Fall of the House of Greenfield* (40), says the sale price was $13 million, but the price has sometimes been reported as $12.8 million, apparently erroneously. In a statement to City Stores stockholders in January 29, 1932, City Stores president Paul Saunders referred to "a $13 million loan made Dec. 1, 1928, in order to acquire controlling interest in Lit Brothers." See HSP, box 171, folder 2; see also Binzen, Daughen, and Friedman, *Rise and Fall of the House of Greenfield*, 47. A suit by stockholders of City Stores Company in 1932 also indicated that the half-interest in Lit's was acquired by City Stores in 1928 for $13 million; see *Philadelphia Bulletin*, February 3, 1932. Oddly, a *Philadelphia Bulletin* article of October 18, 1928, reports that control of Lit Brothers was acquired by City Stores "in association with Bankers Securities Corporation," at a price of $10,521,000 for 501,000 shares, but this appears to refer to the price Bankers Securities paid for Lit's in September, not what City Stores paid for Lit's in October.

40. Binzen, Daughen, and Friedman, *Rise and Fall of the House of Greenfield*, 35, citing a 1928 report in the *Philadelphia Record*.

41. Binzen, Daughen, and Friedman, *Rise and Fall of the House of Greenfield*, 35. The offering took place November 15, 1928. Binzen and colleagues say the offering was for $10 million, but this may be a typographical error; Gus Amsterdam, in an October 30, 1975, interview with me, said that the second offering raised $19 million, bringing the total raised to $31 million by the end of 1928. A Bankers Securities financial statement for December 31, 1929, seems to confirm Amsterdam's recollection: It reports $30,397,222 in total assets, including $18 million in "loans to corporations, fully secured by marketable collateral." HSP, box 116, folder 3.

42. Binzen, Daughen, and Friedman, *Rise and Fall of the House of Greenfield*, 36.

43. Ibid., 36.

44. Ibid., 41.

45. Most accounts say the loan to Lit's was secured by 501,000 Lit's common shares, out of a total of 1 million shares. But in an August 27, 1931, letter to David S. Malis, Esq., Greenfield said the loan was also secured by $6 million of Lit's preferred stock, or half of the total preferred stock of $12 million. HSP, box 155, folder 3.

46. Binzen, Daughen, and Friedman, *Rise and Fall of the House of Greenfield*, 36, 103. Greenfield's new salary took effect April 1, 1929. Bankers Securities' entire payroll in 1931, including Greenfield's salary, was $251,100; see Binzen, Daughen, and Friedman, *Rise and Fall of the House of Greenfield*, 103.

47. Binzen, Daughen, and Friedman, *Rise and Fall of the House of Greenfield*, 36. The loan to Paul Bonwit was transacted in May 1929.

48. Sinclair, *Upton Sinclair Presents William Fox*, 86, 117, 150. Marcus Loew died of a heart attack September 5, 1927, age fifty-seven. Fox paid the Loew family members $50 million for their stock, of which the $10 million loan from Bankers Securities represented one piece; Vanda Krefft, correspondence with the author, November 2011–September 2013.

49. Wainwright, *History of the Philadelphia National Bank*, 203. Tradesmens National Bank formed the Tradesmens Corporation later in 1928; in 1929 securities companies were also formed by Colonial Trust, Corn Exchange National Bank and Trust, Central National Bank, and finally, Philadelphia National Bank.

50. Stern, *Memoirs of a Maverick Publisher*, 169.

51. Letter from J. David Stern to Albert Greenfield, 1962, quoted in Greenfield, "Albert M. Greenfield," 12.

52. Binzen, Daughen, and Friedman, *Rise and Fall of the House of Greenfield*, 27.

53. Stern, *Memoirs of a Maverick Publisher*, 171.

54. "Greenfield Willing to Be Civic Leader of New Type Unlike the Old-Time 'Boss,'" *Evening Public Ledger*, January 22, 1929, HSP, box 900, folder 8.

55. See Harrison, "Mr. Philadelphia," 57–58.

56. Binzen, Daughen, and Friedman, *Rise and Fall of the House of Greenfield*, 29; Harrison, "Mr. Philadelphia," 59.

57. Sinclair, *Upton Sinclair Presents William Fox*, 87.

58. Ibid.; also cited in Binzen, Daughen, and Friedman, *Rise and Fall of the House of Greenfield*, 30.

59. Vare, *My Forty Years in Politics*, 185–186; Harrison, "Mr. Philadelphia," 60–61; "Show Greenfield Responsible for Hoover Triumph," *Philadelphia Record*, June 23, 1928. The *Philadelphia Record* article mentions "A Jew Picks a Candidate for President," an article in the *(Philadelphia) Jewish Times*, published after the convention, which also told the story of Greenfield's purported role vis-à-vis Vare, portraying Greenfield as "one of the few men responsible for the selection of Herbert Hoover as the Presidential candidate of the Republican Party."

60. Harrison, "Mr. Philadelphia," 61.

61. Sinclair, *Upton Sinclair Presents William Fox*, 86–87.

62. Vare, *My Forty Years in Politics*, 185.

63. William Vare, born in 1867, was sixty-one when he suffered the stroke.

64. Harrison, "Mr. Philadelphia," 65.

65. Ibid., 65–66.

66. Ibid., 64.

67. Ibid., 65.

68. Ibid., 62–66.

69. Ibid., 59; Binzen, Daughen, and Friedman, *Rise and Fall of the House of Greenfield*, 29.

70. City councilman Harry Trainer, quoted in *Philadelphia Bulletin*, January 25, 1929.

71. Hagley Museum and Library, "Philadelphia Transportation Company Agency History Record," available at http://research.frick.org/directoryweb/browserecord2.php?-action=browse&-recid=6878.

72. *Philadelphia Bulletin*, October 22, 1928; see also Binzen, Daughen, and Friedman, *Rise and Fall of the House of Greenfield*, 23. The *Bulletin* article says the new company will operate a $12 million bank headquartered in New York. Binzen and colleagues say the merger expanded Bankers Bond's total resources to $42.7 million.

73. *Philadelphia Record*, February 4, 1929; see also Harrison, "Mr. Philadelphia," 26. Albert M. Greenfield & Co. financed the takeover by selling $4 million worth of bonds, nearly half of it to Bankers Securities; see Binzen, Daughen, and Friedman, *Rise and Fall of the House of Greenfield*, 90. Greenfield personally owned 68 to 70 percent of the stock in his real estate firm after the merger, according to his testimony in 1931; see *Philadelphia Bulletin*, March 12, 1931.

74. *Philadelphia Bulletin*, December 22, 1930, provides a list of all banks acquired by Bankers Trust; also see Binzen, Daughen, and Friedman, *Rise and Fall of the House of Greenfield*, 56.

75. Banks, "A Philadelphia Life Underwriter Who Believes in Life Insurance for Himself."

76. Ibid.

77. Arlin Adams, interview by the author, January 16, 2012.

78. Barbara Greenfield, interview by the author, July 18, 2011.

79. Robert Greenfield, interview by the author, October 3, 2011; E. Digby Baltzell, interview by the author, October 16, 1975. Also see Reath, "Older Building Offers Attractive Rental Space."

80. "Greenfield Willing to Be Civic Leader." The office was dismantled in 2013 to accommodate a new tenant, although the building said it might reconstruct it elsewhere on the premises.

81. Ibid.

82. D. Herbert Lipson, interview by the author, October 15, 1975.

83. Emily Sunstein, interview by the author, October 14, 1975, p. 1.

84. Unsigned securities analysis of Bankers Securities, September 23, 1929, HSP, box 185, folder 11. The analyst claimed that the Lit's sale had accounted for "more than two-fifths" of Bankers Securities profits to that date; in fact it was more like three-quarters.

85. Letter from Albert Greenfield and Samuel Barker to Bankers Securities stockholders, September 15, 1929, HSP, box 116, folder 3.

86. *Philadelphia Inquirer*, October 3, 1929. Mitten died on October 1.

87. Ibid.

CHAPTER 6

1. Fox Movietone News, October 21, 1929. Also quoted in "Irving Fisher: Out of Keynes's Shadow."

2. Harrison, "Mr. Philadelphia," 52.

3. Peg Sonenfield, "Albert Greenfield, Quakertown Dynamo, Adds District Hookup," *Washington Post*, September 16, 1951, Historical Society of Pennsylvania (HSP), box 503, folder 5.

4. Stern, *Memoirs of a Maverick Publisher*, 179–180.

5. The Justice Department suit against Fox's purchase was filed in November 1929, after the stock market crash. Vanda Krefft, correspondence with the author, November 2011–September 2013.

6. "William Fox Hurt in Auto Accident." Less seriously injured was Fox's friend and fellow passenger, Jacob L. Rubinstein, secretary and treasurer of the Namquist Worsted Company.

7. Sinclair, *Upton Sinclair Presents William Fox*, 127, 143.

8. Ibid., 117.

9. Ibid., 125.

10. Ibid., 124–126.

11. Ibid., 127.

12. Sinclair, *Upton Sinclair Presents William Fox*, describes the events as "the latter part of November" (140). On page 141, he says that Greenfield's wife "was now in the hospital," but after a couple of weeks Fox learned that her temperature was normal and invited Greenfield to New York. On page 148, Sinclair describes a conversation several days after that meeting as having taken place on "Monday, November 25th." These hints suggest that Fox invited Greenfield in early or mid-November and that their meeting took place perhaps on November 20, 1929.

13. Sinclair, *Upton Sinclair Presents William Fox*, 141. The Ambassador Hotel, where Fox lived, was located at Park Avenue and Fifty-First Street; Penn Station was at Seventh Avenue and Thirty-Fourth Street. If Greenfield had only an hour between trains, the two men would have had at best 45 minutes to dine and converse, and more likely just a half-hour.

14. Ibid., 142.

15. Otterson was president of Electrical Research Products Inc., a subsidiary of Western Electric, which was a subsidiary of AT&T. Vanda Krefft, correspondence with the author, November 2011–September 2013.

16. Sinclair, *Upton Sinclair Presents William Fox*, 143–144.

17. Sinclair notes Greenfield's refusal to sue Fox to recover the loan. *Upton Sinclair Presents William Fox*, 345.

18. Ibid., 144–145. On page 149, Fox notes that from October 28 to November 25 he averaged two hours' sleep per night.

19. Ibid., 144–145.

20. Hints of such perception can found in Sinclair, *Upton Sinclair Presents William Fox*, written in 1933. Fox's biographer, Vanda Krefft, in correspondence with the author (November 2011–September 2013), suggests that Fox may have harbored such feelings only in retrospect.

21. These sound patents were known as Tri-Ergon. Fox also owned a patent for Grandeur, a wide-screen technology, but the Tri-Ergon patents were the ones of interest to AT&T. The patents are referred to in Sinclair, *Upton Sinclair Presents William Fox*, 296–297; see also, Vanda Krefft, e-mail correspondence with the author, May 12, 2012.

22. Sinclair, *Upton Sinclair Presents William Fox*, 223; see also Vanda Krefft, correspondence with the author, November 2011–September 2013.

23. Sinclair, *Upton Sinclair Presents William Fox*, 306.

24. Vanda Krefft, correspondence with the author, November 2011–September 2013.

25. Sinclair, *Upton Sinclair Presents William Fox*, 304. Also see Harley Clarke obituary, *(Fredericksburg, VA) Free Lance-Star*, June 7, 1955.

26. Sinclair, *Upton Sinclair Presents William Fox*, 297. Greenfield acted as Fox's friend, but when he discovered that Alfred C. Blumenthal, a partner with Fox in Foxthal Corp. (with whom Fox had parted company), had had a contract to receive $600,000 if and when Fox sold his voting shares to Clarke, Greenfield told Clarke that if there was to be a commission, Greenfield should receive half, with the result that Blumenthal was forced to give Greenfield $250,000. Blumenthal subsequently sued Greenfield, but Greenfield's commission was ultimately upheld in Federal Appeals Court. See Sinclair, *Upton Sinclair Presents William Fox*, 345; see also *Greenfield v. Blumenthal*, 69 F.2d 294 (1934).

27. The sale is reported in "Big Money." See also Sinclair, *Upton Sinclair Presents William Fox*, 305.

28. "Big Money"; Sinclair, *Upton Sinclair Presents William Fox*, 345; see also Aubrey Solomon, *The Fox Film Corporation, 1915–1935*, 139; Vanda Krefft, correspondence with the author, November 2011–September 2013. Fox Film was merged with 20th Century Pictures in 1935 to become 20th Century-Fox.

29. Clarke was a Christian Scientist.

30. Sinclair, *Upton Sinclair Presents William Fox*, 346.

31. Isman (born 1874) was profiled in the *New York Times* as a "daring real estate speculator," February 10, 1907, when he operated in Philadelphia. See "The Rise of Felix Isman." But after 1915 he was listed in New York City directories, where he never attracted similar press attention.

32. A letter from Jesse J. Schamberg to Albert Greenfield, May 11, 1927, refers to Greenfield's having opened a New York office "a few years ago." HSP, box 90, folder 4. A letter from Albert Greenfield to Watkins & Kronthal, June 26, 1934, and its reply June 29, 1934 (in author's possession), refer to Greenfield's Tuesdays in New York routine.

33. Elizabeth Petrie, interview by the author, October 27, 1975.

34. Harrison, "Mr. Philadelphia," 82.

35. Ibid., 83.

36. Albert Greenfield, "The Closing of Bankers Trust," WFIL radio address, October 17, 1938, HSP, box 238, folder 10.

37. Ibid., 6. The amount on the typed transcript is difficult to decipher—probably $3 million, but possibly $5 million. Andrew Harrison says the amount was $3 million. "Mr. Philadelphia," 83.

38. Albert Greenfield, WFIL radio address. Greenfield said in the broadcast that he was approached by "the executive head of the Pennsylvania Company," apparently a reference to C. Stevenson Newhall, then the Pennsylvania Company's executive vice president.

39. Wayne personally owned one hundred common shares and three hundred preferred shares of Bankers Securities as of March 1930; Bankers Securities list of shareholders, March 14, 1930, HSP, box 140, folder 4.

40. Letter from Joseph Wayne to Albert Greenfield, February 4, 1929, HSP, box 136, folder 8.

41. Letter from C. S. Newhall to Albert Greenfield, August 2, 1928, HSP, box 106, folder 2.

42. Thomas J. LaBrum, interview by the author, October 15, 1975. LaBrum was assistant to David Stern at the *Philadelphia Record* and later represented Greenfield through LaBrum's public relations agency.

43. John R. Bunting Jr., interview by the author, October 15, 1975.

44. One source says that the Bank of Philadelphia & Trust Co. was "heavily involved in real estate, and it was felt that the Greenfield people could best handle the situation." Joseph D. Goodman, "Miracle Man," possibly unpublished article for *Forbes*, 1948, HSP, box 414, folder 16.

45. Albert Greenfield, WFIL radio address.

46. Davenport, "Philadelphia," 188.

47. Binzen, Daughen, and Friedman, *Rise and Fall of the House of Greenfield*, 62, citing Bankers Securities board minutes.

48. Russell Davenport says that the branches opened under the Bankers Trust name on July 22. See "Philadelphia," 188. Greenfield's radio address on October 17, 1938, says July 21, which was a Monday and thus the more likely date.

49. Bankers Trust ad in the *Philadelphia Record*, July 28, 1930, cited in Binzen, Daughen, and Friedman, *Rise and Fall of the House of Greenfield*, 59. Most accounts say Bankers Trust had $50 million in deposits after the merger; the Federal Reserve archives put the figure at $51 million in July 1930. Gary Richardson, e-mail message to the author, April 3, 2012.

50. Letter from Samuel Barker to Bankers Trust employees, August 1, 1930, quoted in Binzen, Daughen, and Friedman, *Rise and Fall of the House of Greenfield*, 62.

51. Letter from Albert Greenfield to Harry Sundheim, August 11, 1930, HSP, box 152, folder 26.

52. Albert Greenfield, WFIL radio address.

53. Lewis and two other former executives of the Bank of Philadelphia & Trust Co. were indicted in December 1931 for allegedly embezzling $100,000. All three were convicted in May 1933 of taking lesser amounts. Each was sentenced in February 1934 to two years in prison. On August 29, 1934, while appealing his case, Lewis committed suicide at age forty-nine. See Binzen, Daughen, and Friedman, *Rise and Fall of the House of Greenfield*, 63–64.

54. Letter from Leon A. Lewis to Albert Greenfield, August 20, 1930, quoted in Binzen, Daughen, and Friedman, *Rise and Fall of the House of Greenfield*, 63.

55. Albert Greenfield, "The Closing of Bankers Trust." Binzen, Daughen, and Friedman, *Rise and Fall of the House of Greenfield*, refers to the "handful of depositors" (64).

56. Wainwright, *History of the Philadelphia National Bank, 1803–1953*, 208. The clearinghouse system is explained on pages 110–111. See also Gorton, "Private Clearinghouses and the Origins of Central Banking."

57. Albert Greenfield, "The Closing of Bankers Trust."

58. Davenport says that the two banks together loaned $7 million. See "Philadelphia," 190. In his "The Closing of Bankers Trust" radio speech on October 17, 1938, Greenfield said the amount was $7.5 million. Joseph Wayne Jr., in a December 22, 1930, letter to the Philadelphia Clearing House Association, said Bankers Trust was indebted to Philadelphia National Bank "for about $6,736,884," suggesting that most of the $7 or $7.5 million was provided by Philadelphia National. See HSP, Clearing House Association papers, collection 1908, box 12.

59. Albert Greenfield, "The Closing of Bankers Trust."

60. Binzen, Daughen, and Friedman, *Rise and Fall of the House of Greenfield* (75), says Bankers Securities had $2,054,865 on deposit at Bankers Trust as of December 22, 1930. Albert Greenfield, "The Closing of Bankers Trust," says, "I was personally responsible for nearly $3.5 million in direct deposits which were there at the time of closing, even after possible set-offs for obligations, and almost $1 million of these were deposited in the last few weeks before closing." Greenfield's total deposits before set-offs for obligations may have been about $4 million.

61. Albert Greenfield, "The Closing of Bankers Trust."

62. Binzen, Daughen, and Friedman, *Rise and Fall of the House of Greenfield*, 65.

63. Ibid., 65–66.

64. Harrison, "Mr. Philadelphia," 85. See also Federal Reserve archives notes re Bankers Trust: It says one-third of the bank's $51 million deposits had been withdrawn, "and the institution was not sufficiently liquid to continue to honor checks." Richardson, e-mail message to the author.

65. Albert Greenfield, "The Closing of Bankers Trust."

66. Ibid.; see also Davenport, "Philadelphia," 190. Greenfield says Philadelphia National and the Pennsylvania Co. loaned Bankers Trust "up to $7.5 million"; Davenport puts the figure at $7 million.

67. Wayne, head of Girard National Bank from 1914, joined Philadelphia National on its merger with Girard in 1926, becoming president of the merged bank as well as a director. See Wainwright, *History of the Philadelphia National Bank*, 194–195.

68. Friedman, *Jewish Life in Philadelphia, 1830–1940*, 18; see also Baltzell, *An American Business Aristocracy*, 244. Loeb was not the first Jewish leader of the Tradesmens National Bank; he succeeded his father, August B. Loeb, as its president in 1915.

69. Harris was president of Franklin Trust and doing business with Greenfield at least as early as 1921; see Franklin Trust statement, September 30, 1921, HSP, box 9, folder 2. Harris is listed as a vice president of Greenfield's Bankers Bond & Mortgage Co. in 1926. See "Bankers Mortgage Co. in New Offices," *Frankford (Philadelphia) Labor News*, 1926, HSP, box 73, folder 6; see also letter from Maurice Wurzel to Albert Greenfield, July 28, 1926, HSP, box 81, folder 4. Harris is listed as a vice president in a Bankers Securities statement of October 10, 1928 (HSP, box 93, folder 9) and on Bankers Securities letterhead of August 13, 1929 (HSP, box 116, folder 2). He is also listed as a Bankers Securities shareholder, with two thousand preferred shares, on a shareholders list as of March 14, 1930 (HSP, box 140, folder 4). In addition, he is listed as a director in attendance at the Bankers Securities meeting of December 20, 1930, that discussed the Bankers Trust crisis. The other Clearing House Committee members were Charles S. Calwell, president of the Corn Exchange National Bank and Trust Co.; William J. Montgomery, vice president of the First National Bank; and J. William Smith, president of the Real Estate-Land Title & Trust Co. See the Clearing House Committee's letter of December 22, 1930. HSP, Clearing House Association papers, collection 1908, box 12.

70. Letter from Albert Jackson to C. H. Batten, April 2, 1929, HSP, Clearing House Association papers, collection 1908, box 7).

71. Wainwright, *The Philadelphia National Bank*, 163, 170. Stotesbury was elected to the board of the Philadelphia National Bank in 1901 and to the Franklin National in 1905. He also served on the boards of Girard Trust, Fidelity Trust, and Philadelphia Trust. His Drexel & Co. partner, Arthur E. Newbold, served as director of the Farmers' and Mechanics' National and the Fourth Street National, the Commercial Trust Company and the Pennsylvania Company; and H. Gates Lloyd, also of Drexel & Co., was a director of the Girard National. All but the Farmers' and Mechanics' National were among Philadelphia's largest banks.

72. Davenport, "Philadelphia," 188. For a discussion of Stotesbury's titles at Drexel & Co., see Rottenberg, *The Man Who Made Wall Street*, 190.

73. Lippincott, "Edward T. Stotesbury," 5.

74. E. T. Stotesbury obituary, *Philadelphia Bulletin*, May 17, 1938, quoted in Dilks, *Morgan, Lewis and Bockius*, 89. Also see Lippincott, "Edward T. Stotesbury," 22.

75. Gray, "Streetscape."

76. Between October 17 and December 11, 1930, the bank's deposits declined from $212 million to $160 million; see "Bank of U.S. Closes Doors."

77. "$1 Billion Union of Banks Completed."

78. For background on the closing of Bank of United States, see Friedman and Schwartz, *Monetary History of the United States, 1867–1960*, 309–310; also Chernow, *The House of Morgan*, 326–327.

79. Richard Sylla, e-mail message to the author, October 14, 2012.

80. Friedman and Schwartz, *Monetary History*, 310.

81. Chernow, *House of Morgan*, 326–327.

82. Letter from J. P. Morgan Jr. to Robert Lowell, quoted in Chernow, *House of Morgan*, 214.

83. Letter from J. P. Morgan Jr. to Henry Fairfield, quoted in Strouse, *Morgan: Financier*, 560.

84. Davenport says that Stotesbury "spent much of his time in New York." See "Philadelphia," 188.

85. Letter from William Fox to Albert Greenfield, November 30, 1928, HSP, box 98, folder 13; letter from Albert Greenfield to William Fox, December 6, 1928, HSP, box 98, folder 13.

86. "It is strange that the only two banks of the 13 banks I was associated with, and which had my personal loans, had their doors closed shortly after I sold out," Fox remarked in 1933. See Sinclair, *Upton Sinclair Presents William Fox*, 201.

CHAPTER 7

1. Benson, *U.S. Immigration and Migration*, 115.

2. Ibid., 115–116; Anderson, "The Lost Founders," 58.

3. See, for example, Solow, "Survival of the Richest?" and "The Merits of Genteel Poverty."

4. Bailyn, *The Peopling of British North America*, 37–38; *U.S. Immigration and Migration*, 117.

5. *U.S. Immigration and Migration*, 138.

6. Bailyn, *Voyagers to the West*, 5.

7. Jay, *The Life of John Jay*, 376.

8. Friend, *Cheerful Money*, 46–47.

9. Ibid.

10. See Ferguson, "Why America Outpaces Europe."

11. This idea is specifically articulated in "The End of America."

12. The first use of the acronym WASP is often attributed to E. Digby Baltzell in his 1964 book, *The Protestant Establishment*. However, Andrew Hacker used the acronym in a 1957 article. Even earlier, it was used by Stetson Kennedy in an African American newspaper, New York's *Amsterdam News*, on April 17, 1948: "In America, we find the WASPs (White Anglo-Saxon Protestants) ganging up to take their frustrations out on whatever minority group happens to be handy—whether Negro, Catholic, Jewish, Japanese or whatnot." See Letters, Sunday Book Review.

13. Friend, *Cheerful Money*, 17.

14. Ibid.

15. Reichley, *The Art of Government*, 104–105.

16. Friend, *Cheerful Money*, 19.

17. Saveth, *American Historians and European Immigrants, 1875–1925*, 74.

18. See Levy, "Henry James and the Jews."

19. Eliot, *After Strange Gods*.

20. Spengler, *The Decline of the West*, 340.

21. The characterization of the Philadelphia Club appears in Baltzell, *The Protestant Establishment*, 138.

22. Davis, *The Bouviers*, 97.

23. Davenport, "Philadelphia," 188. See also "Hopkinson Succeeds Stotesbury as Drexel Senior Partner," *Philadelphia Record*, May 27, 1938.

24. Burt, in *Perennial Philadelphians*, mentions the Lloyd family among "Philadelphia's oldest and best family names" (59).

25. See "Mrs. Stacy B. Lloyd Papers: Biographical/Historical Note," Historical Society of Pennsylvania (HSP), Papers of Eleanor Morris Lloyd, collection 3467. She was descended from Philadelphia's second mayor, Anthony Morris (1654–1721). As of 1911, Effingham Morris (1856–1937) effectively ran seven Philadelphia banks and trust companies: the Girard, Land

Title, Real Estate, Provident, Philadelphia, and West Philadelphia trusts, and the Pennsylvania Company; see Wainwright, *History of the Philadelphia National Bank, 1803-1953*, 174.

26. Auerbach, *Unequal Justice*, 126-127. Robert T. McCracken (1883-1960) was a founding partner of the Philadelphia firm later known as Montgomery, McCracken, Walker & Rhoads, and served as chancellor of the Philadelphia Bar Association and president of the Pennsylvania Bar Association.

27. Allen, *The Great Pierpont Morgan*, 8.

28. Wainwright, *History of the Philadelphia National Bank*, 206.

29. Maurice Wurzel (1888-1949) was a director of Greenfield's Bankers Securities and president of Greenfield's Bankers Bond & Mortgage Co. of America through the 1930s. Greenfield installed him as president of Loft Candy after acquiring it in 1940.

30. Leonard Wurzel, interview by the author, September 23, 2011.

31. E. T. Stotesbury obituary, *Philadelphia Bulletin*, May 17, 1938.

32. Lippincott, "E. T. Stotesbury," 10.

33. Burt, *Perennial Philadelphians*, 168.

34. Wainwright, *History of the Philadelphia National Bank*, 194-195, 220; Davenport, "Philadelphia," 188. Girard National Bank is not to be confused with the Girard Trust Co.

35. Anthony's oldest daughter, Emilie (1851-1883), married Edward Biddle in 1872. See Rottenberg, *The Man Who Made Wall Street*, 104. Anthony J. Drexel's blood descendants subsequently married into such prominent WASP families as the Vanderbilts, Dukes, Roosevelts, Whartons, Wyeths, Whitneys, Mellons, Astors, Ingersolls, Cassatts, and Cadwaladers, as well as the British aristocracy. See Rottenberg, *The Man Who Made Wall Street*, 177. Mother Katharine Drexel (1858-1955) took the veil in 1891 and founded the Sisters of the Blessed Sacrament that year; she was canonized in 2000. See Rottenberg, *The Man Who Made Wall Street*, 187.

36. Joseph Newton Pew Sr. (1848-1912) struck natural gas in Bradford, Pennsylvania, in 1882. In 1901, following the Spindletop oil strike in Texas, he moved his Sun Oil Company to Philadelphia to build a refinery to process the crude oil from Texas. After his death in 1912, his sons J. Howard (1882-1971) and J. N. Pew Jr. (1886-1963) ran the company between them for the better part of a half-century.

37. This insight was suggested by Boyd Barnard, interview by the author, October 20, 1975.

38. For example, Chernow, in *The House of Morgan*, describes the younger J. P. Morgan as "shy, awkward, shambling Jack who had cowered in the corners of Pierpont's life" (161).

39. In any case, Morgan partners enjoyed considerable leeway in regard to the deals they authorized, and they rarely met as a group to approve or disapprove deals.

40. Carosso, *The Morgans*, 304.

41. Stotesbury became a Drexel & Co. partner in 1883 and a Morgan partner in 1894. Jack Morgan became a Morgan partner in 1892 and senior partner upon his father's death in 1913. Of the other key Morgan partners as of 1930, Stotesbury was by far the most senior. The other key partners, and their dates of partnership, were Charles Steele (1900), Henry P. Davison (1908), Thomas W. Lamont (1911), Dwight W. Morrow (1914), Edward Stettinius (1915), Thomas Cochran (1917), George Whitney (1919), Russell C. Leffingwell (1923), and Francis D. Barlow (1926).

42. Chernow, *House of Morgan*, 214-215; Wayne Willcox (Stotesbury's biographer), interview by the author, February 10, 2012.

43. Marion, *Within These Walls*, 168; Skwersky, *Knight of Philadelphia*, 159.

44. Wayne Willcox, e-mail message to the author, May 27, 2012. Louis Magaziner (1877-1957) designed hospitals, movie palaces, college buildings, and department stores.

45. Stotesbury's grandfather, Arthur Stotesbury (1755-1839), a sea captain, had seventeen children by two wives; see Lippincott, "E. T. Stotesbury," 4. E. T. Stotesbury's father, Thomas, had a sugar refinery, called Harris and Stotesbury, on Delaware Avenue in Philadelphia; see ibid., 5. Stotesbury's biographer, Wayne Willcox, says he was a dry goods merchant. Wayne Willcox, interview by the author, February 20, 2012.

46. Willcox, interview by the author, February 20, 2012. The partnership was Harris & Stotesbury, sugar refiners; see Lippincott, "E. T. Stotesbury," 5; see also Stotesbury's entry in Stafford, *Who's Who in Philadelphia in Wartime*.

47. Lippincott, "E. T. Stotesbury," 5. Lippincott says the wholesale grocer was Rutter & Patterson; Stotesbury's biographer, Wayne Willcox, says the correct spelling is Patteson. Willcox, interview by the author, February 20, 2012.

48. Willcox, interview by the author, February 20, 2012.

49. Lippincott, "E. T. Stotesbury," 5.

50. Ibid.

51. Zwicker and Zwicker, *Whitemarsh Hall*, 12.

52. Carosso, *The Morgans*, 306.

53. Dilks, *Morgan, Lewis and Bockius*, 88–89.

54. Wayne Willcox, e-mail message to the author, April 9, 2013.

55. Nevertheless, Stotesbury's two daughters both married into prominent Old Philadelphia families. Edith, born 1877, married Sydney Emlen Hutchinson in 1903; Frances, born 1881, married John Kearsley Mitchell III in 1909.

56. Stotesbury was sixty-two and Eva forty-seven at their wedding. See Dilks, *Morgan, Lewis and Bockius*, 89.

57. Ibid.

58. Ibid., 90.

59. Zwicker and Zwicker, *Whitemarsh Hall*, 12.

60. Maher, *Twilight of Splendor*, 78, cited in Dilks, *Morgan, Lewis and Bockius*, 90.

61. Dilks, *Morgan, Lewis and Bockius*, 89.

62. Willcox, e-mail message to the author.

63. Zwicker and Zwicker, *Whitemarsh Hall*, 18.

64. Burt, *Perennial Philadelphians*, 162.

65. Ibid., 350.

66. Ibid., 162–164.

67. Norris, *Ended Episodes*, 103.

68. Burt, *Perennial Philadelphians*, 162. Wayne Willcox, author of a forthcoming biography of Stotesbury, is skeptical about this account. Willcox, interview by the author, February 10, 2012.

CHAPTER 8

1. For more on Fox's loans and deposits at the Bank of United States, see Sinclair, *Upton Sinclair Presents William Fox*, 200–201. Fox's role as a stockholder at that bank is discussed in Fox's November 30, 1928, letter to Albert Greenfield and Greenfield's December 6, 1928, reply. Historical Society of Pennsylvania (HSP), box 98, folder 13.

2. Sinclair, *Upton Sinclair Presents William Fox*, 1.

3. Ibid., 3.

4. Harrison, "Mr. Philadelphia," 85.

5. "We asked and expected the aid of the banks in the Clearing House Association." Albert Greenfield, "The Closing of Bankers Trust," WFIL radio address, October 17, 1938, p. 7, HSP, box 238, folder 10.

6. Gest is often listed as head of the Clearing House Committee; for example, see the committee's report of January 8, 1931, HSP, Clearing House Association papers, collection 1908, box 12.

7. Joseph Wayne, in a December 22, 1930, letter to the Philadelphia Clearing House Association, said, "Bankers Trust Co. is indebted to the Philadelphia National Bank for about $6,736,884, secured by a miscellaneous assortment of collateral." HSP, Clearing House Association papers, collection 1908, box 12.

8. Albert Greenfield, "The Closing of Bankers Trust," 7.

9. Dilks, *Morgan, Lewis and Bockius*, 104. The lawyers were Francis Bracken and Arthur Littleton. Stotesbury, whose Drexel & Co. was also a Morgan Lewis client, is not mentioned in Dilks's account of the Friday meeting, and, given the events of the following Sunday, it seems unlikely that he attended the Friday meeting or was aware of the plan.

10. The minutes of special Bankers Securities meeting on December 20, 1930 (in the author's possession), say that Bankers Securities had invested "over $2.7 million" in Bankers Trust. Another source says that Bankers Securities had invested $2,750,316 in Bankers Trust; see Binzen, Daughen, and Friedman, *Rise and Fall of the House of Greenfield*, 75. The $2.75 million figure also appears in Greenfield, "The Closing of Bankers Trust," 9. In it, Greenfield says that his personal holding company, Albert Co., had also invested $300,000 in Bankers Trust stock. On page 8, Greenfield refers to Bankers Securities as "the largest stockholder of Bankers Trust Company." Greenfield's right-hand man and successor, Gus Amsterdam, also said that Bankers Securities had $2.75 million invested in Bankers Trust (although Amsterdam was not employed by Bankers Securities at that point); Gustave G. Amsterdam, interview by the author, October 30, 1975.

11. Bankers Securities, minutes of special meeting, December 20, 1930.

12. Ibid.; see also Binzen, Daughen, and Friedman, *Rise and Fall of the House of Greenfield*, 68.

13. Greenfield, "The Closing of Bankers Trust," 8. Bankers Securities, minutes of special meeting, December 20, 1930; see also Binzen, Daughen, and Friedman, *Rise and Fall of the House of Greenfield*, 68.

14. Bankers Securities, minutes of special meeting, December 20, 1930; also Binzen, Daughen, and Friedman, *Rise and Fall of the House of Greenfield*, 68.

15. Greenfield, "The Closing of Bankers Trust," 8.

16. Russell Davenport describes "a final conference during the night of December 21 at Mr. Gest's home on the Main Line." See "Philadelphia," 190. Greenfield's "The Closing of Bankers Trust" radio address says that the meeting took place "the following day" (Sunday, December 21) in "the country home of one of its [the Clearing House Association's] leaders" (8). Gest's entry in Stafford, *Who's Who in Philadelphia in Wartime*, lists his home address as in Merion; the U.S. censuses for 1920 and 1930 list his address as 650 Hazelhurst Avenue in Merion.

17. A summary of Clearing House Association members' claims against Bankers Trust, January 8, 1931, lists thirty-four banks. See HSP, Clearing House Association papers, collection 1908, box 12.

18. Davenport, "Philadelphia," 190; Greenfield, "The Closing of Bankers Trust," 8.

19. Greenfield, "The Closing of Bankers Trust," 8.

20. Joseph D. Goodman, "Miracle Man," possibly unpublished article for *Forbes*, 1948, HSP, box 414, folder 16.

21. Letter from J. David Stern to Elizabeth Greenfield, January 6, 1967, HSP, box 899, folder 6.

22. Stern, *Memoirs of a Maverick Publisher*, 181–182.

23. Greenfield, "The Closing of Bankers Trust," 7.

24. Greenfield preached that when a negotiation soured, one should leave behind an object like a cane, providing an opportunity to reopen contact in the future; see letter from Murry Becker to Elizabeth Greenfield, January 9, 1967, cited in Harrison, "Mr. Philadelphia," 93n. Regarding Greenfield's disparagement of Stotesbury, see Barbara Greenfield, interview by the author, July 18, 2011, and Arlin Adams, interview by the author, January 16, 2012. Barbara Greenfield also blamed Stotesbury in *Mr. Philadelphia*, the 2007 video about Albert Greenfield. Greenfield's private secretary, Alfred Klein, also blamed Stotesbury. See Harrison, "Mr. Philadelphia," 92. Philip Klein, Alfred Klein's brother, said, "Mr. Stotesbury closed the Bankers Trust Company." See Philip Klein, interview by Walter M. Phillips, February 26, 1980, p. 5, Walter Phillips Oral History Project (WPP), Temple University Urban Archives (TUUA). Bob Williams, a *Philadelphia Bulletin* city desk editor at the time, recalled that "Drexel & Co.

wanted to put Al Greenfield out of business." See Bob Williams, interview by Peter Binzen, 1985. These are all secondhand speculations, of course. Wayne Willcox, author of a forthcoming biography of Stotesbury, agrees that Stotesbury was likely responsible; Wayne Willcox, interview by the author, February 16, 2012.

25. This is simply speculation on my part. Harris did attend the Bankers Securities board meeting on Saturday night, December 20, and his name was attached to an announcement from the Clearing House Association released on Monday, December 22; see HSP, Clearing House Association papers, collection 1908, box 12. Harris also attended the Clearing House Committee's meeting on Monday afternoon; see "Phila. Banks Safe, Leading Financiers Assure Depositors." Thus he was surely cognizant of the deliberations and very likely present for the meeting at Gest's home on Sunday night, December 21, as well.

26. Lippincott, "E. T. Stotesbury," 10.

27. This description of the Panic of 1873 is taken from President Herbert Hoover's address to the Gridiron Club, April 27, 1931, cited in Skwersky, *Knight of Philadelphia*, 99. Also see Rezneck, "Distress, Relief, and Discontent."

28. Stotesbury was born at Sixth and Spruce Streets, Philadelphia, and spent his childhood there. See Lippincott, "E. T. Stotesbury," 4.

29. The properties sold in the 1920s included those in Philadelphia suburbs like Radnor, Haverford, and Merion Station, some of which Stotesbury had purchased from Anthony Drexel's estate in 1893. Also sold was the Overbrook Farms development that Stotesbury had created with Anthony Drexel's son-in-law, James W. Paul. Willcox, interview by the author.

30. Albert Greenfield, "Real Estate Outlook for 1951," Albert Greenfield & Co. press release, January 3, 1951, HSP, box 503, folder 5. Greenfield was actually quoting, with approval, an editorial by Herbert U. Nelson of the National Association of Real Estate Boards.

31. Lippincott, "E. T. Stotesbury," 20.

32. Again, it is hard to say who was present or how many bankers attended. Upton Sinclair says only that it was "a meeting of the ruling bankers." See *Upton Sinclair Presents William Fox*, 346.

33. Gray and Rogers, "15th and Walnut Streets Showplace to Be Sold," news release, June 1956 (in the author's possession).

34. Bankers Trust had 135,000 depositors upon its merger with the Bank of Philadelphia & Trust Company in July 1930. By the time of this meeting, the number was down to about 114,000. See "$3,915,792 Paid Out by Closed Banks," *Philadelphia Inquirer*, January 16, 1939, HSP, box 256, folder 6.

35. Sinclair, *Upton Sinclair Presents William Fox*, 345–348. Fox says here that this meeting occurred Sunday night, December 21. It seems unlikely that prominent bankers meeting on the Main Line that day or evening would later reassemble in a downtown bank office. But given the urgencies of the moment, the meeting may have occurred as Sinclair (quoting Fox) relates.

36. Friedman and Schwartz, *Monetary History of the United States*, 310.

37. I am grateful to Vanda Krefft, author of a forthcoming biography of Fox, for her insights into Fox's psyche. Vanda Krefft, e-mail message to the author, May 16, 2012.

38. Telegram from Irland M. Beckman to Albert M. Greenfield, December 22, 1930, HSP, collection 1959, box 140, folder 2, available at http://digitalhistory.hsp.org/bnktr/doc/telegram-irland-beckman-albert-greenfield-december-22-1930.

39. Stern, *Memoirs of a Maverick Publisher*, describes "a rainy Monday morning" (180).

40. Harrison, "Mr. Philadelphia," 89. Precisely how a bank could "temporarily" surrender its assets was not discussed.

41. Sinclair, *Upton Sinclair Presents William Fox*, 347.

42. As of September 30, 1930, Bankers Trust had 135,000 depositors with deposits totaling $45 million; see *Philadelphia Bulletin*, December 22, 1930. But the secretary of banking's final report in 1939 listed 114,000 at the closing. See "$3,915,792 Paid Out by Closed Banks." The difference suggests that some 21,000 depositors closed their accounts between September 30 and December 19.

43. "Crowd Orderly and Composed at Closed Bank," 1.

44. Stern, *Memoirs of a Maverick Publisher*, 180.

45. Binzen, Daughen, and Friedman, *Rise and Fall of the House of Greenfield*, 75. This is the only known recorded comment about the closing made by Greenfield on that day. Binzen says Mayer had invested in Bankers Trust, but more likely Mayer invested in Bankers Securities.

46. Stern, *Memoirs of a Maverick Publisher*, 181; see also letter from J. David Stern to Elizabeth Greenfield, January 6, 1967, HSP, box 899, folder 6.

47. A January 5, 1931, letter from Albert Greenfield to William L. Hoag says he has "himself over $400,000 on deposit in the institution." HSP, box 155, folder 5. But Bankers Securities' corporate secretary Irland M. Beckman, in a statement of October 15, 1938, said Greenfield had only $65,268.31 of his own funds on deposit at Bankers Trust, plus $34,208.71 in savings of his relatives; see Harrison, "Mr. Philadelphia," 91.

48. Greenfield, "The Closing of Bankers Trust," 9.

49. The figure of $11 million is suggested by the long financial statement Greenfield issued when he finally sought bankruptcy protection in 1940. He listed $6.4 million in personal debts and $4.6 million in debts of his personal holding company, the Albert Co. By 1940, he said, about $4.5 million of that total had been settled, and another $4.5 million extended, and $1 million in other obligations were under negotiation. See *Philadelphia Bulletin*, May 31, 1940; see also Binzen, Daughen, and Friedman, *Rise and Fall of the House of Greenfield*, 126–127.

50. Harrison, "Mr. Philadelphia," 92.

51. As late as 1938, Greenfield continued to deny that he had been founder, chairman, or president of Bankers Trust, which was technically true but overlooked his critical role in its creation and the fact that the bank's largest shareholder was Bankers Securities, which he controlled. See "Greenfield Denies He Founded Bank."

52. Anonymous typed letter to Albert Greenfield, December 22, 1930, HSP, collection 1959, box 154B, folder 3, available at http://digitallibrary.hsp.org/index.php/Detail/Object/Show/object_id/5249.

53. Handwritten letter (sender's name illegible) to Albert Greenfield, 1931, HSP, collection 1959, box 154B, folder 3, available at http://digitallibrary.hsp.org/index.php/Detail/Object/Show/object_id/5249 (emphasis in original).

54. Elizabeth Zeidman, interview by the author, October 19, 1975, p. 1.

55. Alfred DiGiovanni, interview by Peter Binzen, 1985.

56. Clearing House Committee press release (signed by the committee's eight members), December 22, 1930, HSP, Clearing House Association papers, collection 1908, box 12.

57. See, for example, Greenfield's December 23, 1941, memo to Samuel Rosenbaum, which says, "I was not a director of Franklin Trust Co., which has a large claim against me." HSP, box 309, folder 2. In a January 17, 1942, letter to Edward Leech, Greenfield denied he ever had any connection with the Franklin Trust Co. HSP, box 309, folder 2.

58. A *Philadelphia Record* article refers to "heavy withdrawals by depositors" at Franklin Trust's central office at Fifteenth and Chestnut "and four branch offices in other parts of the city." See "Bankers Trust Co. Taken Over by State; Plan Reorganization," 1.

59. Binzen, Daughen, and Friedman, *Rise and Fall of the House of Greenfield*, 73.

60. "Phila. Banks Safe, Leading Financiers Assure Depositors." The article lists all twelve bankers who attended, among them Gates Lloyd, Wayne, Newhall, Gest, and Harris. The $20 million credit figure was cited by J. Hector McNeal, a founder (in 1914) of the Franklin Trust, in a speech to depositors in the bank's lobby that afternoon; see "Bankers Trust Co. Taken Over by State; Plan Reorganization."

61. "Bankers Trust Co. Taken Over by State; Plan Reorganization," 1.

62. Ibid.

63. Wainwright, *History of the Philadelphia National Bank, 1803–1953*, 207.

64. Boonin, *The Jewish Quarter of Philadelphia, 1881–1930*, 31–33.

65. Harrison, "Mr. Philadelphia," 90. Greenfield was accompanied by three bankers who did not want their names to go on record. The author is grateful to Serena Skwersky, e-mail message to the author, February 23, 2012, for this tidbit.

66. "400 Bankers Trust Employees Dropped," unidentified newspaper article, January 2, 1931, HSP, collection 3344, box 0, Bankers Trust Co., 1931–32 folder, available at http://digital history.hsp.org/bnktr/doc/400-bankers-trust-employes-dropped-january-2-1931.

67. Greenfield, "The Closing of Bankers Trust," 9.

68. "Want Greenfield Out of New Bank."

69. Harrison, "Mr. Philadelphia," 95; Binzen, Daughen, and Friedman, *Rise and Fall of the House of Greenfield*, 78. The liquidation was ordered by Pennsylvania's new secretary of banking, William D. Gordon, on September 24, 1931.

70. Wadhwani, "Soothing the People's Panic."

71. Wainwright, *History of the Philadelphia National Bank*, 209.

72. Ibid., 210–211.

73. Norris, *Ended Episodes*, 218.

74. Greenfield, "The Closing of Bankers Trust," 1.

75. Ibid., 9–10.

76. The quotation is provided by Barbara Greenfield in the video *Mr. Philadelphia*.

77. Lewis was indicted in December 1931 for allegedly embezzling $100,000, convicted May 1933 of taking lesser amounts, and sentenced to two years. He committed suicide August 29, 1934, while appealing the case. See Binzen, Daughen, and Friedman, *Rise and Fall of the House of Greenfield*, 63–64.

78. The author is grateful to Stotesbury's biographer, Wayne Willcox, for his insights into Stotesbury's mindset and likely actions at the December 21 meeting. Willcox, interview by the author; Willcox, e-mail messages to the author, February 13 and 23, 2012.

79. *Philadelphia Bulletin*, March 12 and 13, 1931. Greenfield said that in addition to the regular commission he received from the owners of Quaker City Cab, he had been paid $95,000 by the PRT.

80. *Philadelphia Bulletin*, March 31, 1931. The cash consisted mostly of $10,000 bills, later changed to $1,000 bills for fear the larger bills could be traced; it was kept in a box in the basement of the Mitten Bank on S. Penn Square. See *Philadelphia Bulletin*, April 14, 1934.

81. *Philadelphia Bulletin*, March 12, 1931. Testifying in Harrisburg, Greenfield said the total fees he received from the PRT ranged between $700,000 and $800,000. This figure included payments from Mitten Management and from Thomas Mitten himself. Greenfield's commissions on real estate transactions for the PRT itself were between $350,000 and $360,000.

82. Ledgers showed that Mitten advanced Greenfield $1,524,375 in 1927. It was speculated that these funds might have been advanced for use in the Republican mayoral campaign of Harry Mackey, who was elected that year. *Philadelphia Bulletin*, May 14, 1931.

83. *Philadelphia Bulletin*, April 11, 1931.

84. Wainwright, *History of the Philadelphia National Bank*, 210.

85. Harrison, "Mr. Philadelphia," 100. Skwersky, *Knight of Philadelphia* (83), says that in June 1931 Albert M. Greenfield & Co. had 125 employees in its Philadelphia office, with a weekly payroll of $4,899.50. See also Albert M. Greenfield & Co. monthly payroll, June 15, 1931, HSP, box 188, folder 19.

86. Harrison, "Mr. Philadelphia," 101. The notes were due November 1, 1931.

87. Draft of letter from Albert Greenfield to Edward T. Leech, December 30, 1941, HSP, box 309, folder 2. Albert M. Greenfield & Co. reached an agreement with its creditors on December 4, 1933, to extend the payoff period on its remaining debentures of $3,960,000 by ten years, to May 1, 1955. The limitations on Greenfield's compensation were included in this agreement. See Harrison, "Mr. Philadelphia," 104. For 1936, Greenfield's compensation totaled $74,000, broken down as follows: $52,000 as chairman of Bankers Securities, $12,000 as chairman of City Stores, and $10,000 as a trustee of the PRT; see Binzen, Daughen, and Friedman, *Rise and Fall of the House of Greenfield*, 105.

88. Harrison, "Mr. Philadelphia," 96.

89. Letter from Albert Greenfield to Edward T. Leech, December 17, 1941, HSP, box 309, folder 2.

90. Binzen, Daughen, and Friedman, *Rise and Fall of the House of Greenfield*, 90, 127.

91. Ibid., 75. Citing Bankers Securities financial statements, Binzen and colleagues say Bankers Securities invested $2,750,316 in Bankers Trust, an investment that was valued at just $1 in Bankers Securities' year-end 1930 financial statement. Bankers Securities' corporate secretary, Irland M. Beckman, in a statement of October 15, 1938, said Bankers Securities had $2,055,726.03 on deposit at Bankers Trust; see Harrison, "Mr. Philadelphia," 91. Bankers Securities owned $1,890,000 worth of Albert M. Greenfield & Co. debentures; see Harrison, "Mr. Philadelphia," 102. Over the years 1929 through 1931, Bankers Securities lost a total of $5,564,243; see Binzen, Daughen, and Friedman, *Rise and Fall of the House of Greenfield*, 88. Securities that Bankers Securities had purchased for $6,244,036 were worth only $1,058,692 by the end of 1932; see Binzen, Daughen, and Friedman, *Rise and Fall of the House of Greenfield*, 91.

92. Binzen, Daughen, and Friedman, *Rise and Fall of the House of Greenfield*, 76. Greenfield's salary was later reduced again to $36,000, but early in 1936, as business conditions improved, it was raised to $52,000 again; see Binzen, Daughen, and Friedman, *Rise and Fall of the House of Greenfield*, 104.

93. That title endured until 2007, when the building was renamed the Philadelphia Building.

94. Stern, *Memoirs of a Maverick Publisher*, 181. See also the letter from Samuel Barker to Albert Greenfield on August 10, 1931, which said, "We properly helped the *Record*, thinking also of ourselves." HSP, box 155, folder 2.

95. Reichley, *The Art of Government*, 74.

96. Josephson, *The Robber Barons*, 114.

97. See, for example, "Edward Hopkinson Jr." The Spoon is one of four "hardware honors" annually bestowed on class leaders at Penn.

98. Gustave G. Amsterdam, interview by Walter Phillips, December 20, 1975, p. 9, WPP, TUUA.

99. An announcement of Greenfield's withdrawal from the PRT board appears in *Philadelphia Bulletin*, February 15, 1962.

100. Dilks, *Morgan, Lewis and Bockius*, 111, quoting Francis Bracken, who represented the PRT's underlying stockholders.

101. Quoted in Brody, "A Richer Life by Seeing the Glass Half Full," D7.

102. Klein, interview by Phillips. Wilson became assistant city controller in 1927 and was elected controller in 1933; see Rossi, "Philadelphia's Forgotten Mayor." This meeting probably took place in 1933 or 1934, when Wilson, as controller, was mulling his mayoral prospects. He subsequently ran and won as a Republican in 1935.

103. Gustave G. Amsterdam, interview by Peter Binzen, 1985.

104. According to Samuel Barker, in January 1931 Greenfield told colleagues that he would never again be a director of any commercial bank. See *Philadelphia Inquirer*, May 12, 1931; see also "Says Greenfield Is Out of New Bank." Actually, at the time of Greenfield's death in 1967, Bankers Securities had become a large holder in the First Pennsylvania Corporation (successor to Stevenson Newhall's Pennsylvania Company), with 112,000 shares worth about $1.8 million; see First Pennsylvania proxy statement for 1975 (in the author's possession).

CHAPTER 9

1. See Binzen, Daughen, and Friedman, *Rise and Fall of the House of Greenfield*, 41, quoting Greenfield's testimony to the Securities and Exchange Commission (SEC) in 1942. Most accounts say the loan to Lit's was secured by 501,000 Lit's common shares, out of a total of 1 million shares. But in a letter of August 27, 1931, Greenfield said the loan was also secured by $6 million of Lit's preferred stock, or half of the total preferred stock of $12 million. Letter from Albert Greenfield to David S. Malis, Esq., August 27, 1931, Historical Society of Pennsylvania (HSP), box 155, folder 3.

2. Letter from Samuel Barker to Albert Greenfield, August 10, 1931, HSP, box 155, folder 2: "The $8 million owing us [from City Stores] constitutes 41% of our assets."

3. Binzen, Daughen, and Friedman, *Rise and Fall of the House of Greenfield*, 40, 47. A *(Memphis) Press-Scimitar* article about R. J. Goerke says City Stores Co. operates "seven large department stores." Eldon F. Roark Jr., "To Succeed, Banish Timidity, Advises Store King Who Did," *(Memphis) Press-Scimitar*, February 28, 1931, HSP, box 160, folder 7. The other stores in the chain were Lit Brothers in Philadelphia (founded 1891), Goerke Co. of Newark (1898), and Goerke-Kirch of Elizabeth, New Jersey (1912); see Binzen, Daughen, and Friedman, *Rise and Fall of the House of Greenfield*, 47.

4. Rudolph J. Goerke obituary, *New York Times*, April 14, 1938. Goerke died April 13.

5. Roark, "To Succeed, Banish Timidity, Advises Store King Who Did."

6. Rudolph J. Goerke obituary. The store was located at Broadway and Bedford Ave.

7. Ibid.

8. See Binzen, Daughen, and Friedman, *Rise and Fall of the House of Greenfield*, 43–44, citing Greenfield's testimony to the SEC in 1941.

9. Binzen, Daughen, and Friedman, *Rise and Fall of the House of Greenfield*, 43. Goerke's son R. J. Jr. was paid $22,000 in 1931, while Howard Goerke received $20,583 and nephew Edmund Goerke was paid $11,000. By contrast, at this time Samuel Barker was earning $10,000 a year as president of both Bankers Securities and Bankers Trust.

10. Roark, "To Succeed, Banish Timidity, Advises Store King Who Did."

11. Binzen, Daughen, and Friedman, *Rise and Fall of the House of Greenfield*, 49, citing letter of City Stores president Paul Saunders to R. J. Goerke, October 6, 1934.

12. Roark, "To Succeed, Banish Timidity, Advises Store King Who Did."

13. Ibid.

14. Binzen, Daughen, and Friedman, *Rise and Fall of the House of Greenfield*, 44.

15. Ibid., 46, 48. The $2.2 million loss was for the fiscal year ended January 31, 1932. City Stores lost another $1.7 million the following year, ending January 31, 1933.

16. Albert Greenfield, memo to himself, April 2, 1931, HSP, box 160, folder 7.

17. A letter from Samuel Barker to Albert Greenfield on August 10, 1931, cites the amount due to Bankers Securities at that point as $8 million and to Halsey Stuart as $2.8 million. HSP, box 155, folder 2. Binzen and his colleagues erroneously say that the principal amount due to Bankers Securities had been reduced by mid-1931 from $8 million to $7.5 million, while City Stores had trimmed its $5 million loan from Halsey Stuart down to $2.5 million. See Binzen, Daughen, and Friedman, *Rise and Fall of the House of Greenfield*, 42. But the reduction they cite actually occurred in January 1932. See the letter from Paul H. Saunders to City Stores stockholders on February 6, 1932, when City Stores' debt to Bankers Securities was reduced from $8 million to $7,407,500. HSP, box 171, folder 2.

18. Letter from Samuel Barker to Albert Greenfield, August 10, 1931.

19. Ibid.

20. Letter from Albert Greenfield to Samuel Barker, August 11, 1931, HSP, box 155, folder 2.

21. Alfred Blasband, interview by Peter Binzen, 1985, p. 2.

22. Letter from Samuel Barker to Albert Greenfield, July 10, 1931, HSP, box 155, folder 3.

23. Letter from Albert Greenfield to Samuel Barker, July 15, 1931, HSP, box 155, folder 3.

24. Letter from Samuel Barker to Albert Greenfield, November 7, 1931, HSP, box 155, folder 2.

25. Letter from Albert Greenfield to Samuel Barker, November 9, 1931, HSP, box 155, folder 2.

26. Harrison, "Mr. Philadelphia," 108. At this point City Stores owned some two hundred thousand shares of Lit Brothers common stock and $1.5 million worth of Lit Brothers preferred. The action failed to produce the funds necessary to avoid default.

27. Binzen and colleagues refer to the Bankers Securities board minutes of November 18, 1931, as the source. See Binzen, Daughen, and Friedman, *Rise and Fall of the House of Greenfield*, 44–45.

28. Binzen, Daughen, and Friedman, *Rise and Fall of the House of Greenfield*, 44. Greenfield does not appear to have exercised his right to the 501,000 Lit's shares as collateral when

City Stores defaulted on the $8 million loan from Bankers Securities on December 1, 1931; the $8 million debt was still listed on the books of City Stores after that date.

29. Letter from R. J. Goerke to City Stores stockholders, November 20, 1931, HSP, box 160, folder 8.

30. Binzen, Daughen, and Friedman, *Rise and Fall of the House of Greenfield*, 44–46. See also the letter to City Stores stockholders from its president, Paul H. Saunders, on February 6, 1932, detailing the agreement among City Stores, Bankers Securities, and Halsey Stuart. As part of the agreement, City Stores' debt to Bankers Securities was reduced slightly, from $8 million to $7,407,500. HSP, box 171, folder 2.

31. Binzen, Daughen, and Friedman, *Rise and Fall of the House of Greenfield*, 46.

32. Ibid., 50. The reorganization plan was approved by City Stores creditors and stockholders on October 28, 1934, and by the U.S. District Court on December 20, 1934.

33. Binzen, Daughen, and Friedman, *Rise and Fall of the House of Greenfield*, 79.

34. Ibid., 81.

35. Harrison, "Mr. Philadelphia," 111. The years refer to fiscal years ending January 31. In the previous fiscal year, ended January 31, 1932, City Stores lost $2.2 million; see Binzen, Daughen, and Friedman, *Rise and Fall of the House of Greenfield*, 46.

36. Davenport, "Philadelphia," 192. Lit Brothers acquired half of radio station WFIL.

37. Harrison, "Mr. Philadelphia," 111. The four prior unprofitable years are deduced from various Lit Brothers balance sheets. As of February 1, 1932, for example, Lit's reported net assets of $23,171,416, down by $4,875,571 from February 1, 1931. HSP, box 170, folder 2.

38. Boyd Barnard, interview by the author, October 20, 1975; Gustave G. Amsterdam, interview by the author, October 30, 1975.

39. Harrison, "Mr. Philadelphia," 112. Other properties that fell under Bankers Securities' control in the 1930s included the Ritz-Carlton, Warwick, and Majestic Hotels in Philadelphia, and the Ritz-Carlton in Atlantic City.

40. *Philadelphia Bulletin*, June 1, 1933. This item may also reflect Greenfield's developing friendship with Edward Hopkinson, who was gradually assuming E. T. Stotesbury's duties as senior partner at Drexel & Co. It could also, of course, be seen as evidence that Stotesbury bore Greenfield no personal ill will in the first place.

41. Letter from Joseph Wayne Jr. to George Roosevelt, Roosevelt & Sons, June 6, 1933, HSP, box 182, folder 4.

42. Letter from C. Stevenson Newhall to George Roosevelt, Roosevelt & Sons, June 6, 1933, HSP, box 181, folder 22.

43. Gustave G. Amsterdam, interview by Peter Binzen, 1985.

44. "Memo from Mr. Greenfield" to Maurice Wurzel, November 13, 1936 (in the author's possession).

45. Letter from Edna's secretary to Rena Mayer (Edna's aunt) in Chicago, February 11, 1932, HSP, box 168, folder 9.

46. Letter from May Schamberg (Mrs. Jay) to Edna Greenfield, June 19, 1932, HSP, box 168, folder 9; letter from Edna to "Blink," 1932, HSP, box 168, folder 10. Stony Lodge is described as a "private psychiatric facility" in Skwersky, *Knight of Philadelphia*, 120. Until 2012 it provided in-patient psychiatric care to children and adolescents.

47. Letter from Albert Greenfield to Edna Greenfield, December 6, 1934, HSP, box 168, folder 9.

48. The affair was mentioned to the author by several of Greenfield's relatives; see also Alfred DiGiovanni, interview by Peter Binzen, 1985.

49. Edna married Paine on October 28, 1935, in Ciudad Juárez, Mexico. See "Mrs. Greenfield Divorced, Reweds." The dispatch, dated November 6, says Edna was divorced the previous week and married Paine after receiving the divorce decree. Also see "Mrs. Greenfield Obtains Divorce." The date of her wedding to Paine appears in "Seeks Reno Divorce," 1936 newspaper clipping, HSP, box 245, folder 5. Little is known about Paine, but he may have been a doctor; see DiGiovanni, interview by Binzen.

50. "Seeks Reno Divorce," cited in Skwersky, *Knight of Philadelphia*, 122.

51. Barbara Greenfield, interview by the author, July 18, 2011.

52. References to the $800 monthly arrangement appear often in Greenfield's correspondence with Edna after 1935. For example, a December 23, 1952, letter to Edna at Prangins, Switzerland, apparently from Greenfield's secretary, Lillian Maeder, details canceled checks for Edna's account. It appears to indicate that Greenfield was sending Edna $800 each month. HSP, box 562, folder 12. Greenfield also specified a lifetime payment of $800 per month for Edna in his will; see Albert Greenfield will, 1967, Register of Wills office, Philadelphia City Hall, Will #131, p. 7.

53. Note apparently written by Edna K. Paine, scribbled in a copy of William B. Terhune, "Adaptation," bk. 1, 1938, HSP, box 338, folder 14.

54. William B. Terhune, "The Nature of Nervousness," bk. 4, 1938, HSP, box 338, folder 15.

55. Morris, *American Catholic*, 188; see also Harrison, "Mr. Philadelphia," 127. Dougherty died in 1951.

56. Binzen, Daughen, and Friedman, *Rise and Fall of the House of Greenfield*, 112.

57. Davenport, "Philadelphia," 192.

CHAPTER 10

1. Harrison, "Mr. Philadelphia," 116.

2. Stern, *Memoirs of a Maverick Publisher*, 200.

3. Harrison, "Mr. Philadelphia," 115–116.

4. Stern, *Memoirs of a Maverick Publisher*, 200.

5. Guffey (1870–1959) subsequently represented Pennsylvania in the U.S. Senate from 1935 to 1947. Lawrence (1889–1966) subsequently served as mayor of Pittsburgh (1946–1959) and governor of Pennsylvania (1959–1963).

6. Stern, *Memoirs of a Maverick Publisher*, 200–201.

7. Harrison, "Mr. Philadelphia," 117.

8. Ibid., 118–119. Barely a month into his term, Roosevelt took the United States off the gold standard altogether. Executive Order 6102, signed April 5, 1933, criminalized possession of monetary gold.

9. Harrison, "Mr. Philadelphia," 123. Morgenthau (1891–1967) was Roosevelt's secretary of the Treasury from 1934 to 1945. Frankfurter (1882–1965) was nominated to the Supreme Court by FDR in 1939 and served there until 1962. Cohen (1894–1983) and Rosenman (1896–1973) served in the administrations of FDR and Harry Truman. Baruch (1870–1965) advised Woodrow Wilson on defense issues during World War I and was later appointed a special adviser to the Office of War Mobilization by Roosevelt. Hillman (1887–1946) was appointed to the National Defense Advisory Committee in 1940.

10. Harrison, "Mr. Philadelpia,"123.

11. *Philadelphia Record* advertising circular, 1935, Historical Society of Pennsylvania (HSP), box 204, folder 8.

12. Davenport, "Philadelphia," 194.

13. *Philadelphia Record* advertising circular. For comparable circulation figures for the two papers in 1936 and 1937, see Cooney, The Annenbergs, 119.

14. Stern, *Memoirs of a Maverick Publisher*, 215–220.

15. Harrison, "Mr. Philadelpia,"128–132. Wilson received 379,299 votes in the election and Kelly 333,811.

16. Harrison, "Mr. Philadelphia," 131–134.

17. Ibid., 134.

18. Rottenberg, "Once There Was Greenfield," 177C. Boyd Barnard of the rival Jackson-Cross firm, for example, said, "Many people resented the way he switched parties. He left the GOP when the going got rough." Boyd Barnard, interview by the author, October 20, 1975.

19. Harrison, "Mr. Philadelphia," 134.

20. William W. Cutler III, quoted in the Albert Greenfield biography film *Mr. Philadelphia.*

21. Alfred Blasband, in an interview by Peter Binzen (1985, p. 2), described the Philadelphia Company for Guaranteeing Mortgages as part of "the bank fraternity in Philadelphia" that resented Greenfield and "would not do anything to help him." That company was established in 1907; the author's search of its pamphlets and annual reports turned up no prominent names among its directors or officers. See HSP, box wi*, folder 796.

22. Thomas LaBrum, interview by the author, October 15, 1975.

23. Letter from Albert Greenfield to Robert M. Hutchins, president of the Fund for the Republic, December 15, 1959, HSP, box 739, folder 4.

24. Peg Sonenfeld, "Albert Greenfield, Quakertown Dynamo, Adds District Hookup," *Washington Post*, September 16, 1951, HSP, box 503, folder 5.

25. Elizabeth Petrie, interview by the author, October 27, 1975.

26. Letter from Albert Greenfield to Robert M. Hutchins.

27. D. Herbert Lipson, quoted in the film *Mr. Philadelphia.*

28. Baltzell, *An American Business Aristocracy*, 222–223. The address was 6399 Drexel Road. Geist had moved to the Main Line in 1933. Serena Skwersky says that Greenfield moved to Drexel Road in November 1936. See *Knight of Philadelphia*, 125. Greenfield married Etelka Schamberg in the Drexel Road house on October 1, 1937; see "A. M. Greenfield Weds." For background about Overbrook Farms, see d'Apéry, *Overbrook Farms*, and http://www.uchs .net/HistoricDistricts/overbrook.html.

29. Baltzell, *An American Business Aristocracy*, 151. Geist moved out in 1933 and died in 1938. Robert Greenfield, Albert's nephew and lawyer, referred to Greenfield's negative feelings about the Main Line in several conversations with the author in 2011 and 2012.

30. Peter Binzen, personal notes. As of this writing, the house at 6399 Drexel Road is the headquarters of the National Catholic Bioethics Center. The house and car are also described in, among others, Sonenfeld, "Albert Greenfield, Quakertown Dynamo."

31. Edna obtained her divorce from Albert October 28, 1935; Jesse Schamberg died December 22, 1935. See Jesse J. Schamberg obituary, *New York Times*, December 23, 1935.

32. Letter from Jesse Schamberg to Albert Greenfield, October 3, 1925, HSP, box 90, folder 4; letter from Jesse Schamberg to Albert Greenfield, May 11, 1927, HSP, box 90, folder 4.

33. A note from Jesse Schamberg to Albert Greenfield on September 11, 1921, refers to purchases and expenses they incurred with their wives in Karlsbad and Vienna. HSP, box 28, folder 2.

34. Impressions of Jesse and Etelka Schamberg are from interviews by the author with Boyd Barnard, October 20, 1975; Irwin Solomon, October 15, 1975; Serena Skwersky, August 4, 2011; and Janet Guth, October 26, 2011.

35. Etelka Joseph Schamberg Greenfield obituary, *New York Times*, May 30, 1949. Etelka was born in 1887, Hetty Goldman in 1881, and Iphigene Ochs in 1893.

36. The marriage took place October 1, 1937, at Greenfield's home at 6399 Drexel Road. See "A. M. Greenfield Weds."

37. Skwersky, *Knight of Philadelphia*, 125–126. The painting hangs in the Philadelphia Museum of Art.

38. Binzen, Daughen, and Friedman, *Rise and Fall of the House of Greenfield*, 116. Yvonne Schamberg married Robert I. D. Straus at Greenfield's home on December 11, 1938; see their wedding announcement, HSP, box 260, folder 9; also box 267, folder 11.

39. Lazar Raditz (1887–1956), born in Russia, taught art at the Philadelphia Sketch Club and the Salamagundi Club. He also lived in New York.

40. Janet Guth, Greenfield's oldest granddaughter, said she learned painting from Etelka at Oak Crest and often visited Greenfield at Oak Crest when Etelka was not there. Janet Guth, interview by the author, October 26, 2011.

41. Dorothy Garrotson, profile of Albert Greenfield, *Philadelphia*, March 1947, HSP, box 394, folder 13.

42. Stern, *Memoirs of a Maverick Publisher*, 237.

43. Hearst launched his evening *Chicago American* in 1900 and the morning *Chicago Examiner* in 1902; Emery and Smith, *The Press and America,* 461.

44. Fonzi, *Annenberg*, 61; Stern, *Memoirs of a Maverick Publisher*, 237-238.

45. Fonzi, *Annenberg*, 61. Max and Moses Annenberg were hired away by the rival *Chicago Tribune* in 1910, bringing with them such thugs as "Mossy" Enright, Red Connors, Walter Stevens, and others who later became prominent in Chicago's gang wars. The Hearst papers responded by hiring their own gang of gunmen. Swanberg, *Citizen Hearst*, 271.

46. Fonzi, *Annenberg*, 63. Moses Annenberg had eight children; his only son was his youngest child, Walter, born in 1908.

47. Cooney, *The Annenbergs*, 65, 77-80.

48. Stern, *Memoirs of a Maverick Publisher*, 239.

49. Fonzi, *Annenberg,* 115.

50. In *Memoirs of a Maverick Publisher*, David Stern says Annenberg was making $14 million a year (see p. 238); Gaeton Fonzi says Annenberg's annual income was "as high as $6 million" (see *Annenberg*, 78).

51. Cooney, *The Annenbergs*, 99. In 1940, when he pleaded guilty to tax evasion in exchange for the government's dropping charges against Walter, Moses Annenberg explained, "I have always had great ambitions for Walter. I purchased the *Inquirer* and have built it up with his future in mind. That's the only thing I'm interested in, and if I can spare Walter the trial, I won't mind doing a year in jail." See Cooney, *The Annenbergs*, 145.

52. Stern, *Memoirs of a Maverick Publisher*, 237. Harold "Red" Grange (1903-1991) was a college and professional football star with the University of Illinois and the Chicago Bears. In 2008, he was named the best college football player of all time by ESPN.

53. Cooney, *The Annenbergs*, 111.

54. Stern, *Memoirs of a Maverick Publisher*, 242; Cooney, *The Annenbergs*, 119.

55. Greenfield said Annenberg's refusal to accept ads from Lit Brothers began in August 1936. See letter from Albert Greenfield to David C. Matt, October 25, 1938, HSP, box 265, folder 8.

56. Stern, *Memoirs of a Maverick Publisher*, 241.

57. Harrison, "Mr. Philadelphia," 138. The other Philadelphia papers were the *Record*, the *Bulletin*, and the *Daily News*.

58. Stern, *Memoirs of a Maverick Publisher*, 241; Cooney, *The Annenbergs*, 107.

59. Stern, *Memoirs of a Maverick Publisher*, 242.

60. Harrison, "Mr. Philadelphia," 138. The apartment is described in Cooney, *The Annenbergs*, 115.

61. Cooney, *The Annenbergs*, 110. Cooney does not cite a source for this anecdote. Greenfield later claimed that he met Annenberg for the first time the previous fall, in October 1936, at which time Greenfield "freely expressed to him my regret that before I met him, and before his arrival in Philadelphia, I had allowed myself to believe some of the things that were printed about him in out-of-town publications and had referred to him in derogatory terms." See letter from Greenfield to Matt.

62. Binzen, Daughen, and Friedman, *Rise and Fall of the House of Greenfield*, 83.

63. Stern, *Memoirs of a Maverick Publisher*, 242.

64. Letter from M. L. Annenberg to Albert Greenfield, April 8, 1937, HSP, box 265, folder 9.

65. Harrison, "Mr. Philadelphia," 138.

66. Andrew Harrison says the attacks began in the summer of 1937 (see "Mr. Philadelphia," 139); Greenfield says the same in his letter to David C. Matt of October 25, 1938. However, a note to Annenberg of July 21, 1938, which Greenfield never sent, refers to Annenberg's attacks on him "ever since last October"; see HSP, box 265, folder 9. See also Harrison, "Mr. Philadelphia," 139; Cooney, *The Annenbergs*, 110.

67. Unsent draft of letter from Albert Greenfield to M. L. Annenberg, July 21, 1938, HSP, box 265, folder 9.

68. Fonzi, *Annenberg*, 92. The law was passed in August 1938.

69. Harrison, "Mr. Philadelphia," 140.

70. Ibid., 140-141.

71. Albert Greenfield radio address sponsored by Democratic City Committee, September 21, 1938, HSP, box 266, folder 9. See also Harrison, "Mr. Philadelphia," 142.

72. "Greenfield Assails *Inquirer* Publisher."

73. Annenberg filed a civil suit for libel and slander against Greenfield and Senator Guffey on October 13, 1938. See Harrison, "Mr. Philadelphia," 144; see also "Annenberg Files $700,000 Claim," unidentified newspaper clipping, October 13, 1938. Greenfield issued a public statement about Annenberg's impending libel suit on October 8, 1938, noting that it had not yet been served. HSP, box 265, folder 9.

74. Daniel G. Murphy, KYW radio address with statewide hookup, October 13, 1938; "Greenfield's Firm Drew $300,000 from Bankers Trust, Lawyer Says"; Albert Greenfield, "The Closing of Bankers Trust," WFIL radio address, October 17, 1938, pp. 2-3, HSP, box 238, folder 10.

75. Greenfield, "The Closing of Bankers Trust," 9-10.

76. Ibid., 11.

77. Fonzi, *Annenberg*, 87.

78. Ironically, both Greenfield and Annenberg belonged to the same congregation, Keneseth Israel. Despite their mutual admiration for Rabbi William Fineshriber, they do not appear to have approached him to mediate their dispute. See Arlin Adams, "Preserving the Voices of History," interview by the Feinstein Center, February 6, 1996, p. 22, Temple University Urban Archives (TUUA).

79. Letter from Morris Goodblatt to Albert Greenfield, October 21, 1938, HSP, box 244, folder 15; box 265, folder 8; quoted in Harrison, "Mr. Philadelphia," 146-147.

80. Elizabeth Zeidman, interview by the author, October 19, 1975, pp. 6-7.

81. Letter from Albert Greenfield to Morris Goodblatt and David C. Matt, October 25, 1938, HSP, box 265, folder 8; also quoted in Harrison, "Mr. Philadelphia," 147.

82. Letter from Stanley Folz to Lemuel B. Schofield, April 13, 1939, and May 5, 1939, HSP, box 265, folder 10.

83. Cooney, *The Annenbergs*, 145, 147; Harrison, "Mr. Philadelphia," 151. Binzen and colleagues say Annenberg paid a total of $10 million. See *Rise and Fall of the House of Greenfield*, 125.

84. Fonzi, *Annenberg*, 96.

85. Robert Greenfield, interview by the author, October 5, 2011. See also Harrison, "Mr. Philadelphia," 151.

86. Unmailed letter from Albert Greenfield to Edward Leech, December 13, 1941, HSP, box 309, folder 2; Stern, *Memoirs of a Maverick Publisher*, 243.

87. Binzen, *Richardson Dilworth*, citing the diary of Treasury Secretary Henry L. Morgenthau.

88. Stern, *Memoirs of a Maverick Publisher*, 243.

89. Binzen, Daughen, and Friedman, *Rise and Fall of the House of Greenfield*, 125.

90. Stern, *Memoirs of a Maverick Publisher*, 243.

91. See McFarland, "Banking's Bell."

92. John C. Bell Jr., public announcement, June 1, 1940 (in the author's possession).

93. Greenfield's statement concerning his bankruptcy, May 15, 1940, listed a total of nearly $11 million in debts: $6,378,032.76 in personal liabilities and $4,604,363.42 owed by his personal Albert Co. See Harrison, "Mr. Philadelphia," 157. See also "Insolvent Plea by Greenfield Blocks Suits."

94. For Kalodner's background, see Harrison, "Mr. Philadelphia," 157; see also Stern, *Memoirs of a Maverick Publisher*, 184-185; Binzen, Daughen, and Friedman, *Rise and Fall of the House of Greenfield*, 126. Whether Kalodner received Greenfield's case coincidentally by lot (as Stern's *Record* reported) or by political manipulation remains a mystery.

95. Harrison notes that at the first meeting with the federal bankruptcy referee, John M. Hill, Greenfield reduced the payoff period to fifteen years, but Bell rejected this period too as

excessively long. See "Mr. Philadelphia," 158. See also "State Attacks Payment Plan by Green-field."

96. Binzen, Daughen, and Friedman, *Rise and Fall of the House of Greenfield*, 127.

97. Harrison, "Mr. Philadelphia," 158–159.

98. Ibid., 160.

99. Letter from Irland Beckman to Albert Greenfield, January 24, 1939, HSP, box 256, folder 6.

100. Letter from Albert Greenfield to Irland Beckman, January 27, 1939, HSP, box 256, folder 6.

101. Albert Greenfield public statement, ca. May 10, 1939, HSP, box 265, folder 9.

CHAPTER 11

1. Binzen, Daughen, and Friedman, *Rise and Fall of the House of Greenfield*, 110, quoting Albert Greenfield's announcement upon purchasing the *Jewish World*.

2. Barbara Greenfield, "Albert M. Greenfield," 4; Harrison, "Mr. Philadelphia," 75.

3. See correspondence between Albert Greenfield and Jacob Ginsburg, 1924, Historical Society of Pennsylvania (HSP), box 36, folder 20. Also see Robert Greenfield, interview by the author, October 5, 2011; Binzen, Daughen, and Friedman, *Rise and Fall of the House of Greenfield*, 110.

4. Letter from Albert Greenfield to Saul Cohn, August 23, 1933, quoted in Harrison, "Mr. Philadelphia," 171–172.

5. Ibid.

6. Albert Greenfield, "What American Jews Can Learn from the Jewish Tragedy in Germany," public statement, 1935, cited in Harrison, "Mr. Philadelphia," 172–173.

7. Letter from Albert Greenfield to Gustavus Kirby, February 18, 1936, cited in Harrison, "Mr. Philadelphia," 173.

8. Letter from Albert Greenfield to Franklin D. Roosevelt, November 17, 1938, cited in Harrison, "Mr. Philadelphia," 174.

9. Harrison, "Mr. Philadelphia," 174.

10. Ibid., 237. Robert Greenfield, in our October 5, 2011, interview, said that Albert "didn't want to be identified as anti-Jewish but didn't attach much importance to it [Judaism]." Emily Sunstein, in our October 14, 1975, interview, said that Greenfield was "not religious in the formal sense but very interested in Jewish culture."

11. Robert Greenfield, interview by the author. He said Greenfield held the same views as William. He also noted that William became a bar mitzvah; Albert apparently did not.

12. Harrison, "Mr. Philadelphia," 241.

13. Barbara Greenfield, interview by the author, July 18, 2011. She recalled the butler's name, circa 1950, as O'Rourke. But the U.S. census for 1940 lists James J. O'Brien as Green-field's butler.

14. For a further discussion of the role of private schools in molding America's upper class, see Baltzell, *The Protestant Establishment*, 127–129.

15. Harrison, "Mr. Philadelphia," 22. Oak Lane went up to eighth or ninth grade when Greenfield's children attended. Later it went only as high as sixth grade.

16. Letter from Albert Greenfield to Edna Greenfield, October 4, 1934, HSP, box 188, folder 20. Carlotta was born May 6, 1920.

17. A letter of December 7, 1936, to Greenfield from Baldwin's associate headmistress, Harriette Dryden Jones, refers to Carlotta as "one of the new girls." HSP, box 238, folder 7.

18. Letter from Albert Greenfield to Edna Paine, June 1, 1938, HSP, box 249, folder 10. Patsy instead followed her sister Carlotta to Baldwin, where she graduated in 1941; Priscilla Luce (Patsy's daughter), e-mail message to the author, November 5, 2012. Presumably, Patsy was finishing ninth grade—her final year—at Oak Lane in June 1938.

19. Binzen, Daughen, and Friedman, *Rise and Fall of the House of Greenfield*, 118. Rosen-baum was also a Philadelphia Orchestra board member; see Welsh, *One Woman in a Hundred*, 126–127.

20. Binzen, Daughen, and Friedman, *Rise and Fall of the House of Greenfield*, 118.

21. Alfred Blasband, Greenfield's longtime lieutenant, told me in 1975 that Greenfield privately blamed the Bankers Trust failure on anti-Semitism but refused to say so in public.

22. "Want Greenfield Fired as Chairman," *Philadelphia Bulletin*, January 28, 1937, HSP, box 227, folder 6; "Governor Earle, Mr. Greenfield and the P.O.S. of A.," *Jewish Exponent*, February 5, 1937, HSP, box 227, folder 6.

23. Albert Greenfield, public response, January 28, 1937, HSP, box 227, folder 6.

24. Estimates of the total number killed in World War II vary from 50 million to 70 million. See, for example, "Counting the Cost," 87.

25. On June 3, 1940, just two weeks after Greenfield filed for bankruptcy protection, the Greenfield interests acquired 473,400 of Loft Candy Corporation's 1,473,2590 shares—less than one-third of Loft's outstanding stock but sufficient to constitute control. Greenfield himself invested none of his own money. Albert M. Greenfield & Co. bought 50,000 shares; Bankers Securities bought 22,700; David Stern's *Philadelphia Record* and *Camden Courier-Post* bought 20,000 shares; Bonwit Teller & Co. of Philadelphia, controlled by Greenfield, bought 60,000; Greenfield's lawyer and childhood friend, David Bortin, bought 20,000; and Greenfield's top real estate executive, George H. Johnson, bought 11,000. See Binzen, Daughen, and Friedman, *Rise and Fall of the House of Greenfield*, 130; see also Harrison, "Mr. Philadelphia," 169–170; "Greenfield and Aides Buy Control of Loft's."

26. Binzen, Daughen, and Friedman, *Rise and Fall of the House of Greenfield*, 131.

27. "Democracy's Arsenal," 92.

28. "C. J. Ingersoll Defense Boss," *Philadelphia Ledger*, October 24, 1940, HSP, box 280, folder 2. Ingersoll was president of Muskogee Company, a holding company for western railroads; he was also a director of the Pennsylvania Railroad, the Girard Trust, Western Saving Fund Society, and the Mutual Insurance Company.

29. Rottenberg, "The Last Run of the Rock Island Line," 197. Crown was born in Lithuania in 1896.

30. Harrison, "Mr. Philadelphia," 160.

31. Greenfield later turned down offers of at least two ambassadorships—one to Turkey and one, after the 1948 election, to the Soviet Union—on the ground that he functioned best at what he knew best, and what he knew best was Philadelphia. Brecht, "The Greenfield Story"; John O'Shea, interview by the author, October 15, 1975.

32. Letter from Albert Greenfield to Gustave G. Amsterdam, August 2, 1943, HSP, box 315, folder 4.

33. These were the so-called B'rith Sholom children, named for the Jewish service organization that sponsored this exodus. Gilbert Kraus (1898–1975) was Edna Kraus Greenfield Paine's younger brother. He secured unused American visas through the help of his friend Francis Biddle, a Philadelphian who two years later became U.S. Attorney General. In 1939 Kraus and his wife, Eleanor, traveled secretly with a pediatrician and a nurse to Austria, where they interviewed some six hundred Jewish children to assess which ones were best suited to endure emigration to America and separation from their parents for an extended period. See Schiavo, "Those Saved from Nazis Honor a Hero"; Brown, "A Four-Month Mitzvah Saving 50 Children."

34. Telegram from Berlin to Americans Friends Service Committee, August 14, 1939, HSP, box 280, folder 5; letter from Albert Greenfield to Henry Katz, September 27, 1939, HSP, box 280, folder 5; letter from Albert Greenfield to G. M. Szalet, February 7, 1941, HSP, box 308, folder 8.

35. Letter from Paul Fantl to Albert Greenfield, April 26, 1939, HSP, box 280, folder 5; letter from Lillian Maeder to Paul Fantl, May 10, 1939, HSP, box 280, folder 5.

36. Harrison, "Mr. Philadelphia," 175.

37. Letter from Albert Greenfield to Edna Paine, June 1, 1938, HSP, box 249, folder 10. See also Harrison, "Mr. Philadelphia," 174–175.

38. Kolsky, "The Opposition to Zionism," 81.

39. Letter from Horace Stern to Albert Greenfield, April 25, 1923 (in the author's possession). Stern (1878–1969) later became chief justice of the Pennsylvania Supreme Court; Weizmann (1874–1952) later became the first president of the State of Israel.

40. Letter from Albert Greenfield to Jacob Edelstein, April 29, 1924, cited in Harrison, "Mr. Philadelphia," 76.

41. Letters from Isaac Serota to Albert Greenfield, May 14 and 31, 1929, HSP, box 126, folder 5; letter from Albert Greenfield to Isaac Serota, June 3, 1929, HSP, box 126, folder 5.

42. Letter from Albert Greenfield to William M. Lewis, April 24, 1926, quoted in Harrison, "Mr. Philadelphia," 76.

43. Harrison, "Mr. Philadelphia," 76–77. Greenfield raised about $105,000 of the total of $123,000 raised in the Philadelphia area, and he personally contributed $1,000.

44. Kolsky, "The Opposition to Zionism," 82–83.

45. William H. Fineshriber (1878–1968) was senior rabbi at Keneseth Israel from 1924 to 1949.

46. Kolsky, "The Opposition to Zionism," 88.

47. Thomas Kolsky, e-mail message to the author, August 24, 2012.

48. Harrison, "Mr. Philadelphia," 175.

49. Letter from Albert Greenfield to Gustave G. Amsterdam, February 10, 1945, HSP, box 345, folder 8. Amsterdam appears to have been stationed in France at the time, although no address is specified.

50. Peg Sonenfeld, "Albert Greenfield, Quakertown Dynamo, Adds District Hookup," *Washington Post*, September 16, 1951, HSP, box 503, folder 5. Strangely, in this interview Greenfield apparently overlooked Washington, Lincoln, and even his personal hero, Benjamin Franklin, in his list of great Americans.

51. Truman's other good Jewish friends included Abraham Feinberg of New York, Jacob H. Blaustein of Baltimore, and Dewey Stone of Boston. See letter from Louis E. Levinthal to Elizabeth Greenfield, July 22, 1968, HSP, box 417, folder 3.

52. Stern, *Memoirs of a Maverick Publisher*, 299–300.

53. Letter from Albert Greenfield to Etelka Greenfield, February 12, 1947, HSP, box 395, folder 14, quoted in Skwersky, *Knight of Philadelphia*, 126.

54. Jonathan Stern (son of J. David Stern), interview by the author, October 18, 2012.

55. Harrison, "Mr. Philadelphia," 190.

56. "Purchase of Camden Papers Due in Week."

57. According to Stern, the deciding factor was neither the strike at the *Record* nor Greenfield's urging but Stern's bitterness over a new strike launched in January 1947 at the *Camden Courier-Post* by its typographers' union. The *Bulletin* bought both papers from Stern. See Stern, *Memoirs of a Maverick Publisher*, 300.

58. Stern, *Memoirs of a Maverick Publisher*, 301. The *Bulletin* also bought Stern's *Camden Courier-Post*, which it continued to publish.

59. Harrison, "Mr. Philadelphia," 193–194.

60. J. Howard McGrath, chairman of the Democratic National Committee, convention statement, July 12, 1948, quoted in Harrison, "Mr. Philadelphia," 195–196.

61. Rosen, "Philadelphia Jewry and the Creation of Israel," 71. Also see letter from Levinthal to Elizabeth Greenfield.

62. Kolsky, "The Opposition to Zionism," 80.

63. The armies of Egypt, Syria, Jordan, Lebanon, Iraq, and Saudi Arabia invaded Israel on May 15, 1948.

64. Lyons, "The Second Shall Be First." The three polling organizations were Gallup, Roper, and Crosley; the Roper Poll was so certain of Dewey's forthcoming victory that it ceased conducting polls more than a month before the election.

65. Harrison, "Mr. Philadelphia," citing interviews with Abraham Feinberg and Greenfield's assistant, John O'Shea. Harrison expresses doubt as to whether this chain of events occurred exactly as it was related to him but concludes that "the story demonstrates Greenfield's financial importance during the campaign" (198).

66. "Lowdown and Inside" column, *Observer*, October 11, 1948, HSP, box 415, folder 4.

67. Letter from Harry Truman to Albert Greenfield, October 2, 1948, collection of Albert M. Greenfield III.

68. Bernadotte's second plan for resolution of the Israeli-Arab conflict was proposed on September 16, 1948. He was assassinated the next day by the LEHI Group, a Hebrew acronym for "Freedom Fighters of Israel," better known as the "Stern Gang." The Stern Gang refused to be held accountable to any Zionist organization, although one of its leaders, Yitzhak Shamir, later became Israel's prime minister.

69. For Levinthal's background, see Rosen, "Philadelphia Jewry and the Holocaust," 42. In the 1920s, Levinthal was a partner of Greenfield's lawyer, Lemuel B. Schofield, and Greenfield's brother-in-law, Gilbert J. Kraus, in the three-man firm of Levinthal, Schofield, and Kraus; see, for example, the firm's letterhead of April 14, 1924, HSP, box 50, folder 15.

70. Letter from Levinthal to Elizabeth Greenfield, July 29, 1968, HSP, box 417, folder 3.

71. Ibid.; "Truman Reaffirms Stand on Israel," 1.

72. Ibid. Truman won the 1948 presidential election with 49.6 percent of the popular vote, against 45.1 percent for Dewey. Dewey carried both New York (his home state) and Pennsylvania, but Truman won other states with large Jewish populations, such as Illinois, California, Massachusetts, and Florida.

73. Harrison, "Mr. Philadelphia," 200.

74. Brecht, "The Greenfield Story"; see also the author's interview with John O'Shea, Greenfield's public relations assistant from 1955 to 1964.

CHAPTER 12

1. John O'Shea, interview by the author, October 15, 1975, p. 2. O'Shea was Greenfield's personal assistant from 1955 to 1964; presumably this incident occurred during that time.

2. O'Shea, interview by the author, 1; D. Herbert Lipson, interview by the author, October 15, 1975.

3. *Philadelphia Bulletin*, December 19, 1951. Bankers Securities began investing in Hoving Corp. in 1946 and bought a 42 percent interest in 1951, leading to its eventual control of Hoving. Bankers Securities sold its 65 percent interest to United Shoe in July 1956 for $10.3 million. See *Philadelphia Bulletin*, July 19, 1956, p. 37; also see "General Shoe Buys Hoving Corp. Control from Bankers Securities"; Binzen, Daughen, and Friedman, *Rise and Fall of the House of Greenfield*, 156; and Harrison, "Mr. Philadelphia," 222. Greenfield's Bankers Securities already controlled the Bonwit Teller store in Philadelphia since 1921; see letter from Albert Greenfield to Harry Sundheim, April 9, 1921, Historical Society of Pennsylvania (HSP), box 6, folder 15.

4. Harris, *Merchant Princes*, 88–89. Also cited in Harrison, "Mr. Philadelphia," 259.

5. See Veblen, *The Theory of the Leisure Class*.

6. Peg Sonenfield, "Albert Greenfield, Quakertown Dynamo," *Washington Post*, September 16, 1951, HSP, box 503, folder 5.

7. In his terminal delirium during his final hospital stay, Greenfield was overheard speaking a steady stream of Yiddish to himself, an apparent throwback to his childhood. Robert Greenfield, interviews by the author, October 5, 2011, and November 21, 2012.

8. Boyd Barnard, interview by the author, October 20, 1975; O'Shea, interview by the author; D. Herbert Lipson, interview by the author, October 15, 1975; Elizabeth Petrie, interview by the author, October 27, 1975.

9. Alice Martell (Grace Fried's daughter), interview by the author, July 25, 2011; see also Robert Greenfield (Grace Fried's brother), interview by the author, October 3, 2011.

10. Gustave G. Amsterdam, interview by the author, September 25, 1975.

11. Robert Greenfield, interview by the author, October 17, 2011.

12. Ibid.

13. Skwersky, *Knight of Philadelphia*, 1–2. Skwersky's father was one of the Shanken brothers.

14. Harrison, "Mr. Philadelphia," 50.

15. Letter from Albert Greenfield to Horace LeLand Wiggins, November 14, 1924, quoted in Harrison, "Mr. Philadelphia," 50.

16. Letter from Albert Greenfield to leasing department, Mastbaum Brothers & Fleisher, April 16, 1921, HSP, box 4, folder 19.

17. Harrison, "Mr. Philadelphia," 51.

18. Bryn Mawr Summer School Concert program, June 1924, HSP, box 49, folder 7.

19. *Philadelphia Bulletin*, October 1, 1951, p. 10.

20. Elizabeth Petrie, interview by the author, October 15, 1975. In *The Lords of Baseball*, the Brooklyn Dodgers traveling secretary Harold Parrott writes that the Ben Franklin rejected the entire Dodger team in 1947 because the club included a black player, Jackie Robinson. If this incident indeed occurred, Greenfield seems to have been unaware of it, and in any case the team soon found lodging at another Bankers Securities hotel, the Bellevue-Stratford.

21. Arlin M. Adams (a retired federal judge), interview by the author, January 23, 2012. The timing is consistent with this scenario. Truman's Executive Order 9981, which desegregated the U.S. Armed Forces, was issued on July 25, 1948—shortly after Truman's nomination at the Democratic National Convention, which was held in Philadelphia from July 12 to 14.

22. Robert Greenfield, interview by the author, January 23, 2012; also Adams, interview by the author. The house was located at 650 N. Eighth St. William, who was then sixty-seven, moved full-time into his summer home in Ventnor, New Jersey. Robert Greenfield (William's son) suggests that the initiative to sell the house to Hastie may have come from William rather than Greenfield.

23. Robert Greenfield, interviews by the author, August 25, 2011, and November 21, 2012; see also Adams, interview by the author. The story is also discussed by Adams in the Greenfield biography video, *Mr. Philadelphia*. Greenfield's lunch companion that day, according to Robert Greenfield, was his vice president, John Herd, who presumably provided this story.

24. *Philadelphia Bulletin*, July 1, 1951. See also "Albert Greenfield Has Said," typed manuscript, HSP, box 884, folder 1. The center was created in conjunction with the National Conference of Christians and Jews, another favorite Greenfield cause.

25. Albert Greenfield, "Acceptance Remarks of Mr. Albert M. Greenfield in Introducing Dr. Martin Luther King," Academy of Music, October 24, 1961 (news release from Bankers Securities; in the author's possession).

26. Janet Guth, interview by the author, October 26, 2011.

27. Harris, *Merchant Princes*, 89.

28. Hopkins, "Stormy Monday," 91.

29. Binzen, Daughen, and Friedman, *Rise and Fall of the House of Greenfield*, 103.

30. Bernard Guth, interview by Peter Binzen, 1985.

31. Bob Olson, interview by the author, September 28, 2011. Olson was corporate secretary of Bankers Securities from 1971 to 1973; Johnson made this remark after Greenfield had died.

32. "A Whiz of a Promoter." See also letter from Albert Greenfield to J. J. Cabrey, June 29, 1951, HSP, box 489, folder 13.

33. Letter from Greenfield to Cabrey. Greenfield's first office boy, John J. Cree, started with Greenfield in 1910, at age fourteen, when Greenfield was still working out of Cahan's print shop on Fourth Street. Over the next fifty years, Cree handled some twenty-five thousand real estate transactions for Greenfield. See Skwersky, *Knight of Philadelphia*, 82–83; page 90n102 lists twenty-six members of Greenfield's twenty-five-year club as of 1963.

34. Hopkins, "Stormy Monday," 23.

35. "Mr. Philadelphia."

36. "Bankers Securities Still Pays Common Arrearages of 1930s," *Philadelphia Bulletin*, November 22, 1953. Bankers Securities' assets were $12,275,000 in 1928; $73,470,000 in 1953.

37. Olson, interview by the author.

38. One example of Greenfield's approach to compensation: Alfred Blasband, whom Greenfield installed as president of the Snellenburg's department store in 1951, was paid $40,000 a year; at the time, Arthur C. Kaufmann, head of Gimbels' Philadelphia store, received a salary of $97,500 plus $36,000 in contingent compensation; see Binzen, Daughen, and Friedman, *Rise and Fall of the House of Greenfield*, 194.

39. "Bankers Securities Still Pays Common Arrearages of 1930s," *Philadelphia Bulletin*, November 22, 1953.

40. Binzen, Daughen, and Friedman, *Rise and Fall of the House of Greenfield*, 92.

41. Letter from Joseph P. Hoenig to Albert Greenfield, December 11, 1958 (in author's possession). See also Binzen, Daughen, and Friedman, *Rise and Fall of the House of Greenfield*, 92.

42. Leonard Wurzel, interview by the author, September 23, 2011.

43. Ibid.

44. Ibid.

45. Ibid.

46. *Philadelphia Bulletin*, January 31, 1949; *Wall Street Journal*, November 4, 1955.

47. Harrison, "Mr. Philadelphia," 222-223. Snellenburg's gross annual volume was about $26 million. Bankers Securities paid $2.1 million to purchase a controlling interest; the company's net value then was $5,456,000. Under Bankers Securities, Snellenburg's lost $2.2 million from fiscal year 1951 through 1957; see Harrison, "Mr. Philadelphia," 226.

48. Binzen, Daughen, and Friedman, *Rise and Fall of the House of Greenfield*, 191-192.

49. Barnard, interview by the author.

50. "A Whiz of a Promoter," *Business Week*, September 25, 1954.

51. Harris, *Merchant Princes*, 87. Harris was the son and grandson of the owners of A. Harris and Co., a Dallas department store.

52. Harrison, "Mr. Philadelphia," 201-203. The quote is from the civic leader Walter M. Phillips. Although the Greater Philadelphia Movement was technically nonpartisan, its membership tended to be Republican and Protestant, composed of the sort of bankers who had rejected Greenfield during the Bankers Trust crisis of 1930.

53. Burt, *Perennial Philadelphians*, 572.

54. Letter from J. J. Cabrey to Albert Greenfield, June 8, 1951, HSP, box 489, folder 13.

55. Letter from Greenfield to Cabrey.

56. Albert Greenfield, interview by *(New York) Daily News*, February 16, 1953, HSP, box 565, folder 2.

57. Edna's lobotomy in the early 1950s was mentioned to the author by many of Greenfield's relatives. Precisely when or where it took place is unclear. Greenfield's granddaughter Priscilla Luce told me that it took place in New York; interview by the author, July 20, 2011. A telegram to Greenfield from Edna at Prangins (near Nyon, Switzerland), January 18, 1953, reads, "Have postponed souling until later date"—a possible reference to her lobotomy. HSP, box 562, folder 12. Some relatives said it was one of the last lobotomies ever performed. Lobotomies, once perceived as an enlightened scientific advance, fell out of favor in the 1960s with the development of effective antipsychotic medications. See Lerner, "When Lobotomy Was Seen as Advanced." Edna's lobotomy apparently relieved many of Edna's anxieties and restored her appetite; from what appeared to her relatives to be the brink of death, she survived another thirty-five years, dying in June 1987 at the age of ninety-two. But Edna retained many of her old germ-wary habits, such as wearing gloves at all times and obsessively cleaning silverware, plates, and pots. Janet Guth (Edna's oldest granddaughter), interview by the author; also Priscilla Luce (Edna's granddaughter), interview by the author, July 20, 2011.

58. Letter from Edna Paine to Albert Greenfield, ca. December 1950, HSP, box 500, folder 15.

59. Cable from Albert Greenfield to Edna Paine, December 26, 1950, HSP, box 500, folder 15.

60. Albert Greenfield Jr., eulogy for his sister Elizabeth Zeidman, March 20, 2005.

61. Letter from Albert Greenfield to Gordon Greenfield, January 27, 1932, HSP, box 168, folder 10. Robert Greenfield, in our interview on January 9, 2012, said, "I learned that Albert held me up to Gordon as a model. Gordon was resentful. He became very cold to me as we got older."

62. For example, Greenfield arranged for Robert to join the Sundheim, Folz & Sundheim law firm, which was located in Greenfield's Bankers Securities Building and handled much of Greenfield's legal work; after a few years, Greenfield arranged for Robert to be listed as a

named partner at the firm, which became Sundheim, Folz & Greenfield. Greenfield put Robert up for membership in a downtown lunch club. Most notably, Greenfield included Robert in the small circle of employees to whom he sold Bankers Securities in 1959 on very favorable terms, "even though I had no claim," Robert said. These were privileges Greenfield did not extend to his own children. "I came to realize that I was a favorite of his," Robert said, "although I never knew it at the time." Robert Greenfield, interview by the author, November 21, 2012.

63. Harrison, "Mr. Philadelphia," 23; Barbara Greenfield, eulogy for Elizabeth Zeidman, March 20, 2005.

64. Letter from Carlotta G. Orchard to Albert Greenfield, April 24, 1947, HSP, box 400, folder 4.

65. Letter from Carlotta G. Vetter to Albert Greenfield, April 2, 1951, HSP, box 508, folder 9.

66. Barbara Greenfield, interview by the author, July 18, 2011. Carlotta married Robert D. Sturgeon on June 12, 1941; see letter from Robert Sturgeon to Albert Greenfield, January 3, 1942, HSP, box 326, folder 20.

67. Sturgeon's wedding to Rosemary Grein is reported in the *Philadelphia Bulletin*, September 18, 1950, HSP, box 477, folder 12.

68. Albert M. Greenfield III, interview by the author, September 22, 2011.

69. Carlotta married Allen Howard on March 7, 1953, in Westport, Connecticut; letter from Allen Howard to Albert Greenfield, February 7, 1953, HSP, box 557, folder 12. Her previous husbands were Stanley H. Goldsmith Jr., Robert D. Sturgeon, Joseph Orchard, and Charles Vetter Jr.

70. Letter from Harry Serwer to Albert Greenfield, September 22, 1949, HSP, box 446, folder 2.

71. Robert Greenfield, quoted in the Albert Greenfield biography film *Mr. Philadelphia*.

72. "Military History of Albert M. Greenfield Jr., Sergeant (1950)," HSP, box 466, folder 7. Albert M. Greenfield Jr. enlisted in the Navy June 16, 1945, and was discharged as a seaman second class, November 20, 1945. He then enlisted in the Marines as a private on April 24, 1947, was promoted to corporal June 1, 1948, and to sergeant April 1, 1950.

73. Albert M. Greenfield III, interview by the author.

74. Albert Jr.'s wife, Barbara Littman, was the daughter of the London entrepreneur Joseph A. Littman, an expatriate American Jew who occasionally did business with Greenfield. After Barbara graduated from high school in 1949, Greenfield arranged for her admission to the University of Pennsylvania. Shortly after she arrived in Philadelphia in September 1949, having just turned eighteen, Greenfield introduced her to his son. They were married July 27, 1950, and Albert Jr. left almost immediately for active duty with his Marine unit, which was bound for Korea. Barbara Greenfield, interview by the author, July 18, 2011; Littman/Greenfield wedding announcement, *Jewish Exponent*, July 28, 1950, HSP, box 466, folder 5.

75. Albert M. Greenfield III, interview by the author; *Mr. Philadelphia*.

76. Greenfield may have extricated his son from the Korean War as a favor to Edna, Albert Jr.'s mother. In a letter to Greenfield from Paris in December 1950, she wrote, "I am glad Albert [Jr.] has finally gotten away from Parris Island, and I hope to heaven he will be a long time on this side (I mean the U.S.A. side) of the ocean" (HSP, box 500, folder 15).

77. An internal memo dated August 7, 1953, announces that Albert Greenfield Jr. "will resume his active association with this office on December 1. . . . He will work in close association with his father and will occupy a desk to be provided near the latter's private office." HSP, box 556, folder 11.

78. Albert M. Greenfield III, interview by the author; Albert Greenfield Jr. obituary, *Philadelphia Inquirer*, June 29, 2005.

79. Janet Guth, interview by the author.

80. Elizabeth Zeidman, interview by the author, October 19, 1975, p. 5. See also Barbara Greenfield, "Albert M. Greenfield," 3.

81. Janet Guth, interview by the author.

82. Luce, interview by the author.

83. Janet Guth, interview by the author.

84. See, for example, *The Observer*, October 11, 1948, HSP, box 415, folder 4.

85. Skwersky, *Knight of Philadelphia*, 126.

86. Letter from Etelka Greenfield (at Homosassa Springs Hotel, Florida) to Albert Greenfield, February 15, 1947, HSP, box 395, folder 14; also cited in Skwersky, *Knight of Philadelphia*, 127.

87. Letter from Albert Greenfield to J. Caprano, April 12, 1949, quoted in Skwersky, *Knight of Philadelphia*, 128.

88. Letter from Albert Greenfield to Nanette Coyne, April 15, 1949, quoted in Skwersky, *Knight of Philadelphia*, 128.

89. Letter from Albert Greenfield to Louis Johnson, May 11, 1949, HSP, box 437, folder 1.

90. Etelka died May 29, 1949; Harrison, "Mr. Philadelphia," 241. The type of cancer does not appear to have been identified in any correspondence or news reports. She is buried in the Greenfield plot at Adath Jeshurun Cemetery, Philadelphia, with her daughter, Yvonne Schamberg Straus (1912-1959).

91. "Woman Banker Makes Things Hum in Trenton," *Philadelphia Inquirer*, September 7, 1952, HSP, box 478, folder 2; Polly Platt, "Interesting Women," *Philadelphia Bulletin*, February 5, 1950, HSP, box 478, folder 2; *Philadelphia Bulletin*, April 21, 1950, HSP, box 478, folder 2. Mary's husband, Siegfried Roebling, was a vice president of John A. Roebling Sons Co. and a director of the Trenton Trust Co. When he died on January 1, 1936, she took his place on the bank's board and was elected president the following year.

92. See correspondence between Albert Greenfield and Mary Roebling, HSP, box 478, folder 2.

93. Letter from Carlotta G. Vetter to Albert Greenfield, ca. January or February 1950, HSP, box 479, folder 3.

94. The Brooklyn Bridge was begun in 1867 by Siegfried's great-grandfather, John A. Roebling (1806-1869) and completed in 1883 by John's son and Siegfried's grandfather, Washington A. Roebling (1837-1926). See Schuyler, *The Roeblings*.

95. Mary Gindhart Roebling was born in 1905 and died in 1994.

96. They were still sending each other gifts and notes at the end of 1950. See their correspondence in HSP, box 478, folder 2.

97. Guinther, *Philadelphia*, 151-158.

98. Burt, *Perennial Philadelphians*, 550.

99. Ibid., 550-555, 572; Harrison, "Mr. Philadelphia," 203.

100. Committee of Seventy, *The Charter*, 7.

101. The Lord Home Rule Bill was approved by the Pennsylvania General Assembly and signed into law by Governor Duff on April 21, 1949; see Committee of Seventy, *The Charter*, 9.

102. Clark and Clark, "Rally and Relapse, 1946-1968," 654.

103. Lois Brunner says that Greenfield was drafted for a one-year term as president of the Philadelphia Chamber of Commerce on February 12, 1951. See "Mr. Albert M. Greenfield," 5.

104. Harrison, "Mr. Philadelphia," 183-184.

105. Elizabeth Hallstrom's *Who's Who* entry listed her date of birth as December 1, 1912, although some news articles say 1913.

106. Elizabeth Hallstrom became executive secretary of the Foreign Policy Association of Philadelphia in 1947 and remained as its executive director when it merged with Philadelphia's United Nations Council to become the World Affairs Council. "Albert M. Greenfield Marries Elizabeth Hallstrom," *Philadelphia Bulletin*, January 14, 1952, HSP, box 525, folder 7; see also Elizabeth Hallstrom Greenfield Petrie, interview by the author, October 15, 1975.

107. Clark and Clark, "Rally and Relapse, 1946-1968," 654.

108. Harrison, "Mr. Philadelphia," 248.

109. Winnet, *Vignettes of a Lucky Life*, 150; see also Harrison, "Mr. Philadelphia," 248.

110. Albert Greenfield, radio address, April 16, 1951, HSP, box 504, folder 4.

111. Barbara Greenfield, interview by the author, July 18, 2011.

112. "Albert M. Greenfield Marries Mrs. Elizabeth M. Hallstrom."

113. Burt, *Perennial Philadelphians*, 532–533.

114. "Albert M. Greenfield Acquires 'Sugar Loaf' in Chestnut Hill," *Philadelphia Bulletin*, December 28, 1952, HSP, box 566, folder 18. In a letter to Albert Greenfield on February 2, 1953, George Wharton Pepper wrote, "I have known this place since 1873, at which time I lived in a tiny gardener's cottage (called Brown's Cottage) which has since been enlarged into quite a sizeable house." HSP, box 566, folder 18. Another source says that Hopkinson lived in the same house at 8700 Montgomery Avenue since 1911, when he was married. Hugh Scott, "Edward Hopkinson Jr.," *Today*, January 20, 1963, p. 4, HSP, box 811, folder 11.

115. "The Evolution of Sugar Loaf," 73.

116. John Harris, Greenfield's grandnephew, mentioned the kosher kitchen to me in a July 11, 2012, interview.

117. The descriptions come from "The $250,000 House"; "The Evolution of Sugar Loaf"; and "Albert M. Greenfield Acquires 'Sugar Loaf' in Chestnut Hill," *Philadelphia Bulletin*, December 28, 1952, HSP, box 566, folder 18.

118. Juliet Six (Greenfield's granddaughter), interview by the author, September 7, 2011; Janet Guth, interview by the author.

119. Harrison, "Mr. Philadelphia," 290. See also Edward Rosen, interview by the author, October 31, 2011; he attended Greenfield's dinner for Mendès-France in 1953.

120. Luce, interview by the author.

121. Brecht, "The Greenfield Story."

122. Irwin Solomon, interview by the author, October 15, 1975.

123. Wurzel, interview by the author.

CHAPTER 13

1. This description is taken from Lowe, *Cities in a Race with Time*, 319–320. See also Harrison, "Mr. Philadelphia," 190–191; LeVan, *The Politics of Reform*, 26–27.

2. Lowe, *Cities in a Race with Time*, 339; see also Boonin, *The Jewish Quarter of Philadelphia*, 56.

3. Lowe, *Cities in a Race with Time*, 339.

4. The earliest known use of the term "WASP" appeared in an African American newspaper, New York's *Amsterdam News*, on April 17, 1948. For further discussion, see note 12 in Chapter 7.

5. Albert Greenfield, "Saving Our American Cities," speech to Urban Land Institute, May 13, 1943, Historical Society of Pennsylvania (HSP), box 320, folder 6.

6. Heller, *Ed Bacon*, 40.

7. Skwersky, *Knight of Philadelphia*, 159–162.

8. Heller, *Ed Bacon*, 40.

9. Bacon was hired by Philadelphia's City Planning Commission as a senior land planner in October 1946; Heller, *Ed Bacon*, 48.

10. Heller, *Ed Bacon*, 50. Lowe, *Cities in a Race with Time* (322–323), says the cost was $400,000 and the exhibition attracted 400,000 visitors.

11. Earl Selby, "In Our Town" column, *Philadelphia Bulletin*, December 14, 1955, HSP, box 633, folder 11. See also Lowe, *Cities in a Race with Time*, 322. The bond between the two men was further cemented in 1953 when Greenfield succeeded Hopkinson as chairman of PTC's executive committee while Hopkinson assumed the newly created post of chairman of the PTC board. "He and I will continue to work together just as we did when we were joint reorganization managers for the Federal Court in the late 1930s," Hopkinson told reporters. Hopkinson had previously been paid $12,000 a year as chairman of the PTC executive committee; under the new arrangement, he and Greenfield were each paid $6,000, suggesting that they functioned as coexecutive officers.

12. In 1946 Greenfield had helped pressure Congress to create the Philadelphia National Shrines Park Commission, and after its passage, he wangled an appointment to the commission.

13. Heller, *Ed Bacon*, 117.

14. Ibid., 119–120.

15. Bacon purchased a townhome at 2117 Locust Street in 1949 and lived there until his death in 2005; Heller, *Ed Bacon*, 54.

16. Ingersoll's house was at 217 Spruce Street, apparently right next door to the home of the stockbroker Henry Watts, chairman of the New York Stock Exchange (although Watts did not move there until 1961). See C. Jared Ingersoll, interview by Walter Phillips, June 28, 1977, pp. 4–5, Walter Phillips Oral History Project (WPP), Temple University Urban Archives (TUUA); see also Heller, *Ed Bacon*, 125.

17. Walter D'Alessio, interview by the author, August 6, 2012.

18. Lowe, *Cities in a Race with Time*, 340. See also Ingersoll, interview by Phillips.

19. Alsop, "The Paradox of Gentleman Joe." Alsop added, "Nothing could be further from the truth."

20. McLarnon and Madonna, "Damon and Pythias Reconsidered," 172–173. See also Lowe, *Cities in a Race with Time*, 329.

21. Richard Schier, quoted in McLarnon and Madonna, "Damon and Pythias Reconsidered," 174.

22. Harrison, "Mr. Philadelphia," 263. The friend was city solicitor Abraham Freedman.

23. Lowe, *Cities in a Race with Time*, 330.

24. This position was expounded by the Citizens' Council on City Planning; Harrison, "Mr. Philadelphia," 252.

25. Harrison, "Mr. Philadelphia," 251–252.

26. See, for example, William Rafsky, interview by Walter Phillips, November 10, 1976, WPP, TUUA; also Harrison, "Mr. Philadelphia," 253. However, the Philadelphia Redevelopment Authority had more direct control over federal funds than the planning commission did; Gregory Heller, e-mail message to the author, May 17, 2013.

27. Lowe, *Cities in a Race with Time*, 330.

28. Ibid., 331.

29. According to Philip Klein, "They were both friends and they were both enemies, Greenfield and Dilworth." See Philip Klein, interview by Walter Phillips, February 26, 1980, p. 9, WPP, TUUA.

30. Binzen, *Richardson Dilworth*, 132.

31. Ibid.

32. Postcard from Richardson Dilworth to Albert Greenfield, December 8, 1957, HSP, box 657, folder 15.

33. In 1956, months after leaving the mayor's office, Clark won the Democratic primary for U.S. Senate over Greenfield's opposition; see Reichley, *The Art of Government*, 38. Clark was elected to the U.S. Senate that November. The Pennsylvania Railroad promised to vacate the Broad Street Station in 1925 but did not do so until 1953. See Lowe, *Cities in a Race with Time*, 331; see also Heller, *Ed Bacon*, 103.

34. "Greenfield Elected Chairman of Planning Commission." Dilworth also cited other goals: to salvage "fringe" areas that had not yet decayed into slums, to develop an all-purpose municipal stadium, and to deal with the city's mounting automobile traffic. See also Lowe, *Cities in a Race with Time*, 337.

35. Dilworth, quoted in *Mr. Philadelphia*.

36. Ingersoll, interview by Phillips, 2.

37. Lowe, *Cities in a Race with Time*, 342.

38. Ibid.; see also Harrison, "Mr. Philadelphia," 258. Greenfield wanted to use every available inch of space at Penn Center for office buildings; by contrast, the ultimate developer, the Binswanger Organization, proposed to set buildings back from the curb to create more open

space. See Alfred Blasband, interview by Peter Binzen, 1985. While the Binswanger plan reduced congestion, Penn Center's open spaces have remained a series of windswept and unappealing plazas, largely devoid of pedestrians, as of this writing.

39. Harrison, "Mr. Philadelphia," 270.

40. "Greenfield Elected Chairman of Planning Commission."

41. Harrison, "Mr. Philadelphia," 269; see also Binzen, *Richardson Dilworth*, 131–133.

42. "Greenfield Elected Chairman of Planning Commission." Greenfield resigned as president of Albert M. Greenfield & Co. effective January 9, 1956. The employees to whom he sold
his stock were Thomas C. Pillion, Maxwell Smolens, John J. Herd, Chester Cincotta, H. Walter
Graves, Harold C. Scott, Albert M. Greenfield Jr., George H. Johnson Jr., Robert G. Hachen-
burg, Henry Hass, Nathan S. Sperling, Howard P. Mulhern, Robert D. Sturgeon (Greenfield's
former son-in-law), Russell D. Atkinson, Joseph West, and John J. Cree (Greenfield's first
office boy in 1910). See "A. M. Greenfield to Retire."

43. Harrison, "Mr. Philadelphia," 216. Greenfield controlled two personal holding companies, Albert Company and the Realty Owning Company; upon leaving Albert M. Greenfield &
Co., he formed a third corporation, the Elizabeth Realty Company.

44. Greenfield also suggested that Hopkinson be asked to stay on as chairman for "another six months to a year" and also said he would be willing to start on the commission as
vice chairman. Dilworth, however, thought "the break should be clean and be made now." See
Selby, "In Our Town" column.

45. "Greenfield Elected Chairman of Planning Commission."

46. Lowe, *Cities in a Race with Time*, 342.

47. Ibid., 343.

48. Ibid., 343, 350; D'Alessio, interview by the author. Some accounts credit Greenfield
with originating the unique approach to restoring Society Hill, others credit Bacon, and some,
like Lowe, credit both men. Clearly, both Bacon and Greenfield were enthusiastic about the
idea.

49. Burt, *Perennial Philadelphians*, 556.

50. *Philadelphia Bulletin*, July 3, 1957; see also Boonin, *The Jewish Quarter of Philadelphia*, 56.

51. Lowe, *Cities in a Race with Time*, 343.

52. Burt, *Perennial Philadelphians*, 539.

53. Lowe, *Cities in a Race with Time*, 344–345.

54. D'Alessio, quoted in *Mr. Philadelphia*. D'Alessio joined the Philadelphia Redevelopment Authority as a young planner in 1961 and rose to executive director before leaving the
agency in 1973; D'Alessio, interview by the author.

55. "GPM Attack Called Unfair by Greenfield," 1.

56. Heller, *Ed Bacon*, 123. Heller says the meeting took place in June 1956, which would
have been after the Old Philadelphia Development Corporation (OPDC) was formally organized in May. William Rafsky says OPDC was developed in a series of meetings involving
himself, Greenfield, Bacon, and Dilworth, and "Greenfield's influence was further extended
because he assigned Gus Amsterdam to help carry this out." See William Rafsky interview,
February 1, 1996, p. 21, Myer and Rosaline Feinstein Center for American Jewish History Collection, TUUA. Walter Phillips said *he* came up with the idea for OPDC but acknowledged
that Greenfield gave it the lift it needed; see Gustave G. Amsterdam, interview by Walter Phillips, December 20, 1975, pp. 12–13, WPP, TUUA.

57. Lowe, *Cities in a Race with Time*, 345. The $2 million capital figure is provided by
"Historic City Shakes Free of Past, Rebuilds." See also Harrison, "Mr. Philadelphia," 272–273.

58. Paul Levy, executive director of Philadelphia's Center City District, e-mail message to
the author, September 9, 2012.

59. Lowe, *Cities in a Race with Time*, 344–346.

60. Amsterdam, interview by Phillips, 14.

61. John O'Shea, interview by the author, October 15, 1975, p. 1.

62. Ibid.

63. Harrison, "Mr. Philadelphia," 278.

64. Letter from William L. Day to Elizabeth Greenfield, January 9, 1967, quoted in Skwersky, *Knight of Philadelphia*, 7. See also Harrison, "Mr. Philadelphia," 278, citing an interview of Holmes Perkins by Kirk R. Petshek, January 15, 1965; *Mr. Philadelphia*. Perkins does not say whom Greenfield called at the White House, which at the time was occupied by a Republican, Dwight D. Eisenhower. The James A. Byrne Federal Courthouse at 601 Market Street opened in 1970.

65. Gutheim, "Philadelphia's Redevelopment," *Architectural Forum*, December 1956, cited in Albert Greenfield, speech to National Citizens Planning Conference, September 3, 1958, HSP, box 681, folder 1.

66. Harrison, "Mr. Philadelphia," 272–273.

67. Letter from Dilworth to Albert Greenfield, February 18, 1957, HSP, box 657, folder 15.

68. Bacon was raised in a strict Quaker household. His mother traced her lineage to Henry Comly, one of the Quakers who fled to Pennsylvania in the seventeenth century to escape religious persecution in England. See Heller, *Ed Bacon*, 17.

69. Edmund Bacon, interview by Peter Binzen, 1985.

70. Edmund Bacon, interview by Walter Phillips, January 9, 1975, pp. 9–10, WPP, TUUA.

71. Society Hill Towers, developed by Webb & Knapp, was completed in 1964. The demolition of Dock Street was publicly funded by federal Title I funds, and the towers were insured by the Federal Housing Administration; Gregory Heller, e-mail message to the author, May 17, 2013. The prominent architect I. M. Pei (born 1917) is best known for the John F. Kennedy Library in Boston, the Louvre Pyramid in Paris, the East Wing of the National Gallery of Art in Washington, the Bank of China Tower in Hong Kong, and the Museum of Islamic Art in Doha.

72. The population of Society Hill was 6,215 in 2014, according to the Center City District website. See http://centercityphila.org/life/nhood_societyhill.php.

73. See "The Success of Downtown Living," 1. It gives the population of Center City in 2002 as 78,902.

74. Lowe, *Cities in a Race with Time*, 313.

75. Rafsky, interview by Phillips, p. 18.

76. Gray and Rogers, "15th and Walnut Streets Showplace to Be Sold," news release, June 1956 (in the author's possession). The palazzo was home to the First National Bank of Philadelphia from 1942 until the bank's acquisition by the Pennsylvania Company in the fall of 1955 (which resulted in the creation of a new entity known as First Pennsylvania Bank); see also John R. Bunting, interview by Peter Binzen, 1985. Albert M. Greenfield III, in our September 22, 2011, interview, said he heard this story from his parents as well as from his uncle, Gordon Greenfield; both his father and Gordon had borne resentments against Greenfield. Greenfield's nephew Robert Greenfield said such an act would have been out of character for Greenfield: "He could be coarse when dealing with coarse people, but when he was dealing with people of standing or money or reputation, he was top of the line." Robert Greenfield, interviews by the author, August 25 and September 15, 2011.

77. Harrison, "Mr. Philadelphia," 211. See also the letter to Albert Greenfield from Edward T. Flood & Son real estate of January 15, 1940, offering to sell Stotesbury's Whitemarsh Hall to Temple University for an asking price of $600,000. HSP, box 278, folder 15.

78. Bankers Securities sold the Drexel building to the developer Martin Decker in 1973 but had to reclaim the building when Decker went bankrupt. Ultimately, it was sold in May 1979 to Jason R. Nathan, former president of Franklin Town Development Corp., for $800,000. See Binzen, Daughen, and Friedman, *Rise and Fall of the House of Greenfield*, 238; also Farber, *The Garbage Man*, 138.

79. "Greenfield Resigns Post." Although Greenfield sold his real estate company and resigned from it in January 1956, his arrival on the planning commission coincided with a period when he became increasingly involved in the affairs of City Stores Company, culminating

with the resignation of City Stores' president Ben R. Gordon on January 31, 1957. See "Gordon Leaves City Stores, A. M. Greenfield Takes Post."

80. Letter from Albert Greenfield to Richardson Dilworth, February 12, 1957, HSP, box 657, folder 15.

81. See resignation letter from Albert Greenfield to Richardson Dilworth, January 17, 1958, HSP, box 788, folder 7; City Council Resolution #220, January 23, 1958, HSP, box 900, folder 10. Skwersky, *Knight of Philadelphia* (181), says Greenfield resigned in January 1959, but this appears to be a typographical error.

82. Letter from Albert Greenfield to Richardson Dilworth, December 15, 1959, HSP, box 735, folder 6. Notwithstanding Greenfield's advice, under Dilworth the city did purchase Broad Street Station in 1961 and subsequently built West Plaza on that site. See Heller, *Ed Bacon*, 111.

83. Telegram from Richardson Dilworth to Albert Greenfield, August 10, 1958, HSP, box 686, folder 16.

CHAPTER 14

1. "Greenfield Resigns Post."

2. *Philadelphia Bulletin*, April 8, 1959.

3. *Philadelphia Bulletin*, January 24,1962; *Philadelphia Bulletin*, February 15, 1962.

4. Howard Magen, interview by the author, January 30, 2012.

5. Binzen, Daughen, and Friedman, *Rise and Fall of the House of Greenfield*, 270. The exact figure was $81.1 million.

6. Of 60,000 Bankers Securities shares outstanding in 1959, Greenfield owned 22,000, and the Albert M. Greenfield Foundation owned an additional 12,000. Gustave G. Amsterdam, interview by the author, October 30, 1975. In the late 1960s, following a stock split, the Greenfield Foundation owned 84,553 shares of Bankers Securities stock, about 21 percent of the total; see Binzen, Daughen, and Friedman, *Rise and Fall of the House of Greenfield*, 243.

7. Farber, *The Garbage Man*, 102. Amsterdam said this was the understanding from the outset: "These debts that were incurred [by the acquiring group] would be paid for out of earnings or assets, as long as creditors were first. We were told by Albert, and believed it ourselves, that there were very substantial surpluses that could be used for the purchase of stock. That was the understanding from the beginning." See Binzen, Daughen, and Friedman, *Rise and Fall of the House of Greenfield*, 269. Bruce Greenfield said Amsterdam's consortium borrowed 85 to 90 percent of the purchase price of the stock; ibid., 269. Greenfield's son Gordon bought one of the twenty units but sold it eighteen months later to Albert M. Greenfield & Co.; ibid., 170.

8. Gordon Greenfield made this remark to Jack Farber in the late 1970s; see Farber, *The Garbage Man*, 102. Gordon remained on the board of Bankers Securities until 1973, when Amsterdam removed him; see Binzen, Daughen, and Friedman, *Rise and Fall of the House of Greenfield*, 243–244.

9. Harrison, "Mr. Philadelphia," 233.

10. See Farber, *The Garbage Man*, 102; Binzen, Daughen, and Friedman, *Rise and Fall of the House of Greenfield*, 170–171, 242–244. See also Gustave G. Amsterdam obituary, *Philadelphia Inquirer*, February 14, 2001.

11. Letter from Eva Fox to Albert Greenfield, March 28, 1959, Historical Society of Pennsylvania (HSP), box 738, folder 2.

12. Harrison, "Mr. Philadelphia," 240.

13. Ibid., 293. The ad appeared in the *New York Times*, the *Washington Post*, and several other papers.

14. Ibid., 296.

15. Ibid., 293.

16. Ibid., 296.

17. Ibid., 296-297. Greenfield paid O'Shea's salary and expenses while O'Shea worked for the Democratic National Committee.

18. See Caro, *The Passage of Power*, 198.

19. Leonard Wurzel, interview by the author, September 23, 2011.

20. Letter from Mark Wurzel to the author, February 29, 2008. See also Farber, *The Garbage Man*, 103. These events took place in 1963 and 1964. Bankers Securities sold its 49.9 percent interest in Loft Candy to Southland Corp. in April 1971 and wrote off its entire $2 million investment in Loft stock; see Binzen, Daughen, and Friedman, *Rise and Fall of the House of Greenfield*, 240.

21. Harrison, "Mr. Philadelphia," 282; Skwersky, *Knight of Philadelphia*, 234. For the trip itinerary, see HSP box 799, folder 13.

22. Harrison, "Mr. Philadelphia," 300. See also "Albert M. Greenfield—Illness," memo listing his hospital stays, September 1963, HSP, box 884, folder 1; "Albert M. Greenfield in Hospital with Ulcer," *Philadelphia Bulletin*, September 22, 1962, HSP, box 884, folder 1; "A. M. Greenfield in Hospital Again," *Philadelphia Inquirer*, September 22, 1962, HSP, box 884, folder 1.

23. Binzen, Daughen, and Friedman, *Rise and Fall of the House of Greenfield*, 222. See also *Philadelphia Bulletin*, May 18, 1964, 42; Bankers Securities minutes, April 30, 1964 (in author's possession).

24. Binzen, Daughen, and Friedman, *Rise and Fall of the House of Greenfield*, 182.

25. Ibid., 222.

26. Ruth Seltzer, "Philadelphia Scene," *Philadelphia Bulletin*, July 7, 1963, cited in Skwersky, *Knight of Philadelphia*, 138.

27. Harrison, "Mr. Philadelphia," 299.

28. Elizabeth Zeidman, interview by the author, October 19, 1975. The same weight loss figure is mentioned by Mildred Custin in Harris, *Merchant Princes*, 89; see also Harrison, "Mr Philadelphia," 300.

29. Harrison, "Mr. Philadelphia," 300.

30. Numerous letters at the Historical Society of Pennsylvania confirm this impression. The earliest I found is one from December 14, 1954, in which Greenfield sends his brother William Greenfield a Christmas gift of two hundred shares of Class B stock of Bonwit Teller & Co. of Philadelphia, with the proviso that "it is my wish that you do not dispose of it during my lifetime." HSP, box 584, folder 16.

31. Letter from Albert Greenfield to Edna Kraus Paine, February 11, 1966, HSP, box 890, folder 6.

32. See, for example, D. Hays Solis-Cohen's January 6, 1967, letter to Elizabeth Greenfield, which says, "Miss Morris [Greenfield's secretary] was kind enough to bring me today a letter he had written to me to be delivered after his death, and its contents in no way diminishes the affection I had for him." HSP, box 899, folder 6.

33. Mildred Custin, quoted in Harris, *Merchant Princes*, 89.

34. Letter from J. David Stern to Elizabeth Greenfield, January 6, 1967, HSP, box 899, folder 6.

35. Letter from Edna Kraus Paine to Albert Greenfield, ca. June 1966, HSP, box 890, folder 6.

36. See, for example, notes to and from "Miss Morris" in 1962, HSP, box 794, folder 9. See also a gift card of August 1963 in which she signs herself "Miss Morris" in quotation marks. HSP, box 814, folder 6. D. Hays Solis-Cohen, in a condolence note to Elizabeth Greenfield, January 6, 1967, referred to a letter delivered to him that day by "Miss Morris," although she was married to Henry L. Reese at the time. HSP, box 899, folder 6. Subsequently, Elizabeth Morris Reese was married to Yetter Schoch and then to Charles Bowden. She was described by Robert Greenfield in an interview by me on November 21, 2012.

37. Elizabeth Morris was born April 16, 1924. She was forty-two when, as Elizabeth Reese, she gave birth to her first child, Suzanne, on November 4, 1966.

38. Elizabeth Zeidman, interview by the author, October 19, 1975.

CHAPTER 15

1. *Philadelphia Bulletin*, January 9, 1967, p. 8. The funeral took place January 8, 1967. For the full text of Rabbi Korn's eulogy, see Historical Society of Pennsylvania (HSP), box 898, folder 4.

2. Yvonne Schamberg Straus was killed in an auto accident in 1959 at age forty-seven. Greenfield was survived by his first and third wives, four siblings, and all five of his children, but for whatever reason, Greenfield was the last of his relatives to be buried in the Greenfield plot at Adath Jeshurun Cemetery.

3. "Albert M. Greenfield Dies at 79; Built Realty and Store Empire."

4. *Philadelphia Inquirer*, August 17, 1969; *Philadelphia Bulletin*, November 18, 1973. Of the $14.9 million in Greenfield's estate, $14 million was in stocks and bonds.

5. Elizabeth Greenfield Zeidman, interview by the author, October 19, 1975; Elizabeth (Greenfield) Petrie, interview by the author, October 27, 1975.

6. Edna Kraus Paine died in June 1987 at the age of ninety-two.

7. Albert Greenfield will, 1967, Register of Wills office, Philadelphia City Hall, Will #131, pp. 1, 7, 18.

8. Ibid., 41.

9. Ibid., 44. This explanation was actually inserted at the urging of Robert Greenfield, Greenfield's nephew and lawyer—and Gordon's cousin—in an attempt to soften the harshness of Gordon's exclusion. Robert said Greenfield had "no confidence" in Gordon. Robert Greenfield, interview by the author, November 21, 2012.

10. In 1968, after Greenfield's death, Bankers Securities also acquired Greenfield's original real estate firm, Albert M. Greenfield & Co. The renamed Greenfield Company was sold in December 1982 for $1 million to Helmsley Enterprises, the global real estate service company based in New York. After Harry Helmsley retired in 1990, his successors sold the Greenfield Company to Albert M. ("Moose") Greenfield III, the founder's grandson, who promptly enlisted the services of his mother, the founder's daughter-in-law Barbara Greenfield, a colorful downtown Philadelphia real estate broker who generated business for the firm well into the twenty-first century, by which time she was in her seventies. See Farber, *The Garbage Man*, 163; see also "Kin Buying Old Greenfield Business."

11. Rottenberg, "Albert Greenfield's Empire Died with Him."

12. Binzen, Daughen, and Friedman, *Rise and Fall of the House of Greenfield*, 257.

13. Farber, *The Garbage Man*, 133.

14. Bob Olson, interview by the author, September 28, 2011. Olson was corporate secretary of Bankers Securities from 1971 to 1973.

15. Binzen, Daughen, and Friedman, *Rise and Fall of the House of Greenfield*, 233.

16. Ibid., 242. The trust agreement was extended as of March 16, 1959, the tenth anniversary of the original agreement.

17. In the fiscal year ended January 31, 1975, for example, Bankers Securities lost $6.7 million. After fiscal year 1974 it had only two profitable years; its cumulative loss for the 1970s was $47.2 million. See Binzen, Daughen, and Friedman, *Rise and Fall of the House of Greenfield*, 267. Its net assets, valued at $81.1 million when Greenfield retired in 1959, had declined to $25.8 million by 1979; and stockholder equity in the company declined to $8 million by the time it was sold in 1979. See Binzen, Daughen, and Friedman, *Rise and Fall of the House of Greenfield*, 270.

18. For the ten years that ended in 1969, Bankers Securities earned only $15 million, partly because of the cost of paying off the debt from the leveraged buyout. Yet at the same time, the Amsterdam group's investors awarded themselves $23 million in dividends. Farber, *The Garbage Man*, 103; also see Binzen, Daughen, and Friedman, *Rise and Fall of the House of Greenfield*, 268. Bankers ceased paying dividends on its common stock after 1970. During Amsterdam's twenty-year regime from 1959 to 1979, Bankers Securities cumulatively lost $32.5 million; during that same period, the company paid out $28.7 million in dividends. By contrast, during the 1950s—Albert Greenfield's last decade in charge—Bankers Securities earned $35.5 million while paying dividends of $11 million. See Binzen, Daughen, and Friedman, *Rise and Fall of the House of Greenfield*, 268.

19. At that point the Greenfield Foundation owned 84,553 shares of Bankers Securities stock, or about 21 percent of the total of Bankers Securities shares; Binzen, Daughen, and Friedman, *Rise and Fall of the House of Greenfield*, 243.

20. The foundation's five-person board then consisted of Greenfield's widow, Elizabeth; Greenfield's two oldest children, Gordon Greenfield and Elizabeth Zeidman; Gus Amsterdam; and Albert Greenfield's nephew Bruce Greenfield, who was Amsterdam's right-hand man at Bankers Securities. When the 1959 voting trust that gave Amsterdam control of the foundation expired in 1969, the other foundation directors agreed to extend it but only for five years; it expired in 1974. See Binzen, Daughen, and Friedman, *Rise and Fall of the House of Greenfield*, 243.

21. Ibid., 244-245. Amsterdam appointed a judge of elections, Steven J. Serling, a law partner of Robert Greenfield, who was a member of Amsterdam's controlling investment group as well as a candidate for Bankers Securities director on Amsterdam's slate. Serling ruled in Amsterdam's favor, and the Amsterdam slate was elected.

22. The 1976 meeting is described in Binzen, Daughen, and Friedman, *Rise and Fall of the House of Greenfield*, 252-254. Also see Farber, *The Garbage Man*, 103.

23. This account is taken largely from Farber, *The Garbage Man*, 101-122. Farber was born in June 1933.

24. City Stores filed its Chapter XI petition on July 27, 1979; see Binzen, Daughen, and Friedman, *Rise and Fall of the House of Greenfield*, 275.

25. At that point, Farber, Amsterdam, and Bruce Greenfield were directors of both Bankers Securities and City Stores. Robert Greenfield was not a City Stores director but had arranged to be present. See Farber, *The Garbage Man*, 134.

26. This account is taken from Farber, *The Garbage Man*, 134-135; also see Binzen, Daughen, and Friedman, *Rise and Fall of the House of Greenfield*, 277. Farber's holding company, Philadelphia Industries, paid Amsterdam $1.4 million for his stock and paid the Greenfield brothers (Greenfield's nephews, Bruce and Robert) slightly more than $2 million. All told, Philadelphia Industries spent $8 million to gain control of Bankers Securities. That outlay bought Philadelphia Industries 68 percent of Bankers Securities voting stock but only 32 percent of its common equity. That is, Farber's company paid $8 million for 32 percent of a company whose *total* common book equity at that point was about $8 million. Technically, Bankers Securities remained a separate entity controlled by Philadelphia Industries until December 31, 1986, when it was formally merged into Philadelphia Industries. At that time the remaining Bankers Securities shareholders were bought out. The Fox interests, whose stake had been worth less than $4 million in 1979, received $17.5 million for their shares—a relatively happy ending to the $3 million investment that William Fox had made in his friend Albert Greenfield's new company in 1928. See Farber, *The Garbage Man*, 163-164.

EPILOGUE

1. Stotesbury died in 1938, Gest in 1939, Wayne in 1942, and Newhall in 1950.

2. Rendell, *A Nation of Wusses.*

3. Prior to 1970, every Ivy League college was led by a WASP male; after 1990, virtually no Ivy League president fit that description. See, for example, Rottenberg, "The Jackie Robinson of Jewish Academia," 64. See also Leonhardt, Parlapiano, and Waananen, "A Historical Benchmark." It notes that in 2012, for the first time, not a single white Protestant could be found in the federal government's highest positions—the presidency, the Supreme Court, the leadership of the Senate or House, or among the presidential and vice presidential candidates of either political party.

4. See Cain, "Hire Introverts," citing research led by the management professor Adam Grant of the University of Pennsylvania's Wharton School.

5. The survey was conducted by the *Boston Review* in 2009 and cited in "Hope Springs a Trap," 83.

6. Campo-Flores, "Why Americans Think Immigration Hurts the Economy," citing a *New York Times*/CBS national poll.

Bibliography

The works in this list that are not explicitly cited in the book were consulted for general background information.

SELECTED PRIMARY ARCHIVAL SOURCES

The Historical Society of Pennsylvania (Philadelphia) is the repository for Greenfield's personal papers—more than one thousand boxes' worth, dating from 1918 to his death in 1967. The papers have been cataloged and indexed, and a two-volume reader's guide is available. An index is also available on the society's website. At this writing the society is in the process of digitizing selected Greenfield papers and making them available on its website. See http://digitallibrary.hsp.org/index.php/Browse/modifyCriteria/facet/entity_facet/id/1252/mod_id/0.

The Temple University Urban Archives (Paley Library, Temple University, Philadelphia) houses the complete clipping morgue of the defunct *Philadelphia Bulletin* (1847–1982). It is also the repository of the Walter Phillips Oral History Project, a collection of transcripts of 145 interviews of prominent Philadelphia politicians and civic leaders during the period 1930–1979. Although Greenfield was not interviewed, he is discussed in many of the transcripts.

The Philadelphia Jewish Archives Center (Paley Library, Temple University, Philadelphia) has been incorporated within the Temple University Urban Archives. It includes several folders dealing with Greenfield; his native village of Lozovata, Ukraine; and other related subjects.

The Albert M. Greenfield Foundation (Philadelphia) has posted many photos and news clippings, as well as excerpts from its biographical video, *Mr. Philadelphia*, on its website: http://www.thegreenfieldfoundation.org.

SUGGESTIONS FOR FURTHER READING

The following books and articles strike me as the definitive sources for their respective subjects. (For full publishing details, see each book's listing under "Books" or "Articles and Manuscripts.")

Philadelphia financial history: Wainwright, *History of the Philadelphia National Bank, 1803–1953.*

Philadelphia business overview: Davenport, "Philadelphia," *Fortune,* June 1936.

Philadelphia's upper class: Burt, *The Perennial Philadelphians.*
America's upper class: Baltzell, *The Protestant Establishment.*
Philadelphia machine politics: McCaffery, *When Bosses Ruled Philadelphia.*
Philadelphia City Charter: Committee of Seventy, *The Charter: A History.*
U.S. urban renewal: Lowe, *Cities in a Race with Time.*

BOOKS

Allen, Frederick Lewis. *The Great Pierpont Morgan.* New York: Harper and Row, 1948.

Auerbach, Jerold S. *Unequal Justice: Lawyers and Social Change in Modern America.* New York: Oxford University Press, 1976.

Bailyn, Bernard. *The Peopling of British North America.* New York: Knopf, 1986.

———. *Voyagers to the West: A Passage in the Peopling of America on the Eve of the Revolution.* New York: Vintage, 1988.

Baltzell, E. Digby. *An American Business Aristocracy.* New York: Collier Books, 1962.

———. *The Protestant Establishment: Aristocracy and Caste in America.* New York: Vintage, 1964.

The Bank, 1781–1976: A Short History of First Pennsylvania Bank. Philadelphia: First Pennsylvania Bank, 1976.

Benson, Sonia G. *U.S. Immigration and Migration: Almanac.* Detroit: UXL, 2004.

Berenbaum, Michael, and Fred Skolnik, eds. *Encyclopedia Judaica.* Vol. 15. 2nd ed. Detroit: Macmillan Reference, 2007.

Biale, David. *Power and Powerlessness in Jewish History.* New York: Schocken, 1986.

Binzen, Peter, with Jonathan Binzen. *Richardson Dilworth: Last of the Bare-Knuckled Aristocrats.* Philadelphia: Camino Books, 2014.

Binzen, Peter, Joseph Daughen, and Murray Friedman. *The Rise and Fall of the House of Greenfield.* Philadelphia: privately printed, 1986.

Boonin, Harry D. *The Jewish Quarter of Philadelphia, 1881–1930.* Philadelphia: Jewish Walking Tours of Philadelphia, 1999.

Bowen, Catherine Drinker. *Family Portrait.* Boston: Little, Brown, 1970.

Burt, Nathaniel. *The Perennial Philadelphians: The Anatomy of an American Aristocracy.* Boston: Little, Brown, 1963.

Caro, Robert. *The Passage of Power.* Vol. 4 of *The Years of Lyndon Johnson.* New York: Vintage, 2012.

Carosso, Vincent. *The Morgans: Private International Bankers, 1854–1913.* Cambridge, MA: Harvard University Press, 1987.

Cave, Roy C., and Herbert H. Coulson. *A Source Book for Medieval Economic History.* 1936. Reprint, New York: Biblo and Tannen, 1965.

Chernow, Ron. *The House of Morgan: An American Banking Dynasty and the Rise of Modern Finance.* New York: Atlantic Monthly Press, 1990.

Clark, Joseph S., and Dennis J. Clark. "Rally and Relapse, 1946–1968." In *Philadelphia: A 300-Year History,* edited by Russell F. Weigley, 649–703. New York: Norton, 1982.

Committee of Seventy. *The Charter: A History.* Philadelphia: Committee of Seventy, 1980. Available at http://www.seventy.org/Downloads/Policy_&_Reform/Governance_Stud ies/1980_-_Charter_History.pdf.

Cooney, John. *The Annenbergs.* New York: Simon and Schuster, 1982.

d'Apéry, Tello J. *Overbrook Farms: Its Historical Background, Growth and Community Life.* Philadelphia: Magee Press, 1936.

Daughen, Joseph R., and Peter Binzen. *The Wreck of the Penn Central.* New York: Mentor Executive Library, 1973.

Davis, Allen, and Haller, Mark, eds. *The Peoples of Philadelphia: A History of Ethnic Groups and Lower-Class Life, 1790–1940.* Philadelphia: University of Pennsylvania Press, 1998.

Davis, John H. *The Bouviers: Portrait of an American Family.* New York: Farrar, Straus and Giroux, 1969.

Dilks, Park B. Jr. *Morgan, Lewis and Bockius: A Law Firm and Its Times, 1873–1993.* Philadelphia: Privately printed, 1994.

Dubin, Murray. *South Philadelphia: Mummers, Memories and the Melrose Diner.* Philadelphia: Temple University Press, 1996.

Eckhardt, Joseph, and Linda Kowall. "The Movies' First Mogul." In *Jewish Life in Philadelphia, 1830–1940,* edited by Murray Friedman, 99–125. Philadelphia: Institute for the Study of Human Issues, 1983.

Eliot, T. S. *After Strange Gods: A Primer of Modern Heresy.* London: Faber and Faber, 1934.

Emery, Edwin, and Henry L. Smith. *The Press and America.* Englewood Cliffs, NJ: Prentice-Hall, 1954.

Farber, Jack. *The Garbage Man.* Philadelphia: Privately printed, 2012.

Fisher, Sidney George. *The Diary of Sidney George Fisher, 1834–1871.* Edited by Nicholas B. Wainwright. Philadelphia: Historical Society of Pennsylvania, 1967.

Fonzi, Gaeton. *Annenberg: A Biography of Power.* New York: Weybright and Talley, 1970.

Friedman, Milton, and Anna Jacobson Schwartz. *Monetary History of the United States, 1867–1960.* Princeton, NJ: Princeton University Press, 1971.

Friedman, Murray, ed. *Jewish Life in Philadelphia, 1830–1940.* Philadelphia: Institute for the Study of Human Issues, 1983.

———. *Philadelphia Jewish Life, 1940–1985.* Ardmore, PA: Seth Press, 1986.

Friend, Tad. *Cheerful Money: Me, My Family and the Last Days of WASP Splendor.* New York: Little, Brown, 2009.

Guinther, John. *Philadelphia: A Dream for the Keeping.* Tulsa, OK: Continental Heritage Press, 1982.

Harris, Leon. *Merchant Princes.* New York: Harper and Row, 1979.

Harrison, Andrew. "Mr. Philadelphia." Ph.D. diss., Temple University, 1997.

Heinzen, Nancy. *The Perfect Square: A History of Rittenhouse Square.* Philadelphia: Temple University Press, 2009.

Heller, Gregory L. *Ed Bacon: Planning, Politics and the Building of Modern Philadelphia.* Philadelphia: University of Pennsylvania Press, 2013.

Hendrickson, Robert. *The Grand Emporiums: The Illustrated History of America's Great Department Stores.* New York: Stein and Day, 1979.

Hodos, Jerome. *Second Cities: Globalization and Local Politics in Manchester and Philadelphia.* Philadelphia: Temple University Press, 2011.

Hunsicker, Henry A. *A Genealogical History of the Hunsicker Family.* Philadelphia: J. B. Lippincott, 1911.

Jay, William. *The Life of John Jay.* New York: J. and J. Harper, 1833.

Jewish Encyclopedia. Vol. 4. New York: Funk and Wagnalls, 1906.

Josephson, Matthew. *The Robber Barons: The Great American Capitalists, 1861–1901.* 1934. Reprint, New Brunswick, NJ: Transaction, 2011.

King, Diane A. "Jewish Education in Philadelphia." In *Jewish Life in Philadelphia, 1830–1940,* edited by Murray Friedman, 235–252. Philadelphia: Institute for the Study of Human Issues, 1983.

Kolsky, Thomas. "The Opposition to Zionism." In *Philadelphia Jewish Life, 1940–1985,* edited by Murray Friedman, 81–106. Ardmore, PA: Seth Press, 1986.

Lafore, Lawrence, and Sarah Lee Lippincott. *Philadelphia: The Unexpected City.* New York: Doubleday, 1965.

LeVan, Ruth S. *The Politics of Reform: An Analysis of the Consequences of Philadelphia's Home Rule Charter Reform Movement.* Philadelphia: Temple University Press, 1963.

Lowe, Jeanne R. *Cities in a Race with Time: Progress and Poverty in America's Renewing Cities.* New York: Vintage Books, 1968.

MacDonogh, Giles. *Frederick the Great: A Life in Deed and Letters.* New York: St. Martin's Griffin, 2001.

Maher, James T. *Twilight of Splendor: Chronicles of the Age of American Palaces.* New York: Little, Brown, 1975.

Marion, John Francis. *Within These Walls: A History of the Academy of Music in Philadelphia*. Philadelphia: Academy of Music, 1984.

McCaffery, Peter. *When Bosses Ruled Philadelphia: The Emergence of the Republican Machine, 1867–1933*. University Park: Pennsylvania State University Press, 1993.

Morris, Charles. *American Catholic: The Saints and Sinners Who Built America's Most Powerful Church*. New York: Vintage, 1998.

Norris, George W. *Ended Episodes*. Philadelphia: John C. Winston Co., 1937.

Parrott, Harold. *The Lords of Baseball*. Lanham, MD: Taylor Trade, 2002.

Polk's Philadelphia Blue Book, Elite Directory and Club List. Philadelphia: R. L. Polk and Co., 1924.

Reichley, A. James. *The Art of Government: Reform and Organization Politics in Philadelphia*. New York: Fund for the Republic, 1959.

Rendell, Ed. *A Nation of Wusses: How America's Leaders Lost the Guts to Make Us Great*. New York: John Wiley, 2012.

Rosen, Philip. "German Jews vs. Russian Jews in Philadelphia Philanthropy." In *Jewish Life in Philadelphia, 1830–1940*, edited by Murray Friedman, 198–212. Philadelphia: Institute for the Study of Human Issues, 1983.

———. "Philadelphia Jewry and the Creation of Israel." In *Philadelphia Jewish Life, 1940–1985*, edited by Murray Friedman, 59–80. Ardmore, PA: Seth Press, 1986.

———. "Philadelphia Jewry and the Holocaust." In *Philadelphia Jewish Life, 1940–1985*, edited by Murray Friedman, 31–58. Ardmore, PA: Seth Press, 1986.

Rottenberg, Dan. *The Man Who Made Wall Street: Anthony J. Drexel and the Rise of Modern Finance*. Philadelphia: University of Pennsylvania Press, 2001.

———. "The Rise of Albert M. Greenfield." In *Jewish Life in Philadelphia, 1830–1940*, edited by Murray Friedman, 213–234. Philadelphia: Institute for the Study of Human Issues, 1983.

———. *Wolf, Block, Schorr and Solis-Cohen: An Informal History*. Philadelphia: Wolf, Block, Schorr and Solis-Cohen, 1988.

Salter, J. T. *The People's Choice: Philadelphia's William S. Vare*. New York: Exposition Press, 1971.

Sarna, Jonathan. *American Judaism: A History*. New Haven, CT: Yale University Press, 2004.

Saveth, Edward N. *American Historians and European Immigrants, 1875–1925*. New York: Columbia University Press, 1948.

Schuyler, Hamilton. *The Roeblings: A Century of Engineers, Bridge-Builders and Industrialists*. Princeton, NJ: Princeton University Press, 1931.

Scranton, Philip B. *Workshop of the World: Philadelphia*. 1990. Revised 2007. Available at http://www.workshopoftheworld.com/index.html.

Semenov, Lillian Wurtzel, and Carla Winter. *William Fox, Sol M. Wurtzel and the Early Fox Film Corporation: Letters, 1917–1923*. Jefferson, NC: McFarland, 2001.

Sinclair, Upton. *Upton Sinclair Presents William Fox*. Los Angeles: Published by the author, 1933.

Skwersky, Serena. *Knight of Philadelphia: The Life and Times of Albert Monroe Greenfield*. Philadelphia: Kopel, 2012.

Solomon, Aubrey. *The Fox Film Corporation, 1915–1935: A History and Filmography*. Jefferson, NC: McFarland, 2011.

Spengler, Oswald. *The Decline of the West*. Oxford: Oxford University Press, 1991.

Stafford, Hartwell. *Who's Who in Philadelphia in Wartime*. Vol. 1. Philadelphia: Stafford's National News Service, 1920. Available at http://archive.org/stream/whoswhoinphilade00 phil/whoswhoinphilade00phil_djvu.txt.

Steffens, Lincoln. *The Shame of the Cities*. New York: McClure, Phillips, 1904.

Stern, J. David. *Memoirs of a Maverick Publisher*. New York: Simon and Schuster, 1962.

Stevens, Robert Bocking. *Law School: Legal Education in America from the 1850s to the 1980s*. Chapel Hill: University of North Carolina Press, 1983.

Strouse, Jean. *Morgan: Financier*. New York: Random House, 1999.

Swanberg, W. A. *Citizen Hearst.* New York: Scribner's, 1961.

Tabak, Robert. "The Transformation of Jewish Identity." Ph.D. diss., Temple University, 1990.

Thorndike, Joseph J., Jr. *The Very Rich: A History of Wealth.* New York: American Heritage, 1976.

Toll, Jean Barth, and Mildred S. Gillam. *Invisible Philadelphia: Community through Voluntary Organizations.* Philadelphia: Atwater Kent Museum, 1995.

Vare, William S. *My Forty Years in Politics.* Philadelphia: Roland Swain, 1933.

Veblen, Thorstein. *The Theory of the Leisure Class.* Mineola, NY: Dover, 1994.

Vernon, Raymond. *The Changing Economic Function of the Central City.* New York: Committee for Economic Development, 1959.

Vitiello, Domenic, with George E. Thomas. *The Philadelphia Stock Exchange and the City It Made.* Philadelphia: University of Pennsylvania Press, 2008.

Wainwright, Nicholas B. *History of the Philadelphia National Bank, 1803–1953.* Philadelphia: Wm. Fell, 1953.

Weigley, Russell F., ed. *Philadelphia: A 300-Year History.* New York: Norton, 1982.

Weiss, Marc. *The Rise of the Community Builders: The American Real Estate Industry and Urban Land Planning.* New York: Columbia University Press, 1987.

Welsh, Mary Sue. *One Woman in a Hundred: Edna Phillips and the Philadelphia Orchestra.* Urbana: University of Illinois Press, 2013.

Whiteman, Maxwell. "Philadelphia's Jewish Neighborhoods." In *The Peoples of Philadelphia: A History of Ethnic Groups and Lower-Class Life, 1790–1940,* edited by Allen Davis and Mark Haller, 231–254. Philadelphia: University of Pennsylvania Press, 1998.

Winnet, Nochem S. *Vignettes of a Lucky Life.* Philadelphia: Privately printed, 1989.

Zwicker, Charles G., and Edward C. Zwicker. *Whitemarsh Hall: The Estate of Edward T. Stotesbury.* Charleston, SC: Arcadia, 2004.

ARTICLES AND MANUSCRIPTS

"Activities of Day in Real Estate." *Philadelphia Inquirer,* December 16, 1921, p. 14.

"Albert M. Greenfield Dies at 79; Built Realty and Store Empire." *New York Times,* January 6, 1967.

"Albert M. Greenfield Marries Mrs. Elizabeth M. Hallstrom." *Philadelphia Bulletin,* January 14, 1952, p. 1.

Alsop, Stewart. "The Paradox of Gentleman Joe." *Saturday Evening Post,* April 27, 1957, p. 40.

"A. M. Greenfield to Retire." *Philadelphia Daily News,* December 7, 1955.

"A. M. Greenfield Weds." *Philadelphia Bulletin,* October 1, 1937.

Anderson, Fred. "The Lost Founders." *New York Review of Books,* September 21, 2006, p. 58.

"Bankers Trust Co. Taken Over by State; Plan Reorganization." *Philadelphia Record,* December 23, 1930, p. 1.

"Bank of U.S. Closes Doors." *New York Times,* December 12, 1930.

Banks, E. S. "A Philadelphia Life Underwriter Who Believes in Life Insurance for Himself." *The Spectator,* 1928, p. 34.

"Big Money." *Time,* April 21, 1930.

Binzen, Peter. "They Came, They Saw and They Built Empire." *Philadelphia Bulletin,* June 27, 1974.

Brecht, Raymond C. "The Greenfield Story: A Titan Looks Back over a Half-Century." *Philadelphia Bulletin,* May 15, 1955.

Brody, Jane E. "A Richer Life by Seeing the Glass Half Full." *New York Times,* May 22, 2012, p. D7.

Brown, Dorothy. "A Four-Month Mitzvah Saving 50 Children." *Philadelphia Inquirer,* April 3, 2013, p. C1.

Brunner, Lois. "Mr. Albert M. Greenfield." *Philadelphia,* March 1951, pp. 5–6.

Buckley, Christopher. "Family Guy." *New York Times Book Review*, November 18, 2012, pp. 1, 20–21.

"Business: Philadelphia Failure." *Time*, December 29, 1930.

Cain, Susan. "Hire Introverts." *The Atlantic*, July–August 2012, p. 68.

Campo-Flores, Arian. "Why Americans Think Immigration Hurts the Economy." *Newsweek*, May 13, 2010. Available at http://www.newsweek.com/why-americans-think-immigration-hurts-economy-72909.

"Counting the Cost." *The Economist*, June 9, 2012, pp. 87–88.

"Crowd Orderly and Composed at Closed Bank." *Philadelphia Record*, December 22, 1930, p. 1.

Davenport, Russell W. "Philadelphia." *Fortune*, June 1936, pp. 67–75, 175–208.

"Democracy's Arsenal." *The Economist*, May 19, 2012, p. 92.

"Edward Hopkinson Jr." *Today*, January 20, 1963, pp. 4–5.

"The End of America." *The Economist*, June 12, 2004, p. 82.

"The Evolution of Sugar Loaf." *Town and Country*, July 1962, p. 73.

Ferguson, Niall. "Why America Outpaces Europe." *New York Times*, June 8, 2003.

Fisher, George. "Sugarloaf." *Philadelphia Reflections*. Available at http://www.philadelphia-reflections.com/blog/1055.htm (accessed January 21, 2014).

"Fox-Stanley Pact." *Wid's Daily*, August 4, 1921, p. 1.

"General Shoe Buys Hoving Corp. Control from Bankers Securities." *Wall Street Journal*, July 19, 1956.

"Gordon Leaves City Stores, A. M. Greenfield Takes Post." *Women's Wear Daily*, February 1, 1957.

Gorton, Gary. "Private Clearinghouses and the Origins of Central Banking." *Business Review*, January–February 1984, pp. 3–11.

"GPM Attack Called Unfair by Greenfield; Financier Alone Blocks Center, They Say." *Philadelphia Bulletin*, August 24, 1955, p. 1.

Gray, Christopher. "Streetscape: The Bank of United States in the Bronx." *New York Times*, August 18, 1991.

Greenfield, Albert M. "I Run a Department Store without Clerks." *Nation's Business*, October 1953, p. 35.

Greenfield, Barbara. "Albert M. Greenfield: A Story for Grandchildren." Unpublished manuscript, 1962.

"Greenfield and Aides Buy Control of Loft's." *Philadelphia Inquirer*, June 4, 1940.

"Greenfield Assails *Inquirer* Publisher." *Philadelphia Inquirer*, September 22, 1938.

"Greenfield Denies He Founded Bank." *Philadelphia Record*, October 7, 1938, p. 19.

"Greenfield Elected Chairman of Planning Commission." *Philadelphia Bulletin*, January 5, 1956.

"Greenfield Resigns Post." *Philadelphia Bulletin*, March 19, 1959.

"Greenfield's Firm Drew $300,000 from Bankers Trust, Lawyer Says." *Philadelphia Inquirer*, October 14, 1938, p. 1

Gutheim, Frederick. "Philadelphia's Redevelopment." *Architectural Forum*, December 1956.

"Historic City Shakes Free of Past, Rebuilds." *San Francisco Examiner*, March 17, 1957, p. 1.

"Hope Springs a Trap." *The Economist*, May 12, 2012, p. 83.

Hopkins, Steven. "Stormy Monday." *Philadelphia*, May 1956, pp. 23–25, 88–91.

"Insolvent Plea by Greenfield Blocks Suits." *Philadelphia Inquirer*, June 1, 1940, p. 1.

"Irving Fisher: Out of Keynes's Shadow." *The Economist*, February 12, 2009.

"Kin Buying Old Greenfield Business." *Philadelphia Inquirer*, November 19, 1990.

Leonhardt, David, Alicia Parlapiano, and Lisa Waananen. "A Historical Benchmark." *New York Times*, August 14, 2012.

Lerner, Barron H. "When Lobotomy Was Seen as Advanced." *New York Times*, December 20, 2011.

Letters, Sunday Book Review, *New York Times*, March 14, 2012.

Levy, Leo B. "Henry James and the Jews: A Critical Study." *Commentary*, September 1958.

Lippincott, Horace Mather. "Edward T. Stotesbury." *Old York Road Historical Society Bulletin,* October 1942, pp. 1–23.

Lyons, Reneé Critcher. "The Second Shall Be First: The 1948 Presidential Election—Truman V. Dewey." *Our White House.* Available at http://www.ourwhitehouse.org/secondshallbe first.html (accessed January 24, 2014).

McFarland, Kermit. "Banking's Bell." *Pittsburgh Press,* May 19, 1940.

McLarnon, John, III, and G. Terry Madonna. "Damon and Pythias Reconsidered." *Pennsylvania Magazine of History and Biography,* April 2012, pp. 171–205.

"The Merits of Genteel Poverty." *The Economist,* August 18, 2007, p. 74.

Moyerman, Esther. "Looking Back on Albert M. Greenfield's Career." *(Philadelphia) Jewish Times,* August 1, 1930, p. 1.

"Mr. Philadelphia." *Time,* September 19, 1949.

"Mrs. Greenfield Divorced, Reweds." *New York Times,* November 7, 1935.

"Mrs. Greenfield Obtains Divorce." *Philadelphia Bulletin,* November 1, 1935.

"$1 Billion Union of Banks Completed." *New York Times,* November 25, 1930.

"Phila. Banks Safe, Leading Financiers Assure Depositors." *Philadelphia Inquirer,* December 23, 1930, p. 1.

"Press Group Hails Old Newsie Greenfield." *Philadelphia Daily News,* May 9, 1963.

"Purchase of Camden Papers Due in Week." *Editor and Publisher,* February 1947.

Putnam, Alfred W. "Mr. Drinker's Desk." Unpublished manuscript, 2002.

Quirk, George, and Howard B. Haas. "Fox Theatre." *Cinema Treasures.* Available at http://cinematreasures.org/theaters/1177 (accessed January 21, 2014).

Reath, Viki. "Older Building Offers Attractive Rental Space." *Philadelphia Bulletin,* August 16, 1981.

"The Residence of Mr. and Mrs. Albert M. Greenfield." *Country Homes,* July–August 1921, p. 52.

Rezneck, Samuel. "Distress, Relief, and Discontent in the United States during the Depression of 1873–78." *Journal of Political Economy,* December 1950, pp. 494–512.

"The Rise of Felix Isman; Audacious Real Estate Speculator." *New York Times,* February 10, 1907.

Rossi, John P. "Philadelphia's Forgotten Mayor." *Pennsylvania History Magazine,* April 1984, p. 154.

Rottenberg, Dan. "Albert Greenfield's Empire Died with Him." *Philadelphia Inquirer,* November 20, 1979.

———. "A Breakthrough against City's 'Anti-leadership' Disease?" *Philadelphia Inquirer,* October 8, 1991.

———. "The Jackie Robinson of Jewish Academia." *Inside,* Spring 1995, p. 64.

———. "The Last Run of the Rock Island Line." *Chicago,* September 1984, pp. 197–201, 234–237.

———. "Once There Was Greenfield." *Philadelphia,* May 1976, pp. 166–192.

"Says Greenfield Is Out of New Bank." *Philadelphia Bulletin,* May 12, 1931, p. 33.

Schiavo, Christine. "Those Saved from Nazis Honor a Hero." *Philadelphia Inquirer,* May 8, 2003, p. B1.

Shaw, John MacKay. "The Life of Thomas Eugene Mitten of Philadelphia." Unpublished manuscript, available at the Free Library of Philadelphia.

Solow, Robert M. "Survival of the Richest?" *New York Review of Books,* November 22, 2007, p. 40.

"State Attacks Payment Plan by Greenfield." *Philadelphia Inquirer,* September 27, 1940, p. 1.

Steffens, Lincoln. "Philadelphia: Corrupt and Contented." *McClure's Magazine,* July 1903, pp. 249–263.

"The Success of Downtown Living: Expanding the Boundaries of Center City." *Center City Developments,* April 2002. Available at www.centercityphila.org/docs/expandingbound aries.pdf.

"Syndicate Seek[s] Philadelphia Academy," *Variety,* May 5, 1920.

T.P. "Taking the Skeleton out of Jewish History's Closet." *Pennsylvania Gazette*, July–August 2009, p. 29.
"Truman Reaffirms Stand on Israel." *New York Times*, October 25, 1948, p. 1.
"The $250,000 House." *Fortune*, October 1955.
Wadhwani, R. Daniel. "Soothing the People's Panic: The Banking Crisis of the 1930s in Philadelphia." *Pennsylvania Legacies*, May 2011, p. 25.
Walzer, Michael. "Imaginary Jews." *New York Review of Books*, March 20, 2014, pp. 31–33.
"Want Greenfield Out of New Bank." *Philadelphia Bulletin*, May 9, 1931, p. 2.
"A Whiz of a Promoter." *Business Week*, September 25, 1954.
"William Fox Hurt in Auto Accident." *Jewish Telegraphic Agency*, July 19, 1929.
"Work, Don't Sleep." *Newsweek*, January 27, 1958.
Zipser, Alfred R. "Along the Highways and Byways of Finance." *New York Times*, June 5, 1955.

OBITUARIES

Gustave G. Amsterdam obituary, *Philadelphia Inquirer*, February 14, 2001.
Harley Clarke obituary, *(Fredericksburg, VA) Free Lance-Star*, June 7, 1955.
Dennis Cardinal Dougherty obituary, *New York Times*, June 1, 1951.
William Fox obituary, *New York Times*, May 9, 1952.
Rudolph J. Goerke obituary, *New York Times*, April 14, 1938.
Albert M. Greenfield obituary, *New York Times*, January 6, 1967.
Albert M. Greenfield obituary, *Philadelphia Bulletin*, January 5, 1967, p. 1.
Albert M. Greenfield obituary, *Philadelphia Inquirer*, January 6, 1967.
Albert M. Greenfield Jr. obituary, *Philadelphia Inquirer*, June 29, 2005.
Bruce H. Greenfield obituary, *Philadelphia Inquirer*, November 18, 2005.
Esther V. Serody Greenfield obituary, *(Philadelphia) Jewish Exponent*, August 17, 1928.
Etelka Joseph Schamberg Greenfield obituary, *New York Times*, May 30, 1949.
Gordon K. Greenfield death notice, *New York Times*, January 10, 2005.
Jacob Greenfield obituary, *(Philadelphia) Jewish Exponent*, May 4, 1928.
Jacob Greenfield obituary, *(Philadelphia) Public Ledger*, April 28, 1928.
William I. Greenfield obituary, *Philadelphia Inquirer*, November 21, 1978.
Cheesman Herrick obituary, *Philadelphia Bulletin*, February 27, 1956.
George H. Johnson Jr. obituary, *Philadelphia Inquirer*, October 26, 2008.
Solomon C. Kraus obituary, *New York Times*, July 30, 1928.
Solomon C. Kraus obituary, *Pluck: A Magazine of Health and Encouragement*, September 1928.
John J. McDevitt Jr. obituary, *Philadelphia Bulletin*, November 15, 1945.
C. Stevenson Newhall obituary, *Philadelphia Inquirer*, December 16, 1950.
Elizabeth Murphy Hallstrom Greenfield Petrie obituary, *Philadelphia Inquirer*, June 18, 2003.
Jesse J. Schamberg obituary, *New York Times*, December 23, 1935.
E. T. Stotesbury obituary, *Philadelphia Bulletin*, May 17, 1938.
Elizabeth Greenfield Zeidman obituary, *Philadelphia Inquirer*, February 23, 2005.

VIDEO

Mr. Philadelphia: The Story of Albert M. Greenfield. Directed by Johnny Boston. Philadelphia: Raw Media Network and Albert M. Greenfield Foundation, 2007. DVD.

Index

Page numbers in italics refer to illustrations.

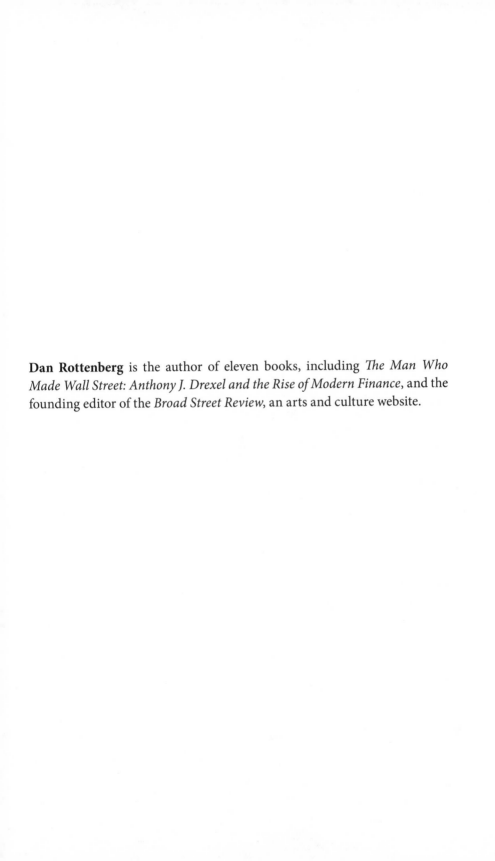

Dan Rottenberg is the author of eleven books, including *The Man Who Made Wall Street: Anthony J. Drexel and the Rise of Modern Finance*, and the founding editor of the *Broad Street Review*, an arts and culture website.